DEALS FROM HELL

DEALS FROM
HELL

M&A Lessons That
Rise Above the Ashes

Robert F. Bruner

John Wiley & Sons, Inc.

Library of Congress Cataloging-in-Publication Data:
Bruner, Robert F.
    Deals from hell : M & A lessons that rise above the ashes / Robert F. Bruner.
      p.   cm.
    Includes bibliographical references and index.
    ISBN-13 978-0-471-39595-9 (cloth)
    ISBN-10 0-471-39595-1 (cloth)
  1. Consolidation and merger of corporations.   2. Business failures.   I. Title.
    HG4028.M4B78 2005
    658.1'62—dc22

                                        2004029114

Printed in the United States of America.

10 9 8 7 6 5 4

A writer doesn't so much choose a story as a story chooses him. I know lots of stories, but for some reason only a few grab hold of me. They catch me and worry me and stick with me and raise questions . . .

—Robert Penn Warren

To my students:

May these stories grab hold of you, worry you,
and continue to raise questions.

Contents

III.   Avoiding the Deal from Hell

Foreword

Students sometimes ask the most amazing and perplexing questions, and oftentimes their innocence and point-blank questioning in the classroom aren't wasted and can prompt a very important reply. If posed to the right professor, the answers can also prove equally delightful and insightful—particularly when a good professor has thought long and hard about the question for more than a dozen years. Such is the case with this book.

I am delighted to introduce you to Professor Robert Bruner of The Darden School. His book with the Dilbertian or apocalyptic title (depending on your point of view) *Deals from Hell* will serve great purpose in bringing more discipline and sharper thinking to the art and science of M&A, and to financial markets.

Whether you are investor or dealmaker, corporate executive or aspiring MBA looking for a career on Wall Street, you are sure to find this book both troublesome and inspiring. Great instruction always is. It cannot be otherwise when you carefully examine a series of M&A "train wrecks" through the same lens as Professor Bruner, a creative teacher in the field of M&A, who has been able to extract the hard, instructive lessons from these disasters. That knowledge, in this book, comes through artful contrasting of failures with other deals where greater discipline and care led to different results.

From my vantage point, this particular trip through M&A hell is very reminiscent of what happened soon after the space shuttle *Challenger* and its crew were destroyed as a result of a catastrophic explosion on January 28, 1986. No one likes to remember that episode, but none of us can forget it. And it was only with great reluctance that the great scientist Richard Feynman accepted a key role as part of the NASA-appointed Rogers Commission to investigate that particular disaster. Little did Feynman know at the time that he would be the one to discover and eloquently explain the direct causes of this disaster, and how it might be avoided in the future.

In the case of Feynman, to show just what a risky business flying a space shuttle truly is, his estimate of the chance of failure was actually closer to 1 in 100, not the 1 in 100,000 calculation used by NASA officials. He also learned that rubber used to seal the solid rocket booster joints using O-rings failed to expand when the temperature was at or below 32 degrees Fahrenheit (0°C), the exact temperature at the time of the *Challenger* liftoff. He simulated and explained this failure to the world by dropping a piece of O-ring material, squeezed with a C-clamp to simulate the actual conditions of the shuttle, into a glass of ice water. As Feynman explained, because the O-rings cannot expand in 32-degree weather, the gas finds gaps in the joints, which led to the explosion of the booster and the loss of the shuttle itself.

Feynman was always a fabulous communicator, and so is Bruner. To find out what causes M&A failure and success, he has dug deep with the people and sources who have built something that failed, and probed for answers. He offers us conclusions (painful as they sometimes are) that promise greater success in the future, not failure.

As Bruner points out, great financial risk in M&A—as with space exploration—is part of the cost of doing business. Either we can stop at potentially greater expense to society, or we can learn how to do it the right way and bat a higher success percentage.

As this book demonstrates, bad deals have led to some titanic failures for shareholders. But success is always there for those who learn how to succeed by understanding failure. There will always be huge winners and losers when it comes to M&A—and knowledge combined with discipline can lead to superior results. From 1982 to 2003, in fact, Warren Buffett's Berkshire Hathaway has acquired companies worth $45 billion, a fact that many investors don't think about. Is he a great investor, or an even greater M&A specialist? In September 2004, the firm's share price was $86,650 for a 27 percent annual compound growth rate.

We simply need greater care and thinking when future M&A deals are on the launch pad. This will lead to even greater wealth for society and investors. It is time we all read on, and let Professor Bruner lead by instruction.

ARTHUR LEVITT, JR.

Westport, Connecticut
February 18, 2005

Acknowledgments

A student's question seeded the research that became this book. "What are the worst mergers?" struck me as superficial when posed more than a dozen years ago. But the question would not let go: It morphed from "what?" into "why?" and "how?" I came to conclude that stories of failure in mergers and acquisitions (M&A) were hugely instructive. And interesting cases never ceased boiling to the surface to offer new lessons. Finally, watching the agony of these deals prompted me to bring these lessons to the public. I believe these stories will change the way you think about M&A and help you to understand—and better yet, to anticipate—such failures to come.

I owe a very great debt of thanks to colleagues, friends, assistants, and students who have contributed to the manuscript over time. Each chapter acknowledges research assistants and colleagues; among these I especially recognize Anna Buchanan, Sean Carr, and Jessica Chan. Research co-authors contributed to work that appears directly or in summary form here: Samuel Bodily, Kenneth Eades, and Robert Spekman. I have benefited enormously from comments by Michael Schill, Don Chew, Saras Sarasvathy, and seminar participants at Virginia (Darden), Harvard, and Indiana universities. Also, the staff at Darden gave helpful support—I especially recognize Frank Wilmot, Stephen Smith (Darden's nonpareil editor), Sherry Alston, and my administrative assistant, Betty Sprouse. The patience, care, and dedication of these people are richly appreciated. This project would not have been possible without the encouragement of Dean Robert S. Harris and the financial support of the University of Virginia Darden School Foundation, the Batten Institute, and Columbia Business School.

I must also acknowledge the support given by my editors at John Wiley & Sons: Bill Falloon, senior editor; Karen Ludke, editorial program assistant; Robin Factor, production manager; and Todd Tedesco, senior production editor. Pamela Van Giessen, executive editor, Joan O'Neil, publisher, and Will Pesce, president, were decisive in my commitment to embark on this project.

Lewis O'Brien checked the manuscript, offered editorial advice, and ferreted out some elusive permissions to quote the material of other authors.

Friends and mentors encouraged me at important moments in the development of this work. Mac and Elsie Thompson urged me into this project during an animated dinner conversation a decade ago. John H. McArthur and David W. Mullins, Jr. ignited my interest in M&A.

In terms of absolute sacrifice, none have contributed more than my wife, Barbara McTigue Bruner, and two sons, Jonathan and Alexander. This book is significantly a product of their faith, hope, and charity. I will remain, forever, in their loving debt.

All these acknowledgments notwithstanding, responsibility for the final product is mine, alone.

ROBERT F. BRUNER

Charlottesville, Virginia
October 31, 2004

1

Introduction

"**M**erger" is the consolidation of two firms that creates a new entity in the eyes of the law. The French have a good word for it: *fusion*—conveying the emergence of a new structure out of two old ones. An "acquisition" on the other hand, is simply a purchase. The distinction is important to lawyers, accountants, and tax specialists, but less so in terms of its economic impact. Businesspeople use the terms interchangeably. The acronym, "M&A," stands for it all.

M&A enters and leaves the public mind with waves of activity, such as those depicted in Figure 1.1. These waves roughly synchronize with equity market conditions and thus carry with them the cachet of excess, hype, and passion that swirl in the booms. Over time, M&A activity radically transforms industries, typically shrinking the number of players, inflating the size of those who remain, and kindling anxieties about the power of corporations in society. Every M&A boom has a bust, typically spangled with a few spectacular collapses of merged firms. These failures significantly shape the public mind, and especially business strategies and public policy. We should study M&A failure not merely as a form of entertainment, but as a foundation for sensible policies and practices in future M&A waves.

Failure pervades business, and most firms fail eventually. Venture capitalists typically reject 90–95 percent of proposals they see. Up to 90 percent[1] of new businesses fail not long after founding. Even mature businesses pass on: Of the 501 firms listed on the New York Stock Exchange in 1925, only 13 percent existed in their independent corporate

Waves of M&A
Number of Deals Per Year

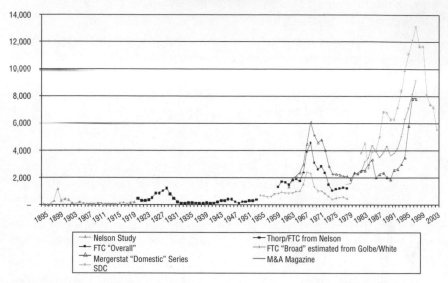

Figure 1.1   **M&A Activity by Year**
Source: Author's analysis with data from indicated sources.

form in 2004. Within healthy growing businesses, failure is a constant
companion. Most patented inventions fail to become commercial successes. Most new products fizzle out not long after the launch pad. Para-
doxically, the success and renewal of capitalism depends on this enormous
rate of failure, what the economist Joseph Schumpeter called the "peren-
nial gale of creative destruction." In the world of M&A, most transactions
fail to close: That deal you may be discussing has perhaps a one-in-ten
chance of consummation. And those transactions that do close, though
profitable on average, tend to fall short of the most optimistic expectations.

Studying M&A failure offers titillating entertainment, worthy of *Cos-
mopolitan*, the *National Enquirer*, or *Geraldo*. However, it is also a springboard
to business insight. All professions understand that the study of failure is the
source of thoughtful advances. Medicine began with the study of pathol-
ogy. Engineers study mechanical and structural failures. And psychologists
study errors, anomalies, and biases in human behavior. At business schools,

the study of cases considers successes and failures. To my knowledge, this book is the first focused study of failure in mergers and acquisitions.

Perhaps the chief insight of this book is that M&A failure is complicated, the result of a convergence of forces. But conventional thinking sees it differently, preferring quick and dismissive explanations arguing, for instance, that merger failure is due to some bad apples in the executive suite, nonobservance of one big Golden Rule ("They took their eye off the customer"), or some kind of industry hoo-doo curse ("Technology mergers have never ever worked"). While these may contain a nugget of reason, they are more remarkable for what they ignore than what they tell us. Most importantly, they are not terribly useful to guide the man or woman on the hot seat toward doing good business. Such bromides remind one of Woody Allen, who took a speed reading course and then read Tolstoy's *War and Peace*. All Allen could say about the book was "It's about Russia."

I wrote this book to fill the gap in our understanding. It addresses four questions:

1. What is "merger failure"? How can we measure it?
2. How prevalent is failure among mergers and acquisitions?
3. What causes merger failure?
4. What are the implications of our answers for managers and policymakers?

OVERVIEW OF THE BOOK

I frame the response to these questions in the three parts of this book. Part I (chapters 2, 3, and 4) offers perspectives on merger failure from the standpoints of previous research. Chapter 2 summarizes what we know about merger failure and success based on more than 130 studies drawn from research in business and financial economics. The research shows that the field of M&A is highly segmented; there are attractive and unattractive neighborhoods. This is the foundation for my argument that *all M&A is local*. Chapter 3 offers a summary profile of the best and worst deals from 1985 to 2000. Chapter 4 gives a perspective on the *processes* of failure, drawn from analyses of real disasters and from concepts in a number of disciplines, including cognitive psychology, sociology, and engineering. Thus, Part I constructs a lens through which to view the causes of merger failure.

Part II lends texture to our understanding of M&A failure through 10 case studies of big M&A disasters. I have paired each of the 10 with a counterpoint or complementary case so that each chapter is actually a paired comparison of what can go wrong and how. The comparison cases are not intended to be deals from heaven; they merely differ in some instructive way. The comparisons suggest how little the situation must differ in order to deliver rather different results.

These 10 cases are not necessarily the worst in any absolute sense. However, judged on common standards there can be little disagreement that they belong on a short list of bad deals. One has a large pool of candidates from which to select. I chose these 10 for several reasons.

- **Size of damage.** *Big* bad deals certainly get one's attention and have face validity. I looked for losses in the billions of dollars, for layoffs, CEO change, tarnished reputation, and possibly, bankruptcy.
- **Diversity** of industry, deal type, and challenges. I could fill a book of M&A disasters drawn from any one of a number of industries. However, as I argue here, industry conditions have a powerful effect on merger success and failure. Thus, diversity of settings sharpens our understanding about how industry has an impact and intrigues us with its local surprises.
- **Access to information.** In half of these cases, I was fortunate to find insiders or knowledgeable outside observers to interview and inform the discussion. However, most participants do not want to discuss their M&A failures. In five instances, I was able to tap valuable archives that lent some insight into senior management's views. For the rest, I relied on a diverse collection of investigative journalism, security analysis, and open commentary. Regardless of sources of information, I aimed to bring a fresh lens through which to view these cases, informed by economics and a scientific mind-set.

I tried to avoid M&A disaster cases caused mainly by crimes, looting, fraud, and sabotage. These are more appropriate for a book on white-collar crime. Such cases are a small fraction of the larger sample of messes we can find and by their notoriety, tend to obscure more important lessons for CEOs and the public. Even so, criminal litigation followed two of the cases described here.

The research and framework from Part I and the case studies in Part II open the door to Part III. There I offer some summary implications for CEOs, investors, and those concerned with public policy.

This is an exercise in *inductive* research, the generation of a way of thinking about failure in M&A, drawn from a detailed look at the research and cases. These were all failures that could have been avoided or sharply mitigated. I hope to show why and how. The result is a volume that seeks to teach, rather than harangue, titillate the reader, or humiliate the protagonists. Where the facts do not fit with sympathetic explanations, I speak plainly; but generally, my bias is to view the challenges facing executives as extremely difficult, arenas in which scholars and the casual reader could easily have done worse. Other analysts may beg to differ on the interpretation of specific events in certain cases or of detailed points in the research stories summarized here. Yet such differences should not obscure the larger point that there are considerable similarities among merger failures and that such similarities lend insight into the causes of failure and the implications for managers.

OVERVIEW OF THE FINDINGS

The key message of this book is that mergers fail because of a "perfect storm" of factors that combine to destroy the new firm. This message invites consideration of the definition, frequency, profiles, and process of failure.

What Is Merger Failure?

The first question is definitional. Though "failure" is commonly understood, it has several differing applications. For instance, the *Oxford English Dictionary* defines "failure" as:

> 1. A failing to occur, to be performed, or be produced; an omitting to perform something due or required; default . . . 2. The fact of becoming

exhausted or running short, giving way under trial, breaking down in health, declining in strength or activity, etc. . . . 3. The fact of failing to effect one's purpose; want of success . . . 4. The fact of failing in business; bankruptcy, insolvency . . .[2]

As the dictionary suggests, "failure" connotes both a *process* ("a failing to occur . . . omitting to perform . . . giving way . . . breaking down") and an *outcome* ("fact of . . . want of," and bankruptcy). In this book, I aim to discuss both process and outcome. My method is to begin with identifiable outcomes and induce from them some insights about process.

What, then, is the outcome of M&A failure? Consider at least these six dimensions:

1. **Destruction of market value.** Harnessing the perspective of the providers of capital, we measure the destruction of value by the percentage change in share values, net of changes in a benchmark, such as a large portfolio of stocks.

2. **Financial instability.** Some of the saddest M&A deals are those that, rather than making the buyer stronger, actually destabilize it. In most of these cases, the buyer overreaches its financial capacity. Degree of financial stability is reflected in debt ratings, earnings coverage ratios, probability of default, and other measures of the ability of the firm to bear risk.

3. **Impaired strategic position.** Many M&A transactions are motivated by a strategic purpose that seeks to improve the firm's competitive position, acquire new capabilities, improve agility, or obtain resources that are vital to future prosperity. Indications of failure in this dimension would include loss of market share, and involuntary abandonment of products, geographic markets, or research and development (R&D) programs.

4. **Organizational weakness.** Knitting together two firms is especially challenging from an organizational perspective. Most CEOs would agree with the old slogan "People are our most important asset." In essence, one could measure organizational strength in terms of depth of talent and leadership, effectiveness of business processes, and the transmission of culture and values. Adverse

changes in human resources appear in unanticipated workforce lay-offs, involuntary changes of leadership in senior management and the board, and defections of talented individuals to competitors.

5. **Damaged reputation.** The M&A deal should improve the reputation of the acquirer and its deal architects. Usually, the realization of these other aims will do just that. But one can imagine deals that depend on acrimony, subterfuge, and a win-lose mentality—in a world of repeated play, the executive must consider how these qualities might affect one's M&A success in future deals. Measurable outcomes in this dimension would include changes in name recognition, reputation, analyst sentiment, and press coverage.

6. **Violation of ethical norms and laws.** You can gain financial, organizational, and strategic objectives in M&A, but in ways that violate norms such as equity, duty, honesty, and lawful observance. After the corporate scandals of recent years, any assessment of outcomes would be incomplete without consideration of laws and ethics. Adverse judgments in criminal and civil litigation would be a rough measure of M&A failure, though they usually follow an extended lapse in ethics.

I was influenced in my selection of the 10 case studies by all of these factors. However, some of these criteria are difficult or impossible to benchmark. As a result, the discussion that follows gives somewhat more attention (though not necessarily more weight) to the financial dimension.

How Prevalent Is M&A Failure?

M&A failures amount to a small percentage of the total volume of M&A activity. Investments through acquisition appear to pay about as well as other forms of corporate investment. The mass of research suggests that on average, buyers earn a reasonable return relative to their risks. M&A is no money-pump. But neither is it a loser's game. Conventional wisdom seems to think otherwise, even though the empirical basis for such a view is scant.

Of more interest to the thoughtful practitioner is not the average result, but the distribution around it. The wide variation in findings about the profitability of M&A suggests that something may be going on to tilt the odds of success and failure. Chapter 2 identifies 18 neighborhoods or dimensions of the M&A market, along which returns to buyers vary significantly. For instance, acquisitions of public companies tend to be much less profitable to buyers than are acquisitions of privately held companies.

The existence of neighborhoods of return suggest that *all M&A is local*. That is, managerial choice can have a huge impact on the results of M&A: Quite simply, where you choose to do business will influence success or failure.

What Causes M&A Failure?

That M&A is local also implies that we might find constructive or destructive patterns of managerial choice in the deals from hell or heaven that they produce. Chapter 3 reports that the extreme outliers of deals, both good and bad, differ from each other and from the middle in at least four general ways.

The first regards strategy. In the best deals, buyers acquire targets in industrially related areas. In the worst deals, targets are in areas that are more distant. This may reflect the benefits of sticking to your knitting: Better knowledge of a related industry may yield fewer surprises and more opportunities to succeed.

In addition, the fit of the buyer and target matter significantly. In successful deals, buyers acquire from strength—the performance attributes of buyers are stronger than their targets suggesting that in good deals, the buyer brings something important to the success of Newco. In the worst deals, buyers acquire from weakness. There, the target is significantly stronger, and one can guess that the buyer hoped to fix some problem by means of the acquisition.

Third, the worst deals show a propensity to occur in "hot" market conditions. The preeminent hot market in business history was the equity market bubble from 1998 to 2000 associated with the emergence of the Internet. Industries can also be hotbeds of activity caused by sudden deregulation, technological change, shifts in consumer demand, and so on. Recent research suggests that many mergers are motivated by strategic turbulence in their industries. The best deals occur in cooler market conditions. Chapters 2 and 3 discuss the possible reasons for this disparity.

Finally, deal tailoring pays. One size does not fit all. Better deals are associated with payment by cash and earnout schemes and the use of specialized deal terms. The worst deals are associated with payment by stock.

Chapters 2 and 3 show that managers' choices matter. However, as the dictionary definition of "failure" suggests, there is more to the story, namely, what can go wrong between the managers' choices and the outcomes. Here is where the case studies of merger failure become vitally important. Chapter 4 shapes a lens through which to view these cases. In that chapter, I turn to research on *real* disasters (those involving the loss of life and property) to highlight six factors that lend traction in understanding the cases of M&A failure:

1. The businesses and/or the deal were complicated. This made it difficult for people on the scene to understand what was going on or to take quick and effective action.
2. Flexibility was at a minimum. Little slack or inadequate safety buffers meant that problems in one part of the business system would radiate to other parts. Trouble would travel.
3. Deliberately or inadvertently, management made some choices that elevated the risk exposure of the new firm.
4. The thinking of decision makers was biased by recent successes, sunk costs, pride, overoptimism, and so on.
5. Business was not as usual. Something in the business environment departed from expectation causing errors or problems.
6. The operational team broke down. Cultural differences between the buyer and target, unresolved political issues, and generally overwhelming stress prevented the team from responding appropriately to the unfolding crisis.

The case studies in Chapters 5 through 14 illustrate these six factors at work in producing the "perfect storm" of merger failure. Each case highlights one or more special aspects of the storm. Chapters 15 and 16 discuss important implications for deal-doers, operating managers, and CEOs.

CONCLUSION: ANTICIPATING M&A FAILURE
CAN ENHANCE SUCCESS

I wrote this book to lift the practice of M&A. Given the sheer complexity of these deals, best practice cannot be reduced easily to a sound bite. For this reason, case studies are excellent for helping the thoughtful practitioner envision what can go wrong and what to do about it. More importantly, the book suggests that success depends vitally on adopting the right attitude about M&A as a path of corporate growth. It is no formula for surefire success; rewards are extremely difficult to sustain over time; risks are legion; it is to be undertaken only with very serious planning and preparation; and the effort should be motivated by the right values and respect for investors. As William Blake said, "Execution is the chariot of genius."

NOTES

1. See Sarasvathy and Menon (2002) and Gartner (1988) for overviews of research on entrepreneurial failure. The research on failure rates of new firms shows wide variation from one study to the next. This is most likely attributable to variations in the length of time after founding from which failure is measured.

2. *Oxford English Dictionary* (Oxford, England: Oxford University Press, 2d ed. 1989), volume V, 667.

I

THE FOUNDATIONS OF
M&A FAILURE

2

Where M&A Pays and Where It Strays: A Survey of Research

How you assess an M&A deal or the whole flow of M&A activity depends on your frame of reference, on beliefs that help you decide whether specific deals represent the average, or what statisticians call the "tails of the distribution." This frame of reference is a hugely important filter for decision makers and their advisers and is typically built on a blend of personal experience, anecdotes, conventional wisdom, and facts. The aim of this chapter is to enrich your frame of reference about success and failure in M&A with the findings of scientific research.[1]

I have two basic criticisms of the way most people think about M&A. First, the conventional wisdom is poorly grounded in the scientific evidence on the subject. The fashionable view seems to be that M&A is a loser's game. Yet an objective reading of more than 130 studies supports the conclusion that M&A *does* pay.[2] These studies show that the shareholders of the selling firms earn large returns from M&A, that the shareholders of the buyers and sellers *combined* earn significant positive returns, and that the shareholders of buyers generally earn about the required rate of return on investment.

Second, conventional wisdom seems to hold that failure is the average outcome of all classes and varieties of M&A, and that, in this sense, M&A, is regrettably homogeneous. Yet the research reveals wide dispersion of returns both within and across studies. And such variation suggests that, like powerful turbulence under the smooth surface of a river, *something* is going on in the world of M&A that differentiates deals and predisposes them to success or failure—and that, like the varying river conditions below the surface, the world of M&A is not homogeneous. In this chapter, I argue that to see the varying states of this world is to build a view that more readily grasps the circumstances and approaches that give rise to success and failure.

Tip O'Neill, the Boston pol who rose to be Speaker of the U.S. House of Representatives, explained that in trying to understand the workings of Congress, it made no sense to focus on lofty national issues or policy debates within the Washington Beltway. Instead, he said, "All politics is local." The mindset of the successful politician begins with his or her constituency and the hopes and fears in town halls, school boards, and police precincts. It is the same in M&A: The best foundation for pursuing success and avoiding failure in M&A lies in seeing the important ways in which individual deals differ from one another. In other words, *all M&A is local.*

CONVENTIONAL WISDOM ON M&A FAILURE: STILL HAZY AFTER ALL THESE YEARS

The popular view is that M&A is a loser's game. The following excerpts from a recent book are representative:

> The sobering reality is that only about 20% of all mergers really succeed . . . most mergers typically erode shareholder wealth . . . the cold, hard reality that most mergers fail to achieve any real financial returns . . . very high rate of merger failure . . . rampant merger failure . . .[3]

I have lost count of the references—in newspaper columns, magazines, and consultants' reports—to this 20 percent success rate: Much is made of how small it is, though it would dwarf success rates of other business activities frequently lauded including new business startups, new product introductions, expansions to new markets, and investments in R&D and new technology. All business is risky. Our purpose in studying failure should be to manage risk better, not eliminate it. Yet there is no body of empirical research that documents this low success rate of M&A activity with a consistency and level of care equal to the gravity of the assertion. What is missing in the popular discussion is a rigorous definition of what the conventional wisdom means by "failure" in M&A. Here, too, the writers tend to refer vaguely to a shortfall between the goals of a merger and its outcomes, without any consideration of the appropriateness of goals or the general conditions in which the merger took place.

Here's an example of how the conventional wisdom on merger failure takes shape. In December 2002, a columnist wrote in the *Wall Street Journal*, "Most mergers don't work . . . A mountain of academic research shows most acquisitions end up costing shareholders . . ."[4] Later, in correspondence with me, he cited as proof a *BusinessWeek* article entitled "Why Most Big Deals Don't Pay Off" and reporting that "61% of buyers destroyed shareholder wealth."[5] That article studied 302 large mergers of public companies from 1995 to 2001 and looked at the changes in the buyer's share price in the year following the bid adjusted for changes in the share prices of peer firms or an industry average.

This example reveals a number of problems in making inferences about the profitability of M&A. First, the conventional wisdom generalizes too readily the findings of a single study (the columnist's use of "*most* mergers"). Second, there is a tendency to exaggerate the extent of failure. By the terms of the *BusinessWeek* study, a share price decline of just a penny would constitute a "failure." But recognizing that most share price movements are subject to a certain amount of noise, a more sensible approach would focus on *significant* failure and would exclude the noise. What's more, the study's period of observation was a once-in-a-lifetime outlier in capital market performance, which should discourage generalization to other time periods. Especially interesting during this time period was the feverish M&A activity in certain industry segments. For instance, a number of the large deals in the sample involved high-tech or Internet-related companies. To what extent was the general finding of the study affected by the price collapse of the technology–media–telecommunications sector that had started in 2000? Most of the deals in the sample were stock-for-stock exchanges, which, as past research has shown, tend to be worse for buyers than cash deals. The deals in the sample were also big deals, which by their nature have more integration and regulatory problems. And the study focused on deals between two public companies while acquisitions of private companies—which are far more common than public deals—tend to be much more profitable for buyers.

So was *BusinessWeek*'s sample representative of all M&A? No. It simply gives us insight into the profitability of big public-company deals in a "hot market." To vault from there to the assertion that "*most* mergers don't work" is unwarranted.[6]

Two recent studies (both by the same authors) offer a cautionary counterpoint to the *WSJ/BW* articles. In the first of the two, the authors examined the two-day abnormal stock market returns to buyers using a large sample of deals announced from 1980 to 2001.[7] They found that the adjusted returns to buyers measured *in dollars* (not percentage returns) over this period were significantly negative (–$25.2 million), on average, consistent with the argument that "most mergers don't work." But the authors also report three other important details. First, the average *percentage* adjusted return to buyers was a significantly positive 1.1 percent and their research shows that the inconsistency between the dollar and percentage returns is due to the extreme unprofitability of a few large deals. Also, in the second study, the authors report that most of the losses from 1980 to 2001 were concentrated in just 87 deals, out of a total sample of 12,023; without these deals, the whole sample would have showed a significantly positive dollar return. Third, the 87 culprits were concentrated in the hot M&A market of 1998 to 2001. Thus, but for a relatively small number of deals in a limited market episode, one reaches a very different conclusion about the profitability of M&A.

The conventional wisdom on M&A thus tends to be either hazy on the evidence or, where solid evidence is offered, too ready to generalize from the findings based on localized conditions. There is more to the story of M&A success and failure. An informed view depends on mastering the scientific findings on the profitability of M&A and on understanding how profitability varies by types of deals and companies.

MEASUREMENT OF M&A PROFITABILITY: BETTER THAN WHAT?

Before looking at the findings, you need to define the tests. The benchmark for measuring performance is investors' required returns, commonly defined as the return investors could have earned on other investment opportunities of similar risk. Against this benchmark, we can see three possible outcomes:

1. **Value is destroyed.** In this case, investment returns are less than those required by investors. Investors could have done better investing in another opportunity of similar risk, and they are justifiably unhappy.
2. **Value is created.** The investment earns a rate of return higher than required. Investors should be happy.
3. **Value is conserved.** The investment just earns its required rate of return. Economically speaking, investors earn "normal" returns. They should be satisfied because wealth is growing at a rate that just fairly compensates the investor. If an investor requires a return of 15 percent and receives it, the value of the investment will double in five years. But value is being just "conserved" in the sense that the investor is merely doing as well as required.

Judgments about the success or failure of M&A transactions should be linked to these measurable economic outcomes. In economic terms, an investment is "successful" if it does anything other than destroy value.

Why do we focus so narrowly on economics? After all, many managers describe a complex set of motives for acquisitions: shouldn't the benefit of M&A activity be benchmarked against *all* of them? In an ideal world, it would be nice to draw on a range of concerns, much as corporations do today with the balanced scorecard. But managers' motives may have little to do with shareholder returns, or with building capabilities that might help achieve them over the longer run. One often hears of M&A deals that are struck for vague strategic benefits, the creation of special capabilities, the achievement of competitive scale, or simply because two organizations or their CEOs are especially friendly. The only way one can prove that such benefits add value is by measuring the economic outcomes rigorously, using a common metric across all deals. Second, special deal-specific definitions of success limit our ability to generalize from the research findings. Increasing shareholder wealth of shareholders is a fundamental objective of all firms; indeed, in the United States, corporate directors are required to implement policies consistent with shareholders' interests, which is generally synonymous with creating value.[8] Fortunately, benchmarking against value creation *does* allow us to make generalizations. In what follows, I focus on economic outcomes in the hope of saying something meaningful grounded in scientific research.

One of the basic conclusions of economics is that where markets are reasonably competitive, players will earn a "fair" rate of return; that is, you just get paid for the risk you take, but no more. The intuition for this is simple: Where information is free-flowing and entry is easy, a firm earning very high returns will draw competitors as surely as honey draws flies. The entry of these other firms will drive returns down to the point where the marginal investor gets just a fair rate of return. This idea, which has been tested extensively in financial markets, leads directly to the concept of market efficiency, which says that prices reflect news quickly and without bias. Whether a free lunch exists in M&A hinges on returns to investors, and, as with tests of capital market efficiency, that hypothesis can be tested using one of three classes of measures:

1. **Weak form.** Did the share price rise? Are the shareholders better off after the deal than they were before? Most simply, was the buyer's stock price higher after the deal than before? Such a before-and-after comparison is widespread, especially in the writings of journalists and securities analysts. But it is a weak test in the sense that it fails to control for other factors unrelated to the deal that might have triggered a price change.

2. **Semistrong form.** Did the firm's returns exceed a benchmark? Are shareholders better off compared to the return on a comparable investment? Introducing a benchmark like the return on the S&P 500 index, or the return on a matched sample of peers that did not merge, strengthens the analysis. This kind of test, which is commonly used in academic research, is more reliable than the weak form tests because it controls for the possibility that the observed returns were actually driven by factors in the industry or the entire economy, rather than were due to the merger. But this kind of test is at best *semi*strong because benchmarks are imperfect.

3. **Strong form.** Are shareholders better off after the deal than *they would have been if the deal had not occurred*? This is the true test of the cost of lost opportunity, the economists' "gold standard" of comparison. And it is what most people *think* they are finding when they

look at weak and semistrong form test results. But the true strong form test could tell a very different story. Consider the case of America Online (AOL)'s merger with Time Warner in January 2001. The weak and semistrong tests would show large losses to AOL's shareholders in the two years following the deal. As Chapter 12 reports, AOL Time Warner outperformed a benchmark portfolio of pure Internet stocks, while underperforming the S&P 500 index and media and entertainment indexes. Given the bursting of the Internet bubble, it seems likely that AOL's shareholders would have been much *worse* off without the merger. It would appear that AOL's acquisition of Time Warner was shrewd and successful for the buyer, despite what the weak and semistrong results show (though Time Warner's shareholders appear to have cushioned the collapse of the Internet bubble for AOL's shareholders). The problem is that strong form results are difficult, if not impossible, to observe.

The distinction among these three kinds of tests is important to bear in mind. The studies summarized in this chapter are, at best, semistrong. Therefore we must exercise humility in drawing conclusions about performance against economic opportunity. We are looking through a glass darkly.

Two main research approaches offer findings that can help us in forming a view of M&A profitability. The first are so-called "event studies," which examine the abnormal returns to shareholders in the period surrounding the announcement of a transaction. The "raw" return for one day is simply the change in share price plus any dividends paid, divided by the closing share price the day before. The *abnormal return* is the raw return less a benchmark of what investors required that day. Typically, the benchmark is the return specified by the capital asset pricing model (CAPM) or, more simply, the return on a large market index like the S&P 500. These studies are based on the assumption that stock markets are *forward-looking* and that share prices are simply the present value of expected future cash flows to shareholders. Since the 1970s, these studies have dominated the field.

By contrast, so-called "accounting studies" examine the reported financial results (i.e., accounting statements) of acquirers before and after acquisitions to see how financial performance changes. The focus of these studies is on variables such as net income, return on equity or assets, earnings per share (EPS), leverage, and liquidity. The best of these studies are structured as matched-sample comparisons in which acquirers' performance is set against that of nonacquirers of similar size that operate in the same industry. In these studies, the question is whether the acquirers outperformed their nonacquiring peers.

If scientific inquiry means anything, it is to frame a hypothesis and test it rigorously against the possibility that the result is due merely to chance. Researchers accordingly test for the statistical significance of a result. But statistical significance is not the same as economic materiality. To say that M&A transactions create or destroy value *on average* requires not only the proof of significance (i.e., that the result is not due to chance) but also some compelling evidence of materiality, namely that the wealth effects of M&A transactions are large enough that shareholders or society should worry about them. Many of the *significant* abnormal returns reported in event studies are as small as 1 percent or 2 percent. But since these returns occur over just a few days, they are large enough, when viewed on an annualized basis, to cause concern or elation among institutions or other sophisticated investors whose performance can be greatly affected by such events.

THE BROAD FINDING: M&A PAYS

Event studies yield insights about market-based returns to target firm shareholders, buyers, and the combined entity.

Abnormal returns to target firm's shareholders. The findings of 25 studies[9] show that target firm shareholders earn returns that are significantly and materially positive, despite variations in time period, type of deal (merger vs. tender offer), and observation period. In short, the M&A transaction delivers a premium return to target firm shareholders.

Abnormal returns to buyer firm's shareholders. The pattern of findings about market-based returns to buyer firms' shareholders is more problematic. About 40 percent of roughly 50 studies report negative announcement returns to buyers; 60 percent report positive returns. When statistical significance is taken into account, the studies of returns to buyer firm shareholders show an even stronger positive bias: Twenty-six percent (14) show value destruction[10] (significantly negative returns); 31 percent (17) show value conservation[11] (insignificantly different from zero); and 43 percent (23) show value creation[12] (significantly positive returns).

A much less buoyant conclusion is offered by 16 studies[13] of the returns to buyers in the years over a multiyear period *after* the consummation of the transaction. Eleven of these studies report negative and significant returns. One possible interpretation of these results is that the buyers' shareholders get second thoughts, perhaps based on new information (generally of a negative character) that emerges about the deal. But a thoughtful consumer of these studies might discount these results somewhat because of confounding events that have little or nothing to do with the transaction. Consider three specific cases:

1. Two Swiss banks, UBS and SBC, merged in June 1998. The next month Russia defaulted on its international debt. This in turn triggered the collapse of Long Term Capital Management, in which the new Swiss bank, UBS A.G., had a sizeable investment. UBS announced a $900 million write-off of its investment, cashiered its CEO, and shook up management. To the uninformed observer of stock price trends, the breathtaking decline in UBS's share price in the months following its merger might appear to confirm the conventional wisdom that M&A does not pay. But closer examination suggests that the decline had less to do with the merger and more to do with external factors.

2. AOL announced the deal to acquire Time Warner just at the peak of AOL's share price. With the benefit of hindsight, we know that AOL's shares were overvalued in the stock market. Thus, the deal was a terrible swap for Time Warner's shareholders, but great for AOL's. As discussed later, the massive evaporation in value was due in part to the market's correction of this overvaluation, a correction that was bound to occur whether or not AOL acquired Time Warner. Several researchers offer findings consistent with the story that acquiring firms tend to pay with stock when they believe their shares are overvalued.[14]

3. Advanced Micro Devices (AMD) acquired NextGen in 1995 and then underperformed its peer group of semiconductor manufacturers in the following year. But the acquisition gave AMD a new future, enabling the firm to introduce its Athlon chip and remain a competitor to Intel. This is a story of an inevitable industry shock

produced by rapid technological innovation. We cannot know how AMD would have performed without the NextGen acquisition, but the consensus appears to be that AMD would not be alive today without it. And suggesting that AMD's case is a representative one, a 1996 study[15] supported the idea that the poor performance of companies following acquisitions is often the result of economic turbulence in the industry rather than the acquisition itself. In other words, when managers see trouble approaching in the form of deregulation, technological change, demographic shifts, or other forms of turbulence, they take action (such as an acquisition) to mitigate the trouble. And in such cases, the subsequent problems have more to do with the foreseen turbulence than the acquisitions themselves.

In short, contaminating events, overvalued stock, and industry shocks could all easily mislead thoughtful practitioners into believing that M&A is fundamentally unprofitable even though these effects may have nothing to do with the transactions themselves. Even more important, buyers are typically much larger than targets, which means that the impact of smaller deals is difficult to measure with any precision. For example, a 1983 study reported that in mergers where the target's market value was equal to 10 percent or more of the buyer's market value, the return to the buyer was a positive (and highly significant) 4.1 percent; but in cases where the target's value was less than 10 percent, the return to the buyer was only 1.7 percent.[16] In other words, what we know about M&A profitability is a blend of noise and large deals. Nonetheless, a reasonable conclusion from these event studies is that buyers essentially break even, which means that acquisitions tend to be investments that earn about their required rates of return.

Abnormal returns to buyer and target firms combined. Findings of positive abnormal returns to the seller and breakeven returns to the buyer raise the question of the *net economic gain* from M&A deals. The biggest challenge here stems from the size difference between buyer and target. Because buyers are typically much larger than the sellers, the dollar value of a large percentage gain to the target shareholders could be more than offset by a small percentage loss to the buyer's shareholders.

A number of studies have examined this possibility by forming a portfolio of the buyer and target firms and examining either their weighted average returns (weighted by the relative sizes of the two firms) or the absolute dollar value of returns. Almost all of a group of 24 studies[17] on combined returns report positive returns, with 14 of the 24 being significantly positive. These findings suggest that M&A activity *does* create net gains for the investors in the combined buyer and target firms and thus, presumably, for the economy as a whole

Reported financial performance of buyers. A second important stream of research on M&A returns is found in a group of 15 studies[18] of profit margins, growth rates, and returns on assets, capital, and equity. Two of these studies report significantly negative performance postacquisition, four report significantly positive performance, and the rest are in the nonsignificant middle ground.

Three of these studies based their comparisons on pre- and post-merger reported financial performance. An early collection of studies of M&A profitability across seven nations concluded that mergers have "modest effects" on firm profitability in the three to five years after the merger.[19] A 1987 study of 471 acquirers between 1950 and 1977 concluded that the buyers' profitability was one to two percentage points lower than that for a group of control firms; these differences are statistically significant.[20] Another group of five studies found that the performance of buyers is not much different from that of nonbuyers.

But the authors of a more recent—and arguably more meaningful—study of the postacquisition operating performance of the 50 largest U.S. mergers between 1979 and mid-1984 concluded that the asset productivity of the acquiring firms improved significantly after the deals, as measured by higher operating cash flow returns relative to their nonacquiring peers.[21] The study also reported that acquirers maintained their rates of capital expenditure and R&D spending relative to their industries, suggesting that the improved performance did not come at the expense of fundamental investment in the business. Perhaps most important, however, was the study's finding that the announcement returns to the stocks for the merging firms were significantly associated with the improvement in post-merger operating performance. That is, the market's reaction to the announcement of a given deal tended to be a reasonably reliable predictor of future operating improvements, with more positive reactions anticipating larger increases in operating cash flow.

Surveys of executives. The findings of scholars in large-sample surveys have been supplemented by studies of smaller samples that often draw some or all of their findings from questions of managers directly. A 1992 survey of the CEOs of 146 large U.K. companies reported that 77 percent said they believed that profitability increased in the short run after mergers, and 68 percent said that the improvement in profitability lasted for the long run.[22]

Surveys conducted by practitioners are often rather casually reported, limiting our ability to replicate the studies and understand the methodological strengths and weaknesses. Still, the similarity between their findings and those of the scholarly surveys is striking. Six of 12 studies[23] by practitioners reported negative results, while the remainder were neutral or positive. And both the practitioner and scholarly studies seem consistent with the view that although M&A does not produce abnormal returns, investments in acquisitions tend at least to cover their cost of capital.

Conclusion about the profitability of M&A. Drawing on the findings from many studies using large samples of observations, the only tenable conclusion is that M&A *does pay* on average.[24] M&A clearly pays for shareholders of target firms. And most studies of targets and buyers *combined* indicate that these transactions create net value. Finally, for bidders alone, two-thirds of the studies conclude that value is at least conserved if not created. The reality appears to be that the bulk of all M&A transactions is associated with financial performance that at least compensates investors for their opportunity cost; buyers tend to earn an adequate return, but no more. Thus, the average, benchmark-adjusted return to corporate investment in M&A is close to zero, as we would expect in any form of corporate investment in competitive markets. But if the average is zero, the distribution of research findings remains wide, which means that many buyers in M&A transactions should prepare to be disappointed.

ALL M&A IS LOCAL

The broad findings invite careful scrutiny of the returns to buyers. Given a mean that is close to zero with considerable variance, one wants to know what might tip the deal into profit or loss. If you handicap likely M&A returns like a bettor at the track, you will probably fail. You must have a view about the underlying drivers of M&A profitability to make intelligent guesses. Scholars have studied the drivers for years and by now have produced some key insights that can help the handicapper get a view.

Joseph Schumpeter observed that firms endure relentless change driven by turbulence in their business environment. He argued that canny entrepreneurs and managers seize opportunities created by this turbulence to make a profit. M&A is one way of capitalizing on turbulence. For example, a 1985 study examined the M&A wave of 1894–1904 when more than 1,800 firms disappeared through the formation of 93 "trusts."[25] The author found that most M&A activity occurred in industries characterized by capital-intensive, mass-production manufacturing processes in which new firms had recently entered with new and devastating technologies. The M&A of this period benefited the broad economy by removing older and less efficient excess capacity from these industries. Similarly, a study reported that mergers during the period 1890–1930 were significantly associated with the diffusion of electricity and the internal combustion engine, and that much merger activity from 1971–2001 involved the diffusion of information technology.[26]

Michael Jensen, in his 1993 Presidential Address to the American Finance Association, argued that restructuring in the 1980s was stimulated not only by advances in information technology, but also by innovations in organizational design, such as the rise of Wal-Mart and the wholesale clubs that introduced a new retailing model. Jensen pointed also to the creation of new markets (such as the high-yield debt market) that stimulated the wave of hostile takeovers and leveraged buyouts.

Consistent with Jensen's argument, a study found that, during the merger wave of the 1980s, industries with the greatest amount of takeover activity were those that experienced fundamental economic shocks like deregulation, technological innovation, demographic shifts, and input price shocks.[27] The study pointed to M&A activity in banking and broadcasting driven by deregulation, in textiles in response to liberalized trade policy, in the energy industry in response to petroleum price changes, and in food processing due to the demographic shift to low population growth.

These academic studies received confirmation of sorts from a 1998 book by well-known M&A adviser Bruce Wasserstein that cited five main

forces driving the merger process: regulatory and political reform, technological change, fluctuations in financial markets, the role of leadership, and
the tension between scale and focus.[28]

If industry and general economic turbulence drive M&A, then success
or failure is likely to be determined in significant part by the context of
the deal. In this sense, as suggested earlier, *all M&A is local.* This view encourages examination of the forces at work in a particular business setting.
Key drivers will vary from one setting to the next. Generalizations about
M&A success won't have much practical content. Useful insights about the
likely drivers of M&A profitability are to be found on a more local basis.

WHERE M&A PAYS AND WHERE IT STRAYS

If all M&A is local, then success and failure will depend on the local story.
Like putting on Mr. Rogers' cardigan, we need to visit some neighborhoods of profit and loss in M&A while wearing the mind-set of the scientific studies. An understanding of these neighborhoods can help the
business practitioner tilt the odds in favor of an economically successful
deal. In the survey that follows, I take the perspective of *the buyer* and survey the neighborhoods in four different cross sections: strategy, market segments, deal design, and governance.

Neighborhood Map 1: Strategy

One of the oldest lines of research on the determinants of M&A profitability has concentrated on strategic choices. Included among these are
attempts to focus or diversify the firm, to grow the firm, to build market
share, to exploit strategic synergies, to use excess cash, and to initiate acquisition programs.

Focus versus Diversification.   Whether strategic focus or diversification
affects the profitability of the buyer has been the subject of considerable
research. The conventional view has been that a strategy of acquiring companies in related fields (so-called "focusing acquisitions") is the most likely
path to the discovery and exploitation of synergies. Executives intuitively
understand that acquiring one's peer competitors offers opportunities for
cost savings, asset reductions, and other efficiencies. Some of the early re-

search suggested that an M&A strategy of focus or *relatedness* pays better than diversification.[29]

On the other hand, the classic motive for diversification is to create a portfolio of businesses whose cash flows are imperfectly correlated with one another and who therefore might improve the company's ability to weather adversity. But since portfolio diversification is something shareholders can do on their own, why should they pay managers to do this for them?

A number of scholars have suggested that diversification might pay when the combination of unrelated businesses within a single entity facilitates knowledge transfer among different business divisions, reduces financing costs, creates a critical mass for competition, and exploits monitoring through internal capital markets.[30] One study examined 21 companies with conglomeratelike structures and found that they produced returns of 18 percent to 35 percent per year by making nonsynergistic acquisitions.[31] Diversification could also pay in cases where the local capital market is less effective or product markets are experiencing deregulation or other sources of turbulence.[32] There is evidence that diversification pays when the buyer and target are in information-intensive industries.[33] In general, however, the research studies tend to find that strategic relatedness explains returns to buyers: Eight studies find that relatedness is a significant factor in returns to buyers; four studies find no significance.[34] Studies of reported financial results are mixed on whether diversified firms over- or underperform their more focused peers.[35] Looking at the mass of relatedness research, it seems reasonable to conclude that diversification does pay, though perhaps in ways more complicated than a variety of studies can capture.

But working against this logic, event studies of acquisitions, joint ventures, divestitures, spin-offs, and carve-outs generally suggest that focus pays more than diversification.[36] Moreover, several studies have found that diversified companies tend to have lower relative market values than more focused firms, though the source and nature of the discount remain the subject of debate. Eight studies have documented a "diversification discount" ranging from 8 percent to 15 percent.[37] On the other hand, nine studies[38] that use finer data and controls have found that diversification has a neutral or even positive effect on value; these authors argue that corporate data have a natural bias in favor of the diversification discount and that the units acquired by diversified firms were discounted *before* the acquisition. Studies of postmerger operating performance and productivity have also generated conflicting findings.[39]

In sum, this diverse research suggests some key ideas about the strategy "neighborhood" of M&A. First, all else equal, *focus and relatedness probably pay better* as an acquisition strategy than does unrelated diversification. Quite simply, merger benefits are more easily discovered and readily exploited when you stick closer to your knitting. Second, the qualifier "all else equal" admits the possibility that a strategy of unrelated diversification can pay where there are unusual skills such as running a leveraged buyout (LBO) association (Kohlberg Kravis Roberts & Co.) or value investing (Berkshire Hathaway). In short, *special managerial skill could trump the need for strategic linkage*, though it's important to keep in mind that many of the lofty claims of managerial skill will not stand up to scrutiny. Large diversified conglomerates (such as ITT, Westinghouse, Gulf+Western, and Ling-Temco-Vought (LTV) were built on the presumption of such skill and then went to the dinosaur boneyard. Third, an acquisition strategy of relatedness and focus warrants critical scrutiny, too. Industries are dynamic; their attractiveness for investment changes over time, making a strategy of diversifying acquisition a potentially valuable mechanism for industrial exit and reentry elsewhere. Just as companies can destroy value by diversifying, they might also destroy value by staying focused. In short, a mindless strategy of focused and related acquisition is no guarantee of success. In some cases, *the fundamental bet on industry attractiveness trumps the need for strategic linkage.*

Strategic Restructuring Pays.   Reinforcing the point about industry attractiveness is the mass of research showing that the sale or redeployment of underperforming businesses is greeted positively by investors. Studies[40] of the announcement returns from divestitures find that they uniformly create value for shareholders of sellers, on the order of 1 percent to 3 percent significant abnormal returns (although the results for buyers are mixed). Generally, the studies[41] of restructurings suggest that the redeployment of assets seems to be what matters, not merely the sale. In particular, there is evidence that the market rewards divestitures that focus the business activity of the firm.[42] Carve-outs, spin-offs, and tracking stock are neutral-to-beneficial for shareholders, with generally consistent abnormal returns: spin-offs return roughly 2 percent to 4 percent, as compared to 2 percent to 3 percent for carve-outs and 3 percent for tracking stocks. As with divestitures, the use of the funds raised in these transactions makes a difference.[43]

Hypotheses about the sources of gains from restructuring center mainly on two possibilities: (1) Increased focus improves efficiency and operating returns on capital, and (2) Market transactions correct the undervaluation of conglomerates by the market. These possibilities are not mutually exclusive. And the research provides support for both, giving perhaps more weight to the conglomerate inefficiency argument on the grounds of the number of studies confirming the value of corporate focus. But either way, the lesson of such studies is that *continually reshaping the business to respond to changes in the competitive environment pays.*

The Initiation of M&A Programs.   When companies announce they are undertaking a series of acquisitions in pursuit of some strategic objective, their share prices rise significantly.[44] The market's systematically positive response to such announcements suggests that most corporate M&A programs tend to create value over the long haul. Investor response to the initiation of M&A programs is consistent with the investor response to restructuring; both encourage a nimble corporate response to evolving conditions.

Strategic Synergies.   The buyer is typically motivated by the synergies to be exploited in the transaction. Synergies include cost savings, revenue enhancements, and financial synergies. These benefits tend to assume different degrees of credibility in the eyes of investors, with several studies showing cost savings discounted the least and the others somewhat more.[45] As a 1996 study of bank mergers concluded, "the market is readily persuaded by the cost-cutting motive for mergers, while subjecting other rationales to considerable skepticism."[46] In short, *M&A will pay where synergies are more credible.*

Grabs for Market Power.   The positive relationship between market share and investor returns is an article of faith among economists and is supported by empirical research.[47] It should follow, then, that acquisitions that increase a company's market share are associated with increased returns to shareholders. And in fact, bidders' returns increase with increases in market share.[48] But as demonstrated in a 1992 study, the stockholder gains from such deals were more attributable to increases in efficiency rather than in product prices.[49] Horizontal mergers (the type of deals that increase market share) are typically motivated by the prospect of cost savings and other synergies mentioned earlier. In other words, the shareholder benefits of larger market share may not be a compelling motive for a deal; bigger is not necessarily better. More efficient is better.

Value Acquiring Pays; Glamour Acquiring Does Not.   A 1998 study reported postacquisition underperformance by glamour acquirers (companies with high book-to-market value ratios) and superior performance by value-oriented buyers (low book-to-market ratios).[50] Value acquirers earn significant abnormal returns of 8 percent in mergers and 16 percent in tender offers, while glamour acquirers earn a significant −17 percent in mergers and an insignificant +4 percent in tender offers.

M&A to Use Excess Cash Generally Destroys Value Except When Redeployed Profitably.   Cash-rich companies have a choice of returning the cash to investors through dividends or reinvesting it through such activities as M&A. A number of studies[51] have reported value destruction associated with the announcement of M&A transactions by firms with excess cash. However, my own 1988 study of this question found that transactions pairing "slack-poor" and "slack-rich" companies tend to be value-increasing.[52] As my study also showed, before the merger, buyers tend to have more cash and lower debt ratios than nonacquirers. And the returns to the buyers' shareholders are positively correlated with changes in the buyers' debt ratios that accompany the merger.

Neighborhood Map 2: Investment Opportunity

A second class of studies suggests that market conditions and the nature of the acquired companies affect the profitability of M&A for buyers. This perspective highlights the segmented nature of the M&A market. Segments that tend to be profitable for buyers are privately owned targets and underperforming targets. More costly to buyers are foreign targets and deals consummated during "hot" market conditions.

Targets That Can Be Restructured.   The opportunity to redirect the target company toward more profitable operation would seem to suggest greater opportunity for a profitable merger. Hostile tender offers are the classic arena for this. Some research suggests that targets of hostile tender offers are underperformers with relatively low share prices.[53] In such cases, bidders expect to earn profits from improving the targets' performance. But other studies are consistent with the view that targets are healthy but happen to fit very well with the buyer's strategy.[54] Thus, the evidence is mixed on the question of whether takeover targets tend to be inefficient firms. They seem not to be basket cases, but nor are they stellar performers. The bulk of these firms have middling-to-mediocre performance in which the bidder sees a profitable opportunity.

One thread that runs through many of these studies has less to do with efficiency than with a key aspect of governance, namely, the entrenchment of target management. Bidders tend to take more forceful measures mainly after target managers reject friendly entreaties.

Privately Owned Assets.   Comparing acquisitions of public and private companies matched by size, industry, and time period, researchers found an average discount of 20 percent to 28 percent in the prices paid for U.S. private firms relative to those paid for their publicly traded counterparts—and discounts of as much as 44 percent to 54 percent for foreign private target firms.[55] Consistent with this finding, several other studies have reported a sizeable positive announcement-day return to bidders when they buy private firms as opposed to public firms.[56] Explanations by researchers point to lack of information on private companies, a discount for lack of marketability of private firm securities, bargaining advantages for public buyers of private firms, the absence of competitive bidding that creates favorable purchase prices, and the creation of new power groups in the buyer company that could motivate the buyer to improve performance.

Crossing Borders.   Cross-border M&A pays in a fashion consistent with the findings for U.S. domestic M&A.[57] That is, targets earn large returns; buyers essentially break even; and on a combined basis, shareholders gain. The chief difference in crossing borders is that foreign bidders appear to pay more than domestic bidders. Two studies report that U.S. targets receive materially higher returns than foreign targets. According to five other studies, the returns to U.S. targets are higher in cases involving foreign rather than domestic buyers.[58] Some researchers have argued that this premium represents payment for the special local knowledge and market access that the target provides the foreign buyer.[59] Also, acquisition offers foreign companies entry into the U.S. legal regime, which itself can serve to increase value. A stream of studies in the 1990s showed that the legal regime in foreign countries has a significant influence on valuation.[60]

Hot and Cold M&A Markets: Misvaluation of Buyer Firms.   Market "windows of opportunity" open and close over time, which creates a very different kind of market segmentation. Two classic sources of this variation are changes in regulation and the appearance of market bubbles. Research shows a slight tendency for bidder returns to decline over time.[61] The returns appear to have been more positive in the 1960s and 1970s than in the 1980s and 1990s, except for deals in technology and banking, where returns to bidders increased in the 1990s. Changing government regulations affect the temperature of M&A markets. These changes take the form of antitrust actions, court decisions, and legislation (such as the Williams Act of 1968).

M&A waves peak during buoyant equity markets, the "hot" markets when security prices are relatively high. The recent equity market peak during the period 1998–2001 was associated with the most M&A activity in U.S. history. Perhaps buyers overpay in hot M&A markets; This might reflect market mania or private recognition by buyers that their shares are overvalued. As mentioned earlier, a 2003 study suggested that the massive wealth destruction in 87 large deals from 1998–2001 reflected the reassessment of buyers' stand-alone valuations.[62] Another study published in the same year reported that the more highly valued (or "overvalued," as indicated by a high price-to-book ratio) is the buyer, the more negative is the investor response to the acquisition announcement.[63] The hot M&A market poses a major dilemma to the CEO of an overvalued company: If you acquire, your shares will drop; if you don't acquire, your shares are also likely to drop. In this can't-win setting, M&A may offer a chance to transfer part of the prospective losses to target company shareholders rather than to have your own shareholders absorb them.

Neighborhood Map 3: Deal Design

A third category of research suggests that the terms of the transaction have a significant influence on profitability of M&A for the buyer. Important terms include form of payment, financing, use of earnouts and collars, tax treatment, and social issues.

Form of Payment: Cash versus Stock.   Several studies report that stock-based deals are associated with negative returns to the buyer's shareholders at deal announcements, whereas cash deals are zero or slightly positive.[64] This finding is consistent with the idea that managers time the issuance of shares of stock to occur at the high point in the cycle of the company's fortunes, or in the stock market cycle. Thus, the announcement of the payment with shares, like the announcement of an offering of seasoned stock, could be taken as a sign that managers believe the firm's shares are overpriced.[65]

This consistent result across these studies can be summarized as follows: First, although target shareholders earn large positive announcement returns, these returns differ materially with the form of payment. In cases where payment is in cash, target shareholder returns are considerably *higher*. When payment is in stock, target shareholder returns are significantly positive, but materially lower than those for the cash deals. Second, although buyer shareholders basically break even, on average, at announcement, the form of payment produces an important difference in returns that complements the returns to targets. Namely, when payment is in cash, estimates of average buyer shareholder returns range from zero to positive, in some cases significantly positive. But when payment is in stock, buyer returns are significantly negative. Tender offers amplify the cash-versus-stock effect; in cases of tender offers paid in cash, the returns to buyers are even higher and the returns from offers paid in stock are even lower. Also, larger cash deals have more positive returns and larger equity deals have more negative returns. The studies also reveal that *stock* tends to be used when a deal is friendly, the buyer's stock price is relatively high, ownership in the buyer is not concentrated, deals are larger in size, and the buyer has less cash.[66]

LBOs.   Shareholders of target companies in LBOs earn large abnormal returns, roughly in line with the target returns found in the general studies of all M&A transactions.[67] The large returns to target and buyer shareholders predict improvements in operating efficiency.[68] LBO transactions are followed by large increases of operating cash flow relative to sales and by large decreases in capital expenditures. Contrary to the belief of some critics, who argued that LBOs were primarily motivated by tax considerations and would transfer wealth from the public sector to the private sector, studies have also found that the gains from LBOs did not come at the expense of the government treasury. On net, tax revenues actually increased as a result of LBOs due to several factors: increased capital gains taxes paid by target firm shareholders, taxes on increased operating earnings; taxes on added interest income earned by creditors; taxes on the capital gains from asset sales; and additional taxes arising from more efficient use of capital.[69]

Use of Earnouts.   Two studies have reported that the returns to buyers are higher when the payment is structured to be contingent on meeting future performance benchmarks.[70] These returns are greater than returns in straight cash or straight stock deals and are larger in cases where the target's management stays. In this sense, earnouts and other contingent payment structures can be viewed as providing stronger performance incentives for selling managers as well as a risk management device for the buyer.

Use of Collars.   A collar is another risk management device, used in stock-for-stock transactions to hedge uncertainty about the value of the buyer. It changes the payment if the buyer's price falls or rises beyond predetermined triggers and often grants either or both of the merging firms the right to renegotiate the deal if the collar is triggered. In this sense, a collar is effectively an option to cancel a merger.

A 2003 study found that the announcement returns to the buyer's shareholders were not significantly affected by the use of collars.[71] At the same time, the announcement returns were lower, and the targets' returns higher, in transactions involving floating rather than fixed collars.[72] Stock offers with collars were significantly more likely to succeed (i.e., to close) than either straight stock or cash offers.

Social Issues: The Merger of Equals.   A great deal of anecdotal evidence suggests that "social" (or "managerial") issues such as appointment of the CEO, board, senior management, headquarters location, and compensation can have a huge influence on deal pricing and profitability to the buyer. Recent research on the "merger of equals" (MOE) deal structure illustrates this influence.[73] These mergers combine partners of roughly equal influence without the payment of a premium by one party to the other. They are typically mergers effected by an exchange of shares with a low or zero implied acquisition premium. The studies show that, despite variation over time, premiums in mergers of equals are typically much smaller than those in other deals. Also, target shareholders earn positive abnormal returns that, although significantly positive, are also smaller than those in other deals. A 2004 study concluded that, in mergers of equals, "CEOs trade 'power for premium.' Specifically, they negotiate control rights in the merged firm (both board and management) in exchange for a lower premium for their shareholders."[74] Others note that the MOE structure, by signaling an absence of dominance of one side over the other, helps reduce resistance in the target company, thereby increasing the probability that the deal gets consummated and building a general sense of teamwork that can pay off in faster postmerger integration.

Tax Exposure. Tax planning considerations are, of course, the focus of considerable professional time and talent in M&A.[75] A 1989 study found that about half of all acquisitions are designed to be "tax-free" or only partly taxable.[76] The form of reorganization is strongly related to the abnormal return at the merger announcement. In taxable deals, the acquisition premium is more than twice as high. Two effects might explain this (though neither explanation is entirely satisfying): (1) In taxable deals, target company shareholders' taxes are due immediately rather than deferred, thus creating a demand for higher payment stimulated by the time value of money; (2) In taxable deals, the buyer is allowed to "step up" the tax basis of the acquired assets, thus affording a larger depreciation tax shield and raising the ceiling on what the buyer can afford to pay. Net operating loss (NOL) carryforwards and debt tax shields can have a similar effect.

Perhaps because of the target's bargaining power, then, or because of a "winner's curse" effect, buyers *do* pay more in taxable deals. The evidence suggests that an even greater percentage of acquisitions of privately held companies tend to be structured to defer tax payments as a means of estate or investment planning for controlling individual shareholders or family groups. But if taxes clearly affect the form of certain transactions, researchers continue to actively debate whether tax considerations *cause* acquisitions.

Neighborhood Map 4: Governance

Research shows that firms with stronger governance practices are more highly valued.[77] Thus, in the M&A map of returns to buyers, we should observe higher returns associated with shareholder-oriented management and protections for shareholder rights and the rights of minority investors. This extends to governance structures, board independence, the use of antitakeover defenses, and activism by investors.

Activism by Institutional Investors. In 1993, institutional investors blocked a merger between AB Volvo and Renault, and the net effect of this action was to restore and then create value for Volvo's shareholders. Institutions such as pension funds and life insurance companies can be distinguished from individual investors by their large size, strong performance orientation, close proximity to markets, ability to bear transaction costs, and, in many cases, degree of sophistication. Research shows that most transactions in which these investors become active (in the sense of seeking to influence the board of directors and management) tend to be associated with the creation of shareholder value.[78] Studies of LBOs,[79] replacement of executives of underperforming firms,[80] and corporate restructurings[81] reveal significant gains in equity value following realignment and improved governance.

What Managers Have at Stake. Studies suggest that returns to buyer firm shareholders are associated with larger equity interests by managers and employees.[82] In assessing the pattern of performance associated with deal characteristics, a 1997 study concluded that "while takeovers were usually break-even investments, the profitability of individual transactions varied widely . . . [and] the transactions characteristics *that were under management control* substantially influenced the ultimate payoffs from takeovers."[83] Such characteristics include the degree of relatedness of target and buyer, the form of payment, and whether the transaction was friendly or hostile.

By far the most compelling evidence of the effect of corporate governance on performance is the remarkable increase in value achieved by buyers in LBOs. In LBOs, managers tend to commit a significant portion of their own net worth to the success of the transaction. As reported by Jensen in testimony to Congress in 1989, the average LBO doubled its enterprise value in its four years as a private company—and with debt-to-total capital leverage ratios that averaged 85 percent, the median equity return to the LBO buyers was 785 percent.[84] Although part of these returns were attributable to tax savings due to debt and depreciation shields, economists have concluded that the largest portion of the gains came significantly from efficiencies and greater operational improvements implemented after the LBO.

Approaching the Target: Friendly versus Hostile. The style of the buyer's approach to the target is influenced by the degree of entrenchment of the target's management. Mergers are typically friendly affairs, negotiated between the top managements of buyer and target firms. Hostile bids, on the other hand, are structured as take-it-or-leave-it proposals made directly to the target firm shareholders, and are often viewed by the target management as coercive. Several studies[85] report larger announcement returns to bidders in tender offers than in friendly negotiated transactions, with successful bidders in hostile takeovers estimated to earn positive abnormal returns of 2 percent to 4 percent. The higher returns from tender offers may reflect bargain prices as well as the expected economic benefits from replacing management and redirecting the strategy of the firm.

Target shareholders also win in that they receive higher acquisition premiums in hostile deals than in friendly deals. When a target successfully rejects a bidder, the target's share price falls, but typically to a price level higher than prevailed before—in part because unsuccessful takeover attempts often lead to restructurings that unlock value for shareholders. And when a hostile bidder offers cash, the returns are more positive still, which could be explained by the poor health and/or investment attractiveness of the target. As noted earlier, the targets of hostile bids tend to be mediocre performers at best. The larger lesson in this case has to do with ineffective governance and the removal of entrenched and inefficient management.

Use of Antitakeover Defenses. Defenses can help shareholders of well-governed companies by enhancing the bargaining power of management, enabling them to extract high prices from bidders. But defenses can also harm shareholders of poorly run firms by entrenching managers who disregard their duty to shareholders. To make sense of market responses to announcements about takeover defenses, one must have a view about the efficiency and governance of the target company. One gauge of the economic impact of defenses is the reaction of investors to the announcement of takeover defense placements. Several studies suggest that the strength of the target's governance mechanisms is a strong determinant of the market reaction to takeover defenses.[86] When the board of directors is strong and independent, and when the CEO's interests are strongly aligned with shareholder returns, the reaction tends to be positive; when governance is poor or the CEO's rewards are misaligned, the reaction is negative.

CONCLUSION: WHAT THE 'HOODS TELL US

All M&A is local. The practical value of M&A research lies in the insights it offers about the local conditions associated with the creation or destruction of value. For this reason, blanket assertions about M&A like the popular claim of general merger failure are not very useful to practitioners or, for that matter, to scholars. Conventional wisdom tends to be hazy about the evidence of success and failure and tends to take findings that apply in one neighborhood as representative of the whole. Critical thinking about M&A steps well beyond the conventional wisdom to focus on patterns of local profit and loss. Table 2.1 summarizes the range of research insights from the articles surveyed here.

The neighborhoods of profit and loss offer a number of warnings to the CEO. You are *more likely* to fail in M&A when:

1. *Your organization enters a fundamentally unprofitable industry, or refuses to exit from one.* A sound industry bet based on expected returns—thinking like an investor—is a necessary precondition for M&A success. Restructurings and the launch of M&A programs reveal careful thought and effort to position the firm strategically for the highest profit. On the other hand, some M&A programs that are cloaked in the language of strategic profitability often harbor serious logical traps, such as momentum and glamour acquiring that should be viewed with skepticism. The CEO needs a sensitive humbug-detector when listening to assertions about the "strategic" value of an M&A transaction.

TABLE 2.1   WHERE M&A PAYS AND WHERE IT STRAYS: ADJUSTED RETURNS TO BUYERS BY "NEIGHBORHOOD"

Returns to buyers likely will be higher if	*Returns to buyers likely will be lower if*
1. Strategic motivation.	1. Opportunistic motivation.
2. Value acquiring.	2. Momentum growth/glamour acquiring.
3. Focused/related acquiring.	3. Lack of focus/unrelated diversification.
4. Credible synergies.	4. Incredible synergies.
5. To use excess cash *profitably*.	5. Just to use excess cash.
6. Negotiated purchases of private firms.	6. Auctions of public firms.
7. Cross borders for special advantage.	7. Cross borders naively.
8. Go hostile.	8. Negotiate with resistant target.
9. Buy during cold M&A markets.	9. Buy during hot M&A markets.
10. Pay with cash.	10. Pay with stock.
11. High tax benefits to buyer.	11. Low tax benefits to buyer.
12. Finance with debt judiciously.	12. Over-lever.
13. Stage the payments (earnouts).	13. Pay fully up-front.
14. Merger of equals.	14. Not a merger of equals.
15. Managers have significant stake.	15. Managers have low or no stake.
16. Shareholder-oriented management.	16. Entrenched management.
17. Active investors.	17. Passive investors.

2. *Your organization steps far away from what it knows.* Generally, focus and relatedness pay better than unrelated diversification. The discovery and exploitation of merger synergies is more likely when dealing with familiar territory. However, a firm's core competency could be in managing a portfolio of unrelated businesses. Thus, the key strategic driver of profitability has less to do with focus and relatedness and more to do with knowledge, mastery, and competencies. What does your company know? What is it good at doing?

3. *The economic benefits of the deal are improbable or not incremental to the deal.* The capital market judges merger synergies skeptically. At the core of best M&A practice is the impulse to do good things for your shareholders that they cannot do for themselves. But what counts for "synergies" within some buyer firms is a host of projects that would have gotten done eventually with or without the acquisition. This is a failure to think "at the margin" by asking what *new* flows of cash an acquisition will trigger. Just as bad is the tendency to imagine benefits that are highly improbable, and treat them as likely. Revenue-enhancement synergies from cross-selling, for instance, are notoriously hard to capture, and research shows that they are discounted rather heavily by investors.

4. *You fail to seek some economic advantage.* Competition drives returns to their minimum. As a buyer, you face competitors in auctions, in the purchase of public firms, and generally whenever you move with the crowd. In settings like these, you will pay top dollar. Positive abnormal returns are more likely to be found in less competitive segments of the market, notably those involving private firms and assets. And making unsolicited offers to the board and its shareholders can preempt interlopers and create bargaining power in negotiations with entrenched managers. In other circumstances, however, bargaining power may reside with the target. A prime example is the target in a foreign country where, because of entry barriers, knowledge of local markets and customs, and market power, the buyer will likely pay a premium.

5. *Your organization is not very creative in deal structuring.* The returns on even a mediocre deal can be enhanced for the buyer through artful deal design. The use of cash, debt financing, tax shields, staged payments, merger-of-equals terms, and earnout incentive structures are all associated with higher buyer returns.

6. *Your organization has poor checks, balances, and incentives.* This begins at the top, with the composition and processes of the board of directors and their willingness to listen to the shareholders whom they represent. And it extends to your oversight of the firm and the manner in which you have delegated decision authority to others in your firm. Throughout the organization, from operating man-

agers to the front line of deal-doers, your people must *think like in-vestors.* The principle is simple: Do you and they have some "skin in the game"?

The survey of scientific research tells us that executives have choices in M&A that, when made thoughtfully, can tilt the odds of success in their favor. This is a very different perspective from what conventional thinking might suggest.

NOTES

1. For helpful comments on this chapter, I thank Don Chew, editor of *Journal of Applied Corporate Finance* where it was published in substantially the same form. It was prepared with research assistance from Anna Buchanan, Jessica Chan, and Chad Rynbrandt and draws some content from my book, *Applied Mergers and Acquisitions* (New York: John Wiley & Sons, 2004).

2. See chapter 3 ("Does M&A Pay?") of my book, *Applied Mergers and Acquisitions* (New York: John Wiley & Sons, 2004).

3. T. Grubb and R. Lamb, *Capitalize on Merger Chaos* (New York: Free Press, 2000), 9, 10, 12, 14.

4. Gregory Zuckerman, "Ahead of the Tape," *Wall Street Journal*, December 30, 2002, C1.

5. "Why Most Big Deals Don't Pay Off: A BusinessWeek Analysis Shows that 61% of Buyers Destroyed Shareholder Wealth," *BusinessWeek*, October 14, 2002, 60.

6. Beyond wishing for more discussion of the sample and research methodology in the *BusinessWeek* article, I offer no criticism about the execution of the research. As far as I can tell the researchers used an approach that is conventional in academic work.

7. See Moeller, Schlingemann, and Stulz (2003 and 2004).

8. For brevity, I will follow the lead of most academic researchers and focus on the economic consequences for the shareholders of the acquirer and the target, although the impact on other stakeholders is certainly of interest. This is also consistent with the fact that the primary fiduciary responsibility of directors is to their shareholders.

9. Studies reporting returns to target firm shareholders include these: Langetieg (1978); Bradley, Desai, and Kim (1988); Dennis and McConnell (1986); Jarrell and Poulsen (1989); Lang, Stulz, and Walkling (1989); Franks, Harris, and Titman (1991); Servaes (1991); Bannerjee and Owers (1992); Healy,

Palepu, and Ruback (1992); Kaplan and Weisbach (1992); Berkovitch and Narayanan (1993); Smith and Kim (1994); Schwert (1996); Loughran and Vijh (1997); Maquieira, Megginson and Nail (1998); Eckbo and Thorburn (2000); Leeth and Borg (2000); Mulherin and Boone (2000); Mulherin (2000); DeLong (2001); Houston et al. (2001); Kuipers, Miller, and Patel (2003); Renneboog and Goergen (2003); Billett, King, and Mauer (2003); and Beitel et al. (2002).

10. Studies reporting significantly negative returns to buyer shareholders include Dodd (1980); Asquith, Bruner, and Mullins (1987); Varaiya and Ferris (1987); Servaes (1991); Jennings and Mazzeo (1991); Bannerjee and Owers (1992); Byrd and Hickman (1992); Kaplan and Weisbach (1992); Sirower (1994); Mitchell and Stafford (2000); Walker (2000); DeLong (2001); Houston et al. (2001); and Kuipers, Miller, and Patel (2003).

11. Studies reporting insignificantly negative returns to buyer shareholders are Langetieg (1978); Morck, Shleifer, and Vishny (1990); Franks, Harris, and Titman (1991); Healy, Palepu, and Ruback (1992); Berkovitch and Narayanan (1993); Eckbo and Thorburn (2000); Mulherin and Boone (2000); and Ghosh, A. (2002). Studies reporting insignificantly positive returns are Asquith (1983); Malatesta (1983); Wier (1983); Lang, Stulz, and Walkling (1989); Smith and Kim (1994); Schwert (1996); Lyroudi, Lazardis, and Subeniotis (1999); Beitel et al. (2002); and Billett, King, and Mauer (2003).

12. Studies showing significantly positive returns to buyer shareholders are Dodd and Ruback (1977); Kummer and Hoffmeister (1978); Bradley (1980); Jarrell and Bradley (1980); Bradley, Desai, and Kim (1982); Asquith, Bruner, and Mullins (1983); Eckbo (1983); Denis and McConnell (1986); Jarrell, Brickley, and Netter (1987); Sicherman and Pettway (1987); Bradley, Desai, and Kim (1988); Jarrell and Poulsen (1989); Loderer and Martin (1990); Maquieira et al. (1998); Eckbo and Thorburn (2000); Leeth and Borg (2000); Mulherin (2000); Kohers and Kohers (2000); Kohers and Kohers (2001); Floreani and Rigamonti (2001); Fuller, Netter, and Stegemoller (2002); Renneboog and Goergen (2003); and Moeller, Schlingemann, and Stulz (2003).

13. Studies of long-term returns to buyers are Mandelker (1974); Dodd and Ruback (1977); Langetieg (1978); Asquith (1983); Bradley, Desai, and Kim (1983); Malatesta (1983); Agrawal, Jaffe, and Mandelker (1992); Loderer and Martin (1992); Gregory (1997); Loughran and Vijh (1997); Rau and Vermaelen (1998); Louis (undated); Pettit (2000); Moeller, Schlingemann, and Stulz (2003); Ferris and Park (2001); and Kohers and Kohers (2001).

14. Shleifer and Vishny (2001); Moeller, Schlingemann, and Stulz (2003); and Dong, Hirschleifer, Richardson, and Teoh (2003).

15. Mitchell and Mulherin (1996).

16. Asquith, Bruner, and Mullins (1983).

17. Twenty-four studies reporting positive returns: Halpern (1973); Langetieg (1978); Firth (1980); Bradley, Desai, and Kim (1982); Bradley, Desai, and

Kim (1983); Malatesta (1983); Varaiya (1985); Bradley, Desai, and Kim (1988); Lang, Stulz, and Walkling (1989); Franks, Harris, and Titman (1991); Servaes (1991); Bannerjee and Owers (1992); Healy, Palepu, and Ruback (1992); Kaplan and Weisbach (1992); Berkovitch and Narayanan (1993); Smith and Kim (1994); Leeth and Borg (2000); Mulherin and Boone (2000); Mulherin (2000); Houston et al. (2001); Fan and Goyal (2002); Kuipers, Miller, and Patel (2003); Gupta and Misra (undated); and Beitel et al. (2002).

18. Fifteen studies of financial performance: Meeks (1977); Salter and Weinhold (1979); Mueller (1980); Mueller (1985); Ravenscraft and Scherer (1987 article); Ravenscraft and Scherer (1987 book); Herman and Lowenstein (1988); Seth (1990); Healey, Palepu, and Ruback (1992); Chatterjee and Mecks (1996); Dickerson, Givson, and Tsakalotos (1997); Healy, Palepu, and Ruback (1997); Parrino and Harris (1999); Parrino and Harris (2001); Ghosh (2001); Carline, Linn, and Yadav (2001); and Sharma and Ho (2002).

19. Mueller (1980).

20. Ravenscraft and Scherer (1987).

21. Healy, Palepu, and Ruback (1992).

22. Ingham, Kran, and Lovestam (1992).

23. Twelve practitioner studies: Johan Brjoksten, 1965 (cited in Lajoux and Weston (1998)); McKinsey & Co., 1987 (cited in Lajoux and Weston (1998)); PA Consulting (cited in Lajoux and Weston (1998)); McKinsey & Co. (cited in Fisher (1994)); Mercer Management and *BusinessWeek*, October 1995 (cited in Lajoux and Weston (1998)); David Mitchell of Economists Intelligence Unit, 1996 (cited in Lajoux and Weston (1998)); Kenneth Smith, in research for Mercer Consulting, 1997, and for Mitchell Madison Group, 1998 (cited in Lajoux and Weston (1998)); Michael Mayo, Lehman Bros. (cited in Lajoux and Weston (1998)); Andersen Consulting (cited in Bahree (1999)); KPMG LLP (Kelly, Cook, and Spitzer (1999)); Chaudhuri and Tabrizi (1999); Booz-Allen & Hamilton (2001); and Adolph et al. (2001).

24. This is the conclusion also of five major surveys of the research literature that predate this one: Dennis Mueller (1979); Jensen and Ruback (1983); Weidenbaum and Vogt (1987); Datta, Pinches, and Narayanan (1992); and Caves (1989).

25. Lamoreaux (1985).

26. Jovanovic and Rousseau (2002).

27. Mitchell and Mulherin (1996).

28. Wasserstein (1998).

29. See, for example, Rumelt (1974, 1982), who found higher equity returns for strategies of related diversification. Rumelt's work prompted a critical reappraisal of the conglomerate diversification movement of the 1960s and early 1970s.

30. See, for example, Salter and Weinhold (1979). But the evidence about the effectiveness of internal capital markets is mixed. For instance, a study of the behav-

ior of oil companies during the oil price collapse of the mid-1980s found evidence that "large diversified companies overinvest in and subsidize underperforming segments" (Lamont, 1997, 106).

31. See Anslinger and Copeland (1996). They explained the superior performance of these firms as due to seven principles: "Insist on innovating operating strategies. Don't do the deal if you can't find the leader. Offer big incentives to top-level executives. Link compensation to changes in cash flow. Push the pace of change. Foster dynamic relationships among owners, managers, and the board. Hire the best acquirers" (127).

32. The distinction between developed and developing countries is also interesting as a possible focus for diversification strategies. Hubbard and Palia (1999) found that the returns from conglomeration were positive and significant during the 1960s, a time when the authors believed that U.S. capital markets were less efficient in allocating capital than they are today. This is consistent with Chandler (1977) who documented the rise of the modern corporation and showed that enhanced methods of monitoring and information transfer enabled senior executives to manage larger and more diverse operations effectively, though he was also highly critical of the conglomerate form of organization. Khanna and Palepu (1997, 2000) made a similar argument in studying conglomerates in India. The authors concluded that these industrial groups enjoyed greater efficiency because of their ability to allocate resources better than the capital market there. Fauver, Houston, and Naranjo (2002) studied 8,000 companies in 35 countries and concluded that "internal capital markets generated through corporate diversification are more valuable (or less costly) in countries where there is less shareholder protection and where firms find it more difficult to raise external capital" (1). The research of Lins and Servaes (1999, 2002) reinforces such a comparison by reporting diversification discounts of 0 percent in Germany, 10 percent in Japan, and 15 percent in the United Kingdom. Nevertheless, in seven emerging markets, they found a diversification discount of about 7 percent, and concluded that the discount was concentrated among firms that are members of industrial groups. This suggests that differences in corporate governance and/or rule of law across countries may have a material impact on the benefits of a diversification strategy.

33. See Morck and Yeung (1997).

34. Studies finding no or low effect of relatedness on returns to buyers include Leeth and Borg (2000); Switzer (1996); Lubatkin et al. (1997); and Linn and Switzer (2001). Other recent studies report results of a significant effect of relatedness on buyers' returns: Healy, Palepu, and Ruback (1992); Datta and Puia (1995); Weech-Maldonado (2002); Lubatkin and O'Neill (1987); Loree et al.(2000); Flanagan (1996); Scanlon et al. (1989); and Chatterjee and Lubatkin (1990).

35. Studies that have looked at accounting performance: Though accounting-based operating results are easily managed by executives and are vulnerable to

exogenous effects unrelated to diversification, they are an easy focus of investigation. Four studies (Rumelt (1974, 1982); Ravenscraft and Scherer (1987); and Kaplan and Weisbach (1992)) showed that firms following strategies of unrelated diversification underperform those firms who focus more. Yet four others (Kruse (2002); Healy, Palepu, and Ruback (1992); Parrino and Harris (1999); and Cornett and Tehranian (1992)) found *improvements* in operating performance following diversifying acquisitions. In addition, Anslinger and Copeland (1996) found that firms pursuing a conscious strategy of unrelated diversification realized high abnormal returns for sustained periods.

36. Event studies of acquisitions, joint ventures, divestitures, spin-offs, and carve-outs:

Acquisitions. Seven studies (Morck, Schleifer, and Vishny (1990); Sicherman and Pettway (1987); Morck (1990); Maqueira et al. (1998); Nail, Megginson, and Maqueira (1998); Delong (2001); and Megginson, Morgan, and Nail (2002)) find cumulative average residuals (CARs) at the announcements of transactions that are significantly more negative for diversifying deals than for focusing deals. These studies suggest that mergers that focus the firm enhance the buyer's share value by 1percent to 3 percent more than diversifying deals. Yet six other studies (Carow (2001); Hubbard and Palia (1999); Schipper and Thompson (1983); Elgers and Clark (1980); Matsusaka (1993); and Ferris et al. (2002)) show significantly positive CARs for diversifying acquisitions; most of these, however, are studies of conglomerate acquisitions in the 1960s (e.g., Hubbard and Palia (1999)) or are associated with the relaxation of regulatory constraints on diversifying acquisitions (e.g., Carow (2001). On balance, the event studies of acquisition announcements suggest that focus pays more than diversification.

Joint ventures and alliances (JVs). Three studies consider the effect of focusing or horizontal JVs. Ferris et al. (2002) find that focus-increasing JVs show materially larger CARs than diversifying JVs. Chan et al. (1997) report that horizontal alliances involving technology transfer have a materially higher CAR. And Gleason et al. (2003) find that horizontal deals in the financial services industry have materially higher CARs than diversifying deals. The event studies of JV and alliance announcements suggest that focus pays more than diversification.

Divestitures, spin-offs, and carve-outs. Generally, divestitures, spin-offs, and carve-outs are good news for investors; and since these deals shed assets, the results would seem to be roughly supportive of focusing. But what matters is the nature of the assets being disposed. Two studies of carve-outs suggest a materially larger announcement CAR when the carved-out unit is not from an industry related to the parent's core business (Hurlburt et al. (2002) and Vijh (2000)). Three studies of spin-offs show a materially larger announcement CAR when the transaction is focus-increasing (Veld and Veld-Meruklova (2002); McNeil and Moore (2001); and Johnson et al. (1996)). Regarding divestitures, Donaldson

(1990) reports materially larger positive CARs at the announcement of sale of noncore assets compared to core asset sales. Dittmar and Shivdasani (undated) report that, over the year following the divestiture, firms that became single-business firms had a 3 percent higher return than those that remained diversified. In short, the event studies of divestitures, spin-offs, and carve-outs are consistent with benefits from focusing and penalties from diversification.

37. The "diversification discount" (see Berger and Otek (1995)) is computed as the market value of a company's equity plus the book value of liabilities divided by the company's "imputed" value—measured as the sum of its segment values estimated by the product of a valuation multiple for single-business peers (total capital divided by assets, sales, or operating earnings times the accounting value for the segment). Eight studies document the diversification discount: Berger and Ofek (1995, 1999); Lang and Stulz (1994); Servaes (1996); Comment and Jarrell (1995); Lins and Servaes (1999); Mansi and Reeb (2002); Denis, Denis, and Yost (2002); and Lamont and Polk (2002) find negative excess values for diversified firms, in the range of 8 percent to 15 percent. Studies showing that diversified firms have lower market values: "Tobin's Q" is a measure of economic efficiency that is estimated as the ratio of the market value of assets divided by book value. The higher the Q, the higher the efficiency. Typically these studies regress Q against a variety of independent variables, including measures of diversification and focus. Three studies give findings consistent with the benefits of focus. Lang and Stulz (1994) find that diversified firms have lower Qs than single-business firms. Morck and Yeung (1997) find that diversification is associated with lower Q except where the industry is information-intensive. Aggarwal and Samwick (2003) report that diversification has a significantly negative effect on Q.

38. Nine studies that find no discount: Chevalier (2000); Hyland and Diltz (2002); Klein (2001); Graham, Lemmon, and Wolf (1998); Campa and Kedia (1999); Villalonga (1999, 2003a); Mansi and Reeb (2002); and Whited (2001).

39. Studies that have examined postmerger productivity: Lichtenberg (1992) found lower total factor productivity with increases in diversification. But Schoar (2002) reported that plants in diversified firms were 7 percent more productive than plants in single-business firms. Nevertheless, increases in diversification are associated with a net decrease in productivity. Plants that had been acquired actually increased their productivity, whereas incumbent plants decreased in productivity. But since there were fewer acquired than incumbent plants, the total effect on productivity was negative. She wrote, "Diversified firms experience a new toy effect, whereby management focus shifts towards new segments at the expense of existing divisions. As a whole, these results indicate that diversified firms have a productivity advantage over their stand-alone counterparts. They even increase the productivity of their acquired assets. With each diversifying move, however, these firms lose some of their productivity advantage" (2380).

40. Studies of announcement returns from divestitures: One study reported positive and significant returns (Hite et al. (1987)), a second reported positive and insignificant returns (John and Ofek (1995)), and a third reported negative and insignificant returns to buyers (Allen and Phillips (2000)).

41. Studies of restructurings: Lang et al. (1995) found an announcement return of 4 percent when the firm committed to returning the divestiture proceeds to investors (e.g., in the form of reducing the firm's debt). In comparison, the announcement return was insignificantly different from zero when the firm planned to reinvest in the business. Announcements of plant closings (Blackwell et al. (1990)) are frequently the prelude to divestiture or liquidation and produce small but significantly negative returns to shareholders. Announcements of plant closings can signal to investors the failure of a strategy. Complete voluntary liquidations of a business, which is the ultimate divestiture program, deliver the highest returns to shareholders, in the range of 12 percent to 13 percent.

42. Evidence that the market rewards focusing divestitures: John and Ofek (1995) document a significant relation between the announcement returns at divestiture and the degree of increase in strategic focus of the firm after divestiture. In his study of a 20-year restructuring program at General Mills, Donaldson (1990) found that announcements of the sale of noncore assets were associated with higher abnormal returns than was the sale of correlated assets (+2.03 percent versus −0.43 percent). Kaiser and Stouraitis (2001) studied the refocusing effort of Thorn-EMI and reported positive and significant abnormal returns.

43. Allen and McConnell (1998) found that investors reacted positively to carve-outs that would generate cash to be paid to creditors, but were neutral in instances where the funds were to be reinvested in the business.

44. Evidence of share price rise on series of strategic acquisitions: Asquith, Bruner, and Mullins (1983); Fuller, Netter, and Stegemoller (2002); Gregory (1997); and Schipper and Thompson (1983).

45. Research finds cost savings are discounted the least and the others somewhat more: Houston, James, and Ryngaert (2001) studied the association of forecast cost savings and revenue enhancements in bank mergers and found a significant relationship between the present value of these benefits and announcement-day returns. The market appears to discount the value of these benefits, however, and applies a greater discount to revenue-enhancing synergies and a smaller discount to cost-reduction synergies. DeLong (2003) also studied bank mergers and found that investors responded positively to mergers where one partner was inefficient, and where the merger focused geography, activity, and earnings: All are symptomatic of synergy gains.

46. Houston and Ryngaert (1996), 76.

47. Studies revealing that M&A efforts to enhance market position yield no better performance: Ravenscraft and Scherer (1987); Mueller (1985); and Eckbo

(1992). Studies of share price movements of competitive rivals: Stillman (1983) and Eckbo (1983).

48. Ghosh (2002).

49. Eckbo (1992).

50. Rau and Vermaelen (1998).

51. Studies reporting value destruction associated with the announcement of M&A transactions by firms with excess cash: Servaes, Lang, Stultz, and Walkling (1991); Harford (1999); and Jensen (1986).

52. Bruner (1988).

53. Research showing that targets of hostile tender offers are underperformers with relatively low share prices: Targets of hostile bids show lower sales growth, debt, returns on equity, insider ownership, and price/earnings ratio; they also show higher liquidity and unused debt capacity. Schwert (1997) writes that the differences in performance are "consistent with the notion that targets of hostile offers suffer disproportionately from entrenched management . . . inefficient use of corporate assets." Prior to hostile bids, institutional investors have been defecting from the target firm (see Ambrose and Megginson (1992)). Studies of the likelihood of takeover find numerous predictive factors consistent with underperformance. Hasbrouck (1985) found that high market/book ratios and large size reduced the probability of takeover. Palepu (1986) found that high sales growth, high leverage, and large size reduce the probability. Morck et al. (1988) confirmed the effect of size and market/book ratio. Medium or small size might predict takeover if these firms are followers or otherwise at a size-induced competitive disadvantage. Trimbath (2002) concluded that "relatively inefficient firms have a higher probability of being taken over" (71). Comparisons of targets in hostile and friendly deals reveal that hostile targets show higher management turnover, lower profitability, and lower indebtedness. Management and board turnover increases following hostile takeovers as does corporate restructuring (see Dahya and Powell (1998) and Shivdasani (1993)).

54. Studies that are consistent with the view that targets are healthy but happen to fit very well with the buyer's strategy: Some evidence suggests that targets are not particularly different from other firms, and no less efficient (see Ravenscraft and Scherer (1987) and Schwert (2000)). Franks and Mayer (1996) found that "there is little evidence of poor performance prior to bids." McWilliams (1990) found that the exploitation of synergies better explains returns from takeovers than does the replacement of entrenched managers or redirection of underperforming firms. Models that attempt to predict likelihood of takeover do not select measures of valuation such as market/book or price/earnings (see Ambrose and Megginson (1992); Shivdasani (1993); and Comment and Schwert (1995)).

55. Comparing acquisitions of public and private companies: Using a multiples-based approach, Koeplin, Sarin, and Shapiro (2000) estimated an "as-if public" valuation for acquisitions of private firms, 84 in the United States and

108 outside, between 1984 and 1998. Then using the actual transaction prices, they calculated the discount from this public value. Bruner and Palacios (2004) model the so-called marketability discount for private firms as an option to switch securities and derive results in simulation that are consistent with the observed discounts.

56. Several studies report a sizeable positive announcement-day return to bidders buying private firms: Chang (1998) found a positive 2.64 percent cumulative average return to bidders who buy private targets with stock. The return in cases where a new significant shareholder is created in the deal is a positive 4.96 percent. Chang hypothesized that the new block holder will help to monitor the public firm's management. Hansen and Lott (1996) reported that, in buying private firms, bidders earn a 2 percent higher cumulative average residual (CAR) than when buying a public firm. Fuller, Netter, and Stegemoller (2002) reported a 3.08 percent higher CAR for acquisitions of private companies. Moeller, Schlingemann, and Stulz (2004) report that over a very large sample of transactions, the equal-weighted (value-weighted) CAR for buyers of public firms is +0.76 percent (−1.249%). In comparison the equal-weighted (value-weighted) CAR for buyers of private firms is +2.318 percent (+1.272%).

57. Regarding returns on cross-border M&A transactions, returns to target shareholders are significantly positive (see Conn and Connell (1990); Biswas et al. (1997); Wansley et al. (1983); Shaked et al. (1991); Harris and Ravenscraft (1991); Marr et al. (1993); Kang (1993); Pettway, Sicherman, and Speiss (1993); Servaes and Zenner (1994); Dewenter (1995); Eun, Kolodny, and Scheraga (1996); Kiymaz and Mukherjee (2000); and Kuipers, Miller, and Patel (2003)).

58. Wansley et al. (1983) and Marr et al. (1993) report that U.S. targets receive materially higher returns than do foreign targets. In five studies returns of U.S. targets are higher with foreign buyers than domestic buyers (in addition to Wansley and Marr see Shaked et al. (1991); Harris and Ravenscraft (1991); and Kang (1993)).

59. Kohers and Kohers (2001).

60. See La Porta et al. (1998, 1999, 2000); Bris and Cabolis (2002); and Rossi and Volpin (2001).

61. Research showing a tendency for bidder returns to decline over time, especially due to regulatory changes: Bradley, Desai, and Kim (1988) reported that average announcement returns to bidders fell from 4.1 percent in the 1963–1968 period to −2.9 percent in the 1981–1984 period. Moeller et al. (2003) reported a dramatic decline in bidders' returns from 1997 to 2001. Fan and Goyal (2002) found that the average return to bidders and targets combined rose from 1962 to 1996. One explanation for why M&A returns vary over time has to do with the impact of changes in business regulation. Wier (1983) and Eckbo (1983) found evidence suggesting that Federal Trade Commission antitrust actions benefit competitive rivals of the buyer and target. Jarrell and Bradley (1980) and Asquith,

Bruner, and Mullins (1983) found that returns to merging firms were significantly higher before than after implementation of the Williams Act of 1968. Schipper and Thompson (1983) considered four regulatory changes between 1968 and 1970 and found wealth-reducing effects associated with increased regulation.

62. Moeller, Schlingemann, and Stulz (2003).

63. Dong, Hirschleifer, Richardson, and Teoh (2003).

64. Studies of stock versus cash deals: Asquith, Bruner, and Mullins (1987); Huang and Walkling (1987); Travlos (1987); Yook (2000); and Heron and Lie (2002).

65. Evidence on returns associated with form of payment: Emery and Switzer (1999) found that tax, size, Tobin's "Q," and the amount of cash or unused debt capacity were significant drivers. Hayn (1989) compared the returns to bidders and targets in taxable and nontaxable deals: Taxable deals are often for cash; nontaxable deals are almost always for stock. Hayn found a pattern of returns to bidders that closely mirrors the pattern associated with form of payment, which implies that taxes are a factor in the choice. Yook (2000) found that changes in the firm's bond ratings were significantly associated with these returns, which emphasizes the financing dimension of the choice of medium of exchange. Focusing on reported financial results, two studies found no evidence that operating performance varied by form of payment. But focusing on investor returns, Loughran and Vijh (1997) found a sizeable difference over the five years following the deal: Share-for-share deals yielded average excess returns of +14.5 percent to investors, while cash deals yielded +90.1 percent. The disparity between the two sets of studies is a clue that the use of stock is designed mainly to exploit overvaluation of the buyer's shares in the market.

66. The use of stock when a deal is friendly: Zhang (2001) found that cash payment is strongly associated with tender offers, which tend to be hostile. When the buyer's stock price is high: The better performing is the buyer's stock, the greater is the likelihood of a share-for-share deal. The typical measure here is the firm's Tobin's "Q" ratio (market value divided by book value). Several studies have identified this effect (Zhang (2001); Heron and Lie (2002); Chang and Mais (2000); and Martin (1996)). Carleton et al. (1983) and Martin (1996) found that the acquiring firm's investment opportunities are an important determinant of the form of payment: Acquirers with high "Q" are significantly more likely to issue stock than cash or a blend. When ownership in the buyer is not concentrated: Two studies (Chang and Mais (2000) and Yook et al. (1999)) found that when the ownership of the target and/or the buyer is concentrated, the deal tends to be settled in cash. By not paying with stock, the buyer possibly avoids bringing in a new significant shareholder, with the potential to destabilize the internal politics of the equity ownership group. When Time Warner acquired Turner Enterprises for stock, it made Ted Turner the largest single shareholder of the firm. Turner, known for his temper and outspoken views, must have contributed to lively board meetings until he resigned

in disagreement. In larger deals: The larger the size of the target relative to the buyer, the greater the likelihood that the buyer will pay with stock. This may well reflect nothing more than the buyer's ability to "write a check." See Hansen (1987) and Zhang (2001).

When the buyer has less cash: Zhang (2001); Heron and Lie (2002); and Chang and Mais (2000) all found that the ability of the buyer to pay with cash (measured as the buyer's cash balance relative to the size of the target deal) was a significant determinant of whether the form of payment was cash or stock.

67. Returns to shareholders in LBO targets: DeAngelo, DeAngelo, and Rice (1984) found a 25 percent abnormal return over a period from 40 days before to 40 days after the announcement. Marais, Schipper, and Smith (1989) reported a 13 percent abnormal return at the announcement, and Lee (1992) found a 14.9 percent abnormal return. The shareholders of the buyer group fared even better. Jensen (1989b) cited findings of Steven Kaplan that the total net-of-market return to buyers over the life of their equity investment is a remarkable 785 percent. Estimated on the entire capital base used to purchase the target firm, the net-of-market returns are 42 percent.

68. Changes in LBO operating cash flows and capital expenditures: Critics noted several prominent defaults by LBO targets, challenging the existence of improved efficiency in LBOs. Kaplan (1989a) and Kaplan and Stein (1993) found that in the early stage of the LBO wave, defaults were infrequent, about 2 percent. But in the late 1980s, almost 27 percent of LBOs defaulted on loans. Jensen (1989b) said, "LBOs frequently get in trouble, but they seldom enter formal bankruptcy. Instead they are reorganized in a short time (several months is common), often under new management, and at apparently lower cost than would occur in the courts"(43). He called this the "privatization of bankruptcy." Kaplan and Andrade (1997) studied financially distressed highly leveraged transactions (HLTs) and found that they had viable businesses with operating margins greater than the median for their industries. These firms were financially distressed, not economically distressed. Also, they found that from before the HLT transaction to after the resolution of distress, the value of the target firm actually *increased*. Lee (1992) and Amess (2002) reported significant gains in efficiency. Smith (1990) found sustained increases in operating returns following buyouts owing to tighter management of working capital rather than to layoffs, or cuts in advertising, R&D, maintenance, or capital spending. Opler (1992) examined LBOs in the late 1980s, a time when LBO profitability was believed to have declined. He found that even during this period operating margins in LBOs increased on a par with increases in earlier deals. Lichtenberg (1991) and Jensen (1989b) reported significant gains in productivity.

69. See Jensen, Kaplan, and Stiglin (1989).

70. Earnout returns: Kohers and Ang (2000) studied acquisitions using earnouts and found that the returns to buyers at the announcement of earnout

transactions were a positive (and significant) 1.4 percent. Also, the buyer's returns were significantly more positive in cases where management stayed and a payout was actually made under the earnout. Most of the gains from these acquisitions appear to be captured at the announcement, since over the three to five years after the deal the buyers' share prices perform in line with the market. The acquisition premiums were larger in earnout deals than in straight cash or stock deals. The premiums in earnout deals tend to be higher for private targets than for divested subsidiaries. Earnouts are used predominantly in two kinds of deal situations: divestitures of corporate divisions and acquisitions of privately held targets (which comprised two-thirds of the sample). Smaller acquirers are more likely to use earnouts than larger acquirers. Foreign buyers from countries with common law traditions (similar to the United States) are more likely to use earnouts than foreign buyers from countries with civil code traditions (e.g., France). Earnouts are more likely to be used where the buyer and target are from different industries. Kohers and Ang concluded that the use of earnouts was consistent with two explanations: Earnouts help (1) to manage the buyer's risk and (2) to retain and motivate management. Datar, Frankel, and Wolfson (1998) reported similar profiles and conclusions for a sample of earnouts.

71. Fuller (2003).

72. A floating collar allows the buyer's share price a range within which to vary but imposes a ceiling and floor on the value to be delivered to target shareholders. A fixed collar establishes a fixed value for the target's shares as long as the buyer's share price remains within the predetermined range; outside that range, the exchange ratio is adjusted. See Bruner (2004b) for a detailed discussion of collars.

73. Premiums in mergers of equals versus other deals: Wulf (2001) and Becher and Campbell (2002) showed that buyers in mergers of equals earn zero-to-positive abnormal returns, while buyers in other transactions earn significantly negative returns.

74. Wulf (2004), 60.

75. Researchers continue to actively debate whether tax considerations *cause* acquisitions: Scholes and Wolfson (1992) analyzed changes in the volume of merger and acquisition activity before and after changes in the tax laws passed in 1981 and 1986 and concluded that the evidence "very strongly" suggested that these changes affected M&A activity. M&A is associated with three possible tax benefits, including the use of net operating loss tax carryforwards (NOLs) and other tax credits; the "step-up" or increase in the basis or value of assets on which tax shields such as depreciation expense are computed; and the exploitation of debt tax shields through increased financial leverage. Scholes and Wolfson argued that each of these benefits can be realized through means other than M&A, possibly at lower transactional cost. Moreover, targeted studies by Auerbach and Reishus (1988a, 1988b, and 1988c) suggested that NOLs, basis step-up, and leverage changes are probably significant in only a small number of mergers.

76. Hayn (1989).

77. Research shows that firms with stronger governance practices are more highly valued: Shleifer and Vishny (1997) and Maher and Anderson (2000) surveyed the recent literature as it pertains to the United States and the Organization for Economic Cooperation amd Development (OECD). Gompers, Ishi, and Metrick (2001) studied firm-specific governance practices in the United States. Worldwide, firms with stronger governance practices tend to trade at higher market values. Shareholder protections vary significantly among countries. Differences in laws and their enforcement are associated with variations in valuations. La Porta et al. (2000) noted that efficiency of investment, breadth and depth of capital markets, dividend policies, ownership structures, and new security issuance are associated with how well legal systems protect shareholders and creditors. Even a firm in a country with strong governance laws and practices can "opt out" of certain governance provisions through amendments to the firm's charter and bylaws. Finally, looking across the entire range of firms and countries, Klapper and Love (2002) found a significant relation between strength of governance and valuation of the firm. This finding extends even to emerging countries where governance institutions at the national level may be relatively weak, but governance at the firm level is strong. The study also found that firm-level governance is weaker in countries with weak legal systems, suggesting that enhancing the legal system should remain a priority for policymakers.

78. Research showing that active investors are associated with the creation of shareholder value: Black (1992a, 1992b) has argued that institutional voice is potentially valuable because of the need for someone to monitor corporate managers. It can add value by increasing the independence of corporate directors, discouraging bad takeovers, encouraging more efficient governance rules, discouraging cash hoarding, and establishing a more arm's-length process for setting CEO pay. The empirical evidence is consistent with the hypothesis that voice is valuable. Nesbitt (1994) found that intervention by CalPERS, a large pension fund, is associated with excess returns of 41 percent over the five years following intervention. Agrawal and Mandelker (1990) discovered that companies with high institutional ownership experience event returns that are much more positive in response to antitakeover amendment proposals. Pound (1988); Jarrell and Poulsen (1987); Brickley, Lease, and Smith (1988); and Gordon and Pound (1993) gave evidence that the presence of institutional ownership is associated with a higher probability of dissidents winning proxy contests, with lower adoption of value-decreasing antitakeover proposals, and with the success of shareholder-sponsored proposals to change corporate governance structures.

79. Several studies of LBOs: Kaplan (1989); Muscarella and Vetsuypens (1990); Smith (1990); Opler (1992); and Andrade and Kaplan (1998).

80. Studies of replacement of executives of underperforming firms: Warner, Watts, and Wruck (1988) found a significant association between poor stock performance and the frequency of management turnover, but no significant excess

returns to shareholders at the announcement of management change. Other studies (Bonnier and Bruner (1988); Furtado and Rozeff (1987); and Weisbach (1988)) documented significantly positive returns in response to management change.

81. Studies of corporate restructurings: Denis and Denis (1993); Denis (1994); Donaldson (1990); Holderness and Sheehan (1991); Murphy and Dial (1992); and Wruck (1994).

82. See the article that follows in this issue of the *JACF* by Sudip Datta, Mai Iskandar-Datta, and Kartik Raman.

83. Healy, Palepu, and Ruback (1997), 55.

84. See Jensen (1989).

85. Studies of bidder returns in hostile takeovers versus friendly deals: Jensen and Ruback (1983) gave a survey of returns in contested and friendly deals. Numerous studies have reported positive significant returns to bidders in hostile transactions (Asquith, Bruner, and Mullins (1987); Gregory (1997); Loughran and Vijh (1997); Rau and Vermaelen (1998); Lang, Stulz, and Walkling (1989); and Jarrell and Poulsen (1989)). On the other hand, Healy, Palepu, and Ruback (1997) found that hostile deals were associated with insignificant improvements in cash flow returns, owing possibly to the payment of higher acquisition premiums.

86. Studies on the effect of strength of the target's governance mechanisms: McWilliams (1990, 1993) showed that strong governance is associated with a positive reaction of investors at the announcement of antitakeover defenses while weak governance is associated with a negative reaction. Bhaghat and Jefferis (1991) found that voting power of employee stock ownership plans (ESOPs) and the CEO play a prominent role in whether a firm will adopt antitakeover charter amendments. The announcement of takeover defenses benefits shareholders where internal governance mechanisms work well (see Malekzadeh and McWilliams (1995) and Malekzadeh et al. (1998)). Targets of hostile bids have lower percentages of insider shareholdings (see Song, Stulz, and Walkling (1990) and Mikkelson and Partch (1989)). For contrasting findings see Ambrose and Megginson (1992). CEO shareholdings are inversely related to resistance to a tender offer and positively related to the likelihood of bidder success (see Cotter and Zenner (1994)). Models estimated to predict takeover find that larger CEO shareholdings reduce the likelihood of a hostile bid (see Mikkelson and Partch (1989) and Shivadasani (1993)). And the percentage of ownership held by insiders is negatively related to the number of takeover defenses (Boyle et al. (1998)). The number of takeover defenses placed by a firm is inversely related to the percentage of shares held by insiders (Boyle et al. (1998)).

3

Profiling the Outlying M&A Deals

F. Scott Fitzgerald: "Ernest, the rich are different from you and me."
Ernest Hemingway: "Yes, they have more money."

itzgerald romanticized the rich, suggesting that they had a different
sensibility toward life, an appreciation for art and luxury, and special
problems that went along with it. "Sensibility, schmensibility," Hemingway seemed to say. His famous retort implied that the rich are not
smarter, harder working, or more creative. They got that way by luck, such
as inheritance or a good evening at the casino. The contrasting views have
implications for how you think about success and failure. To what extent
is either a matter of random occurrence versus attributes that create a
predisposition?[1]

The research summarized in Chapter 2 gives evidence to suggest relationships among attributes of buyers, targets, and deals and success or failure in M&A. Such research offers an "outside-in" exploration, starting
from a population and asking what factors explain the variation in returns
within the population. But a Fitzgerald/Hemingway debate also invites an
alternative, "inside-out" exploration. Start from groups whose variation is
given, such as high and low achievers, and identify the factors that distinguish them from each other. Though it is a road less taken in business research, the inside-out approach has yielded some useful insights and a lot
of popular attention.[2]

EXTREME PERFORMERS

This chapter draws a profile of the extreme performers from 1985 to 2000, the cases of severe failure and vaulting success. What generalizations can one draw from quantitative data about these transactions? Statistical analysis offers three important distinctions between best and worst performing groups.

First, strategic considerations play a material role in success and failure. Looking at returns over the long run, the best deals are done in related fields; the worst are much less related. Acquiring into the same or a related industry is more closely associated with success than diversifying into unrelated fields. There is a benefit to sticking to your knitting.

Second, the worst deals are associated with "hot" equity market climates; the best deals are associated with colder markets. There are at least two explanations for this association. Behaviorists might point to the tendency toward unthinking, herdlike activity during hot markets: Carelessness lowers one's luck. Alternatively, some economists argue that rather than being careless, managers are carefully calculating; they recognize when their firm's shares are overvalued and exploit that by issuing shares in an M&A deal.

Third, the best deals seem to be improvements of the target company, rather than improvements of the buyer. Buyers go into the best deals as healthy, well-performing firms, seeking to spread their best practices to the targets. The worst deals show buyers who perform poorer than targets leading up to the deal.

Identifying the Best and Worst Transactions

Chapter 2 argues that returns to investors are a reasonable metric for assessing merger performance. It also notes that returns measured in a short window of time around the announcement of a deal tend to bear little relationship with returns measured over the years following. In statistical terms, the association is quite weak,[3] a fact that could be explained by the intervention of confounding events unrelated to the merger, or to the fickleness of markets.

For this reason, the identification of best and worst transactions considered returns to investors over both the short term (11 days around the announcement of the deal), and for the long term (three years after the announcement). The returns were calculated "net-of-market," meaning that they reflected a benchmark of performance rather than simply being absolute returns. These market-adjusted returns to stockholders were estimated day by day, and cumulated over time, producing the basic metric, *cumulative market-adjusted return* or CMAR. Ranking on the basis of CMARs screened out those transactions that might appear to be best or worst simply because the stock market had an episode of positive or negative performance. There are more refined ways to gauge abnormal returns to investors,[4] but the simple CMARs suffice to offer some rough-and-ready insights in addition to those in Chapter 2.

The word "return" bespeaks profit and could be measured in two ways: as a percentage, and in dollar terms. The dollar CMAR is simply the percentage CMAR for the buyer times the market capitalization for the buyer six days before the announcement of the deal. The two measures address *economic materiality* very differently. Two transactions may have a CMAR of 2 percent but very different dollar adjusted returns: Consider that a 2 percent CMAR on ExxonMobil will produce a dollar return that dwarfs that associated with a 2 percent CMAR on a small biotech firm. The percentage return helps to gauge the impact of the transaction on an equal-weighted portfolio return of a well-diversified investor. The percentage return ignores the impact of size and embraces the possibility that best and worst performance can accrue to companies of any size. The dollar return suggests the absolute magnitude of damage or benefit and is perhaps more interesting as a measure of CEO performance and from a macroeconomic policy perspective.

I drew a sample of 2,804 transactions from 1985 to 2000.[5] Using the three measures of performance, I ranked the transactions and identified the top 2.5 percent and bottom 2.5 percent of the distribution as the "best" and "worst." This corresponds to the outliers defined by the 95 percent confidence interval used by social scientists. All of these transactions are significantly different from the mean in a statistical sense, which, in plain English, means that there is a very small likelihood (5 percent) that they fell into either category by random chance.

Next, I sought to compare the best, worst, and middle of the distribution of deals on the basis of numerous factors. Some of these factors have been identified in previous research surveyed in Chapter 2. I explored others more opportunistically on a simple trial-and-error basis. Since factors can interact in unusual ways, I tested the various factors *simultaneously* using multivariate analysis. The findings enlarge our perspective of success and failure in some important ways.

Returns for the Best, Worst, and Entire Sample

Measured in terms of percentage return, the whole sample of 2,805 transactions yields a mean adjusted return of −0.51 percent to buyers' shareholders over 11 days and +11.72 percent over 3 years. These percentage returns are significant at the conventional 5 percent level. When measured in dollar value terms, the mean returns are −$95 million for the 11-day period and −$386 million over 3 years. The 11-day dollar return is statistically significant while the 3-year return is not. In short, this sample shows value destruction from M&A shortly around the announcement of deals, and value creation or conservation associated with the 3 years following a deal. Measured either way, the short-term returns are significantly negative, though economically, they are small and not sustained over the longer term. The difference in results between the two measures suggests that a small number of especially value-destroying deals depresses the averages when they are measured in dollar value terms. This is consistent with other recent research on M&A activity in the 1990s.[6]

Figure 3.1 presents a graph of the cumulative return from day −5 to day +756 for the whole sample and "best" and "worst" subsamples as determined by percentage returns over the three-year period. The slightly positive trend for the whole sample differs from other studies of long-term returns that find negative drift in performance. Here, the mean return is significantly positive by the end of the third year.[7]

The trends for the two subsamples reveal interesting differences. The first difference concerns the immediacy of appearance of a trend of returns. The subsample of best transactions realizes a material gain over the market within the first 20 days after the announcement. But the worst transactions show no similarly sharp response right away. For them, the returns are only modestly negative for the first 99 days. In short, the standout winners reveal themselves quickly; the standout losers take longer to mature.

The second difference concerns the sustainability of winning and losing streaks. For the best deals, the returns climb sharply for the 310 days after announcement, and then the rate of gain slows. For the worst deals, the

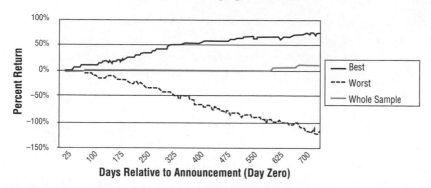

Figure 3.1 **Cumulative Adjusted Returns for Whole Sample, Best, and Worst, from Day −5 to Day +756**

Source: Author's analysis.

rate of decline after day 75 is unerring: no breathers; no slowing of the deterioration; no hints at a turnaround.

The graph is roughly consistent with the observations of M&A practitioners that success or failure is determined within a short span of time after doing a deal. Their rule of thumb is that the first 100 days after consummation are the crucial window of opportunity within which success or failure is determined.

Profiles of the Outlying Performers

The distributions of the best, worst, and whole sample of deals differed on a number of dimensions. A process called "univariate analysis" considers the importance of these dimensions one at a time.

Strategic Factors. These prove to offer the most significant explanation of variance of returns and incidence on a univariate basis. For instance, the degree of relatedness of the buyer's and target's industries represents a significant factor. Previous research has shown that higher M&A performance is associated with higher industrial relatedness of buyers and targets. The best deals show a heavier concentration in industrial sectors closer to the buyer; the worst deals show a heavier concentration in sectors further from the buyer.

Also of strategic note is that transactions in three industries account for a disproportionate share of the total M&A activity in the sample. The technology-media-telecommunications (TMT), biomedical, and finance sectors account for 63 percent of the total sample, 59 percent of the best, and 48 percent of the worst-performing deals, when percentage returns are measured over 11 days. These industries experienced major strategic turbulence due to deregulation and technological innovation.

Time Periods and Hot Markets.   The best and worst are significantly different from the whole sample in their distribution across time periods. Generally, both of the extreme samples are more concentrated in the 1998–2000 time period, a time that was characterized by high M&A activity and security prices, and hot market conditions. Whereas this period accounted for 31 percent of all deals in my sample, it accounted for between 60 and 100 percent of the best and worst, depending on the type of return with which you rank them.

Three findings associate the worst deals with hot market bidding. First, the best deals more often bid below the target's two-year high, while the worst deals more often bid above it. Second, the worst deals are associated with a strong positive run-up in the buyer's share price before the announcement; the best tend to be announced after a period of underperformance in the buyer's share price. Finally, when I contrast the distribution of observations by the performance of the S&P 500 index in the year prior to the announcement, the worst deals are particularly associated with a recent period of market buoyancy.

Deal Design and Deal Attitude.   Form of payment distinguishes the best from worst: The best are more frequently cash-based deals; the worst are more frequently paid for with the buyer's shares. Measures of the specific characteristics of a deal and of the attitude (i.e., friendliness) of a deal prove to be statistically insignificant in explaining the outlying deals. Only the presence of a termination agreement is important. However, further research reveals that the termination agreement is highly correlated with large deals in which stock is used as a basis for payment.

Fit between Targets and Buyers.   One line of research and practical thought is that targets and buyers combine in complementary ways. To test such complementarity, I studied the attributes of the target *relative* to that of the buyer. The comparison reveals that targets in the best deals have relatively lower profit margins, liquidity, and leverage, and higher activity and growth, consistent with the notion that they represent opportunities to restructure and reinvigorate the target. The worst deals show the opposite. It is logical to infer that the best deals arise when the buyer brings something in the way of best processes and practices to the target, making it a transformation of the target; in the worst deals it seems that the target is the superior performer possibly acquired to help transform the buyer.

Multivariate Analysis.   The research tested the explanatory power of numerous variables together. The estimates confirmed the association of hot markets with worst-case outcomes. Deal design seems to matter only a little. And finally, the strategic setting of the buyer and the pairing of buyer and target are important. Generally, the multivariate analysis of returns is consistent with the univariate analysis of incidence: The categories of factors that seem to matter most are strategic and market environment variables.

The Question of Size: Is Bigger "Badder"?   Consistent with earlier research, deals that are large relative to the size of the buyer are associated with worse returns than smaller deals. But perhaps this is a result of a relationship among three factors: relative size of the deal, form of payment, and time period. The existence of such an association is consistent with previous research. Researchers[8] have argued that managers will be more prone to undertake acquisitions when they perceive the share price of their firms to be overvalued. This implies an association between time period (reflecting "hot market" conditions) and form of payment. Recent studies[9] find an association between relative size and time period: Large deals done in the late 1990s are associated with material destruction of value. But if size, time period, and equity forms of payment converged in the late 1990s, perhaps the apparent conclusion about the malignancy of large deals is more justifiably a conclusion about *equity* deals. This complicated interaction of key effects may be important in helping us understand the tendency toward best or worst outcomes.

Consistent with previous research, I find that large deals are associated with significant negative returns in the short period around the announcement. Deals in which stock is used for payment have negative returns. Cash deals have a small positive return. Small cash deals have a significant positive return. But decomposing the returns for the entire 1985–2000 time period into subperiods shows that most of the returns' action comes from the late 1990s, and that most of the negative returns are due to large deals in which equity was the form of payment. This convergence of effects challenges the simplistic conclusion that large deals are bad, that they destroy value more than smaller deals. Instead, perhaps large size is a proxy for other factors that are also associated with value destruction, namely, the use of stock as form of payment, and the hot M&A market conditions of the late 1990s. I used cross-sectional regression to tease out which effects dominate. The findings suggest that it is the choice of form of payment and the time period that dictate the extreme performance rather than the size of the deal, which is merely an amplifier.

Conclusions and Implications

The important insight from inside-out research on the attributes of extreme performers is that listing among the best and worst M&A deals is not simply a matter of luck. The strategic situation of buyer and target and the capital market environment dominate other classes of determinants such as deal design features, investment opportunities, and deal attitude. The factors interact in complex ways to suggest that returns from large deals are contingent on form of payment and the capital market environment. In this sense, big deals are not better or "badder" than small deals. Instead, we should consider other deal attributes rather than size to explain the results. The mosaic of findings suggests that the best and worst deals *are* different from the broad middle. The best make strategic sense; they are conceived in cooler capital market environments; they seem to be more artful in the design of terms; and vice versa for the worst deals.

The analysis reminds the thoughtful practitioner to view lists of "best" and "worst" deals with care. Nettlesome measurement issues challenge the robustness of such lists. Instead, more understanding may be found in the broader comparisons of larger samples or in the more detailed analysis of individual cases. We might lament the absence of a simple and definitive story of success and failure, but the very complexity of business and M&A is what creates opportunity and danger, a theme explored in the following chapters.

NOTES

1. This chapter derives from original research developed by myself and prepared with research assistance from Yakup Asarkaya and Anna Buchanan. The research is summarized in a working paper by Bruner, Robert F., "Profiles of outlying M&A transactions, 1985–2000," (Charlottesville, University of Virginia, November 2004)—it may be downloaded from http://ssrn.com/abstract =681282. Other studies cited in this chapter and that influenced the research include the following:

Dong, M., D. Hirschleifer, S. Richardson, and S. H. Teoh. "Does Investor Misevaluation Drive the Takeover Market?" Ohio State University Working Paper (September 27, 2003).

Gugler, K., D. G. Mueller, and B. B. Yurtoglu. "The Determinants of Merger Waves," University of Vienna Working Paper (undated).

Moeller, S., F. Schlingemann, and R. Stulz. "Do Shareholders of Acquiring Firms Gain from Acquisitions?" Ohio State University Working Paper (February 2003).

Moeller, S., F. Schlingemann, and R. Stulz. "Wealth Destruction on a Massive Scale? A Study of Acquiring-firm Returns in the Recent Merger Wave," Ohio State University Working Paper (2004).

Shleifer, A., and R. Vishny. "Stock Market Driven Acquisitions," working paper downloaded from http://papers.ssrn.com/sol3/papers.cfm?abstract_id=278563 (June 2001).

2. The inside-out research literature in business is exemplified by James Collins' *Good to Great*, Collins and Porras' *Built to Last*, and Peters and Waterman's *In Search of Excellence*.

3. The correlation between the 11-day and the 3-year percentage returns is 10.8 percent; it is only 2.6 percent for the dollar returns.

4. Exploring the returns and rankings associated with more refined asset pricing models is the focus of ongoing research by Michael Schill and me. Our preliminary findings are generally consistent with the *qualitative* insights offered in this chapter, though detailed results to be reported eventually may differ in specific ways.

5. I drew a sample of U.S. transactions from January 1, 1985 to December 31, 2000 from the Securities Data Corporation U.S. Mergers and Acquisitions database. The universe of transactions was screened for those deals in which

- The acquisition is announced in the period 1985 to 2000.
- The acquirer buys 100 percent of the target company and had no interest in the target before the announcement.
- Both the buyer and target were public companies.

- The transaction was successfully consummated.
- The transaction was not a creeping purchase, self-tender or open market repurchase of stock, minority freezeout (purchase of minority interests), going private transaction, spin-off, split-off, restructuring, or formation of alliance or joint venture.

From the universe of 153, 087 transactions, I found 3,189 that met these criteria. A second level of screening was imposed by the need for data on the acquirer to be found on the CRSP and Compustat databases. Daily equity returns to buyers for these transactions from day −5 to day +762 around the announcement were obtained from the CRSP database; financial accounting data for the buyer and target firms were obtained from the Compustat database. After excluding observations for which data could not be found on these databases, the resulting sample consisted of 2,805 transactions.

6. See, for instance, the study by Moeller, Schlingemann, and Stulz (2004).

7. Sixteen studies consider returns well after the consummation of the transaction, of which 10 report significantly negative returns: Langetieg (1978); Asquith (1983); Bradley, Desai, and Kim (1983); Malatesta (1983); Agrawal, Jaffe, and Mandelker (1992); Gregory (1997); Rau and Vermaelen (1998); Louis (undated); Pettit (2000); and Ferris and Park (2001).

8. Shleifer and Vishny (2001).

9. Moeller, Schlingemann, and Stulz (2004).

4

Real Disasters and
M&A Failure

M&A FAILURE AS DISASTER

In 2001, the business world seemed to be coming unglued. The collapse of the Internet bubble, the onset of recession, the terrorist attacks on the Twin Towers, and the distress of businesses were capped by the death-spiral of Enron Corporation—a *business* Chernobyl. Real disasters entail the destruction of physical assets, death, and injury to people. When businesses melt down, they destroy monetary value, social capital, reputation, market position, and fictional persons (such as corporations in the eyes of the law).

The parallels between real disasters and merger failures can yield important insights that augment our understanding of the kinds offered in Chapters 2 and 3.[1] To my knowledge this book is the first exploration of these parallels. Such explorations can synthesize a large body of research and wide field of evidence. The investigations and extensive documentation of facts surrounding real disasters tells us a great deal about them (though given the toll in human life, what we know will never feel like enough). Studies of real disasters arise from fields as disparate as engineering (why buildings and aircraft fall down), economics (how costly is safety?), cognitive psychology (why do humans err?), military history (why do armies lose battles?), epidemiology (how does disease spread?), sociology (why do structures of social control fail to reduce risk?), politics (can public policy prevent accidents?), and operations management (how can we improve employee safety?). A reading of this wide literature shows that the world is a dangerous place and that very bad things can happen suddenly and surreptitiously. Worse, at the heart of most disasters is an element of human choice or action that might have averted the outcome.

This chapter summarizes lessons for M&A to be drawn from the analysis of real disasters. Deals from hell are sufficiently similar to real disasters to invite knowledge transfer about the latter to an understanding of the former. Moreover these lessons fill a glaring gap in our understanding about M&A failure: *how* it happens. Chapters 2 and 3 illuminate the *what* and *where* of M&A failure but say little about the processes that lead to those outcomes. From case studies of real disasters, this chapter synthesizes a framework for understanding the process drivers of M&A failure.

REAL DISASTERS AND THEIR ORIGINS

The *Oxford English Dictionary* defines "disaster" as "anything that befalls of ruinous or distressing nature; a sudden or great misfortune, mishap, or misadventure; a calamity."[2] The catalog of disasters is quite long and engages virtually all institutions of society. Governments would probably dominate the list, by virtue of the scale of problems they grapple with. For instance, one thinks of war (Napoleon's defeat in Russia that destroyed an army of 500,000), economic mismanagement (China's Great Leap Forward in 1969 that induced deaths by famine for 30 million), and public health (HIV by 2003 had infected more than 38 million[3] and continues to grow at double-digit rates in some regions of the world). Some technological disasters stand out not for their size, but rather for the asymmetry between small errors and large costs. For instance, the total loss of the $125 million Mars Climate Orbiter in 1999 was due to software whose instructions were denominated in pound seconds while the orbiter required instructions in Newton seconds; a small flaw in the $1.5 billion Hubble Space Telescope mirror stymied operation of the telescope for three years until another space shuttle mission could be sent to repair it.

Consider the following five sketches of real disasters. I selected these for the diversity of issues they raise with the aim of finding common elements that might be extended to the world of M&A.

Collapse of the Walkway at the Kansas City Hyatt Regency Hotel, July 1981

The atrium at the Hyatt hotel was crossed by three walkways, suspended from beams in the ceiling by steel rods. The beauty of the space and a band attracted a large crowd for dancing. The floor of the atrium was packed with people on the evening of July 17. Onlookers and dancers swarmed onto the walkways adding weight and vibration to the bridge structures. Later that evening, two of the three walkways crashed to the floor, killing 114 people, and seriously injuring 200 more, creating the worst structural disaster in U.S. history to that time.[4] Within days, forensic engineers determined that the collapse had been due to a flawed design that provided insufficient support for the number of people the walkways could be assumed to carry, only 60 percent as strong as they should have been under the Kansas City Building Code.

During installation of the walkways, modifications were made to the way the supporting rods connected to the bridges that, in effect, doubled the stress on washers and bolts. These modifications aimed to simplify the installation of the walkways. But workers installing the walkways complained that heavy wheelbarrow loads caused swaying and vibration in the walkways. Rather than investigating the structural weaknesses, project managers ordered the workers to divert their wheelbarrows to other routes than the walkways. The Attorney General of Missouri sued the engineers of the walkways for gross negligence, charging a failure to test the load capacity and adequacy of design.

Henry Petroski, professor of engineering at Duke University, noted that good structural designs provide several alternative load-bearing paths, so that if one fails, the other paths will bear the load, at least temporarily, until the structural failure can be fixed. He wrote, "[H]ad the structure not been so marginally designed, the other rods might have redistributed the unsupported weight among them and the walkway might have sagged a bit at the broken connection. This would have alerted the hotel management to the problem and, had this warning been taken more seriously than the signs of the walkway's flimsiness during construction, a tragedy might never have occurred."[5] The walkways at the Hyatt had no alternative paths.

Chernobyl, April 1986

Attempting to conduct an equipment experiment, workers at the V. I. Lenin Chernobyl Power Station, 80 miles north of Kiev, Ukraine, caused reactor number four to go "super critical" (begin fissioning) and explode at 1:24 A.M. on April 2.[6] Some hypothesize that the event actually consisted of two explosions, a violent release of steam and a small atomic bomb. The explosions ejected the 1,100-ton containment lid on the reactor and spewed molten core fragments over the surrounding countryside and a cloud of fission material across Eastern Europe and Scandinavia. It contaminated 400 square miles of farmland, rendering them unfit for cultivation. The fire and attempts to contain the damage killed 30 people. By some estimates, 70,000 people received dangerous levels of radioactivity.[7]

The aim of the equipment experiment was to see whether the momentum remaining in a spinning steam turbine generator would be sufficient to power the Emergency Core Cooling System (ECCS) in the event of a loss of other sources of power, until diesel generators could be started. This experiment followed an order from Moscow requiring it to be conducted. The Chernobyl reactor was of a unique Soviet-era design that proved to be efficient at high operating rates and dangerously unstable at low rates. A key design flaw was the self-damping tendency of the reactor that would draw it naturally into the danger zone. Appointed to operate the plant during the period of the experiment were electrical engineers from Moscow, not nuclear engineers familiar with the local facility. The plan for the experiment did not provide a safety net in the event that conditions went out of control. Reactor managers at Leningrad, Kursk, and Smolensk had refused to carry out the experiment for safety reasons.

The experiment necessitated a reduction of the reactor power and a shutdown of the ECCS so that it would not override the experiment. The reduction of reactor power triggered the self-damping feature of the reactor. This took the reactor core into a dangerously unstable mode of operation where small unpredicted reactions could produce rapid changes in activity. Trying to increase reactor power back into the safe zone, the operator overreacted, overrode the automatic system, and manually removed all but 6 of the 211 control rods, well below the safe minimum of 15 rods in the reactor. This produced a surge of heat. At 1:22 A.M. the workers reduced the flow of water into the reactor, concluding that the steam pressure was adequate for conducting the experiment. In effect, this reduced the coolant, amplifying the intensity of heat in the reactor. Next, the operators shut off the steam to the turbines, a necessary part of the experiment. This caused a surge in steam pressure within the reactor. At 1:24 A.M. the workers evidently realized that conditions were out of control and tried to reinsert control rods into the reactor core but found that the extreme heat had warped the control rod tubes, making it impossible to reinsert them and contain the reaction. Within a minute the reactor exploded.

A government report noted that the operators had "lost any feeling for the hazards involved."[8] The operators had been on duty for at least 12 hours, having been forced to delay the experiment to meet a surge in power demand during the afternoon of April 25. Fatigue probably affected their ability to recognize and respond to problems. The impending shutdown of the reactor for routine maintenance imposed on the operators a psychological time pressure to get the job done. In addition, the Chernobyl plant had recently received an award for operational excellence, perhaps creating a sense of overconfidence. The use of manual overrides on the automatic system suggests impatience and a tendency to overcorrect by the operators.[9] Dietrich Dorner wrote, "In the behavior of Chernobyl's operators we find difficulty in managing time, difficulty in evaluating exponentially developing processes, and difficulty in assessing side-effects and long-term repercussions, that is, a tendency to think in terms of isolated cause-and-effect relationships."[10]

Bhopal, December 1984

A leak of toxic gas (methyl isocyanate, or "MIC," a highly toxic intermediate compound used in the production of pesticide) from a plant owned by Union Carbide Corporation killed about 4,000 people and injured some 200,000 others in Bhopal, India.[11] The plant was located near a high-density population area, around the walls of which people had built shanties. The close proximity of the population left no room for error in the operation of the plant. Some critics suggest that the design of the

Bhopal plant was flawed. Union Carbide operated a plant of identical design in Institute, West Virginia, at which a small accident eight months after Bhopal triggered a detailed review by OSHA. The agency cited Union Carbide for numerous "willful" and "serious" violations in its operations of the plant.[12]

The Bhopal plant opened in 1980 with four safety systems that would have mitigated the disaster: scrubber, flare tower, refrigeration system, and water spray system. The first three systems were shut down for maintenance reasons in December 1984, and the fourth, water spray, was not designed to reach the top of a 100-foot-tall vent tower from which the MIC would seep. The operator tried to bring the scrubber on line in response to the crisis, but was unable to. An inattention to safety systems in general failed to inform employees of the toxicity of MIC, to provide for gas masks or evacuation plans, or generally to emphasize system safety—this despite the fact that the plant had been criticized in previous safety audits and had had six accidents in as many years. Also, recent downsizing of the workforce and turnover of experienced operators had left the plant with workers who were relatively new and stretched for coverage. Finally, for some reason the plant had overproduced the amount of MIC needed for steady operation and thus faced a relatively long period of storage of the risky substance.

By 1984 the safety systems had turned into maintenance problems. The refrigeration system was diverted to more pressing uses at the plant. The flare tower was shut down, awaiting a part from the United States. The scrubber had been shut down as well. The holding tanks for MIC were having trouble maintaining the integrity of their contents against seepage from the outside. An effort to clean the pipes connected to the MIC holding tanks failed to prevent further seepage. The proximate cause of the gas leak was the entry of water into the holding tank full of MIC. The mixture produced a volatile reaction and generated a gas that was vented into the atmosphere. A clear night, with families in their homes, and a breeze blowing in the direction of the center of population compounded the exposure.[13]

Public authorities responded inadequately to the unfolding crisis, urging the population to flee. This drove people out-of-doors, to maximum exposure to the gas when staying indoors and breathing through a wet towel would have saved many. The venting began at 10:00 P.M. shortly after a shift change in the operations. The fresh shift operators were unfamiliar with the chain of events that had led to the volatile reaction and venting and were reduced to responding to a surging crisis with inadequate safety remedies. Initial assertions by the operators to the public authorities that the gas was *not* toxic may have reflected incomplete knowledge about the plant system. James Reason wrote that this is a "tangled story of botched maintenance, operator errors, improvised bypass pipes, failed safety systems, incompetent management, drought, agricultural economics, and bad governmental decisions."[14] Union Carbide alleged that the disaster was caused by sabotage: an employee disgruntled by a demotion sought to destroy a batch of product by altering the component flow—but even if true, the absence of monitoring, checks, and safety devices amplified the deadly impact of sabotage.

Ocean Ranger, February 15, 1982

The world's largest oil drilling rig when it was built, the *Ocean Ranger* was positioned for drilling on the Grand Banks off Newfoundland when a gale-force storm assaulted it on February 14. The rig had survived at least 50 other storms in its 6-year life, proving a capacity to withstand 110-foot waves and winds of 100 miles per hour. When it sank in the middle of the storm at 3:00 A.M. on February 15, it carried 84 lives and $100 million in asset value to the bottom.[15]

The rig was eventually salvaged. An inquest concluded that a rogue wave shattered a porthole glass, thus permitting water to enter an electrical equipment room. For some reason, the steel storm shutter that could have protected the porthole glass was not closed. The water entering the room through the porthole short-circuited the equipment, causing valves in giant ballast tanks to open and close erratically. The operators shut off the electricity to the shorted panel, and then at midnight, inexplicably turned it on again. The accumulated effect of the valves opening and closing had been to admit water into the pontoons that supported the rig, deep below the surface of the ocean. The rig began to settle down sharply on the port side. This brought the rig's anchor chain locker within reach of the waves, admitting tons of water into an interior storage area of the rig. At 1:05 A.M. the captain of the rig called for assistance from a ship five miles away and ordered the crew to the lifeboats. Unfortunately, as these were lowered to the water, the waves and wind hammered them against the sides of the rig, smashing them before they could escape. The assisting ship found mainly life vests and parts of lifeboats floating on the water. One lifeboat was intact but shipping water. The occupants were so cold in the zero degree weather that none was able to climb aboard. Instead all fell into the freezing water and were lost.

The inquest identified, in addition to the system failure of the porthole and electrical controls, other contributing factors. Key operators of the rig were undertrained compared to the preparation specified in the company's operating policies. The investigating commission wrote, "The training program did not provide an understanding of the electrical and mechanical operations of the ballast control system nor the effects of ballast gravitation. A thorough knowledge of what might go wrong and how to detect and remedy the situation were also lacking. The training emphasis was based on the erroneous assumption that the ballast system was fail-safe."[16] The operators were not familiar with the complex system of ballast, valves, and pumps that would keep the rig upright. And second, the response of the controls was slow and uncertain under the best of conditions. But in the context of a howling gale, the fatigue, distraction, and imperfect systems feedback made the task of responding properly much harder.

Mount Everest, May 1996

On May 10, 1996, 23 people attempted to climb to the summit of Mount Everest in Nepal. Of these, five people lost their lives. Others barely survived, sustaining injuries and frostbite that required amputation and other emergency medical care—this, despite the fact that the expeditions that day were led by two of the most accomplished high-altitude climbers. This disaster ranks as one of the most dramatic examples of mission failure by a team.[17]

Conditions on Mount Everest are harsh: ice, glaciers, crevasses, snow, avalanches, high winds, subzero temperatures, and lack of oxygen. Adjustment to the thin air takes several weeks of conditioning at a base camp. The physical demands of living and climbing in that environment are so severe that they can cloud judgment. The remote location creates a logistical nightmare where bottled oxygen, food, and specialized equipment must be packed on the backs of Nepalese sherpas. The task of the ascent itself was complex, requiring coordination, observance of safety procedures, and proper use of technical equipment. The fact that food, water, and oxygen had to be carried to the summit kept supplies scant. There is little margin for error in the ascent of Everest.

However, by 1996, guided climbing expeditions of Everest were a growing business. That spring, 30 expeditions were scheduled to climb Everest, with 10 of them for commercial purposes.[18] Two of the commercial expeditions began the ascent to the summit on May 10. One commercial expedition was organized by Adventure Consultants and led by Rob Hall with two experienced climbers and seven sherpas. This group served eight clients, only two of whom were experienced in high-altitude ascents. The other expedition was organized by Mountain Madness and led by Scott Fischer with two other guides and eight sherpas; this expedition served eight clients. While the three professionals on each team were known to one another, both teams were largely comprised of strangers not experienced in working together.

Hall and Fischer were icons in the field of high-altitude climbing, with numerous ascents and lifetimes of climbing experience. Jon Krakauer described Scott Fischer as outgoing, energetic, one who craved celebrity, and highly self-confident. Fischer said, "I believe 100 percent I'm coming back . . . because I'm gonna make all the right choices."[19] Later Fischer said, "Hey, experience is overrated. It's not the altitude that's important, it's your attitude, bro."[20]

The general practice was for expedition leaders to suppress possible dissent as a foundation for maintaining safe coordination. Both Hall and Fischer advocated a rule of beginning the descent—whether having reached the summit or not—by two o'clock in the afternoon. Rob Hall took firm command of his expedition, saying, "I will tolerate no dissension up there. My word will be absolute law, beyond appeal. If you don't like a particular decision I make, I would be happy to discuss it with you afterwards. But not while we're on the hill."[21] Later, one of the professional guides working for Scott Fischer complained that Fischer did not listen to his concerns.

The teams left Kathmandu, Nepal, at the end of March and arrived at the base camp (17,600 feet) a week later. Through a series of practice climbs, the guides sought to acclimatize their clients to the atmosphere.

The expeditions had a brief window in weather conditions that experience showed would produce calm weather at the summit. Then on May 6, the teams began their ascent to camps II, III, and IV, each 2,000 feet successively higher. Over that ascent, the teams were met by climbers who had attempted to reach the summit, but had been turned back by extremely high winds. Still, on the evening of May 9, Hall and Fischer directed their teams to prepare for the final ascent, to start at midnight.

Four of the clients decided to turn back before reaching the summit; the rest pushed on, reflecting "summit fever" in Jon Krakauer's words. The climbers discovered that safety ropes had not been affixed in the final 500 feet. Fischer had simply assumed that a previous expedition had done this and had dismissed the extra rope as a burden. This created bottlenecks and delays in progress while sherpas went back for rope. The exhaustion of all climbers was expected, though it became evident to all that the leaders, Hall and Fischer, had become extremely worn out since the ascent from base camp, probably reflecting the interruptions to their own acclimatization routines due to logistical and managerial problems. By 2:00 P.M., most of the clients were still on the ascent; the last one arrived at 4:00 P.M.

Without warning in late afternoon, a snowstorm enveloped the mountain, producing a windchill of −100 degrees Fahrenheit and "whiteout" conditions that prevented visual contact and coordination among climbers. The teams lost cohesion. Stragglers were left behind. A dozen climbers huddled for a while out of the wind until a break in the weather permitted them to proceed. Most returned after midnight, clocking more than 24 hours of the most grueling physical experience. Exhaustion and exposure claimed the lives of Hall, Fischer, a professional guide, and two clients.

In assessing the mission failure of the two expeditions, Michael Roberto wrote:

> One explanation, drawn from behavioral decision-making research, suggests that cognitive biases may have impaired the climber's judgment. These biases include overconfidence, a failure to ignore sunk costs, and a tendency to overestimate the probability of recent events. A second analytical lens focuses on group dynamics. The evidence strongly suggests that the conditions and beliefs required for effective team learning and

performance did not exist. Finally, the complex systems perspective suggests that multiple, interconnected breakdowns occurred within the human, technological, and natural systems involved in the Everest ascent. . . . factors at each level—individual, group, and organizational system—reinforced and interrelated with one another.[22]

SOME COMMON ELEMENTS OF REAL DISASTERS

These cases offer a number of common points, of which I choose to highlight six that are especially relevant for our understanding of M&A failure. In essence, the real disaster story goes as follows:

> At the outset, the setting is complex, making it difficult for decision-makers to understand what is going on at any moment, and for operators to organize and coordinate response to the unfolding disaster. Moreover, there is very little operating slack, such as buffers or safety stocks that leave a margin for error. Thus, small errors can compound and radiate through the larger system. And the leaders have made choices that expose the enterprise to risk and/or amplify it.

> Leaders and operators aren't mentally prepared for disaster, possibly reflecting overconfidence, past success, or trust that someone somewhere else knows what's going on. Then something goes awry: An external condition that deviates from normal or inadvertent operator error triggers dangerous conditions that begin to spread out of control. The team of operators at the scene reacts inappropriately due, perhaps, to poor training, lack of information, or dysfunctional coordination. Disaster ensues.

The six key elements embedded in disasters are these: complexity, tight coupling, management choices, cognitive biases, business not as usual, and failure of the operational team. Table 4.1 sketches how the five real disaster cases reflect these six elements. It remains for us to explore why these six elements matter individually and how they combine to produce disasters. Research has illuminated the role of these elements. Consider each in turn.

TABLE 4.1   SUMMARY OF THE FIVE CASES

	Hyatt Hotel Walkways	Chernobyl	Bhopal	Ocean Ranger Oil Rig	Everest Expedition
Complexity: rapid spread of problems; difficulty to understand what is going on.	System of suspension bridges with tie rods from supports in the ceiling. Points of failure out of sight.	Nuclear power plant, 211 fuel rods operated by remote control.	Complex chemical plant. Movement of toxic fluids and gasses by remote control. Possible design flaws promote chance of errors and accidents. Shift change—new workers are unclear about evolving conditions.	Large drilling rig. Ballast system operated by remote control.	Complicated logistics management and coordination of the ascent. Teams unused to working together.
Tight coupling: no margin for error.	No secondary paths of load-bearing. No safety-net. Failure of one washer materially increases stress on others.	Emergency core cooling system shut down. Self-damping tendency reduces margin for error.	Maintenance problems reduce margin for error. Four safety systems inoperable or useless. Population housed near plant.	Manual override on ballast system is difficult to use. No effective backup system for ballast management.	Limited supply of oxygen. Limited time between sunrise and sunset. Limited climate "window" before monsoons.
Management choices: create risk exposure or amplify it.	Alter the construction of the bridges from the stronger original design to one 60% as strong, to simplify installation.	Run the test. Appoint electrical engineers from Moscow to run the test rather than nuclear engineers from the local plant.	Operate the plant with no safety systems. Inattention to safety systems despite six previous accidents.	Reliance on inadequate operational and safety training.	Decision to proceed on May 9–10.

Cognitive biases impair anticipation of, or response to, disaster.	Optimism. Belief in the integrity of the revised bridge design without adequate testing.	Mindlessly follow orders from Moscow. Optimism and recency bias derived from late awards for operational excellence. Impatience to complete task. Fatigue.	Overconfidence in the integrity of the system. Acceptance of incomplete knowledge.	Optimism and recency bias: The rig had survived 50 previous storms.	Overconfidence. Recency bias. Sunk cost thinking. Escalation of commitment. Suppressed dissent. "Summit fever." Extreme fatigue producing impaired judgment.
Business not as usual: the trigger.	Overcrowding. Packed floor below. Dancing on the bridge added weight and vibration.	Simulated equipment malfunction. Self-damping draws reactor into danger zone.	Temporary oversupply of MIC at plant. Leakage of water into holding tank. Sabotage or operator error that channeled MIC into holding tank.	Severe storm; rogue wave. Smashed porthole glass. Short in electrical system.	Severe winds. Extremely low temperatures. "Whiteout" blizzard conditions.
Inappropriate response by operational team.	Ignored instability (vibrations) in the bridge system both during construction and the evening of the disaster.	Overreacted to self-damping nature of the system; removed too many fuel rods. Simultaneously shut off feed water.	Inattention. Failure to contain leakage. Initial denial to public authorities that the gas was toxic. Public authorities urge populace to flee.	Operated ballast pumps despite short-circuiting and malfunctioning. Failure to close steel storm shutter.	Failure to begin descent by 2:00 P.M. Loss of team cohesion. Abandonment of stragglers.

Complexity

The Hyatt bridge system, Chernobyl reactor, Bhopal chemical plant, *Ocean Ranger*, and Everest expeditions were all complex systems. Though the nature of the complexity can vary, complexity is a precursor of disaster because it makes it difficult for decision-makers to understand what is happening and organize a response. This introduces an element of guesswork into the decision-making process, guesses based on the operator's mental model of how the system works. Complexity enables the rippling of side effects through the system that create dynamic complexity, compounding the difficulty of comprehending the problems. In short, complex systems are more difficult to manage than simple systems. In defining system complexity, Dietrich Dorner wrote:

> Great complexity places high demands on a planner's capacities to gather information, integrate findings, and design effective actions. The links between the variables oblige us to attend to a great many features simultaneously, and that, concomitantly, makes it impossible for us to undertake only one action in a complex system. . . . A system of variables is "interrelated" if an action that affects or is meant to affect one part of the system will also always affect other parts of it.[23]

The human mind tends to look for simple explanations to problems. Dorner studied the behavior of decision-makers in complex simulations and wrote, "It appears that, very early on, human beings developed a tendency to deal with problems on an *ad hoc* basis. . . . The need to see a problem embedded in the context of other problems rarely arose."[24] Simplification of complex problems may not merely prevent one from grasping the essence of the problems, but through misspecified solutions could make them worse. Thus, the anticipation of potential disaster requires rigorous discipline that humans may not be naturally disposed to muster.

Tight Coupling

The five real disasters each featured little margin for error. The Hyatt bridge system had no backup paths of support. Safety systems at Chernobyl and Bhopal were shut down or inoperable. The manual override on the *Ocean Ranger*'s short-circuited ballast management system was extremely difficult to use. The Everest expeditions had limited time and oxy-gen for the final ascent. In all of these situations, the absence of a backup or buffer meant that the disaster, once triggered, would be very difficult to stop. This is "tight coupling."

To illustrate the concept of tight coupling, imagine two auto manufac-turers with different operating strategies. Manufacturer A has a just-in-time system in which the parts plant delivers parts to the assembly plant in the nick of time to produce a car. The virtue of this system is that it mini-mizes costly inventory; its vice is that a glitch in the supply chain can shut down the whole operation. Manufacturer B has a system of ample buffer stocks of parts inventory. This is more costly but the buffer stocks cushion the system against the usual uncertainties that the manufacturer faces. Manufacturer A has a more *tightly coupled* system of manufacturing in comparison to Manufacturer B.

In general, the push for efficiency and cost reduction will drive opera-tions toward tighter coupling. A consequence is that the system becomes less forgiving of variations. Loosely coupled systems are more flexible; the standards of performance in such systems are more ambiguous; and the parts of such systems can "express themselves according to their own logic or interests," as Charles Perrow writes.[25]

High volume mass production manufacturing processes are usually tightly coupled. At the opposite extreme, custom manufacturing opera-tions are loosely coupled. To apply a metaphor from the field of music, a quartet that plays Mozart is necessarily tightly coupled; a quartet that plays improvisational jazz is loosely coupled.

Charles Perrow first highlighted the role of tight coupling in disasters and noted that tightly coupled systems feature several important attrib-utes.[26] First, such systems are time-dependent: The operation cannot wait for a subsystem to "get around to" its obligation as a part of the larger sys-tem. Second, such systems are inflexible. Tight coupling requires the parts to play a determinate role, and not vary from it. Third, the sequences are typically invariant: Tightly coupled systems require that step A must be performed before step B. And fourth, tightly coupled systems have rela-tively low internal buffers with which to cushion the impact of uncer-tainty. For a tightly coupled system to tolerate *any* variation, it must be explicitly designed into the system in advance: Variation must be *antici-pated*. Loosely coupled systems are more forgiving in the sense that their internal buffers may accommodate unanticipated variations more readily.

Tight coupling hastens the spread of problems in a system. Perrow combined complexity and tight coupling into a theory of "normal accidents." He argues that the design of modern systems virtually dictates accidents for "no matter how effective conventional safety devices are, there is a form of accident that is inevitable. . . . Most high-risk systems have some special characteristics . . . that make accidents in them inevitable, even 'normal.' This has to do with the way failures can interact and the way the system is tied together."[27] Thus, accidents and disasters that are unacceptable and avoidable become "normal" defined in the context of the design of the systems in which they occur. Edward Tenner wrote, "Complexity makes it impossible for anyone to understand how the system might act; tight coupling spreads problems once they begin."[28]

Perrow arrayed different kinds of activities on the dimensions of complexity and coupling. For Perrow, the nuclear power plant is the exemplar of high complexity and tight coupling. In comparison, hydroelectric power plants are simpler systems though they still offer tight coupling of internal subsystems. Custom manufacturing operations by an artisan would illustrate simple operations with loose coupling. And universities and R&D firms would illustrate complex operations with loose coupling. Perrow argues that the propensity for "normal accidents" increases where complexity is combined with tight coupling. Reviewing a series of disasters, Perrow disagrees that they are due to "dumb operators . . . technology, capitalism, and greed."[29] Instead, he argues that the problem resides in the design of systems.

Cognitive Bias

All of the disaster stories offer evidence that the thinking of decision-makers was *biased* against evidence or actions not consistent with a prevailing mindset.[30] In all of the cases, overconfidence figured prominently in the mindset. Chernobyl (recent operating award) and *Ocean Ranger* (survival of previous storms) show that optimism can derive from successful past experience. Bhopal and the Hyatt walkways suggest that optimism can derive from ignorance or a general faith that someone else knows what is going on and has matters under control. The leaders of the Everest expeditions displayed optimism to the point of bravado, based in part on their own recent successes. Knowing what we know now, such optimism was unwarranted. Other cognitive biases include adherence to sunk costs and goal momentum ("summit fever" or impatience to complete a task). Fatigue (Chernobyl and Everest) has been associated with compart-mentalized thinking (so-called "silo mentality") and errors in perception and judgment.

Cognitive biases matter for the understanding of disasters because they filter information and shape action-taking. Based on direct testimony or inference from actions, we can say that in each of the disaster cases, warnings were discounted and remedies pursued consistent with overoptimism.

Cognitive biases such as overoptimism are hard to square with an ideal of a rational decision-maker. But research suggests that they are *pervasive* in business life. Table 4.2 gives a sampling of some biases documented by researchers. In addition to cognitive biases, researchers have explored cognitive *errors* such as inattention, ignorance of trends, and failures of coordination. Dietrich Dorner has written, "Failure does not strike like a bolt from the blue; it develops gradually according to its own logic."[31] A chief of the National Transportation Safety Board said, "When has an accident occurred which has not had a precursor incident? . . . basically never."[32] B. M. Turner studied disasters and concluded that they were preceded by a series of danger signals, events that did not conform to normal operation but were overlooked or misinterpreted. Turner found that these signals accumulated or incubated over a long period of time. The fact that they went unnoticed for so long meant that they could not receive immediate attention and correction or enrich a vision of how failure might occur. Turner calls this a "failure of foresight." Inattention seems to grow following an extended period of quiet or even success. Henry Petroski wrote, "Failures appear to be inevitable in the wake of prolonged success, which encourages lower margins of safety. Failure, in turn, leads to greater safety margins and, hence, new periods of success."[33] Inattention has two dimensions: getting no facts and failing to check the facts for changes. Much of the history of airplane accidents, particularly in-flight collisions, attributes the accident to inattention due to familiarity or overconfidence stemming from reliance on automated systems.[34] A NASA report said:

> . . . many pilots . . . tend to relax their visual scan for other aircraft until warned of its presence; when warned of a conflicting aircraft, they tend to look for it to the exclusion of within-cockpit tasks and scanning for unreported traffic.[35]

TABLE 4.2   SOME COGNITIVE BIASES DOCUMENTED BY RESEARCHERS

Loss aversion, endowment effect, and status quo bias. People will pay more to avoid a loss than to acquire a gain of equal size. This *loss aversion* led to a better understanding of two related phenomena of great importance in M&A: *endowment effect* in which people tend to ask more in selling an asset than they would offer to buy it; and *status quo bias* in which people tend to stick with their current situation because the disadvantages of changing seem larger than the advantages.

Hindsight and confirmation bias. After an event, people have a tendency to believe that they "knew it would happen." They overestimate the likelihood that what happened would happen; this is hindsight bias. Displaying confirmation bias, decision makers observe more, give more weight to, and solicit evidence that confirms their beliefs.

Representativeness heuristic and stereotyping. People tend to use a "heuristic" (or problem-solving routine) for making judgments about similarity based on how closely they resemble one another. This depends on superficial rather than essential characteristics and stimulates inferences about the representativeness of what is being judged. Stereotyping attributes particular characteristics to a class, ignoring meaningful variation within the class. Stereotypes of people based on race or economic status are examples.

Anchoring effects. Experienced negotiators move first to offer terms on a deal. Typically the opening terms are at the extreme of a feasible range (low if a buyer, high if a seller). This has the effect of dragging the counterparty's expectations in the direction of the extreme. This is called "anchoring" the expectations of the counterparty.

Context effects. The preferences people express depend on the choice alternatives presented to them, the "context" for their decision. For instance, they are drawn disproportionately to compromises that lie between extremes. And they choose the best alternative available even though that alternative might lie outside a desirable range.

Sunk cost bias. People tend to set asking prices relative to what they paid for the asset, rather than relative to what the asset might actually be worth in the market.

Home country bias. People tend to overinvest in the country they live in even though that may not be the optimal strategy.

Immediacy bias. When asked to defer consumption that would have been immediate, people discount the value of that future consumption more than implied by ordinary time value.

Money illusion. People easily make decisions on nominal values rather than adjusting for inflation. For instance, a person may feel wealthier simply by receiving a 10 percent raise in line with 10 percent inflation.

(Continued)

TABLE 4.2   *(Continued)*

Overconfidence (or hubris). Optimistic or pessimistic attitudes significantly influence the prices one will pay for an asset. Thus, optimism in the form of overconfidence about the ability to realize merger synergies could promote overpayment for a target. This is the essence of the "hubris hypothesis" offered by Richard Roll to explain why buyers tend not to realize significantly positive returns from merger.

Winner's curse. Someone auctions a jar full of pennies. It is highly probable that the winner will pay more than the value of the jar and pennies. This is the winner's curse, a phenomenon first identified in the analysis of bidding for oil leases. Winning buyers tend to be the most optimistic, and optimists tend to overpay. The winner's curse is hugely important in M&A and has been offered as a possible explanation for the poor returns to buyers.

Running computer simulations of evolving crises, Dietrich Dorner found that the overinvestment of a decision-maker in a current set of policies can blind her to emerging needs and opportunities. Good decision-makers are nimble and responsive; bad decision makers "lock-in" on a set of policies and make measurably fewer decisions.[36] Related to this is the tendency of humans to extrapolate a trend, in linear fashion, rather than to suppose the possibility of jump-steps in a trend, or of nonlinearities. Linear thinking is appealing because it is simple, a simplifying assumption that under time pressure can be especially appealing. Commenting on the Chernobyl meltdown, Dietrich Dorner wrote:

> We find a tendency, under time pressure, to apply overdoses of established measures. We find an inability to think in terms of nonlinear networks of causation rather than of chains of causation—an inability, that is, to properly assess the side-effects and repercussions of one's behavior. We find in inadequate understanding of exponential development, an inability to see that a process that develops exponentially will, once it has begun, race to its conclusion with incredible speed. These are all mistakes of cognition.[37]

Reflecting on the role of cognition in M&A results, Professor Stewart Myers, said:

> And it finally came to me that, in mergers, the ratio of "noise" to "signal" is very high, and that the noise is a helluva lot more fun. . . . They're

idiosyncratic things that happen in a particular case, once people get into it, and once people start trying to win . . . the lesson about noise and signal is really very important. If we pose the problem of valuing a merger candidate, what you want to do is find the signal and avoid the noise. The great danger is that you start out trying to be rational and end up as a noisemaker. . . . People start out trying to be rational but they end up making mistakes in the analysis; they end up getting carried away in the heat of the battle, and they lose the kind of rationality, the kind of power, that financial analysis can bring to this kind of a problem. As Pogo used to say, "We've met the enemy and he is us."[38]

Management Choices

The role of managers and leaders in the cause and unfolding of disasters is unquestionably significant but all too often is the sole focus of investigators, trial lawyers, and journalists. Instead, the perspective offered in the cases of real disasters is that managerial choices are important contributors; they expose the enterprise to risk and/or amplify the risk exposure. However, bad management choices alone are usually insufficient to cause the disaster: It remains for the other five elements to turn a bad choice into a catastrophe. Moreover, the hunt for one large bad choice may well be frustrated: In some cases we see instead a compounding of several smaller bad choices.

The decision to redesign the Hyatt walkways to facilitate construction weakened the system. The revised design used sections of supporting rods bolted together, rather than one long (stronger) supporting rod. At Chernobyl, the decision to run the simulation of an equipment malfunction is the obvious bad choice, though choice of personnel (visiting electrical engineers to run the simulation) and timing contributed to the disaster. In the instances of Bhopal and *Ocean Ranger* we see a general willingness to conduct operations without proper staffing, safety systems, and/or training. At Everest, the decision to proceed with the final ascent given indications of severe weather looks like one big bad decision, but closer examination suggests that the leaders erred in decisions about training, supply of rope and oxygen, and rules for turning back.

Poor management choices may be linked to cognitive biases such as overoptimism or incomplete information due to complexity. This underscores the compounding or mutually-amplifying nature of these causes.

Business Not As Usual

In each of the disaster cases, conditions departed from normal or expected conditions. Heavy traffic (Hyatt walkways), simulated equipment failure (Chernobyl), leakage of water (Bhopal), and storm (Everest and *Ocean Ranger*) triggered a series of events that led to the disaster. The rest of the enabling conditions permitted these triggers to turn into full-blown catastrophes.

Inappropriate Response by the Team on the Scene

In the face of the preceding five conditions, disaster might seem inevitable. Yet, like the Dutch boy who stuck his finger into the dike to save the village, people on the scene such as laborers, supervisors, and lower-level managers can avert or sharply mitigate the effects of disaster. The real disaster cases summarized here suggest that inattentive, awkward, or perverse responses to the developing disaster conditions can sustain or even amplify them. Thus, the overreaction of the nuclear fuel rod operator at Chernobyl created far too much power; at the same time, lack of coordination with other workers resulted in shutoff of water intakes to the reactor and steam outflow, which increased the heat and pressure in the reactor. The maladjustment of ballast on the *Ocean Ranger* caused the rig to tip far enough to begin flooding through a chain locker. Construction supervisors at the Hyatt walkways elected to divert workers with wheelbarrows rather than to alert the architects or hotel that the walkways were unstable under heavy loads. At Bhopal, workers botched the cleaning of pipes into tanks holding the MIC; and later, public authorities actually drove the populace out of doors, to maximum exposure to the toxic gas. On Everest, the expedition teams lost discipline (not turning back by 2:00 P.M.) and cohesion, resulting in loss of stragglers.

In assessing the failure of the Everest expeditions, Michael Roberto wrote:

> . . . the climbers did not perform effectively as a team. At critical junctures, the teams did not discuss mistakes openly, exchange information freely, and challenge prevailing views and assumptions. The absence of these learning behaviors impaired the effectiveness of the two expedition

teams. In particular, the lack of open and candid discussions made it more difficult for the teams to identify and address the cognitive biases that impaired individual decision-making.[39]

Roberto argues that effective team performance depends on "psychological safety," that is, the comfort level in taking interpersonal risks as reflected in high trust and respect. The ability to object, to present contrary evidence, to offer alternatives for action, is taken more freely in a psychologically safe environment. Leadership is the vital mechanism for creating such an environment. Amy Edmondson and her co-authors studied the *Columbia* shuttle disaster and concluded that psychological safety is vital for the proper functioning of organizations in high-risk settings. Such settings require an aggressive learning orientation in which information is rapidly gathered and all alternatives are explored.

FORESTALLING REAL DISASTERS: SYSTEM REDESIGN AND THE HIGH RELIABILITY ORGANIZATION

Some direct managerial implications of the research on real disasters may be grouped into perspectives concerning the enterprise, the operational team, and the individual (the manager or leader).

Redesigning the Enterprise

Complexity and tight coupling play a foundational role in the rise of disasters. Therefore one path of disaster avoidance would entail system redesign. Complexity limits awareness of problems and action-taking. And tight coupling promotes the spread of problems. Complexity and tight coupling might be mitigated through the aggressive use of information management resources that promote transparency about conditions within the enterprise. And buffer stocks or safety nets that can absorb shocks might prevent the further spread through the system. It is possible to design complex systems that self-adapt to changing conditions. Consider the following three examples of self-correcting systems:

1. *U.S. Constitution.* By providing for checks and balances among the three arms of the federal government, the Constitution assures that

one arm will not overwhelm the others. It is instructive that the founders of the U.S. form of government did not fashion a system based on idealized behavior. Rather, they anticipated power-seeking behavior, errors, and disagreements. Thomas Jefferson argued for a system that assumed fallible human beings.

2. *Free markets.* Economic research shows that prices incorporate information rapidly. Episodes of panic or contagion do occur, but markets self-equilibrate. The adaptive quality of market systems depends on the free flow of information and the easy entry (or exit) of participants and money.

3. *Scientific process.* The means by which science advances, the process of hypothesis testing, the primacy of the null hypothesis, use of statistical tests, replication of findings, and stringent procedures for publication of results is based on an understanding of ways in which humans can do science incorrectly. The scientific process is a self-correcting system that anticipates and expects error.

In short, systems that adapt well to error anticipate it, actively seek information, use checkpoints to control the spread of error, and invite countervailing forces to oppose error. Within firms, the design of organization structures and business processes could employ similar principles to thwart M&A failures.

Fighting Biases and Bad Managerial Choices

Cognitive biases filter information and affect action-taking. Therefore the manager needs to check his or her thinking, the adequacy of information, and the reasonableness of action-taking. Discussing problems and actions with a diverse group of advisors is a preeminent check on bias in thinking. Not merely permitting, but actively soliciting contrary information is crucial. Constructing a culture of psychological safety is vital to the resolution of biases and testing of choices.

Preparing the Operational Team for High Reliability

Organizational processes and culture play a role in disaster avoidance. High reliability organizations (HROs) produce quality outcomes repeatedly even though working conditions produce surprising variations.[40] They do this by building a vigilance in everything they do, from recruiting employees, to the greeting of customers, the fulfillment of orders, the design of products, and quality of manufacturing.

Edgar Schein defined culture by six formal properties: "(1) shared basic assumptions that are (2) invented, discovered, or developed by a given group as it (3) learns to cope with its problem of external adaptation and internal integration in ways that (4) have worked well enough to be considered valid, and therefore, (5) can be taught to new members of the group as the (6) correct way to perceive, think, and feel in relation to those problems."[41] From the standpoint of disaster avoidance, important cultural attributes that distinguish error-prone firms from reliable firms are

- Tolerance for unsafe conditions and practices.
- "Methodism," the reliance on rituals, tradition, what has succeeded before. Dietrich Dorner notes that a wide range of research shows that people tend to act in terms of preestablished patterns.
- A focus on the condition of a narrow department rather than on the whole system. This is "silo" thinking. Such thinking fails to see side effects of actions and unintended consequences.
- A focus on symptoms rather than root causes. Surface problems are relatively easier to fix than deeper problems. Fixing the surface problems helps a worker to show activity and accomplishment. Dietrich Dorner calls this "repair service" behavior, searching for things that are malfunctioning and fixing whatever seems broken without a sense of priorities. He notes, "A mayor who is guided by a randomly generated list of complaints risks giving far too much attention to relatively unimportant problems and either overlooking the truly important ones or failing to assess them properly."[42]

Society offers various examples of high reliability organizations, enterprises that regularly face serious risks, have a low tolerance for error, and deliver reasonably reliable performance over time. Such organizations include hostage negotiation teams, hospital emergency rooms, flight decks on aircraft carriers, nuclear power plants, and teams of firefighters. From the study of such organizations, Karl Weick and other scholars found a number of common attributes:

- *A preoccupation with failure.* HROs are obsessive about the potential for things to go wrong. These organizations do not relax under threatening conditions; they do not trust that somehow things will work out okay.
- *A reluctance to simplify.* HROs take little for granted. As Perrow and others have noted, looking for simplistic explanations in the context of a complex system is dangerous. HROs make redundant checks of conditions.
- *A continuous sensitivity to operations.* HROs do not let themselves get distracted from their central mission and the operations it requires. The entire organization is focused on the critical operations. The operational leaders are present, visible, and in continuous communication with the front line.
- *A commitment to resilience.* HROs take surprise as a given and prepare to respond flexibly to it, tailoring a response often at the front line.
- *A deference to expertise.* HROs trust that the people closest to the problem are better informed and more capable of dealing with it. This implies a decentralization of decision-making.

Weick and Sutcliffe wrote:

[I]t is impossible to manage any organization solely by means of mindless control systems that depend on rules, plans, routines, stable categories, and fixed criteria for correct performance. No one knows enough to design such a system so that it can cope with a dynamic environment. Instead, designers who want to hold dynamic systems together have to organize in ways that evoke mindful work. People have to find it easy and natural and rewarding to adopt a style of mental functioning whereby they include, as part of their job description, the responsibility to engage in continuous learning as well as in the ongoing refinement and updating of emergent expectations.[43]

Mindfulness is a focus on updating one's information. One looks for anomalies, the unexpected, the disconfirming, and the disagreeable. The aim is to correct for possible blind spots. Thus, HROs encourage error reporting and the analysis of close calls. For instance, high performance medical units report more errors, not because they make more errors, but because they are more vigilant.

CONCLUSIONS

Real disasters offer important insights and practical guidance for the failures we see in M&A. This chapter describes five cases and from them abstracts six drivers of disaster. These include complexity, tight coupling, managerial choices that increase risk, cognitive bias, business not as usual, and inappropriate responses by the operational team. No single factor is destructive—but in unison they are lethal. The convergence of disaster causes is, I think, the most important foundation required of the thoughtful practitioner for understanding M&A failures, or for that matter, all business failures. The search for the single explanation is fruitless and wrong. Worse, it enables decisions and processes that are fundamentally unprepared for the multiple drivers of failure.

NOTES

1. The chapter has benefited from conversations and correspondence with Amy C. Edmondson, Michael A. Roberto, and Saras Sarasvathy.

2. *Oxford English Dictionary*, 2d ed. (Oxford: Oxford University Press, 1989), volume IV, 723.

3. Data as of December 2003, Joint United Nations Programme on HIV/AIDS.

4. The discussion of the Hyatt walkway disaster draws upon Petroski (1982).

5. Quoted from Petroski (1982), 92.

6. The discussion of Chernobyl draws upon accounts in Perrow (1999), Chiles (2001), Dorner (1996), and Reason (1990).

7. The human toll is at best a rough estimate. The 30 deaths are attributable to the explosion and fire suppression effort. More died later from burns and radiation sickness. The 70,000 figure is quoted in Chiles (2002), 162.

8. Quoted in Reason (1990), 255.

9. These points were argued in Dorner (1996), 33.

10. See Dorner (1996), 34 and 35.

11. The discussion of the Bhopal disaster draws upon discussions in Reason (1996) and Perrow (1999).

12. Quoted from Bill Dawson, "Union Carbide Fine 1.3 Million" *Houston Chronicle,* April 2, 1986, 1.

13. The neglect of maintenance is discussed in Chiles (2001), 262–266 and Reason (1990), 252.

14. Reason (1996), 191.

15. The discussion of the *Ocean Ranger* draws on Chiles (2001), 17–36.

16. Quoted in Chiles (2001), 28.

17. The summary of events surrounding the Everest expeditions draws particularly on Krakauer (1997), Roberto (2002), and Roberto and Carioggia (2002).

18. Facts reported in Krakauer (1997), 26.

19. Krakauer (1997), 84.

20. Krakauer (1997), 85.

21. Krakauer (1997), 216–217.

22. Roberto (2002), 139. Copyright © 2002, by The Regents of the University of California. Reprinted from *The California Management Review* Vol. 45, No. 1 by permission of the Regents <www.hans.berkeley.edu/cmr/>.

23. Dorner (1996), 38.

24. Quoted in Dorner (1996), 5 and 6.

25. Perrow (1999), 92.

26. Perrow (1999) discusses these four elements on pages 93 and 94.

27. Perrow (1999), 3 and 4.

28. Tenner (1996), 20.

29. Perrow (1996), 339.

30. The discussion of research on cognitive biases benefited from the comprehensive survey, "Behavioral Economics: Past, Present, and Future," by Colin F. Camerer and George Lowenstein, in Advances in Behavioral Economics, Colin F. Camerer, George Loewenstein, and Matthew Rabin, eds. (Princeton: Princeton University Press, 2003).

31. Dorner (1996), 10.

32. Quoted in Chiles (2001), 183.

33. Petroski (1992), viii.

34. See Billings (1980).

35. Billings (1980) quoted in Perrow (1996), 154.

36. Dorner (1996), 21.

37. Dorner (1996), 33.

38. Stewart Myers, "The Evaluation of an Acquisition Target," in *The Revolution in Corporate Finance,* Joel Stern and Donald Chew, eds. (New York: Basil Blackwell, 1986), 394.

39. Roberto (2002), 143. Copyright © 2002, by The Regents of the University of California. Reprinted from *The California Management Review* Vol. 45, No. 1 by permission of the Regents <www.hans.berkeley.edu/cmr/>.

40. For a fuller discussion of this definition, see Weick et al. 1999, 86.

41. Schein (1985), as adapted from Chapter 1 in Weick and Sutcliffe (2001).

42. Dörner (1996), 59.

43. Weick and Sutcliffe (2001), 49.

II

CASE STUDIES OF
M&A FAILURE

5

February 1968: Merger of the Pennsylvania and New York Central Railroads

BEFORE AND AFTER

At midnight on February 1, 1968, the Pennsylvania Railroad and the New York Central Railroad merged.[1] This was the largest merger to date: It created America's sixth largest corporation and the nation's largest transportation company. The new company, Penn Central, owned 20,000 miles of track in 16 states and served an area embracing 55 percent of America's manufacturing plants. It carried 300,000 passengers and a million tons of freight each day. Were the company to be closed, the government estimated that the U.S. gross national product (GNP) would fall by three percent, and unemployment would rise by three percent.[2] A merger of such size and consequence was without precedent. The CEOs of the merging firms had testified confidently to the U.S. Interstate Commerce Commission that:

> . . . it is my judgment, based on my forty-five years of experience in railroading, that the merged company will be far more susceptible to efficient management than either company alone was only a few years ago.[3]

... no two railroads in the country [are] in a better position than the Pennsylvania and the Central, by reason of their location, duplicate facilities and services, and similarity of traffic patterns, to consolidate their operations and at the same time substantially increase efficiency and provide an improvement in service at lower cost.[4]

Just 29 months later, on June 21, 1970, the railroad filed for bankruptcy in the most spectacular business failure up to that time. The wreckage was considerable. Between the merger and bankruptcy filing dates, shippers had lost millions of dollars measured in delays, spoiled goods, or outright disappearance of shipments. Passengers suffered a sharp deterioration in service. The three most-senior executives of the company were fired shortly before the filing. Investors in the Penn Central lost $1.84 billion as the company's stock price fell from a peak of $86.50 in July 1968 to just $6.50, the day after it filed. Figure 5.1 shows that by June 1970, the cumulative lost opportunity to investors amounted to –153 percent of their investment. The bankruptcy triggered seven government investigations[5] and numerous lawsuits. The U.S. government guaranteed

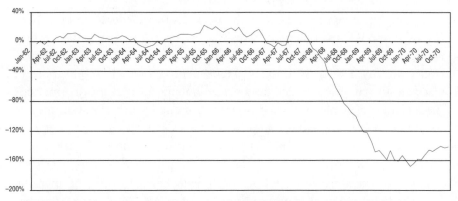

Cumulative Market-Adjusted Returns to Shareholders in Penn Central

Note: The monthly market-adjusted return is computed by estimating the total return to shareholders from price changes and dividends and subtracting the return on the S&P 500 index. The monthly market-adjusted returns are summed over time to produce the cumulative market-adjusted return. Returns before the date of merger are weighted averages of those of the Pennsylvania and New York Central, weighted by the percentage of shares in Penn Central. Computations are by the author.

Figure 5.1 **Cumulative Market-Adjusted Returns to Penn Central Shareholders, February 1968 to July 1970**

Source of data: Datastream.

loans to Penn Central of $125 million, bought Penn Central's rail assets for $2 billion, formed Conrail in 1976 from Penn Central and five other bankrupt railroads, and provided operating funds of another $7 billion— all until Conrail was privatized in 1987 in an initial public offering that fetched the government $1.9 billion: In round numbers, the failure of Penn Central and other railroads in the Northeast cost taxpayers $7 billion.[6] In describing the failure of Penn Central, government investigators abandoned the neutral language of bureaucracy in favor of words more colorful: "fiasco"[7] and "drastic blow to the economy."[8] The *bons mots* offered by other writers to summarize this story include, "the mother of American business debacles,"[9] "misjudgment . . . malfeasance,"[10] "cataclysm . . . a disaster,"[11] "swindle,"[12] and "inefficiency, incompetency, gross miscalculations, practices bordering on fraud and a public-be-damned attitude."[13] The collapse of Penn Central hastened the revolution in deregulation that affected a range of industries including airlines, trucking, broadcasting, and banking and that ultimately shuttered the Interstate Commerce Commission on December 31, 1995.

WORSENING FUNDAMENTALS FOR U.S. RAILROADS AT MID-CENTURY

Railroads in the United States reached their zenith in profitability in the 1920s. Thereafter, new technology in the form of the automobile, truck, and airplane, abetted by government subsidies for the construction of airports, roads, river locks, and interstate highways, slowly displaced the railroads. Figure 5.2 depicts this shift in modes of transportation. Substitutes and regulation put price pressure on the railroads. Laws and labor agreements restricted the ability of the railroads to improve productivity. Standard compensation gave a day's pay for 100 miles of travel. But with improvements in equipment, a train crewman could do a week's work in one day. "Featherbedding" was a practice of carrying excess train crewmen such as firemen on a diesel engine that had no need for a stoker. For all these reasons, returns on investment in the railroad industry worsened sharply after World War II. In 1962, David Bevan, chief financial officer of the Pennsylvania testified that the railroad industry was unable to earn a return to investors to compensate them adequately and that "the railroad is not supporting itself, and we are living on past glories, and we are in slow

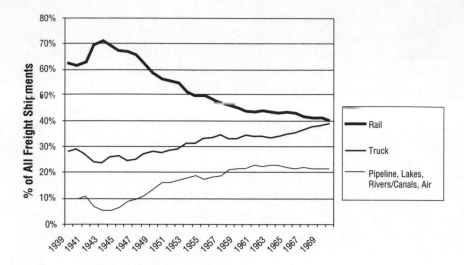

Figure 5.2 **Intercity Freight by Modes**
Source of data: U.S. Senate Committee on Commerce (1972), page 24.

liquidation."[14] Figure 5.3 shows that both the Pennsylvania and Central were unable to cover their cost of capital, by a wide margin. Stuart Saunders, chairman of Penn Central testified after the bankruptcy:

> The problems were far deeper and much more deep-seated. . . . This has been going on since World War II. Neither the Pennsylvania Railroad nor the New York Central have ever made any money. . . . this is basically a sick industry. And it's been sick for years.[15]

At mid-century, the railroad industry was "grossly overbuilt,"[16] relative to the demand for its services. The worsening fundamentals triggered a wave of restructurings aimed at removing excess capacity from the industry. Bankruptcies, always a feature of the industry, especially after panics and recessions in the nineteenth century, again cascaded through the industry, including New York, New Haven, and Hartford (1961), Jersey Central (1967), Boston & Maine (1970), Lehigh Valley (1970), Reading (1971), and Erie–Lackawanna (1972). Stephen Salisbury wrote that "Almost all other northeastern railroads either preceded or followed the Penn Central into bankruptcy."[17] Bankruptcy is an awkward process of industrial restructur-

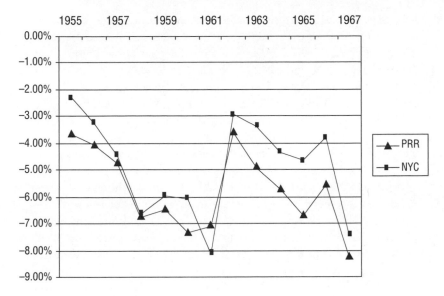

Figure 5.3   **Return on Total Capital Minus Weighted Average Cost of Capital**
Source: Author's calculations.

ing that weighs competing claims and interests, and may or may not generate an economically desirable outcome.

The other major instrument of industrial restructuring was merger.
The U.S. Senate Committee on Commerce noted that "beginning about
1957, a great wave of mergers has swept through the railroad industry, involving virtually every carrier and leading to substantial structural realign-
ments."[18] Each new merger triggered others as competitors reacted to
strategic changes in the landscape. All researchers agree that the Penn Central merger was motivated significantly by other mergers in the sphere of
the Pennsylvania and Central. The Senate committee described the
domino effect:

> The interlocking pattern of rail mergers, with one spawning another in a
> snowballing process, is best illustrated by developments in the East. The
> Eastern railroad story began in 1958 when the ICC approved the merger
> between the Norfolk & Western and the Virginian, two financially strong
> railroads heavily engaged in the movement of coal. Their merger
> promised cost savings; and, looked at as an isolated event, appeared to be
> of no great significance for the structure of rail transportation. Innocent

though it seemed at the time to be, that merger unleashed a wave of mergers that did not expire until the entire Eastern rail system was completely restructured and the Penn Central, the great house of cards, had been created. The Virginia–N&W merger ended the New York Central's access to the Pocahontas coal territory. With its valuable coal traffic threatened, the New York Central sought protection in a merger with the B&O. Pressed to consider merger, the B&O decided to merge instead in a two-way arrangement with the C&O. When the C&O and B&O merged, the N&W was threatened because it gave the C&O access to St. Louis and to transcontinental traffic. To counter this move the N&W merged with the Nickel Plate and the Wabash railroads (the latter through a lease arrangement), an affiliation that, in a sense, "one-upped" the C&O-B&O since it gave the N&W access not only to St. Louis but to Chicago, Kansas City and Omaha as well. These moves placed the NYC in even greater jeopardy. With what it regarded as its more desirable partners having already merged, the NYC finally agreed to join with the Pennsylvania in their ill-fated union. When the Penn Central merger was authorized in 1968, only ten years had passed since the Virginia–N&W merger but the entire Eastern railroad industry had been restructured.[19]

This process continued until by 2004 the North American railroad industry had been rationalized into six über-systems: Norfolk Southern (NS), CSX, Union Pacific, Burlington Northern Santa Fe, Canadian National, and Canadian Pacific. Like bankruptcy, this great wave of consolidation in the twentieth century was an awkward process, governed chiefly by the Interstate Commerce Commission (ICC) and various antitrust considerations. The ICC was notoriously slow in its process of reviewing merger applications—three years was a typical elapsed time; the high tide was the Rock Island merger case, a "bureaucratic horror story"[20] in which the ICC took 10 years to decide. Delay bred internal indecision in the merging firms, which when combined with the growing impatience of shippers and the inflexibility of labor unions to accommodate changes in work rules, neutered the hoped-for cost savings, productivity improvements, and revenue growth.

HISTORY OF THE DEAL

More than 10 years elapsed from the initial discussions to closing of the deal. CEOs James Symes and Robert Young (from the Pennsylvania and

New York Central, respectively) began discussing merger in 1957 and announced publicly on November 1 that they were studying the possibility. Young died in January 1958, leaving Alfred Perlman CEO of the Central. Perlman preferred a merger with the Chesapeake & Ohio (C&O) rather than with the Pennsylvania. So, jilting Symes, Perlman proposed marriage to the C&O. But the C&O preferred to merge with the Baltimore and Ohio (B&O), leaving the Central with no alternative but to deal with the Pennsylvania. After the B&O and C&O announced their merger, Alfred Perlman reluctantly agreed to resume discussions with James Symes in 1961. They reached an agreement for a merger of equals in January 1962.

The terms called for a share-for-share exchange of 1.3 shares of Pennsylvania for 1 Central share. The chairman and CEO would come from the Pennsy. After Symes retired in October 1963, Stuart Saunders would assume the title in the new company; Alfred Perlman of the Central would be president. Though the share ownership would be divided about 60:40 percent between Pennsylvania and Central shareholders, respectively, the Pennsylvania would account for 14 directors and the Central for 11 (a 56:44 percent balance). No formal announcement was made regarding the headquarters location, though it ultimately settled in Philadelphia. The public stance of both firms was that it was to be a merger of equals. Neither firm would dominate and instead the new company would appropriate the best of each firm. But later Perlman testified, "If you notice the people at the heads of the departments of the merged company, everyone was from the Pennsylvania Railroad except myself. To me it was not a merger, it was a takeover, frankly."[21]

Viewed in its strategic context, the prime motive for the merger of the Pennsylvania and the Central was survival. With competitors preempting freight traffic and generally encroaching on expansion possibilities, the only path to survival was to merge and focus on improving the efficiency of the core business. During the 12 years from 1952 to 1963, the Central's average return on investment was 1.84 percent. This was only slightly better than that of Pennsylvania at 1.28 percent, but far worse than the 6 percent to 9 percent returns for other utilities. With the exception of 1966, neither railroad would realize returns greater than two percent in the five-year period 1963–1967.

Cost savings formed the chief argument for the deal, though the estimates of these forecasts varied through time. Robert Young, CEO of the Central, said in 1958 that he thought it possible to save $200 million per year.[22] Later, Stuart Saunders, CEO of the Pennsylvania, advanced an estimated savings of $100 million per year "so often that they actually seemed to believe that somehow, on merger day, $100 million would come floating down to net income."[23] Finally, Robert Patchell, vice president of the Pennsylvania, estimated merger savings of $81.1 million per year, a figure ultimately used in the ICC merger application and as a target over the next decade. Offsetting the savings were $75 million in capital requirements less $45 million in disposals triggered by the merger. Netting these against the savings and recognizing the slow integration process, the savings would build up gradually from $3.4 million in the first year following the merger to $81.1 million by the ninth year. In the final event, Penn Central far exceeded targeted savings in the first two years, clocking $74.5 million[24] in 1968 and 1969 combined, compared to the $33.3 million[25] that Patchell had forecast for those two years. Unfortunately, these savings were swamped by other merger-related cash outlays.

A six-year hiatus followed in which the merging firms sought regulatory approvals and fended off challenges. Of these, the ICC, U.S. Department of Justice, and labor unions are notable. In August 1962, the two firms applied to the ICC for permission to merge. The Commission embarked on a process of 128 public hearings and rendered a decision in April 1966: The two firms could merge *if* they also took over the bankrupt New York, New Haven, and Hartford ("New Haven") at a high price and with guarantees for labor that exceeded benchmarks. By 1970 this proved to be an expensive albatross.

Saunders, a lawyer and adept at government lobbying, dealt with opposition at the city, state, and federal levels of government. In October 1963, the Department of Justice (DOJ) Antitrust Division announced its opposition on the grounds that the merger would impose restraints on railroad competition and endanger service. But a year later, the DOJ approved the merger subject to the Pennsylvania divesting its holding of Norfolk & Western (N&W) stock. The impact of this was to cut off a healthy dividend stream from the N&W which was difficult to replace because of restrictions on the redeployment of the funds. The proceeds of $300 million were used as collateral for a loan to fund investments in real estate, oil, and aviation. The opposition of key cities and states melted when Saunders reassured them that the merger would not reduce employment or service in their areas.

Saunders also surmounted the vehement opposition of labor unions with assurances of employment. In May 1964, the Central and Pennsylvania agreed with 17 unions to grant lifetime job protection for all those employed at the date of the merger and to rehire up to 5,000 employees who had previously been let go for reasons unrelated to the merger. The unions conceded to Penn Central the right to reduce the labor force five percent per year, but only through attrition—a method of workforce rationalization that gave little choice to management over which jobs to eliminate. Saunders and Perlman estimated that the Merger Protective Agreement would cost Penn Central a total of $78 million spread over eight years. In reality it cost $92.7 million[26] in the first three years following merger, diminishing the cost savings from merger that had been projected for those years. One director who joined Penn Central's board in 1969 thought the terms of the agreement were so onerous as to cancel the merger: "The day Stuart Saunders signed the deal with the unions he gave the farm away. It was all downhill after that. It was impractical and impossible."[27]

As the wait for approval to merge lengthened, the two firms faced the pressure to maintain reported earnings. The exchange ratio of 1.3:1 was predicated on share prices prevailing when the merger agreement was signed. Significant declines in the share prices of either firm would rupture the parity implied by the exchange ratio, triggering a wealth transfer from the relatively richer firm's shareholders to the poorer firm's shareholders. And generally, a decline in both firm's shares might threaten the deal if shareholders believed that a better price was to be found by selling to another buyer altogether. The deterioration in operating profitability of the railroads during the six years threatened the deal. To maintain the fragile exchange ratio relationship, the two firms sharply increased their dividends (see Figure 5.4), began to manage earnings, and undertook a set of operating policies aimed at conserving cash and minimizing borrowings—thus accelerating a process of underinvesting and deferring maintenance that affected service. Figure 5.5 shows that measured in terms of capital expenditure per mile of track, Penn Central underspent its peers. Also, the limbo of waiting for merger approval triggered a mentality of delay so that whatever investing was done would be consistent with the view of the new firm.

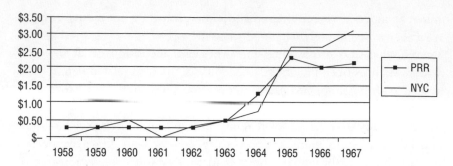

Figure 5.4   **Dividend Payment per Share**

Source of data: U.S. Senate Committee on Commerce (1972), page 68.

Remaining litigation over the merger was resolved on January 15, 1968, in a decision by the U.S. Supreme Court in favor of the deal. The transaction was consummated two weeks later.

THE MERGER TEAM

An important factor in the demise of Penn Central was the organizational friction between the Pennsylvania and New York Central. In large part, this sprang from the historical rivalry between the two railroads, the so-

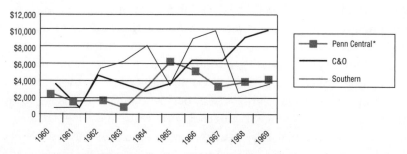

*A pro forma combination of the Pennsylvania, Central, and New Haven RRs.

Figure 5.5   **Capital Expenditures per Mile of Track Operated**

Source of data: U.S. Senate Committee on Commerce (1972), page 94.

called "red team" (Pennsylvania) and "green team" (Central), so named because of the color of their freight cars. The respective corporate legacies would challenge the integration of these two corporate cultures, as Daughen and Binzen describe:

> The Pennsylvania, stolid, steady and traditional, carried ore over mountains. It was "volume oriented," and its operations were highly decentralized. It generally promoted from within its own ranks. The Central was smaller, scrappier, hungrier, more inclined to abandon the book and innovate. . . . The Central carried manufactured goods along its "water-level route." It was profit oriented and centralized. PRR critics conveyed the impression that the Central was run "out of Perlman's hat." But Perlman often went outside the company for promising executive talent. . . . The Central, for example, used in-cab locomotive signals; the Pennsylvania used visual signals along its right-of-way. Central locomotives came equipped with cushioned armrests for engineers; Pennsylvania locomotives didn't. (Central engineers refused to operate PRR locomotives until the armrests were installed.) The two railroads even used different railroad spikes."[28]

With time, training, and collaboration in running the railroad, the two sides might be expected to blend their cultures. But the cultures clashed significantly at the top of the organization. Saunders and Perlman differed socially. The polished Saunders was readily accepted by Philadelphia society upon his appointment as CEO of the Pennsylvania; he joined the most prestigious sports and social clubs. Perlman, on the other hand, was not a joiner; others saw him as proud, hardheaded, temperamental, sarcastic, and antagonistic. More importantly, the professional experiences of these two railroad executives contrasted sharply. Perlman was known as an operations man, with a solid record of turning around failing railroads (including the New York Central). However, Saunders, a lawyer by training, came from Norfolk & Western, one of the wealthiest railroads around.

Compounding matters, both Saunders and Perlman disliked Penn Central's Chief Financial Officer David Bevan. By all accounts, Bevan performed well. However, his strong personality was off-putting to many in his company, as well as in the general banking community. Bevan was thought to be Symes' heir apparent to the CEO of the Pennsylvania, making relations with Saunders particularly delicate. But the situation would worsen after the merger. Saunders excluded Bevan from the new 25-member board of directors of Penn Central (he had been a board member of the Pennsy). Bevan lost to Perlman key staff functions such as accounting and budget administration. Accordingly, Bevan tightened his grip on the part of Penn Central he did control. Since Bevan was responsible for raising money, and Perlman for spending it, this change in assignment would prove to be the source of friction for the new Penn Central.

THE AFTERMATH

The official merger ceremony commenced at 12:01 A.M. on February 1, 1968. Perlman remained inside his private car on the train at Pennsylvania Railroad's Thirtieth Street Station in Philadelphia, while the ceremony—commemorating a deal that he still didn't prefer—was conducted outside. Even eight years after signing the merger agreement with Saunders, Perlman wished that the Central had merged with the C&O and harbored resentments about the structure of management in the new company.

Despite having nearly $7 billion in assets, the new company started with only $13.3 million in cash. Saunders, Perlman, and Bevan likely believed that cost savings from the merger and cash from diversification would relieve the cash shortfall. But these did not.

Bevan had favored a diversification strategy since 1963. He argued that Penn Central's nonrail activities—which included holdings in real estate, oil, and aviation—could give the return necessary to offset the losses from passenger service and therefore could provide for the continued operation of the railroad. Indeed, nonrail activities were able to bolster the Penn Central's dismal earnings statement in the short term. The evidence is that diversifying investments did divert funds away from the core business *and* that the profits from those investments helped to support the sagging core. After its bankruptcy, Penn Central's trustees concluded that the diversification strategy had been a mistake. But none of the government investigations concluded that diversification was a material cause of the merger failure. This question absorbed the investigators because at the time the business community was coming to grips with the financial underperformance of the diversified conglomerates created in the 1960s. But diversification, like the firm's dividend payments and earnings management, helped create the image of a healthy firm that masked the rot in its core operations. The image permitted the company to gain merger approval from shareholders, unions, and regulators, and to obtain loans.

From February to June 1968, the two firms operated separate lines in parallel. The hiatus reflected the extraordinarily complex task of stitching together two rail systems so that freight could move seamlessly and quickly from origin to destination. Compounding the difficulty was the fact that the two management teams undertook the integration *with no plan.* Saunders and Perlman had commissioned a task force to prepare an integration strategy for the new firm. This produced a six-volume study prepared over two and one-half years. But by November 1967, Perlman and Saunders had decided to accelerate the rate of integration and ordered that the plan be shelved and the sequence of key construction projects be accelerated. As one manager testified to the SEC:

> We were in the same situation as if we had planned the invasion of Europe without having General Eisenhower named until D-Day. . . . Here we have a plan [of] which [it] has never been said, "This is it. Do it this way." The man who was going to run the railroad has not said, "This is what we're going to follow.[29]

Chaos ensued when the process of operational integration began in July 1968. Richard Saunders called it "the mother of all operating breakdowns."[30] Locomotives were in short supply, as were freight cars. As Figure 5.6 shows, accident rates rose above those of peers. Waybills, the paperwork accompanying the cars and directing them to their destinations, got lost or

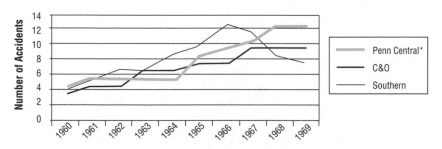

*A pro forma combination of the Pennsylvania and New York Central.

Figure 5.6 **Railroad Accidents per Million Units**

Source of data: U.S. Senate Committee on Commerce (1972), page 96.

to the same effect were poorly completed. An internal memorandum described the ripple of routing errors:

> The principal effect of these [merger] changes was to create congestion and confusion at major gateways and to shift the classification functions of those terminals to internal yards, thus spreading the congestion eastward. This initial disruption triggered a number of collateral effects: it widened the margin for error by clerical personnel who were unfamiliar with stations and consignees to which they were routing traffic; it disrupted the cycling of locomotives and thereby produced sporadic power shortages; it placed an unmanageable trading demand upon a data processing system already beset with the problems in incompatibility; it causes separation of cars from billing as emergency steps were taken to clear congested yards; it prompted short-hauling of Penn Central, thereby increasing the switching burden at interchange points with other eastern carriers—and as these adversities snowballed one after another the speed and reliability of our service deteriorated steadily.[31]

Train yards were clogged with lost cars, by accelerated construction projects in the yards, and by the overflow from the closing of other yards. Shippers defected to other railroads or modes of transportation.

Integration plans for those critical areas such as consolidating duplicate facilities in 35 cities—as well as the separate computer and marketing systems—were still unresolved one year after the merger. An inspector for the Interstate Commerce Commission wrote:

> Nearly all shippers said the attitude of station employees, which was none too good prior to merger, became almost intolerable within a few months after the merger. It was my experience, when making agency checks, that these employees were flooded with requests to trace delayed traffic. When this became almost impossible, they had to face, day after day, irate shippers and receivers, and suffer the caustic comments made toward them and their company. This plus the failure of their railroad to provide any semblance of the service they had known on their separate railroads before the merger, dropped their morale to near zero. It was not confined to station employees, but happened to sales people, yard police, and any other department that had contact with the general public.[32]

The accelerated capital spending and operational problems worsened the flow of cash. As the Securities and Exchange Commission (SEC) later reported, the adverse cash impact of the merger was "grossly underestimated"[33] by management. In 1968 and 1969, the merger triggered a total of $250 million in extra cash outlays, of which operational chaos consumed $30 million in lost income and rental of equipment from other roads. The rest was accounted for by capital improvements ($90 million), rehabilitating the New Haven ($45 million), labor protection ($64.6 million), and training, excess overtime, and purchase of homes ($18.6 million).[34] As the Senate Committee noted, the operational chaos accounted for a small fraction (12 percent) of the total excess outlays. The rest was a predictable consequence of the merger speed-up. This was offset by the cost savings from the merger mentioned earlier, producing a net cash outflow of almost $176 million.

The merger coincided with a dramatic turnover in human resources at the company. The Senate report noted that "The rush to consolidate effectively destroyed the organizations of the predecessor companies and the Penn Central was unable to generate in time its own new cohesive and coordinated organization."[35] In the two and one-half years following merger, the organization lost 5 senior executives (associates of Saunders, Perlman, and Bevan), 8 of 20 vice presidents, and 100 of the former Central's marketing department. An internal report shortly before the bankruptcy noted a high level of front-line supervisors in their jobs less than one year: 61 percent of train masters, 81 percent of transportation superintendents, and 44 percent of division superintendents. "Rampant disorganization" was the summary judgment of the Senate Committee.[36]

The merger brought no respite from another worsening trend, the management of reported earnings. In Penn Central's first annual report, Saunders was upbeat. He wrote:

> ... our merger has been smoother and more rapid than we had anticipated. Sound and comprehensive planning while we awaited consummation enabled us to evolve a close working relationship between the two companies. A remarkable spirit of cooperation and enthusiasm is manifest throughout our new organization.[37]

However, the actual operating and financial performance of the firm was much worse than presented. Costs were higher; revenues were lower. As

Figure 5.7 shows, the operating ratio of expenses to revenues was the highest among Penn Central's peers and increased sharply in 1968.

Though the health of the railroad was deteriorating through the year, the Board of Directors approved a dividend payout of $55.4 million in 1968 (equal to 63 percent of reported net income) and sustained the New York Stock Exchange (NYSE)'s longest streak of dividend payments. In the first two years of operation, Penn Central's board approved cash dividend payments of nearly $99 million, funded by loans at interest rates of up to 10.5 percent. The dividends diverted capital from rail improvements. Board minutes and testimony during the bankruptcy and investigative hearings show that the board asked few penetrating questions about operations or finances and dwelled on minutiae instead. This may have reflected a process of internal "information management" by Saunders and Perlman (that paralleled the external "earnings management"). SEC investigators concluded that the Board plainly failed to respond to clear warnings about the failing condition of the railroad, as well as questionable conduct among its top officers.[38]

The reported financial performance did not match the buoyant dividend declarations. Figure 5.8 gives the quarterly railroad and holding company earnings following the merger. The investigation by the Securities and Exchange Commission found numerous examples of mislead-

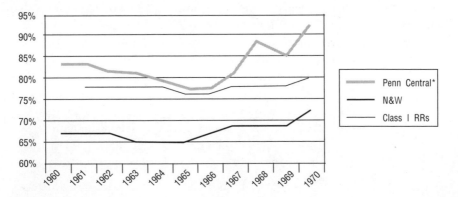

Figure 5.7 **Operating Ratio (Operating Expenses Divided by Operating Revenues)**

Source of data: U.S. Senate Committee on Commerce (1972), page 96.

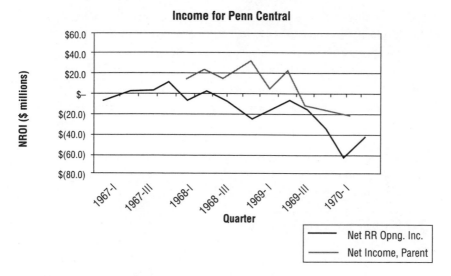

Figure 5.8 **Quarterly Railroad and Holding Company Profits**
Source of data: SEC (1972) pages 30 and 202.

ing—bordering on fraudulent—financial reporting. Earnings management began with an order from the top: Stuart Saunders, the CEO, put the accounting department under a mandate to "create the most favorable income at all times by the best favorable transactions."[39] Saunders consistently sought to understate or underaccrue those charges that would not be fully known until after the close of an accounting period (e.g., per diem charges, inventory losses, and increases in reserves for damages, personal injuries, etc.) and conversely to overstate estimates for revenue forecast figures. For example, it was assumed that since revenues could not be documented with absolute certainty, revenue figures could be legitimately manipulated within a one percent to two percent range. Additionally, Saunders encouraged his accountants to charge all costs that could be considered merger related against a $275 million reserve account for that purpose, so that they would be treated as an extraordinary item (in contrast, all merger savings were allowed to flow through to increase reported earnings). Finally, in this vain attempt to boost quarterly earnings statements, Penn Central managers were tasked with achieving arbitrarily determined cuts in costs. However, the result of these budget restrictions was a further deterioration of rail service, an increase in the already large number of complaints from shippers, and ultimately a further loss of customers to other modes of transportation. The SEC concluded:

It is clear   that throughout the entire period from February 1, 1968 until June 1970, when top management and Penn Central parted company, the public was being fed misleading information on a virtually continuous basis. Disclosure was made only to the extent that it was not feasible to do otherwise, because it could not be hidden. The tone presented to the public throughout 1968 was one of great optimism with respect to all aspects of the business—financing, earnings, operations, etc., an optimism clearly not justified by the facts. The picture was altered only when facts about the service problems became known anyway. The company then admitted the existence of these merger-related problems and their related earnings impact, but indicated repeatedly that the situation had turned the corner and things were definitely on the upswing. The rest of the picture was rosy. It was not until early 1970, when the end was near, that the rosiness was tempered. There was no mention yet of financing problems or the course of conduct being pursued in the earnings area. The company did give increased indication of problems in the critical railroad segment of the business, although management rejected internal suggestions that it might be in the economic interest of the company to lay these problems bare in their entirety.[40]

Ominously, the firm's merger coincided with rising inflation, interest rates, the onset of recession, and the nation's turmoil over Vietnam (see Figure 5.9). The rise in interest rates coincided with the firm's declining creditworthiness. Penn Central started 1969 with a working capital deficit of $171 million as interest payments on debt rose more than 40 percent in one year. By the end of 1969, Penn Central's working capital deficit had grown to $206.5 million. Meanwhile, Penn Central's stock price had plummeted to $29. By 1970, Penn Central was bleeding cash at the rate of $1 million a day. Figure 5.10 shows that the cumulative cash deficit would amount to −$750 million by the bankruptcy filing in 1970. Bevan, who had already borrowed more than $400 million since the merger, was forced to find more sources of capital in order to meet the debt maturities and interest payments coming due that year. These included $106 in long-term debt, $30 million in other bank loans, $193 million in commercial paper, and $132 million in interest charges. Assuming the bank loans and

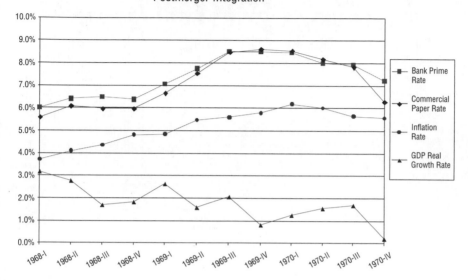

Figure 5.9   Inflation, Growth, and Interest Rates

Source of data: WRDS database, Federal Reserve Bank *Bulletin*, Bureau of Economic Analysis.

commercial paper could be rolled over, the financial need for 1970 could be filled with a $100 million bond issue by a subsidiary of Penn Central. The goal was to float the bond issue in spring 1970.

Three fresh developments in early 1970 killed the bond issue. First, deep snows and low temperatures in January and February 1970 jammed the Penn Central system. The firm spent $8.5 million to free the blocked tracks. Switches froze and equipment broke; the cold weather slowed or prevented repairs. Stuart Saunders later testified, "It was worse than any strike we ever had. For . . . over three weeks the Penn Central was paralyzed over a great portion of its railroad. We couldn't get a car through Selkirk yard for days. . . . You have to expect bad weather every year but the unprecedented bad weather we had in the first quarter of this year cost Penn Central at least 20 million."[41] Reflecting the weather, Penn Central reported a first quarter total loss of $17.2 million, with losses on rail operations at $65.8 million.[42]

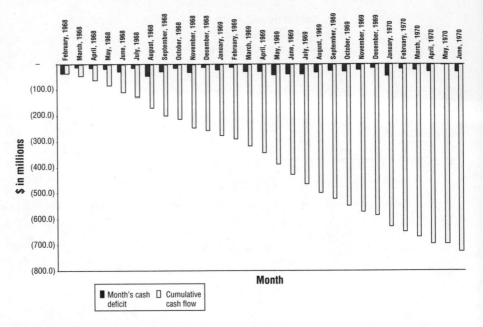

Figure 5.10 **Monthly and Cumulative Cash Flow Deficits**
Source of data: ICC filings.

In spring 1970, a stock market downturn depressed the value of the company's investment portfolio so that it could not provide sufficient collateral for the debenture issue. The offering prospectus for the bond issue revealed that Penn Central was caught in a financial squeeze spurred by dwindling confidence in the firm. The squeeze took the form of a "run" on its commercial paper, similar to bank depositors seeking to withdraw their savings from a shaky bank. The commercial paper investors chose to move their funds elsewhere as the instruments matured. In April 1970, $41 million of commercial paper financing had evaporated. In May, another $94 million disappeared. Shareholders followed shortly thereafter with a fire sale of the company's stock. Turnover in Penn Central stock increased as investors sold off 6,727,000 shares—more than 27 percent of all outstanding stock—in the second quarter of 1970.

In mid-May, Standard and Poor's downgraded Penn Central's credit rating to "junk bond" status, unacceptable to large institutional investors. This accelerated the run on commercial paper and the selling of shares. On May 25, the Board of Directors voted to withdraw the bond issue from the market. At that point, the only source of liquid funds remaining for the company was a circle of money-center banks, led by First National City Bank. However, the banks were no longer willing to lend money to Penn Central without government loan guarantees. When legislation to authorize such guarantees failed to gain support in Congress, Penn Central filed for bankruptcy on June 21, 1970.

EPILOGUE

Penn Central operated its rail system under the management of a bankruptcy court-appointed trustee. In 1976, the U.S. government formed the Consolidated Rail Corporation (Conrail) from the rail assets of Penn Central and five other bankrupt railroads in the Northeastern United States. The privatization of Conrail in 1987 and acquisitive breakup in 1997 left the Northeast served by two large rail systems, CSX and Norfolk Southern (NS), an outcome not very different from that envisioned by Robert Young and James Symes in 1957.

Penn Central Corporation emerged from bankruptcy on October 24, 1978; the day before, its shares had ceased trading on the New York Stock Exchange at $1.62 each. After extended litigation over the value of the rail assets folded into Conrail, the government agreed in December 1980 to pay Penn Central $1.46 billion for the assets and $650 million in accumulated interest. This cash, plus a considerable tax-loss carryforward funded a program of diversifying acquisitions by Penn Central. The financier, Carl Lindner, took over the company on March 24, 1995, changing the name of the company to American Premier Underwriters; it continues to operate in nonrail businesses, including real estate and insurance.

COUNTERPOINTS: SUBSEQUENT RAILROAD MERGERS

The collapse of Penn Central left a long legacy of distrust of railroad mergers. Writing in 1972, the Senate Commerce Committee concluded:

> In the preponderance of the mergers that have been approved since 1959 the record reveals that cost savings forecasts have typically been overblown, that where some savings have resulted they have been

exceedingly modest, that savings are far more difficult to realize and require far longer than is anticipated, and that merger can lead to rising rather than falling costs. . . . The available evidence, as borne out by the experience of the last 15 years, simply does not establish that mergers are a generally useful way of increasing [railroad] efficiency, eliminating excess capacity, or improving rail service. By and large, they are more likely to be harmful than beneficial.[43]

The judgment of the U.S. Senate's Committee on Commerce is mirrored by historians such as Richard Saunders Jr., writing in 2003:

> . . . mergers produced little of the benefits ascribed to them and left the industry as a whole a bleeding mess. . . . None of the ones that remained in the works after the Penn Central's crackup were successful. . . . The mergers had not eliminated duplicate routes and excess mileage except for a few bits and pieces. They had not saved much money.[44]

But Saunders noted that the M&A environment for railroads changed in the late 1970s with a wave of deregulation that, in combination with changes in technology, constituted a "revolution." These changes promoted the development of coast-to-coast trunk lines in which the expensive and time-consuming interchange of cars was reduced. Regulatory consideration of merger applications was accelerated. Railroads had more latitude to pursue productivity improvements. Figure 5.11 shows the dramatic increase in ton-miles per employee that occurred starting around 1980. Thus, the character of industry consolidation changed over the next 20 years. This is reflected in five large transactions.

Transactions

CSX formed by the merger of the Chessie System and Seaboard Coast Line.

Merger discussions between Chessie and Seaboard began in September 1978; the merger was announced in January 1979 and consummated on November 1, 1980, creating the first behemoth in the Eastern United States, in a transaction worth more than $1 billion. One employee said that the name CSX stands for "Chesapeake Seaboard Expansion"; another source said it means "Chesapeake Seaboard Together." The Chessie/Seaboard union was structured as a 50:50 partnership (versus the

Millions of Ton-Miles per Employee

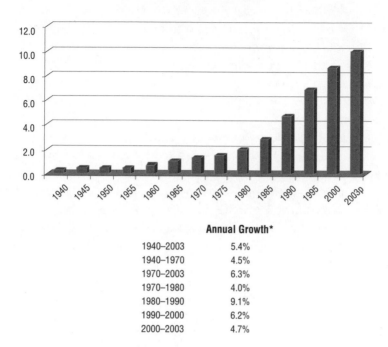

Annual Growth*

1940–2003	5.4%
1940–1970	4.5%
1970–2003	6.3%
1970–1980	4.0%
1980–1990	9.1%
1990–2000	6.2%
2000–2003	4.7%

* Compound average annual growth rate.

Figure 5.11   **Increase in Labor Productivity (All U.S. Railroads)**

Sources of data: Mergent/Moody's Transportation Manual, 2002; Statistical Abstract, 2003, and Association of American Railroads.

60:40 split between PRR and Central). Each company provided one-half of the initial directors, as well as a co–CEO determined by the new board. The new company sought gradually to integrate the policies and adminis-tration of its two separate rail systems. Most importantly, the CSX union involved two relatively healthy companies. While its nonrail subsidiaries were doing well, CSX's rail services were the principal source of earnings growth. CSX was already a leading carrier of metallurgical coal for export; a growing demand for steam coal further augmented the growth of ship-ments. Yet another important advantage for Chessie and Seaboard was that ICC hearings on the proposed merger took just eight months.

From the start, CSX executives consciously sought to avoid the mistakes made by their counterparts at Penn Central. At first, the Chessie and Seaboard Coast systems were operated independently. Integration took a deliberate pace. Only a small headquarters staff existed for overall planning purposes. Integration planning had been completed in advance of the merger. The two companies' computer infrastructure was aligned in advance of the merger, eliminating one of the vexing problems of the Penn Central combination.

The Chessie/Seaboard union delivered impressive financial results in the following year. In the first quarter of 1981, CSX's earnings rose 59 percent from the earnings for the combined companies in the same period the previous year; quarterly revenues on transportation and non-transportation segments rose 12 percent and 18 percent, respectively. The results were attributed to continued cost–control measures and strong export coal shipments (up 31 percent from the year before). An 80-day coal miner's strike caused profits to lag in the second quarter. However, CSX's profits rebounded in the third quarter, up 87.5 percent from the previous year. In short, CSX concluded the year with no visible signs of distress.

Norfolk Southern Corporation formed by the merger of Norfolk & Western and Southern.   Announced on June 2, 1980, and consummated on June 1, 1982, this deal was a domino-like reaction to the CSX merger. Norfolk & Western was a direct competitor of the Chessie System, and Southern had sought to acquire Seaboard Coast Line. Richard Saunders commented, "Both were profitable and successful railroads in peak physical condition, well managed, and proud."[45] There was little operational disruption following this merger.

Acquisition of Santa Fe by Burlington Northern.   Following a bidding war between Union Pacific and Burlington Northern, Burlington Northern (BN) acquired Santa Fe (SF) on September 22, 1995. While BN was already among the largest lines in the Western United States, this acquisition created the largest rail system in North America. The merger integration proceeded smoothly, though the earnings of the new firm fell in 1995 due to merger-related costs. Key to this success was the installation of master computer software that gave managers clarity about bottlenecks and system requirements. Some observers believed it would not have been possible to handle the surge in freight that hit the system in the late 1990s without this software.

Acquisition of Southern Pacific by Union Pacific. On September 11, 1996, this deal was consummated after a year-long fight with shippers, regulators, and competitors, who argued that the merger represented an excessive concentration of railroad power. By trading trackage rights with competitors, soliciting support from shippers, and lobbying the government intensively, Union Pacific (UP) management turned the tide and won approval for the deal. Portending a difficult integration, UP management ordered rapid integration of the two lines like Saunders and Perlman had at Penn Central 18 years earlier. More than 3,000 employees would be laid off, and another 3,000 transferred. A large number of Southern Pacific (SP) middle managers took buyouts and left.

In June 1997, a crucial hub rail yard in the UP system at Houston (a former SP yard that needed investment and was easily congested) began to clog up. The congestion radiated outward from there and was measured in terms of slower train movements, accidents, and mistakes in car tracking. The booming national economy loaded all the railroads with increased traffic.

By October 8, 1997, 550 trains in the UP system were stalled for want of locomotives or crews. The gridlock threatened to spill over into the Burlington Northern Santa Fe (BNSF) system and others. Shippers became intensely angry. The Surface Transportation Board threatened intervention. Only by working its employees arduously long hours, rationalizing yards, and undertaking track-sharing agreements with BNSF and other lines did the plugged traffic gradually work its way through the railroad system.

In June 1998, almost two years after the merger, the Surface Transportation Board declared the traffic emergency at Houston to be over. Richard Saunders wrote:

> This was called a meltdown, a loss of managerial control of Penn Central dimensions. It was national news. By October 1997, the damage to the economy was reckoned at over a billion dollars. . . . By Christmas the estimates went to $2 billion. . . . But with the 1997 meltdown, the great railroad rebirth somehow lost focus. The industry as a whole was never quite as vibrant or optimistic again. A vulnerability had been exposed and an innocence lost.[46]

Split-up of Conrail to Norfolk Southern and CSX.   Following a months-long bidding war between CSX and Norfolk Southern (NS), the Surface Transportation Board (successor to the Interstate Commerce Commission) intervened bringing both suitors and target to the bargaining table. There, the parties settled on a carve-up of the Conrail system to NS and CSX. The date of consummation was August 22, 1998. Conrail was functioning well at that time, with good records for on-time delivery and safety, good equipment condition, and high employee morale. One indicator of Conrail's health was its share price: Taken public at a split-adjusted $13.00 per share in 1987, CSX and NS paid $115.00 per share, giving investors a compound annual return on investment of 22 percent.

Conrail actually continued operation of its system until NS and CSX were ready to assume control of their respective assets. The date of operational takeover was delayed until June 1, 1999, when both buyers declared themselves ready. Information technology systems on both lines functioned imperfectly, declaring loaded cars as empty, and changing destinations. Congestion built up at some of the rail yards. And some shippers defected to truckers. Richard Saunders rendered this judgment:

> Both CSX and NS had paid way too much for Conrail and the fortunes of neither recovered quickly. CSX was hit by Hurricane Floyd in September 1999. . . . Norfolk Southern's net income plunged 59 percent in the second quarter of 1999 and 88 percent in the third quarter, which was attributed to congestion in the Conrail breakup and the desertion of customers because of it. . . . For both CSX and Norfolk Southern, all this came simultaneously with a steep slide in export coal . . . [a] lucrative business for these railroads. . . . The Conrail breakup was not a meltdown like the one at Union Pacific, but it was more than a year before the congestion and confusion was over. . . . Workers felt they had been overworked and then thanked with massive dismissals. Middle managers were frustrated. Some were leaving because the stress level was great, hours long, job security nil, and the pay less than that for union members. Tonnage was no longer growing at the bounding rates of the 1990s.[47]

The stress of merger integration was a significant factor in the poor performance of CSX and NS following the merger. It is also true, however, that CSX and NS would have suffered from Hurricane Floyd and declining shipments of export coal whether they had acquired halves of Conrail.

It is a matter of speculation whether the merger or the exogenous effects did more damage.

Have these mergers paid off? Figure 5.12 gives the cumulative market-adjusted returns to investors in the acquiring firms in these deals for five years following consummation. It shows winners and losers, but on average, a cumulative return insignificantly different from zero. Figure 5.13 gives the standardized change in reported earnings by quarter for each of the buyers for the 20 quarters after merger. Two conclusions stand out: Every deal shows a period of sharp volatility—no one is spared. But the Union Pacific/Southern Pacific merger volatility dominates the others, consistent with its "meltdown." Also, it seems that the sharp volatility ends after two and one-half years from the merger. This long period underscores the difficulty of mergers in transportation. Finally, unlike the Penn Central case, all of these subsequent deals emerged as survivors who recovered after their merger difficulties.

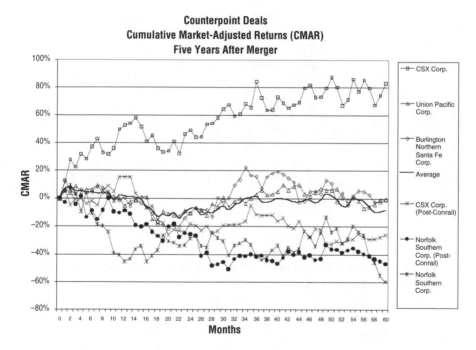

Figure 5.12 **Cumulative Market-Adjusted Returns to Shareholders Following Other Major Railroad Transactions**

Source of data: Datastream.

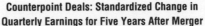

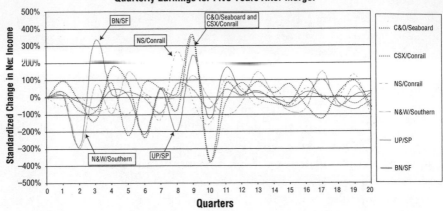

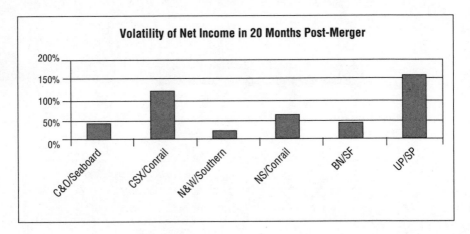

Note: "Standardized Change in Quarterly Earnings" is the change in net income in the current quarter over the previous quarter, divided by the standard deviation of net income over the 20-quarter observation period. "Volatility" is the standard deviation in quarterly net income over 20 quarters divided by the mean net income for that period. Division by the mean adjusts for size differences among the firms.

Figure 5.13 **Volatility of Earnings for Major Railroads, Following Merger**

Source of data: Datastream. Author's analysis.

CONCLUSION

The Senate Commerce Committee concluded that "It will perhaps be a disappointment to those expecting the root cause to be found in a litany of sordid events to learn that the railroad's failure cannot be written off as resulting from evil men's schemes. Rather, the major contributors were much broader in scope: . . . the failure of men, institutions, and laws."[48] Indeed, what distinguishes Penn Central from the other railroad mergers surveyed here is a convergence of forces—a perfect storm—on the transaction. The merger failure framework offered here highlights the dimension of these forces.

Business was not "as usual": The decline of the railroad industry accelerated during the 1960s; regulatory delays were unforeseen, as were a wave of inflation, rising interest rates, and the severe winter of 1970. The nature of the companies and the deal allowed little flexibility to meet these difficulties. The *tight coupling* of the financial fortunes of the two railroads through the deal design with a fixed exchange ratio forced the two roads to overpay dividends, manage earnings, and skimp on capital spending during the long wait for approval. The operations of each road were *complex* to begin with, and would be very complex upon merger of the operations. Expectations of shippers required that operations be tightly coupled and synchronized upon merger. The *decision* by Saunders and Perlman to dispose of the integration plans and instead to opt for an accelerated ad hoc integration, while motivated by the urgency of harvesting cost savings quickly, reminds one of management's decision at Chernobyl to operate the reactor despite a shut-down of the emergency core cooling system: perhaps justified in the abstract but foolhardy in this particular situation. The lack of training and cultural differences worsened the possibility that the employees of the new firm would work well as a *team* to respond to unforeseen challenges. Through it all, the public optimism of top management suggests a *cognitive bias* so strong as to discount the urgency and severity of the problems. Saunders and Perlman seemed too willing to hide the problems of the two railroads. Harold Geneen, CEO of International Telephone and Telegraph, a leading conglomerate firm at the time, argued that the big mistake of Saunders and Perlman had been their lack of transparency about the weakness of the core railroad operations.[49] Cognitive bias was highlighted in the Senate Commerce Committee report:

> [T]he merger became such an *obsession* that the managements were willing to "pay" a considerable amount for the merger. It may be argued that they "paid too much." They took on the loss-ridden New Haven as a condition of merger. In addition they assumed labor protection costs, amounting to $64 million in the first two years as it turned out. It must be remembered that the two railroads were not forced to merge; if they believed that the conditions imposed were too costly they could always have withdrawn from the agreement. But withdrawal never seemed to be an alternative and the architects of the merger drove to completion at whatever the cost." (italics added)[50]

NOTES

1. This chapter was prepared with research assistance from Sean Carr, David Eichler, and Sanjay Vakharia. Also, I am grateful for insights gained in interviews with Ernest R. Varalli, Controller's Office, Penn Central; Eileen Drelick, Research Administrator at Blank, Rome, Comiskey, and McCauley, LLP; and John H. McArthur. And I consulted primary archives at the Center for the History of Business, Technology, and Society, Hagley Museum and Library, Wilmington, Delaware; and the Pennsylvania State Archives and Pennsylvania Historical and Museum Commission, Harrisburg, Pennsylvania.

2. Estimates of the impact of closing the Penn Central Transportation Company by the U.S. Department of Transportation, reported in Senate (1972), xix.

3. Testimony of Alfred Perlman, CEO of the Central, before the Interstate Commerce Commission, as quoted in Daughen and Binzen (1971), 63.

4. Testimony of James Symes, CEO of the Pennsylvania, before the Interstate Commerce Commission, as quoted in Daughen and Binzen (1971), 52.

5. The investigations were led by the Securities and Exchange Commission, the Interstate Commerce Commission, the House Banking and Currency Committee, the House Committee on Interstate and Foreign Commerce, the Senate Committee on Commerce, the Department of Justice, and the Philadelphia District Attorney. Summarized in Salisbury (1982), 198, and Senate (1972), v.

6. Figures of cost to the U.S. government are drawn from "Bank Runs and Bailouts: A Short and Costly History Lesson," *U.S. News & World Report*, February 20, 1989.

7. Harley O. Staggers, Chairman of the House Special Subcommittee on Investigations, *Financial Collapse of the Penn Central Company*, U.S. Government Printing Office (1972), vi.

8. Senate (1972), xix.

9. Saunders (2003), 143.

10. Saunders (2003), 45.

11. Daughen and Binzen (1971), 12.

12. A quotation of Milton Shapp, critic of the merger, in Daughen and Binzen (1971), 78.

13. Daughen and Binzen (1971), 308.

14. Quotation of David Bevan to the ICC, given in Daughen and Binzen (1971), 63.

15. Quotation of Stuart Saunders at Senate hearings, given in Daughen and Binzen (1971), 312 and 314.

16. A quotation of John Weller of the brokerage firm of Hayden Stone writing in *Fortune*, September 1970, 62. Quoted in Saunders (2003), 61.

17. Salisbury (1982), 209.

18. Senate (1972), 283.

19. Senate (1972), 285.

20. Saunders (2003), 110.

21. Daughen and Binzen (1971), 112.

22. Daughen and Binzen (1971), 53.

23. Saunders (2003), 10.

24. SEC (1972), 29.

25. SEC (1972), 16.

26. The estimated cost is given in Daughen and Binzen (1972), 221.

27. Daughen and Binzen (1971), 222.

28. Daughen and Binzen (1971), 90–91.

29. SEC (1972), 20.

30. Saunders (2003), 10.

31. Internal memorandum quoted in SEC (1972), 22.

32. Statement of ICC inspector quoted in Saunders (2003), 11.

33. SEC (1972), 29.

34. Senate (1972), 171.

35. Senate (1972), 164.

36. Senate (1972), 164.

37. Quotation of Stuart Saunders' Chairman's Letter to Shareholders, in Penn Central Annual Report, March 15, 1968, given in Daughen and Binzen (1972), 223.

38. SEC (1972), 153.

39. SEC (1972), 34.

40. SEC (1972), 200.

41. Testimony by Stuart Saunders at U.S. Senate Commerce Committee, quoted in Daughen and Binzen (1972), 254.

42. SEC (1972), 202. The size of the losses depended on the method of accounting. The figures given in the text reflect ICC reports. Yet, for the bond offering circular, the company reported losses on rail operations of –$101.5 million.

43. Senate (1972), 285–286.

44. Saunders (2003), 143.

45. Saunders (2003), 229–230.

46. Saunders (2003), 331 and 336.

47. Saunders (2003), 344–345.

48. Senate (1972), 16.

49. Geneen's comments reported in a letter from William L. Day to Stuart Saunders, December 1, 1969, and quoted in Daughen and Binzen (1972), 261.

50. Senate (1972), 184.

6

December 1986:
The Leveraged Buyout
of Revco Drug Stores

Revco was in trouble from the day it went private. Sales and earnings projections were strictly from dreamland.[1]

Revco Drug Stores was taken private on December 29, 1986, at a
48 percent premium to the firm's stock price 12 months earlier.
Nineteen months later, it filed for bankruptcy. The means by
which the firm had been "taken private," a leveraged buyout, was a hall-
mark of the 1980s and 1990s.[2] In this transaction, management and a
group of investors, acquired from public shareholders Revco's common
stock with a cash payment that was financed substantially by debt. At closing in December 1986, Revco's leveraged buyout (LBO) was one of the
largest ever ($1.4 billion) and certainly one of the most complex, featuring
nine discrete layers of financing.

A counterpoint to the story of Revco is the leveraged buyout of its direct competitor in the retail pharmacy industry, Jack Eckerd Corporation.
Eckerd was taken private in May 1986, also in response to a threatened
hostile bid. As was typical of most LBOs, Eckerd reported losses but positive cash flows, sufficient to purchase 220 of Revco's stores in 1990. Subsequently, Eckerd submitted an unsolicited bid to purchase the entire

company. Revco's management and creditors resisted. In 1993, Eckerd went public again, netting its equity investors a hefty return. Why Eckerd prospered and Revco didn't offers lessons about governance, deal design, and financial leverage.

THE DEMISE OF REVCO

The buyout consummated a long episode of anxiety for Sidney Dworkin, the CEO of Revco, about possible takeover threats, internal fighting over control of the firm,[3] and declining financial performance.[4] The performance of Revco's common stock over the period 1984–1986 provides a clear picture of how poorly the company performed prior to the 1986 LBO.

An analysis of the market-adjusted returns and cumulative market-adjusted returns (CMARs) to shareholders during the period 1984 to 1986 paints a dismal picture of Revco before the leveraged buyout. Shareholders suffered a −40 percent CMAR in 1984–1985. This performance reflected several events. In April 1984 the U.S. Food and Drug Administration (FDA) announced a possible link between E-Ferol, a vitamin E supplement produced by a Revco subsidiary, and infant deaths. Analysts estimated that Revco's liability could mount to $75 million; yet the drop in market value associated with this event was $160 million. Further deterioration in returns later in 1984 is associated with the announcements of worse-than-expected financial performance. In 1985, the declines in CMAR in February–March are associated with management changes and the removal of dissident directors; later in 1985, additional declines are associated with worsening financial performance and the downgrading of Revco's debt ratings by the major rating agencies.[5] Generally, Revco underperformed its peer group over the 1984–1986 period, reporting lower annual sales growth and earnings before interest and taxes (EBIT) margins (EBIT/Sales).

An independent investment banker first proposed the idea of an LBO to Sidney Dworkin on September 17, 1985. Shortly thereafter, Revco retained Salomon Brothers Inc. to advise on the feasibility of an LBO. Salomon rationalized Revco's poor recent financial results as being due to "temporary problems"[6] and solicited Wells Fargo to develop a syndicate of banks to provide senior debt in the transaction. Wells Fargo provided a commitment letter in early March 1986; and on March 11, 1986, Sidney Dworkin presented a proposal for an LBO to the Revco directors. The proposal called for shareholders to receive $33 per share in cash, and $3.00 per share in exchangeable preferred, a 17.6 percent premium to the previous day's price per share on the New York Stock Exchange.

The LBO announcement produced a two-day market-adjusted return of 8.4 percent for Revco shareholders. However, Dworkin's announcement generated a vigorous debate within the financial community regarding the adequacy of the bid. Two securities analysts, issuing separate reports, believed the offering price to be "fair."[7] Other analysts believed the bid to be too low: William Blair & Company issued a report[8] saying, "$38-40 is more equitable." Also, the Dart Group, operator of a chain of discount drug stores, approached the directors about a possible acquisition of Revco. Later Dart asked to join the LBO group, and threatened to mount a hostile tender offer if excluded. Jamie Securities, a risk arbitrage boutique, expressed an interest in raising its holding of shares to more than the 9 percent it already owned.

On June 2, 1986, Dworkin presented a revised offer to the board for $38.50 in cash. The directors accepted the offer on August 15. Revco stockholders voted to approve the acquisition on December 17. The LBO closed on December 29.

Notable about this deal was its complex financial structure. It featured nine layers of financing and included exotic forms of securities rarely seen on Wall Street. These included the following:

- *Preferred stock*, like common stock, serves to "cushion" the creditors. The amount of cushion the firm needs is probably dictated by expectations about the firm's cash flows, particularly its strength and stability. The capital structure is like a serving line, with the senior creditors at the front, and the equityholders at the back. If the food is likely to run out, the cooks would rather have customers at the end of the line who will not boycott the cafeteria. Preferred holders cannot initiate a bankruptcy proceeding in the event a dividend is passed. At the same time, preferred stock is probably cheaper than common stock; dividends on preferred stock are not tax deductible, although corporate investors do enjoy an 80 percent preferred-dividend exclusion that creates a tax savings, which investors and issuers frequently share (via a lower dividend).

- Bundling the *subordinated notes into units* with common stock shares and common stock puts essentially "kicks" the expected return on the notes upward (if one is optimistic). The natural question is why Revco did not simply issue the notes with a coupon of 15 percent or 20 percent? The answer must be that the financial engineers did not anticipate sufficient strength of cash flow. The strategic role of the equity kick is also applicable to the convertible preferred stock.

- The *exchangeable preferred* was perhaps the most interesting layer in the deal structure. In essence, it was a "pay-in-kind" (PIK) preferred for the first five years, thereafter reverting to an ordinary current-cash-dividend preferred. In addition, the company retained the option to exchange the preferred for subordinated debt carrying the same yield, 15.25 percent. Upon exchange, investors would lose the 80 percent dividend exclusion but would gain modestly higher seniority in the event of liquidation. The company, on the other hand, would gain a new tax deduction with which to shelter its cash flow.

  Was the exchangeable preferred issue really debt or equity? The answer must be found in the anticipated economic behavior of management, and in the economic role this issue plays. One should anticipate that Revco will exercise its right of exchange as soon as the firm gets a whiff of tax expense in 1992. Over the 1987–1989 period, this issue could just as easily have been carried as a debt issue; either way, additions to retained earnings would have been the same. It is a preferred stock in name only, so named in order to exploit a curious feature of the tax code.

- The *junior preferred* was to be purchased entirely by Salomon Brothers, and Transcontinental Services Group (TSG), another investor group. These investors could just as easily have committed the capital in the form of common equity; they probably chose to take a portion of their return in the form of PIK preferred to exploit the dividend exclusion. Economically speaking, one could view the junior preferred as common equity.

Revco's ornate capital structure could be explained as a sophisticated solution to a complex financial problem: (1) Raise a lot of money to pay the buyout premium; (2) get as much as possible from the senior lenders (it's the cheapest capital); (3) get as little as possible from the equity investors (they want to maximize returns); (4) tailor the terms of the capital in the "mezzanine" to be serviceable by the expected flow of cash and yet to be attractive to the providers of that capital (i.e., where necessary use contingent forms of payment).

Through the summer and fall of 1986, management watched the performance of the firm fall short of budget, which management attributed to the entry of new discounters into the discount-drug retailing industry. Net income for the year ended May 31, 1986 was down 17.6 percent versus the prior year. During the first quarter of fiscal 1987 (i.e., May–August 1986), operating income was 21.8 percent lower than plan. In October 1986 the operating budget was revised to provide a forecast for use in the prospectus. However Revco's actual performance failed even to meet the revised budget. Nonetheless, during 1986, shareholders had realized a CMAR of 27 percent.

An internal memo written by Revco's treasurer and dated January 2, 1987—four days after the LBO closed—expressed serious concerns about the firm's worsening cash flows:

> I am very concerned about cash flow since the sales for the past six weeks have been poor resulting in approximately $30 million less cash flow. It will be very difficult to make up this loss of funds. In fact, we have no excess cash going forward.[9]

The reports for the 4- and 32-week periods ending January 10, 1987 showed an extremely disappointing Christmas season.

What followed was progressive financial asphyxia. Anxious bankers met with Revco in February and March. On March 31 the banks were informed that Sidney Dworkin would step down as CEO, though he would remain board chairman, a move that reflected the sentiments of the banks and Salomon that Dworkin "was more entrepreneurial and not experienced or capable of running the operations on a day-to-day basis in a highly leveraged environment.[10] Daily operating control would be shifted to President William B. Edwards. At this same meeting, the banks were informed that progress on asset sales was delayed, operating income was running below budget, and inventories were higher than plan. In May 1987, Revco's operating profits for the fiscal year were 12.5 percent below plan, and its chief financial officer believed that the firm "was in serious danger of not being able to make debt service payments."[11]

The changing of the guard brought with it a change in Revco's strategy. Management abandoned Revco's strategy of "everyday low prices" and adopted a strategy that included weekly sales and promotions. In addition, the product mix was broadened to include TVs, knockdown furniture, and VCRs. Store layouts were changed in an effort to increase pharmacy sales. These changes complicated operations and confused customers.

The internal power struggles split staff loyalty and caused infighting among management. Management struggles were taking precedence over running the company in the efficient manner necessary to make the LBO work. In September 1987, a new management team was installed at Revco, including Boake A. Sells, a former president of Dayton Hudson. Following this change in senior management, Dworkin sold his stake in the Revco venture for $8 million in cash and assets (the amount of his original investment in the LBO), and after 30 years of service, left the company he had so badly wanted to control.

Following the departure of Dworkin, asset sales stalled and cash became scarce. Due to the cash shortage, the company was unable to stock adequate inventory in the fall of 1987 and the Christmas season was a disaster. More generally, the stock market crash of October 1987 dampened consumer demand for the kind of goods toward which Revco was shifting its merchandising strategy. Revco was in serious trouble.

The extent of the problems became known when Revco filed its 10-Q for the quarter ended February 6, 1988. The disclosures indicated that asset sales to date had not been adequate to meet interest payments and the company had drawn down all but $15 million of its revolving line of credit. Furthermore, Revco was in violation of certain financial and nonfinancial debt covenants.

On March 10, 1988, Salomon's high-yield bond sales force stopped making a market for Revco's debt securities. Twelve days later, Salomon deleted Revco from its monthly report, The Safest of High Yields. At the same time, Boake Sells met with Salomon and expressed his displeasure with the level and quality of Salomon's advisory services. On April 13, Salomon presented a restructuring proposal to Revco; Sells virtually rejected it, soliciting restructuring proposals two days later from Drexel Burnham, First Boston, and Goldman Sachs. Revco retained Drexel on April 19 to devise a restructuring plan. The hiring of outside advisors was triggered by internal projections, which indicated that Revco would not be able to meet a $46 million interest payment on its publicly held subordinated debt. Management planned to miss the debt payment so that working capital could be increased, that vendors could be paid, and that store operations could be improved.

On June 16 1988, Revco missed its first interest payment and omitted a quarterly preferred stock dividend. Drexel appealed to the firm's investors to grant Revco "breathing room." When these appeals were rejected, the firm filed for bankruptcy on July 28, 1988.

Drexel's attempts to restructure were fruitless for several reasons. As management had suggested might happen, Revco missed a $46 million interest payment in June 1988. Transcontinental Services Group (TSG), which controlled 60 percent of Revco's common equity, refused to give up a controlling interest in the firm in exchange for $703 million in concessions from bondholders. When a major bondholder refused to consent to a standstill agreement until January 15, 1989, the fate of the highly leveraged company was sealed. On July 28, 1988, 19 months after going private, Revco filed for court protection under Chapter 11 of the bankruptcy code.

Revco's bankruptcy sent tremors through the financial community. From the buyout to July 1988, investors in these securities lost about 80 percent of their capital. The Revco LBO was one of the most prominent highly leveraged transactions in the late 1980s. The rapidity of its demise raised questions about the safety of these transactions and the ability of financial engineers to mitigate the foreseeable risks. This realization strained the junk bond market. The bankruptcy announcement coincided with a rise in junk bond risk premiums.

Revco was Salomon Brothers' first foray into the field of large merchant banking deals: Salomon largely designed the transaction, placed the securities, and invested its own capital as a principal. The failure of Revco and other deals temporarily impaired Salomon's franchise in merchant banking.

In 1990, while in bankruptcy, Revco divested almost one-half of its stores to Jack Eckerd Corporation, Reliable Drugs, Perry Drugs, and Harco, among others. Revco successfully fended off takeover threats by Rite Aid and Eckerd during almost four years of bankruptcy proceedings. Management, creditors, and competitors between November 1990 and

February 1992 submitted at least 10 reorganization plans. In early 1992 both Rite Aid and Eckerd withdrew their bids for Revco. Revco ultimately paid Eckerd to go away, covering $7.5 million in expenses associated with Eckerd's yearlong pursuit of Revco. The company finally emerged from bankruptcy protection in June 1992.

COUNTERPOINT: THE LBO OF JACK ECKERD CORPORATION

Based in Clearwater, Florida, Eckerd had 1,547 drugstores in 15 states. It was second to Revco in the number of outlets and behind both Revco and Walgreen in annual income. Drugstore chains accounted for 59 percent of the $43.2 billion in drugstore sales in 1984 (up from 57 percent in 1983), and their rapid growth over the past 10 years gave them excess cash to invest in other unrelated ventures . . . some of which went sour. Drugstores in general were considered an attractive takeover target in the early to mid-1980s because of the high profitability of the pharmacy end of the business, even though increased competition from supermarkets had cut profitability of health and beauty product sales. Besides Eckerd, other recent acquisitions in the industry had included Kroger's purchase of Hook Drugs for $159.1 million in February 1985, K Mart's $500 million purchase of Pay Less Drug Stores one month later, and the $325 million acquisition of Peoples Drug Stores by Imasco Ltd in April 1984. However, the larger drugstore chains such as Walgreen and Rite Aid were more immune to takeovers because of their high P/E multiples. Eckerd faced increasing competition in the Sunbelt region of the United States and saw a new threat from "deep-discount" chains, which operated on thinner profit margins than the typical drugstore chain. Eckerd, a Fortune 500 company, had sales of $2.5 billion in FY 1985 (ended August 3), but posted a loss of $8.3 million (compared with earnings of $85.4 million in 1984). Poor financial performance made it a prime takeover target.

In June 1985, Dart Group Corporation disclosed that it owned five percent of the shares of Jack Eckerd Corporation. Eckerd stock fell 68.5 cents to $26.25 after weeks of rising prices on takeover rumors. Dart's purchase came weeks after an announcement by Eckerd that third-quarter earnings were expected to be only one-half that of the prior year's period of $17.9 million. Eckerd responded by filing a lawsuit to stall Dart

Group, and by selling divisions that were ancillary to the core business. On July 15, 1985, Eckerd announced the repurchase of Dart's stake for $29.50 a share ($55.6 million total). News of the agreement sent Eckerd stock down $3.125 a share to $26.375.

In August Eckerd announced that it was considering a possible "sale, merger or business combination." Analysts viewed the announcement as intended to increase the stock price (Eckerd was nine percent owned by management, including its chairman, president, and chief executive, Stewart Turley) as well as fend off any further hostile takeovers. The company also announced that it expected a 30 percent drop in earnings for the year to between $56–61 million, attributing the decline to unusually heavy markdowns on merchandise and write-offs associated with the sales of divisions.

On October 10, 1985, Jack Eckerd Corporation announced that it had entered into a definitive merger agreement providing for the acquisition of the company by a new corporation to be owned by its employees and management, in addition to a group of investors organized and led by Merrill Lynch Capital Partners Inc. The LBO was seen by analysts as a move to discourage further takeover attempts (Dart Group Corporation had made a play for the company earlier in the year). The LBO also enabled Eckerd to concentrate on getting its business back in order without having to worry about short-term stockholder earnings. Initially, analysts viewed the LBO deal as good, but not great, thinking the company might be worth somewhat more than the buyout offer. The offer consisted of an all-cash bid valued at $33 per share for a total $1.2 billion.

On April 30, 1986, the acquisition was consummated following shareholder approval at the company's annual meeting. Stewart Turley, chairman and chief executive officer of the new private company, said that going private would not affect the way he and his team would run the drugstores and that the change would be invisible to customers. Jack Eckerd, the founder of the firm, announced that he would sell all of his stock (1.1 million shares) and would not hold any position in the new company. He further noted that a person who had invested $1,000 in the original issue of Eckerd stock in 1961 would receive $158,000 as a result of the LBO.

Jack Eckerd Corporation had a negative net worth of about $252 million at the end of fiscal 1990, and payments on debt contributed to a net loss of $32.6 million. But Eckerd also paid down its $785 million in senior debt to $460 million from 1986–1990, as sales rose from $2.6 billion to $3.5 billion (despite the fact that the number of stores rose by only about

100). In June 1990, Revco agreed to sell 220 of its drugstores to Eckerd for an undisclosed price (later estimated to be about $60 million).

A year later, Eckerd announced an unsolicited offer to buy Revco out of bankruptcy. The offer was resisted by management and the creditors' committee as being insufficient. Eckerd revised the offer upward again. But management countered with an offer of a greenmail payment in 1992, which Eckerd accepted.

The decision to go public again in 1992 was widely anticipated because of low interest rates. The company was able to refinance its debt inexpensively and buy back preferred stock that was getting 14.5 percent yields, thus saving money and improving the balance sheet. Meanwhile, high stock prices meant that investors would be willing to pay more for shares of Eckerd than before.

Although Eckerd had lost money annually since the buyout, the company maintained sufficient cash flow to pay off its debt and was considered one of the more successful companies to have undergone an LBO. By paying down and refinancing the outstanding debt at a lower rate, the IPO was expected to make Eckerd profitable again. Moreover, improved cash flow would enable the company to channel more resources into store construction/renovation and other capital improvements.

Eckerd tested investor interest with a small issue of stock in 1993, rather than dive in with a larger issue and have it not be well received. The proceeds from the IPO were used to pay down the nearly $1 billion in debt still outstanding from the 1986 LBO. Even though sales growth had been respectable, annual debt service payments approaching $150 million were eroding profits. In 2004, CVS Pharmacy acquired Eckerd.

THE PROBLEM OF CAPITAL ADEQUACY

The bankruptcy of Revco spawned a flurry of litigation centered on the question of whether, as a result of the LBO, the firm was (1) left insolvent, or (2) left with "unreasonably small capital." If so, penalties for fraudulent conveyance could be invoked.

The test of insolvency considers whether the sum of liabilities at the date of the LBO was greater than the value of the firm's assets. The bankruptcy examiner retained Alex. Brown & Sons to perform a solvency analysis comparing the par value of liabilities to the market value of assets—where market value was determined under three different approaches, comparable market multiples, comparable merger multiples, and discounted cash flow. Notwithstanding the numerous difficulties of applying these approaches, the examiner concluded, "it appears that under most tests Revco would have been solvent, although not in all cases."[12] The difficulties included scientifically estimating a discount rate, and accounting for the uncertainty about forecast assumptions.

The alternative explanation is that the structure of Revco's deal was too aggressive, that it left the firm with too little financial slack with which to withstand the ordinary risks of business. "Financial slack" is conventionally thought of as excess cash and unused debt capacity, the cushion for adversities. Of course, there are two measures for slack, both of which are linked. One looks at the amount of equity relative to debt, and asks how large an erosion of enterprise value could be sustained before the value of debt exceeded the value of the enterprise. The other view would be to compare the projection of cash flows to the annual debt service obligations of the firm. One view looks at stocks of value; the other looks at flows. These two perspectives are linked if the market value of the enterprise and its securities is simply the present value of expected future cash flows.

In choosing how to finance the firm, managers choose the mix of equity and debt. Ordinarily, the higher the proportion of debt in the capital structure, the greater is the expected return, and the risk of default. The higher return derives from exploitation of debt tax shields, a phenomenon understood since the early work of Nobel prize winners, Franco Modigliani and Merton H. Miller. The higher risk derives from the lower margin for error that high debt service obligations create: As leverage rises, it takes relatively smaller surprises to bring the firm to ruin. The Examiner's report cites evidence testing these hypotheses.

From analysis by Alex. Brown using a base case scenario assuming 12 percent revenue growth and 7.7 percent EBITDA margins, the Examiner concluded that Revco "appears to have adequate capital."[13] But testing another scenario, which relied on assumptions drawn from a Marine Midland Bank projection,[14] the Examiner found that Revco would be unable to meet its cash requirements starting in 1989. Further scenario analysis by Alex. Brown projected financial difficulty in 1988, 1989, and 1990. The

Examiner offers other evidence to suggest that the deal was economically unattractive.

- There was no stampede of lenders trying to get into the deal: Of 33 banks invited to participate in the syndicate, only 11 actually did; the initial round of commitments was insufficient to finance the deal. Increases in fees to the banks were necessary to induce them to increase their lending commitments.
- The appraised values of Revco were less than the purchase amount.
- Although other bidders were rumored to be preparing offers, in fact none appeared to top Dworkin's bid.
- The rating agencies, Moody's and S&P, plainly declared Revco's LBO to have a "negative outlook" more than a month before the deal was consummated.
- Internal bank memoranda acknowledged that the firm would survive only with aggressive asset sales.
- The performance of the firm had been declining for years and was so significant in the fall of 1986 as to necessitate a rebudgeting of fiscal year 1987.

The Examiner concluded, "A strong case can be made that Revco was left with unreasonably small capital as a result of the Revco LBO."[15]

The quantitative tests of insolvency and inadequate capital are driven by point estimates of forecast assumptions. Yet given the crucial role of uncertainty about the future in this case, it is the *probability of failure* rather than a point estimate in a scenario that should be the governing economic test. Kenneth Eades and I[16] used Monte Carlo simulation to test the ability of Revco to cover its annual cash obligations, and in particular, to yield an estimate of the *probability* of failure to cover. At issue is the sensitivity of the coverage of cash interest and preferred dividend payments to variations in operating assumptions: those used by Revco and Salomon, versus assumptions consistent with the performance of comparable companies and Revco's own historical performance.

The simulation model forecast two ratios, EBIT coverage and Cash Flow coverage from May 31, 1986 to May 31, 1989. One could look at a longer forecast period, but the first three years feature the maximum risk exposure for Revco and thus warrant the most scrutiny. We considered two different debt service coverage ratios for these years. The first ratio was Earnings Before Interest and Taxes (EBIT) divided by projected interest and principal payments on long-term debt and cash dividends on convertible preferred stock. We call this the "EBIT Coverage Ratio." The second ratio was EBIT plus proceeds from asset sales divided by interest, principal, and cash dividends. We call this second ratio the "Cash Flow Coverage Ratio."

The Examiner's report reveals strongly contrasting views about Revco's future performance among insiders and outsiders. Salomon and Revco advocated operating assumptions that others deemed aggressive in light of the performance of comparable companies and of Revco's own operating history. The Examiner noted that the lowest sales growth rate contemplated by Salomon was 8 percent, while the lowest EBIT margin used was 6.5 percent.[17] However, the investor group provided its banks with forecasts assuming 12 percent sales growth—Wells Fargo ran a "worst case" scenario assuming 8 percent sales growth.[18] Goldman Sachs, the advisor to Revco's outside directors, determined that a 12 percent growth rate assumption was "too aggressive" (a more reasonable assumption was 8 percent), and the assumption of a 7.7 percent gross margin was "a bit aggressive."[19] Ironically, Goldman ultimately opined that the investor group's projections were "realistically attainable."[20]

To some extent, Revco's sales growth rate depended on the rate at which it planned to open new stores: The company planned to open 100 new stores per year for the next five years, to discourage new entry by competitors into Revco's own market areas.[21] The wisdom of the aggressive expansion strategy, however, is questionable in light of the resulting drag on operating performance: the Examiner noted that 70 percent of Revco's stores that had been open less than one year lost money; the figure dropped to 48 percent for stores open between one and two years.[22] In short, a case could easily be made for using much more conservative forecast assumptions than were used by principals in evaluating the Revco LBO. We modeled the impact of both sets of assumptions.[23]

The analysis suggests that Revco had a probability of between 5 percent and 30 percent of successfully servicing its financial obligations in the first three years after going private. These survival possibilities are so low as to suggest that Revco was undercapitalized in the sense that the new debt obligations exceeded its expected cash flow and the buyout was doomed to fail from the start. It is only when Revco's earning power is assumed at almost double that of its recent past that the survival probability (assuming independence of cash flows) approaches 50 percent. The survival probabilities are relatively insensitive to assumptions concerning asset sales and growth of sales, suggesting that it was the *structure of the deal*, rather than flawed execution of the strategy by management that drove Revco down. The results for optimistic and pessimistic forecast assumptions are summarized in Table 6.1 and Figure 6.1. Figure 6.1 gives a representation of the probability distribution of Revco's cash flow coverage ratio for the entire three-year period, 1987–1989. The graph reveals that only about 30 percent of the outcomes are higher than a coverage ratio of 1.0. The average coverage ratio is about 0.91, well below the minimum coverage of 1.0.

In comparison we applied the same assumptions (though different base year sales and debt service figures) to the Jack Eckerd Corporation, one of Revco's competitors in discount drugstore retailing and itself the subject of a leveraged buyout in 1986. Eckerd's base year financial figures differed from Revco's. Perhaps most importantly, its annual interest and principal payments had a substantially deferred payment schedule as compared to Revco. The

TABLE 6.1   SENSITIVITY ANALYSIS OF MONTE CARLO SIMULATION RESULTS

	Probability of Survival under Independent Annual Cash Flow Coverage Ratios	Probability of Survival under Cumulative Three-Year Cash Flow Coverage Ratios
Base Case	0.05	0.30
Margin = 6.6%		
Growth = 5.0%		
Stores = 100/year		
Variations on Margin		
Revco's 1984–1985 margin = 4.17%	0.00	0.00
Salomon's assumption = 8.0%	0.48	0.94
Variations on Growth		
1.0% under base case = 4.0%	0.02	0.20
1.0% over base case = 6.0%	0.06	0.40
Variations on Store Openings/Year		
50 under base case = 50	0.02	0.23
50 over base case = 150	0.10	0.40

Source: Bruner and Eades, 1992. Reprinted from Financial Management (Spring, 1992) with permission from the Financial Management Association International, College of Business Administration #3331, University of South Florida, Tampa, FL 33620 (813) 974-2084.

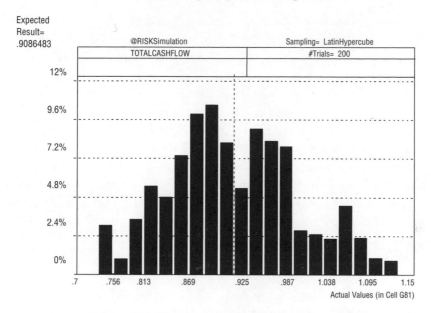

Figure 6.1 **Probability Distribution of Revco's Cash Flow Coverage Ratio for the Three Years 1987–1989 Cumulatively**

Source: Bruner and Eades, 1992. Reprinted from Financial Management (Spring, 1992) with permission from the Financial Management Association International, College of Business Administration #3331, University of South Florida, Tampa, FL 33620 (813) 974-2084.

simulations for Eckerd reveal annual coverage ratios well in excess of 1.0 for the first three years and a cumulative probability of survival of 95 percent. We concluded from this comparison that the low coverage ratios for Revco revealed in the simulation analyses were a feature of Revco's projected schedule of debt service rather than a result of the functioning of the model or reasonableness of the growth and margin assumptions. Moreover, it seems clear that the Revco LBO had a very high likelihood of failing within the near term and that our probabilistic analysis is qualitatively consistent with the opinions of the rating agencies at the time.

CONCLUSION: WHAT WENT WRONG

Revco collapsed merely 19 months after going private, a lifespan astonishing for its brevity. Jack Eckerd Corporation survived and prospered. Common to both stories was a turbulent product market in drug retailing (specifically, the rise of the discount chains), the threat of hostile raiders, and the stock market crash of 1987 that produced a depressed holiday selling season that year. Clearly, *business was not as usual*. The retail chain of more than 1,400 stores was *complex* to supply and manage. Relatively high acquisition premiums left little room for error at Revco. Its financial performance was *tightly coupled* to its operating performance. Eckerd, on the other hand, had a little more slack with which to absorb shocks. The *operating team* was hampered by divided staff loyalties, infighting, executive turnover, and an inexperienced financial sponsor. It was working in crisis mode from the date of going private. Finally, overoptimism as a *cognitive bias* is strongly apparent in the aggressive financing terms designed into the deal. Fundamentally, however, the Revco case illustrates the forceful effect of bad management choices during and after the transaction. This is apparent in three areas.

1. *Aggressive strategic change*. A typical LBO candidate would have most of the following features:

   • Strong cash flow.
   • Low level of capital expenditures.
   • Strong market position.
   • Stable industry.
   • Low rate of technological change (and low R&D expense).
   • Proven management with no anticipated changes.
   • No major change in strategy.

   Revco departed from this profile in a number of ways.

   Management intended to sustain the firm's aggressive rate of new-store openings, about 100 per year. This strategy would demand approximately $10 million per year in capital expenditures, assuming costs of $100,000 each. At the rate of 100 stores per year, however, Revco might be on the verge of exhausting the desirable opportunities for new stores in small towns. Expansion into larger cities might bring higher setup and operating costs. Aside from the possible financial and marketing instability induced by this growth strategy, it also promised to divert the attention of senior management, and to strain the capabilities of middle- and junior-level managers. It made little sense simultaneously to impose on the firm huge financial risks, and market expansion demands. The change in merchandising strategy contradicts the profile of stability. Rearranging store layouts and introducing a range of bigger-ticket consumer goods risks confusing and driving away the customer, and increasing Revco's inventory risk.

2. *Aggressive transaction structure.* The comparison of Revco and Eckerd revealed dramatically different probabilities of financial survival, as summarized in Table 6.2. In comparison to Eckerd, Revco's deal displayed a materially higher acquisition premium, much smaller percentage of equity capital, lower cash flow coverage of interest— so low, in fact, that it would need to be supplemented by an aggressive program of asset sales, and a net *withdrawal* of cash by managers and key institutional investors in equity. Revco's operating cash flow was simply insufficient to satisfy the demands for principal repayment in 1987–1988. For instance, timely service of the term loan assumed that Revco could sell its nonretail assets (about $230

TABLE 6.2   COMPARATIVE SUMMARY: LBO OF REVCO DRUG STORES VERSUS LBO OF JACK ECKERD CORPORATION

	Revco	*Jack Eckerd*
Date	December 29, 1986	April 30, 1986
Acquisition premium	48%	13%
Total LBO financing	$1.448 billion	$1.341 billion
Common equity/total financing	2.41%	8.75%
Cash flow/cash interest	87%	173%
Complexity: number of layers in financial structure of Newco	9	7
Required asset sales in first year	$255 million	$72 million (maximum)
Total net cash flow received (paid) by stockholder groups in Newco	$21.4 million ($78 million in fees)	–$116.8 million ($25 million in fees)
Principal payments, first three years	$305 million	$300 million
Probability of survival, over three years after LBO	5%–30%	95%

million) by the end of fiscal year 1988. Thereafter, the operating cash flow was expected to be sufficient to service the debt. In short, the first 18 months after the buyout were to be a dangerous, "bet-the-ranch" time for the firm.

Arguably, Sidney Dworkin and his financial advisers were credit abusers. To compensate in part for a high purchase price, they exploited the credit bonanza prevailing in 1986 for LBO investments.

- They borrowed quite a lot relative to their equity base (only 2.4 percent of the total purchase price was financed by common equity).
- They borrowed too much relative to Revco's expected operating cash flow (the probability of survival in the first three years based on reasonable historical performance was quite low).
- They structured their borrowings in ways that would make it difficult to negotiate breathing room if Revco should encounter difficulty (nine layers of debt financing, all sold to different lenders or investors).
- They predicated the payment of principal in early years on asset sales rather than on operating cash flow, thus betting the survival of the firm on the buoyancy of the M&A market.

The case of Revco Drug Stores offers an important lesson for sound practice in M&A. Deal designers must preserve some financial slack in the structuring of their transactions. Bad things can happen to good companies. It is through the maintenance of slack that buyers can withstand the vicissitudes of business life. Intuitively, one knows that slack can be valuable. Slack is like an insurance policy, to be drawn upon in times of adversity.

3. *Failure of governance.* The appeal of the leveraged buyout has been that it proves the wisdom of governance that is up close and personal. Michael Jensen and others[24] have properly argued that the LBO invokes closer scrutiny (from banks, managers, and the LBO sponsor), aligns managerial incentive payments much more closely to the success or failure of the firm, binds managers to deliver cash to investors, rationalizes internal organization, and reduces costs—all this produces material improvements in the efficiency of firms taken private. Revco's proxy statement cited these and other virtues

as motives for the LBO. It offered several reasons why the buying group regarded the purchase of Revco as "an attractive investment opportunity":

- Favorable business prospects.
- Being private would permit Revco to have a higher debt-to-equity ratio and thus realize higher return on equity and higher growth in net worth
- The value of Revco depended on long-term expansion of the business, rather than on quarterly results to which the public investors give undue attention.

Indeed, the examiner's report suggests that some progress was made toward these ends.

The case of Revco Drug Stores illuminates what can happen when the systems of governance and control fail to function. Karen Wruck (1991, 90) wrote:

Stating that too much leverage was the *fundamental* cause of Revco's problems does not offer much insight into what went wrong. Management disarray, a weak and inexperienced LBO sponsor, a fee structure almost guaranteed to produce overpayment, and a disastrous midstream shift in strategy all conspired with the use of debt financing to put Revco into Chapter 11.

She reminds us of the fatal effects of managerial choices that elevate risk and failures of the operational team—these are two of the six factors highlighted in Chapter 4.

NOTES

1. Phillips (1988), 46.
2. This chapter draws on collaborative research with my colleague, Ken Eades, who deserves special recognition as a co-developer of the perspective offered here. In addition, the study refers throughout to the historical data given in the bankruptcy examiner's report on Revco (Zaretsky (1990)). This chapter derives from court records, public news reports, and data analysis developed with the

help of Ty Eggemeyer, Greg Graves, and David Eichler, all research assistants. Thanks also go to the Financial Management Association International, publisher of *Financial Management*, for permission to republish tables and findings from the Bruner–Eades (1992) article.

3. CEO Dworkin had been concerned about possible takeover threats (Zaretsky (1990), 30) since April 1984 when the firm's stock price was battered by the sudden announcement by the Food and Drug Administration of a possible link between E-Ferol, a vitamin product, and infant deaths. In the week of the FDA announcement, Revco's market value of equity fell by $160 million, more than twice the $75 million liability, which analysts estimated (see Kully (1984)). Dworkin, who owned 2.3 percent of the firm's common shares, had hoped to pass the reins of senior management to his two sons, both of whom were senior vice presidents of Revco. Within six days of the FDA announcement, Revco announced an agreement to acquire Odd Lot Trading, Inc., a retailer of close-out goods, in an exchange of shares—the transaction would put 12 percent of Revco's new total shares in the hands of two of Dworkin's closest friends, Isaac Perlmutter and Bernard Marden, who were the owners of Revco, and who would become officers of Revco.

The peace of mind acquired with Odd Lot was short-lived: In less than three months from joining the firm, Perlmutter and Marden found evidence of purchasing irregularities in the firm, centering on Elliott Dworkin, Sidney's son. A week later, Perlmutter and Marden announced that they might make a hostile tender offer for the firm, that they wanted 6 of 12 seats on the board of directors, and that they had retained Drexel Burnham Lambert to advise them. Shortly thereafter, the board largely exonerated the purchasing department; Perlmutter and Marden were fired in February 1985; Revco repurchased their shares in July 1985.

4. For the five years up to 1984, Revco's sales had grown at a compounded annual rate of 19 percent; earnings per share had grown at about 18 percent. Its stock price had risen 60 percent, as compared to a 49 percent increase in the S&P 500 index. Revco's stock price never recovered from the E-Ferol controversy, the purchase of Odd Lot Inc., and from the ensuing management infighting. Nor was the stock price helped along by a decline in the firm's financial performance in 1985 and 1986—though revenues grew at a comparatively slow rate, operating profits declined, blamed in large part on losses at the new Odd Lot subsidiary.

5. Performance deteriorated in 1985 because of unsuccessful price discounting programs, significant store relocating and remodeling expenses, turmoil in the purchasing department arising from the departure of the dissident directors, legal fees associated with the dissidents, and losses associated with an unsuccessful division.

6. Zaretsky (1990), 36.

7. The two analysts' reports were mentioned in Winter (1986).

8. See Kully (1986).

9. Zaretsky (1990), 199.

10. Zaretsky (1990), 133.

11. Zaretsky (1990), 137.

12. Zaretsky (1990), 177.

13. Zaretsky (1990), 177.

14. Marine's "Reasonable Case" assumptions were sales growth varying from 7 percent to 6.5 percent over five years, and EBDIT margin ranging from 5 percent to 7.5 percent. See Zaretsky (1990), 178.

15. Zaretsky (1990), 196.

16. Bruner and Eades (1992).

17. Zaretsky (1990), 34.

18. Zaretsky (1990), 42.

19. Zaretsky (1990), 52–53.

20. Zaretsky (1990), 54.

21. Revco D. S. Proxy Statement, November 14, 1986, 11.

22. Zaretsky (1990), 42.

23. Detailed assumptions for the simulation analysis may be reviewed in Bruner and Eades (1992).

24. See, for instance, Baker and Wruck (1989); Bull (1989); DeAngelo, DeAngelo, and Rice (1984); Jensen (1989); Kaplan (1989a and 1989b); and Schleifer and Vishny (1988).

7

September 1989:
The Acquisition of Columbia
Pictures by Sony Corporation

BEAMING ONTO THE BIG SCREEN

In September 1989, Norio Ohga, CEO of Sony Corporation, announced the agreement to buy Columbia Pictures Entertainment Inc.[1] The purchase price, $3.4 billion for Columbia's stock and another $1.4 billion in debt to be assumed by Sony, was soon augmented by the settlement of a $1 billion breach-of-contract lawsuit by Warner Brothers, and a spree of internal spending to rebuild sickly Columbia. All told, Sony would invest about $6 billion in Columbia.

The public reactions were sharp: "They clearly overpaid," noted the chief at one studio,[2] "stunned disbelief,"[3] "no relationship to the worth of the entity,"[4] "an epic of excess, a drama involving big egos and bigger sums of money . . . not just a public relations disaster for Sony, but a financial debacle as well."[5]

Over the ensuing five years the unit gave a meager return and failed to lift its share of market materially. Sony wrote off $2.7 billion in November 1994. The writeoff was one of the largest in Japanese corporate history. A housecleaning of senior management ensued: Gone were the CEOs of Columbia, Sony Corporation of America, and Sony Corporation. Akio Morita, co-founder and CEO of Sony and in ill health, resigned within 14 days of the writeoff. Sony denied that his departure was related to the debacle in Hollywood, though he had been the unmistakable champion of Sony's entry into film production. In 1995, the new CEO of Sony, Nobuyuki Idei, summed the episode in a classic expression of Japanese understatement, "It is difficult to say that our management of the studio operations has been a total success over these past five years."[6]

MOTIVES FOR THE ACQUISITION

The buyer and major seller came to the bargaining table in 1989 chastened and looking for change. Coca-Cola had acquired Columbia Pictures in 1982, as an investment of cash gushing from its consumer beverages business and in the belief of some synergy between film production and the promotion of Coke's brands. Neither the profits, nor the synergies, materialized. Coke made the acquisition at a 75 percent premium over market value. This move surprised many analysts. Columbia's film production record was dogged by a series of changes in management, a strike by the Writers Guild of America, a number of stunning film flops, and the embarrassment of a check-forgery scandal by the studio's president, David Begelman, in the late 1970s. There were no obvious economic links between the leading producer of soft drinks, and the venerable but struggling film studio. Therefore, there would be little basis for creating economic value through synergies. After a few years of mediocre financial results from the studio, Coca-Cola partially spun off Columbia in September 1987, retaining a 49 percent interest in the firm. Therefore, Coca-Cola would be the gatekeeper to any acquisition of the studio. Then, after the stock market crash in 1987 and a particularly weak performance in the following fiscal year, Coke was ready to sell the rest.

Sony Corporation built its business on novel consumer electronics founded on miniaturization. The transistor radio, Trinitron TV, Handycam, Walkman, and other products created new markets. But competitors quickly imitated Sony's advances, which meant that Sony's growth had to come from continuing new product development rather than building out existing products. Sony had been stung by the failure of its Betamax video recording system to dominate the inferior VHS technology after its introduction in 1974. Akio Morita came to believe that proprietary programming (music, films, and software) would give Sony the edge in the intensely competitive consumer electronics industry. He said, "If I owned a movie studio, Betamax would not have come out second best."[7] In 1988, Morita pointed to Phillips N.V., Sony's Dutch competitor, and said, "Phillips benefited from software—it owned Polygram Records, and that helped its compact discs."[8] Thus, Sony's strategy assumed that technological innovation would stimulate a convergence between consumer electronics ("hardware") and entertainment property, such as recorded music and films ("software").

Gaining traction on this strategy, however, would prove to be a huge challenge. In large part, convergence simply remained an interesting abstraction. The merger proxy statement vaguely acknowledged it:

> For the last few years, Sony and its subsidiaries have studied methods of implementing a strategic policy of developing their interests in the entertainment industry, in part to diversify Sony's operations and in part as a means of developing "software" to be used with its entertainment "hardware"—tape players, televisions, video cassette recorders and related equipment. Sony's 1986 acquisition of CBS Records from CBS Inc. was the first result of that policy.[9]

Michael Schulhof, vice chairman of Sony Corporation of America, said that the acquisition "extends Sony's long-term strategy of building a total entertainment business around the synergy of audio and video hardware and software,"[10] though he did not elaborate on the size or nature of the synergy. Norio Ohga noted that Columbia's film and TV libraries (which contained titles such as *Gandhi, Ghostbusters, Wheel of Fortune, Who's the Boss?* and *Married with Children*) could provide cross-marketing avenues for Sony products such as its new 8-millimeter Video Walkman, VCRs, high-definition TV, and other video hardware.

One investment banker declared that "Sony has a clear strategic intention," to which entertainment analyst Harold Vogel responded that Coke did, too, and had exited profitably only because of the rising asset value for film studios rather than because of synergies or special skills in deal-making.[11] Benjamin Stein, lawyer and actor, scoffed at the strategy: "It's like saying that people who own a restaurant must also own a huge ranch. Studios are not that profitable. So why take the gamble?"[12] Critics noted that if such synergies existed, there were cheaper routes to harvesting them (such as joint ventures) as opposed to acquisition, that Columbia's small share of market would prompt relatively few sales of consumer electronics, and that Sony's purchase of CBS Records had not been exploited very aggressively toward hardware sales beyond CD players.

It would not be until 1993 that Sony could offer a tangible example of the synergy of hardware and software, in the form of Columbia's release of *Last Action Hero*, starring Arnold Schwartzenegger. The strategic synergy was to link the Sony-made film to a soundtrack made by Sony Music. The theatres exhibiting the film would use an enhanced digital sound system made by Sony. Sony planned to sell digital games based on the film. Finally, Sony planned joint marketing of TVs, VCRs, and the film. The film bombed at the box office, losing $124 million, and the write-off of which depressed Sony's earnings for 1993. One securities analyst concluded, "Synergy: big wind, loud thunder, no rain. It's great to talk about conceptually . . . but at the end of the day it's minimal."[13]

In 1987, Sony acquired CBS Records for $2 billion. Leaving the existing management team in place, Sony used stars Michael Jackson, Bruce Springsteen, and Barbra Streisand to boost sales of its CD players. The stock market seemed to bless the strategy, boosting Sony's shares at a 33 percent compound average growth rate since the acquisition (see Figure 7.1).

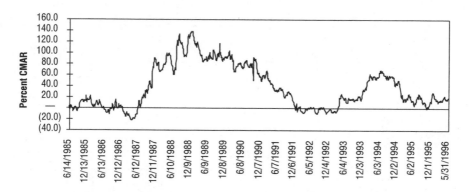

Figure 7.1 **Cumulative Market-Adjusted Return to Sony Corporation Shareholders**

Source of data: Datastream.

Meanwhile, the dollar had fallen 50 percent against the yen from 1984 to 1989 (see Figure 7.2), making Japanese investment in the United States relatively cheaper and unleashing a wave of cross-border investment to the United States that would raise fears of a Japanese economic takeover. Japanese were buying flagship real estate properties such as Rockefeller Center. This was, no doubt, an opportune moment for Sony to move.

The executive in charge of the Sony music unit, Walter Yetnikoff, lobbied actively for an acquisition of a film studio. Griffin and Masters describe Yetnikoff, who struggled with substance abuse throughout his time at Sony, as intensely driven by money and power. Yetnikoff said, "I wanted to be Steve Ross [CEO of Warner Brothers]. I wanted to have dominion over an empire."[14]

Finally, doubts about the synergies and champions of the deal were filtered by Sony's self-confident optimism. This began at the top. When con-

Figure 7.2   **Yen/Dollar Foreign Exchange Rate**

Source of data: Datastream.

fronted by financial concerns about the deal, Akio Morita said, "Don't worry about it. We can always recover money. The opportunities like this come once in a lifetime."[15] Later, the *Economist* opined that the investment in Columbia was one of the "biggest, grandest examples of Japanese corporate hubris in the late 1980s, as that country's relentless economic growth combined with its stock-and-property market bubbles to make anything seem possible, any price seem affordable."[16]

STRIKING THE DEAL

Sony retained Michael Ovitz, the president of Creative Artists, the dominant agency representing actors, to open doors for the Japanese firm. Sony approached Coca-Cola in November 1988 with a proposal to purchase its interest in Columbia. Ovitz' approach to Coca-Cola had followed earlier discussions about a possible joint venture with Columbia, and acquisition discussions with Paramount, Fox, MCA/Universal, and MGM/United Artists studios. In February 1989, rumors circulated that Coca-Cola had been approached by several parties, including Sony, Matsushita, and L'Oreal. Possibly Coca-Cola had fanned these rumors in the interest of stoking bidding fever for its stake.

Coca-Cola, represented by Herbert Allen of Allen & Co., opened with an asking price of $35.00 per share. Sony countered with an offer in the low $20s. Discussions moved forward very slowly. The price offered a 148 percent premium over the average price prevailing in November 1988 and a 59 percent premium over Columbia's highest share price in 1989. This represented the largest takeover by a Japanese firm in the United States to date.

In July 1989, Sony's board approved the acquisition of Columbia if an American manager could be found to run it (Columbia's CEO had declined to stay on under Sony's ownership). The public accounts of Sony's governance process give no indication that Sony's board hesitated over the price.

The search for a studio executive triggered a second round of dealmaking. Not experienced in studio management, Sony said that it would keep most of Columbia's existing management, though Columbia's senior management announced that they would depart. Griffin and Masters (1996) wrote:

> Finding someone with the brains, guts, and instincts to run a studio has al-ways been difficult. The job calls for an individual who can make constant decisions involving hundreds of millions of dollars. Business sense isn't enough; a studio chief needs to have some intuition about what will en-tertain the fickle public and some rapport with temperamental actors and directors. Indecision is intolerable: The distribution system is a gaping maw that needs to be filled with one picture after another. Aside from movies, there are television operations, home video, and theaters. Over-head roars along at more than $100 million a year. Failures are public.[17]

Walter Yetnikoff first recommended that Michael Ovitz be appointed CEO. But when negotiations with Ovitz deadlocked, Yetnikoff then rec-ommended Jon Peters and Peter Guber to serve as co-CEOs.

Peters and Guber had produced two blockbuster hits in recent years, *Batman* (1989) in which they were actively involved, and *Rain Man* (1988) in which they played an insignificant role. Guber was a lawyer by training; Peters had been a hairdresser before getting into films. Still, with their blockbusters and a raft of lesser titles to their names, Guber and Pe-ters would nudge their way onto the A-list of producers. They were on a roll of success.

> Longtime Hollywood associates described Mr. Guber as the intellec-tual powerhouse of the two, a man with a flair for deal-making and marketing. . . . Mr. Peters, on the other hand, has fewer fans in Holly-wood, and his detractors like to characterize him as something of a hot-tempered bully. He gets better reviews as a creative whiz, an en-thusiast, an idea man. . . . Thrice married but now single, Mr. Peters got plenty of ink last summer for an on-set romance with actress Kim Basinger during the making of "Batman." Mr. Guber, by contrast, has been married to one woman for more than 20 years. But for all their intellectual and stylistic differences, they make the perfect "good cop, bad cop" team, Hollywood associates say.[18]

Director Brian De Palma said, "They're the best production talent around."[19] Certainly, the profiles of the two were colorful. "Hollywood's two most successful self-promoters . . . talentless fast-talkers [who] bootstrapped themselves with the help of Mike Milken's money machine, to the very pinnacle of Hollywood power."[20] Angry at their defection to Sony, Steve Ross of Warner Brothers said, "If Morita knew what he was getting himself into, he wouldn't have touched those guys with a 10-foot pole."[21] "Guber and Peters are where they are because they are shameless self-promoters, profligate loose cannons and generally larger-than-life. They are showmen . . . and they speak fluent hyperbole, which translates nicely into modern Japanese."[22] Despite this, Michael Schulhof of Sony declared, "I was immediately attracted [to Guber]. I found him very sympathetic. . . . the chemistry was wonderful. I didn't hear anything that made me feel uncomfortable at all."[23]

The two had recently founded a production company, Guber-Peters Entertainment Company (GPEC), and had signed a five-year exclusive production agreement with Warner Brothers. Sony agreed to buy GPEC for $200 million, by some estimates, 40 percent above market value[24]— which a GPEC board member called "a dramatic overpayment; one of the greatest deals of all time."[25] Their 28 percent share of GPEC would net Guber and Peters $56 million. In addition, Sony agreed to pay each co-CEO an annual salary of $2.7 million (rising with cost of living adjustments for the Los Angeles area), various perquisites, an 8 percent share of any increase in the firm's value over the 5 years, up to 10 percent of Columbia's future cash flow, and a $50 million bonus pool at the end of 5 years. This was one of the largest compensation packages ever seen in Hollywood.

Industry observers were incredulous upon hearing the deal and its terms: "handsomely rewarded . . . most generously compensated moguls."[26] "Most entertainment executives agreed that Sony paid far too much . . . [and] blamed Pete Peterson and the Blackstone Group for endorsing a price that, as one executive close to the negotiation put it, 'had no relationship to the worth of the entity,'" wrote Griffin and Masters.[27] The *Wall Street Journal* reported, "Sony . . . has apparently decided to accept Columbia's projections that it will substantially improve its results and its cash flow in 1990 . . . Blackstone led Sony to be overoptimistic about the studio's earning power . . . [a knowledgeable Sony insider said] 'they simply didn't understand the business.'"[28] In Japan, the head of the Keidanren, the powerful alliance of businesses, told Akio Morita, "Morita-san, you're making a big mistake. Making movies is different; it's a special kind of business. You don't understand Hollywood. It won't work. You're asking for trouble. You're getting into a business that you won't be able to control. Don't do it."[29]

THE GUBER–PETERS YEARS

The beginning was inauspicious. Shortly following the merger announcement on September 25, 1989, Warner Brothers sued Sony for promoting a breach of contract. Guber and Peters were under a five-year production contract to Warner at the time. The size of the suit ($1 billion) and high publicity amplified the pressure on the Sony executives.

Unfortunately, they had no time for deliberation. Indeed, the events of late 1989 suggest pressure and haste. The basic agreement with Coke was clinched in July, with Sony's board approval *subject to* finding a new CEO.[30] Schulhof and Yetnikoff raced to find a candidate for fear that news would leak and an interloper (such as L'Oreal or Matsushita) would appear before they had wrapped up the deal. Michael Ovitz had warned Walter Yetnikoff about the Warner contract, but the warning apparently never affected the deal design. Perhaps Schulhof took a calculated risk that, presented with a fait accompli, Warner would go away. Agreement on the purchase of GPEC occurred on the same day as Sony and Columbia agreed on a final price. Then, with a cash tender offer ticking (it began on October 2 and would expire on November 1) Sony *needed* to reach agreement rapidly to dispel any uncertainty about the deal and leadership of the studio.

Sony and Warner announced a settlement of the lawsuit in the nick of time: A deal was announced on October 31, just before the tender offer ended. Obtaining release from the Warner contract entailed a swap of studio properties that cost Sony an estimated $300–525 million.[31]

In addition, some Columbia investors sued Sony, charging fraudulent disclosure that artificially depressed stock prices before the $27 buyout offer. Such claims are not uncommon in American M&A and amount to a game to extort higher payments from the buyer. To the self-effacing Japanese, the litigation can have only compounded the nightmare. The deal also triggered a barrage of xenophobic press from politicians and the media. Accounting for the litigation settlements, the final tab for buying Columbia is summarized in Table 7.1. This included one other item, rebuilding the studio.

TABLE 7.1   Investment Base in Sony Pictures Entertainment
(in $ millions)

	Low Est.	High Est.
Purchase of equity of Columbia Pictures Entertainment	$3,400	$3,400
Assumption of CPE's debt	1,400	1,400
Settlement with Warner Brothers★	300	525
Buyout of RCA joint venture★	350	350
Studio Refurbishment★	50	250
Acquisition of GPEC	200	200
High-Priced personnel★	300	300
Total	$6,000	$6,425

Sources: This is a compilation of amounts published in filings with the SEC and press accounts. Starred items (★) are estimated or drawn from various sources. Estimates of the RCA joint venture and high-priced personnel are based on "Out in Hollywood: Revisiting Sony's Show Biz Acquisitions," *M&A Europe* September/October 1991, 6. Studio refurbishment range is drawn from *M&A Europe* and Laura Landro, *Wall Street Journal*, August 20, 1990. The settlement with Warner is based on Griffin and Masters (1996), 240, 249.

Nominally, Columbia Pictures Entertainment was a major force in the film industry. It had a 2,700-title film library, a 23,000 TV episode library, and through its Loew's theater chain, owned more than 800 screens. What Guber, Peters, and Sony discovered upon taking over was not heartening. Evidently, there were about 40 projects in preproduction planning, and none in actual production. "We opened the door in the vault, and it was virtually empty," said a new senior executive of Columbia.[32] There were not many pictures in the pipeline because Columbia executives did not want to take on additional risk as the company was preparing itself to be sold.

Columbia was in poor condition in 1989. Its share of market had been dropping steadily for five years from 19 percent in 1985 to 9.9 percent in 1988. Its financial performance was worse. In the three reporting years since its partial spin-off from Coca-Cola, sales and net income had fallen steadily (see Figure 7.3). Returns on equity were low or negative, never larger than the firm's cost of equity.

The challenge posed by the disarray of Columbia was compounded by adverse industry trends. In essence, production costs were rising much faster than the rate of inflation, spurred in part by aggressive bidding for star talent. The industry had caught blockbuster fever, the allure of the film

Financial Performance of Columbia Pictures

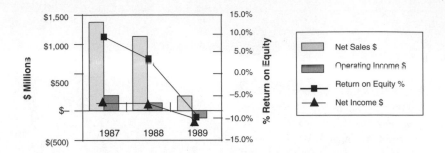

Figure 7.3   **Profitability of Columbia Pictures Entertainment**
Source of data: Columbia merger proxy statement, filed with SEC, 1989.

that would gross more than $100 million at the box office, and have a long "tail": sequels and sales of merchandise, games, music, and so on. To achieve this required more coordination, longer lead-times, star casts, and expensive advance marketing. Each blockbuster covered the losses on box office bombs. But the blockbuster amplified the consequences for failure: absent the occasional big hit, financial performance of a studio would look comparatively bad. The net effect on industry profitability was negative. Though industry revenues had doubled from 1979 to 1989, operating profit had risen only 15 percent.

In addition, the studios were caught in a dramatic consolidation wave in the media and entertainment industry. Fox had been acquired by Rupert Murdoch's News Corporation in 1986; Warner Brothers by Time Inc. in 1989; MGM/UA by Quintex Group in 1989; Columbia by Sony in 1989; MCA by Matsushita in 1990; and Paramount by Viacom in 1993. These acquisitions brought more capital to the industry but also imposed higher performance standards, as the new owners sought to earn a competitive return on their investment.

Over the year following the acquisition, rumors of Peters and Guber's extravagant use of studio money dominated Hollywood news: "the wildest and most profligate ride that Hollywood had ever seen . . . and became a symbol for the worst kind of excess in an industry that is hardly known for moderation."[33] Other adjectives used to describe the Guber–Peters years include "shameless," "obscene," and "vulgar."[34] The elements of excess included lavish decoration of the firm's headquarters, high promotion expenses, huge cost overruns on film projects, large severance payments to sacked executives, high prices paid for scripts and talent, use of the corporate jet to fly flowers to a girlfriend, and high compensation for a bloated staff.

Journalist Laura Landro wrote:

> Sony Corp. faces several years of heavy expenditures before it can expect a return. It will cost $500 million to $700 million for the Columbia and Tri-Star units to crank out 20 to 30 movies annually. And Sony will have to spend plenty more on marketing, distribution and television operations. Another $50 to $100 million will go to massive renovation and new construction at the Culver City studio over the next two to three years, while annual overhead costs have been increased to about $50 million from $35 million because of the heavy influx of new executives and staff. Sony acknowledges that it expects Columbia to have a negative cash flow of $250 million to $350 million—or about $100 million in operating losses—for each of the next two years, and possibly beyond. Annual cash flow of about $150 million from Columbia's healthy television operations and its Loews Theaters won't be nearly enough to offset the investment required, and it will take 18 months to two years to get a steady flow of new films made and released. But Sony dismisses industry speculation that it faces a bottomless pit of losses and huge unexpected writeoffs. . . . Messrs. Guber and Peters, who declined to be interviewed, have been spending at a breakneck pace, paying top dollar for writers and directors, buying scripts at record prices and generally making a big splash around town. Much of the attention, though, has been on the seeming excesses of Mr. Peters, the former hairdresser who is by far the more flamboyant of the Guber–Peters team. Hollywood has been buzzing in recent months as Mr. Peters put his ex-wife, a girlfriend, and his son's girlfriend on the Columbia payroll."[35]

"Everything they do is too much, too loud, and too expensive," said one Columbia executive.[36] Publicly, Sony officials in Tokyo dismissed criticism and took a longer-term view of the business. "For Columbia, Sony is the perfect parent. It provides the two essentials of survival in Hollywood: time and money."[37] With the lavish spending of Guber and Peters, annual overhead costs rose 50 percent. A *Forbes* article asked "Whatever happened to the Japan that can say no?"[38] An article in *Fortune* summed up the situation this way: "The two (Guber and Peters) essentially said to their Japanese masters, 'You don't understand how to make movies. We do. You need to

160 CASE STUDIES OF M&A FAILURE

give us a whole lot of money and leave us alone. Trust us.' And the Japanese did, to the tune of $8 billion."[39]

Perhaps reflecting the negative press, Jon Peters resigned as co-CEO in May 1991. He would start his own company to produce films, music, and television episodes under contract to Columbia. Peters' affiliation with Sony ended completely in March 1994.

In August 1991, Sony renamed the enterprise Sony Pictures Entertainment (SPE), though it retained the names of its two studios, Columbia Pictures and Tri-Star Pictures. Also that month, Sony announced that it was weighing the sale of a 25 percent stake in SPE for $3 billion. This was motivated by the large ongoing investments in SPE and the slowing demand for consumer electronics as the recession of 1991–1992 appeared. But Sony found no takers. The deal would have valued the studio at $12 billion, a very high price relative to its peers, but another telltale about Sony's view of its accumulated investment. Management problems, exacerbated by the resignation of the motion picture group president, plagued the studio and caused an increase in Sony's involvement in studio management. Rumors spread that Guber needed the New York office's permission on projects costing more than $40 million and Japan's permission for projects in excess of $60 million.

The number of film releases by Columbia and Tri-Star increased sharply in 1991, reflecting the aggressive expansion led by Guber and Peters. Figure 7.4 shows that, consistent with the higher rate of film production, SPE's share of market increased in 1991 as well. Despite the lavish spending, the studio was unable to produce the box office smash envisioned by Sony. The release of Arnold Schwarzenegger's *Last Action Hero* in 1993 failed badly at the box office. Other Columbia movie disappointments for the year included *Geronimo: An American Legend* and *I'll Do Anything*. Worse yet, increases in sales from the integration of entertainment and consumer electronics failed to materialize. No films were released by Columbia in the first half of 1994, suggesting to industry observers creative, rather than fiscal, problems.

Meanwhile, the parent, Sony Corporation, experienced a worldwide downturn in hardware sales, increased competition from Asia, and eroding profitability due to the relatively higher value of the yen. Sony's debt burden increased to $12 billion by 1994. Figure 7.5 shows that up to fiscal year 1995, Sony's profitability had been in decline; in 1995 it took a dramatic turn for the worse.

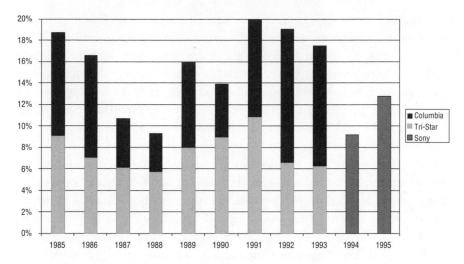

Figure 7.4 **Columbia, Tri-Star, and Sony Box Office Market Share (1985–1995)**

Source of data: Standard & Poor's *Industry Surveys.*

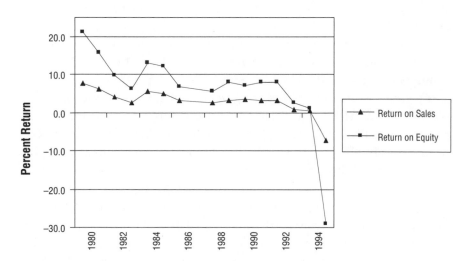

Figure 7.5 **Profitability of Sony Corporation**

In April 1994 Sony announced a reorganization, consolidating and dividing the whole company into eight separate, autonomous units. In November 1994, dozens of SPE staff members were fired, including Guber who had been unable to produce one blockbuster movie during his five-year tenure. Simultaneously, Sony announced losses of $3.2 billion, one of the largest in Japanese corporate history, and wrote down the book value of the studio by $2.7 billion to $3.1 billion. Of this $510 million reflected the discontinuation of projects in development. Fourteen days later, Akio Morita, Sony's chairman and co-founder, resigned due to health problems. In December 1995, Michael Schulhof, the head of American operations resigned. Reflecting on the previous five years, analysts[40] faulted management for the failure to control overhead expenses, the overexpansion of the film development pipeline (many projects were started; few hit the theaters), and their "big event" strategy, backing expensive films like *Last Action Hero*.

In the five years following Sony's acquisition, SPE underperformed badly as an investment. Figure 7.6 shows that in the best year, SPE's yen-denominated return on total capital was less than one-half of one percent.

Starting in 1995 Sony Pictures Entertainment began the slow process of turnaround that should have begun in 1989. Share of market recovered and the unit reported modest profitability. This resulted from some moderate successes at the box office, combination of the distribution arms of Columbia and Tri-Star, overhead reduction of $100 million, and an improvement in the development process to yield higher releases of projects started. Finally, SPE abandoned the big event film strategy in favor of less risky (and less costly) productions.[41]

Still, the change in strategy and management could not free Sony from the boom-and-bust cycle of the film industry. SPE's revenues and profits slumped badly in 1997 and 2001 and boomed in between (1998). Through 2001 the unit's return on assets employed did not exceed 5.1 percent, hardly enough compensation for the risks taken.[42] It is hard not to be skeptical about the value proposition in this industry.

Thirteen years after Sony's acquisition of Columbia, some analysts were optimistic again about the linkage of Sony's hardware and software businesses, based on the rapid spread of DVD technology to households. For instance, UBS reported:

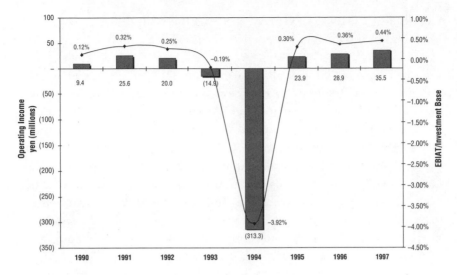

Figure 7.6 **Sony Pictures Group Performance**

Source of data: Sony Corporation Annual Reports and author's analysis.

The Sony Entertainment division represents the "glue" in the integration of hardware and software and will become an increasingly important value enhancer across Sony's portfolio with the integration of content, consumer electronics and network communications. Put simply, we believe Sony Entertainment has the potential to enhance margins in the consumer electronics divisions, while driving new in-home network applications and strengthening Sony's global brand. . . . Over time, we believe the development of network distributed digitally encoded content can enable Sony Entertainment to disintermediate direct to home audio video channels such as broadcasters, multisystem cable and satellite systems with subscription services.[43]

The crucial words here are "has the potential" and "over time." In March 2007, the directors of Sony signaled their impatience with waiting for convergence to pay and with the lack of major new consumer electronics products. They shuffled CEO Idei into retirement, and appointed Sony's first foreign-born CEO, Howard Stringer.

COUNTERPOINT: UNILEVER'S ACQUISITION OF BESTFOODS

On April 20, 2000, Unilever PLC made an unsolicited written proposal to the directors of Bestfoods Corporation, to acquire the shares in that firm for a price between $61 and $64 each.[44] Management assessed the proposal and submitted it for consideration to the Bestfoods directors at a special meeting on May 2. But on May 1, Unilever increased its offer to $66 per share, or about $18.4 billion (including Bestfoods' debt). Shares of Bestfoods soared 21 percent the day after; in London, Unilever stock fell 2 percent (see Figure 7.7). However, the Bestfoods board rejected the offer as inadequate. A key point of debate was the size of possible synergies, and the resulting impact on the offering price: Unilever estimated cost savings of $500 million annually; Bestfoods' guess was $1 billion.

The combined company would have 1999 revenues and operating income of roughly $52.3 billion and $6.2 billion, respectively. A Bestfoods

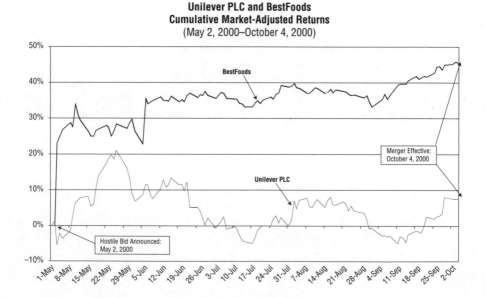

Figure 7.7 **Investor Reaction to Unilever's Bid for Bestfoods**

Source of data: Datastream.

and Unilever combination would create leading global positions in the areas of culinary products ($7.5 billion), spreads ($4.5 billion), tea ($2.4 billion), ice cream ($4.7 billion), and frozen foodS ($3 billion). It would also strengthen the companies' position in food services, with global combined sales of $2.2 billion.

The bid was also consistent with Unilever's planned overall strategy to grow its business. "This transaction will accelerate Unilever towards the achievement of our path-to-growth objectives—it will make a good plan better," said N. W. A. Fitzgerald, chairman of Unilever PLC and A. Burgmans, chairman of Unilever N. V. "The complimentary nature of our geographic coverage and our combined product portfolio, together with Bestfoods' strong food service operations, will enable us to further raise our growth ambition."[45]

In sharp contrast to the reach of the Sony/Columbia deal, Unilever sought to acquire in fields close to home. A Unilever official described the company's acquisition approach: "The target should be in or closely adjacent to our existing categories. It should have a good record of growth and growth potential into the future. We would look for new capability and access to new channels. It should be strongly branded and have the potential to support and/or accelerate our own process of focus and simplification. It must be able to manage the acquisition process and post management plan along existing priorities. It must be value creating for our shareholders."[46]

Indeed, acquiring Bestfoods would provide Unilever with leading positions in key food sectors and provide a platform for growth, at a time when many of Unilever's product categories, such as margarine and tea, were flat or declining. Bestfoods' Hellmann's mayonnaise, for example, was a logical extension of Unilever's margarine business. Knorr, with more than $2 billion in annual sales, would become Unilever's biggest food brand. With Bestfoods on board, Unilever bulked up its operations in North America and in Latin America, where it was weak, and lessened its dependence on Europe, which accounted for 59 percent of total food sales of $21.8 billion in 1999.

Unilever was also one of the world's largest buyers of oil, thanks to its dominance in margarines, while Bestfoods manufactured a range of oil-based products. Unilever's purchasing clout would bring discounts. Wall Street analysts believed that acquiring Bestfoods would give Unilever the ability to use new distribution channels to market its own products, while consolidating the costs of the two operations. Unilever officials anticipated that the combination would result in cost savings of approximately $500 million annually from the elimination of duplicate functions, combined purchasing savings, greater efficiencies in operations and business processes, synergies in distribution and marketing, streamlining of general and administrative functions, and increased economies of scale. Bestfoods told investors $1 billion of cost savings could be realized from a combination of the two companies. Analysts specifically pointed to the Bestfoods Baking Company unit, which included brands such as Entenmann's, Thomas' English Muffins, Boboli and Oroweat bread, as an unlikely fit with Unilever's portfolio. Graham Jones, an analyst with Dresdner Kleinwort Benson in London took a more middle-of-the-road view. "The truth is that the savings would be more in the $700-to-$800 million range," he said.[47] It was also expected that to achieve these cost savings, the combined company should be ready to spend around $1.25 billion for restructuring. In addition, it was expected that the merger would result in a one percent increase in revenues from cross-selling and manufacturing between Bestfoods' and Unilever's products. However, some industry observers were skeptical that the combination of Bestfoods brands such as Knorr, Hellmann's, Sloppy, and Entenmann's would meld seamlessly with Unilever's Lipton, Ragu, and Ben & Jerry's brands—let alone with Calvin Klein or Mentadent.

Some analysts saw Unilever's bid in the context of a new wave of consolidation. The last significant M&A activity in the food industry was focused on Pillsbury, Kraft, and General Mills in the 1980s. This was followed by a wave of restructurings in the 1990s. Now, two major companies were in play—Bestfoods and Nabisco Group Holdings Corporation, which had been put up for sale the past month after the threat of a partial tender offer from financier Carl Icahn. Analysts said the acquisition was a remedy for a global food industry faced with slow growth. As food company executives were under pressure to expand their markets and at the same time to cut costs, the best approach was to acquire well-known brands that could be sold through the existing distribution system—a distribution system that has narrowed as the retail grocery sector has consolidated.

Bestfoods had strong takeover defenses, such as a poison pill and a staggered board of directors so that it was not possible to mount an effective proxy fight to gain control of the board in any given year. If Bestfoods simply refused to negotiate with Unilever, it could easily remain independent, according to investment bankers not involved in the deal. Thus, Unilever's cash tender offer was contingent on Bestfoods' board rescinding their poison pill.

The sentiment among analysts was that Bestfoods would be sold—albeit for not less than $70 a share. Analysts noted that only a few companies, such as Kraft Foods and Nestle SA, could afford such a price tag, though they would not want to get into a bidding war with Unilever. While there was considerable speculation that Bestfoods would try to pull off a stock-swap merger of equals with Heinz or Campbell Soup Company, which were closer in size to Bestfoods, takeover professionals noted that such a deal would require shareholder approval, which would be nearly impossible to obtain in the face of a competing cash bid of $66 a share. "The market will assume that Bestfoods will get sold, because there is an actual cash offer with a price tag,"[48] said Andrew Lazar, an analyst at Lehman Brothers, noting that the offer was reasonably priced.

"As a long-suffering owner of consumer companies I would urge the company to take the money and run,"[49] said William Hackney, managing partner of Atlanta Capital Management (a major shareholder in Bestfoods), assuming Bestfoods "can get $70 a share, that's a fair price." Analysts who had believed that Bestfoods was one of the most attractive companies in the sector began thinking that Bestfoods might be running out of excuses to fend off potential acquirers. "To justify your independence because you've outperformed a pathetic food group is not enough,"[50] said John McMillin, an analyst with Prudential Securities Inc.

Bestfoods took evasive action by encouraging competing bids and seeking to acquire. On May 7, HJ Heinz reportedly offered $72 per share for Bestfoods. Although the price Heinz offered was higher than that offered by Unilever, Heinz's offer was a stock-for-stock deal, less attractive to some investors than Unilever's cash bid. On May 23, Bestfoods began initial conversations with Diageo PLC to acquire its Pillsbury division. Indeed, Bestfoods continued to talk to a number of other companies for potential acquisitions, figuring that since the company had stated it was not for sale, it should continue to explore takeovers, a strategy it was pursuing prior to Unilever's unsolicited bid. Bestfoods found Campbell Soup as a potential merger partner.

On June 4, Unilever increased its bid from $66 to $72 per share. At the same time, Bestfoods was in merger talks with Campbell Soup. The board of Bestfoods would decide whether to accept the offer of Unilever for $20.5 billion or to acquire Campbell Soup for at least $15 billion in cash and stock, or more than $35 per Campbell share, which was clearly undervalued. Bestfoods' biggest shareholders already started urging Bestfoods to make a deal with Unilever for about $72 a share. Montag & Caldwell, Bestfoods' largest institutional shareholder with 12.2 million shares, or 4.3 percent of the shares outstanding, publicly spoke in favor of the Unilever deal.

On June 6, Unilever increased its bid from $72 per share to $73 per share, for a total value of $25 billion. Bestfoods' board, after rebuffing Unilever for more than a month, approved the offer after seven hours of deliberations. The board gave serious consideration to a proposal to acquire Campbell Soup Company for about $36 a share, or $16 billion, in a complicated stock-and-cash deal that would have bypassed approval by Bestfoods' shareholders.

Unilever and Bestfoods foresaw cost savings of $750 million annually and also a one percent increase in revenues. After shareholders of both firms had approved the merger of the two companies, Unilever named seven Bestfoods executives to important positions within its newly created Foods Division. The company also said that Bestfoods' CEO would not have an executive role at Unilever, but instead would serve in an advisory capacity.

The merger of the two firms was consummated on October 4, 2000. The integration of Bestfoods into Unilever avoided indigestion. Six months later, Unilever sold Bestfoods Baking Company, the subsidiary that produced baked foods that were not consistent with Unilever's strategic product focus. Sales growth in the consumer foods industry slowed in 2003, causing some skeptics to question the revenue enhancements projected from the acquisition of Bestfoods. Figure 7.8 gives the cumulative market-adjusted returns for Unilever for the three years following the announcement. The figure suggests that Unilever performed reasonably well.

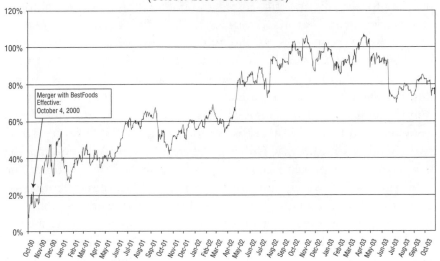

Figure 7.8   **Performance of Unilever Shares versus S&P 500 Index over Three Years after Acquiring Bestfoods**

Source of data: Datastream.

CONCLUSION: WHEN STRETCH TURNS INTO STRAIN

All six failure factors drove the demise of the Sony/Columbia deal. Film production is a *complex* business. Commitments made today echo financially over the next three years, and the uncertainty about consumer tastes and fads amplify the consequences for the decision-maker. Paying a high price leaves little room for error in stretching to achieve a reasonable return on investment. The large outlay *tightly coupled* the operating decisions and financial results. The higher the price, the less tolerance for operational glitches and overspending. Guber, Peters, and their overly-tolerant parent ignored this and suffered accordingly. A number of *management choices* in this case seem as unreasonable today as they did in

1989: the high purchase price, the decision to hire Guber and Peters, the size and structure of their compensation, and most importantly, the decision to diversify into filmed entertainment. Sony bought Columbia at a moment when *business was not usual*: Columbia was sick and needed mending; the economics of the film business were shifting toward blockbuster "bet-the-ranch" projects; technological changes faced both Sony and Columbia with expensive implications. All of these introduced a wildcard into the cash flow forecasts of Columbia. This required the outlay of larger sums and the assumption of more risk. When Sony acquired Columbia, that firm's production pipeline was dry. These two conditions meant that Guber and Peters would likely commit the firm to a stream of massive investments in a short space of time. The management *team* was dysfunctional: a parent that was distant both geographically and culturally; Guber and Peters, who were out of their depth and, responding to aggressive incentives, spent money aggressively; and generally a tolerance for aberrant behavior that would be grounds for dismissal in many organizations, including Yetnikoff's drug addiction and Peters' abusive temper and nepotism.[51] Finally, a *cognitive bias* shaped Sony's management of its film entertainment business: Overoptimism or hubris stimulated the unusual bets made by management and delayed the action-taking in response to the worsening crisis.

This case highlights the role of two kinds of culture gaps between the buyer and target organizations that merit close consideration: national and industrial. Unilever's acquisition of Bestfoods was blessed with a fairly narrow gap. Unilever has an Anglo-Dutch heritage, closer to American culture than any (perhaps except Canadian). And Unilever targeted a firm in its own industry, meaning that executives could understand and assess each other's skills and performance.

In stretching to acquire Columbia, Sony was reaching across two very large cultural divides. First, the stretch from Japan to the United States would, ethnographically, be rather far. Second, Sony stretched far across industry groups as well: The entertainment industry is, by wide acknowledgement, culturally very dissimilar from other industries. Sony's reach was ambitious.

Cross-border M&A worldwide accounts for about 20 percent of the number of deals over time, with the United States being the largest recipient of cross-border bids. Such deals are an important laboratory for studying success and failure in M&A simply because they are so challenging to negotiate, structure, and implement. The comparison of these two cross-border deals suggests why: The stretch to reach across borders and industries turns into strain because of surprises about culture. Large cultural difference is an *amplifier* of several of the drivers of failure: It creates a tin ear for danger; it heightens the complexity of decision processes; and it may introduce cognitive biases, management choices, and operational practices that are inappropriate for the situation of the merger.

Failures in the choice of cultural "bridges" may also explain why Sony made no headway on the integration of filmed entertainment and consumer electronics during the first five years following its acquisition of Columbia. Certainly, the leaders of Columbia had no motivation to make such a connection. And Sony's preoccupation with technological changes and changes in consumer demand distracted the firm from pursuing the hypothesized synergies.

Unilever's acquisition of Bestfoods contrasts sharply in all these dimensions. The Bestfoods management remained largely intact. There was no disruptive change in people or strategies following the acquisition. The synergies in cost savings and revenue enhancements were clearly understood and testable against experience in other markets and products. Though the rise of global branding may be as significant as the rise of blockbuster production that Columbia faced in 1989, Unilever had the confidence and experience with which to face the change.

NOTES

1. This chapter was prepared with research assistance from Sean Carr, David Eichler, Ali Erarac, Chad Rynbrandt, and Sanjay Vakharia. Important resources for this chapter were Nancy Griffin and Kim Masters' *Hit & Run: How Jon Peters and Peter Guber Took Sony for a Ride in Hollywood* (New York: Simon and Schuster, 1996), and John Nathan's *Sony* (Boston: Houghton Mifflin, 1999).

2. Jack Egan, "Sony's Big-Picture Strategy," *U.S. News & World Report*, October 9, 1989, 35.

3. Griffin and Masters (1996), 237.

4. Griffin and Masters (1996), 231.

5. Paul Farhi and Steven Mufson, "Lights! Camera! Contract!; Sony's Pursuit of Guber, Peters, Produces a Mega-Million-Dollar Gamble," *Washington Post*, December 17, 1989, H1.

6. Steve McClellan, "Sony Wants to Be in Pictures, Says New President," *Broadcasting & Cable*, November 27, 1995, 58

7. Quotation of Akio Morita in Griffin and Masters (1996), 184.

8. Quotation of Akio Morita in Griffin and Masters (1996), 196.

9. Merger Proxy Statement, Sony Corporation, filed with the SEC, October 3, 1989, 21.

10. Quotation of Michael Schulhof from Paul Richter, "Sony to Pay $3.4 Billion for Columbia Pictures," *Los Angeles Times*, September 28, 1989, Part 1, 1.

11. Quotation drawn from, and paraphrase based on Nina Easton, "After Long Wait, Sony May Have Columbia's Price," *Los Angeles Times*, September 26, 1989, Part 4, 1.

12. Quotation of Benjamin Stein in Nancy Perry, "Will Sony Make It in Hollywood?" *Fortune*, September 9, 1991, 158.

13. Quotation of Jeffrey Logsdon in Johnnie Roberts, "Global Entertainment (A Special Report): Hollyworld—Missing Links: Synergy Benefits Have So Far Eluded the Entertainment Giants," *Wall Street Journal*, March 26, 1993, R9.

14. Quotation of Walter Yetnikoff in Griffin and Masters (1996), 175.

15. Quotation of Akio Morita in Griffin and Masters (1996), 230.

16. "On the Cutting Room Floor," *The Economist*, April 8, 1995, 16.

17. Griffin and Masters (1996), 220.

18. Laura Landro, "Dynamic Duo: Producers of 'Batman' Stir Whammo! Battle over Future Services," *Wall Street Journal*, October 20, 1989, 1. Copyright © 1989 by Dow Jones & Co. Inc. Reproduced with permission of Dow Jones & Co. Inc. in the Format Trade Book via Copyright Clearance Center.

19. Quotation of Brian De Palma in Laura Landro, "Dynamic Duo: Producers of 'Batman' Stir Whammo! Battle over Future Services," *Wall Street Journal*, October 20, 1989, 1.

20. Christopher Byron, "Filmland Flimflam," *Wall Street Journal*, June 11, 1996, A12.

21. Quotation of Steve Ross in Paul Farhi and Steven Mufson, "Lights! Camera! Contract!" *Washington Post*, December 17, 1989, H1.

22. Griffin and Masters (1996), 297.

23. Quotation of Michael Schulhof in Griffin and Masters (1996), 224.

24. Griffin and Masters (1996), 233, report that this price was about 40 percent above GPEC's assessed market value.

25. Griffin and Masters (1996), 239.

26. Paul Farhi and Steven Mufson, "Lights! Camera! Contract!" *Washington Post*, December 17, 1989, H1.

27. Griffin and Masters (1996), 231.

28. Quoted in Griffin and Masters (1998), 231.

29. Quoted in Griffin and Masters (1998), 232.

30. Date of approval by the Sony Board is given in Griffin and Masters (1996), 218.

31. Griffin and Masters (1996, 240, 249) report that the payment consisted of a swap of valuable studio lots, and cable television rights to Columbia's library. The range of valuation represents the high and low estimates from various observers.

32. Griffin and Masters (1996), 270.

33. Griffin and Masters (1996), 9.

34. Griffin and Masters (1996), 297.

35. Laura Landro, "Movies: At Columbia, Comeback Is the Big Production," *Wall Street Journal*, August 20, 1990, B1. Copyright © 1989 by Dow Jones & Co. Inc. Reproduced with permission of Dow Jones & Co. Inc. in the Format Trade Book via Copyright Clearance Center.

36. Griffin and Masters (1996), 281.

37. "Will Sony Make It in Hollywood?" *Forbes*, September 9, 1991.

38. *Forbes*, September 9, 1991.

39. "Hollywood's Hell-Raising Duo," *Fortune*, July 22, 1996.

40. The critique is paraphrased from *Recommendation Follow-up*, Bear Stearns, February 2, 1996.

41. Steps taken are paraphrased from *Recommendation Follow-up*, Bear Stearns, February 2, 1996.

42. My assessment of growth, profits, and returns is based on data given in C. Dixon, K. Hata, Y. Punj, and S. Ehlers, "Music and Movies—Key Elements of Evolving Strategy," December 4, 2002, UBS A.G. Global Equity Research Report, 23.

43. C. Dixon, K. Hata, Y. Punj, and S. Ehlers, "Music and Movies—Key Elements of Evolving Strategy," December 4, 2002, UBS A.G. Global Equity Research Report.

44. This section of the chapter draws substantially upon research by Ali Erarac under the direction of Robert Bruner.

45. Pamela Sauer, "Satisfying the M&A Hunger," *Chemical Market Reporter*, May 2000, 2.

46. Pamela Sauer, "Satisfying the M&A Hunger," *Chemical Market Reporter*, May 2000, 2.

47. Judith Rehak, "Profiting from Mergers: Bestfoods Nibbles for Bids That Top Unilever's Offer," *International Herald Tribune*, May 20, 2000.

48. Nikhil Deogun, "Unilever Offers $18.4 Billion for Bestfoods—Target Firm Rebuffs Move; Bid May Spur Shake-Up in the Food Industry," *Wall Street Journal*, May 3, 2000.

49. Ernest Back, Shelly Brench, and Nikhil Deogun, "Unilever Won't Rule Out Hostile Bid for Bestfoods—Deadline for Response Set for Today, As Shares of Target Soar by 22 Percent," *Wall Street Journal*, May 4, 2000.

50. Ernest Back, Shelly Brench, and Nikhil Deogun, "Unilever Won't Rule Out Hostile Bid for Bestfoods—Deadline for Response Set for Today, As Shares of Target Soar by 22 Percent," *Wall Street Journal*, May 4, 2000.

51. Griffin and Masters (1996), 220–221, discuss Yetnikoff's health problems and Peters' temper (151, 161).

8

September 1991: The Acquisition of NCR Corporation by AT&T Corporation

AT&T: COLLECT CALL

After a bruising hostile takeover fight, Robert Allen, CEO of American Telephone & Telegraph (AT&T) Corporation, and Charles Exley, CEO of National Cash Register (NCR) Corporation, announced in May 1991 an agreement for AT&T to acquire NCR for $7.48 billion.[1] This represented a 132 percent premium over NCR's market value prevailing at the end of October 1990, shortly before AT&T commenced a hostile tender offer for NCR. By May, the two men were buoyant. Then and earlier, Allen had said that the merger would "create an enduring American institution with the technological, financial and marketing strength to succeed against foreign competition in the emerging global information market,"[2] and "will be uniquely equipped to meet what customers will need in the future."[3] "I am absolutely confident that together AT&T and NCR will achieve a level of growth and success that we could not achieve separately. Ours will be a future of promises fulfilled."[4]

Five years later, in May 1995, AT&T announced that it would spin off NCR leaving an entity with a market capitalization of $3.4 billion, about a fourth of the value of AT&T's total investment in the computer segment.

The press was remorseless: "Fiasco . . . a lesson in just about everything that can go wrong . . . one of the biggest flops in the computer industry,"[5] and an "unmitigated disaster for all concerned."[6] Reflecting on the experience, Robert Allen said that AT&T's entry into computers "was made with no experience and a belief that technology would drive the industry."[7] He also said, "The complexity of trying to manage these different businesses began to overwhelm the advantages of integration. The world has changed. Markets have changed."[8]

ORIGINS OF THE ACQUISITION

In 1919, after a bitterly-fought consolidation effort, AT&T was tacitly sanctioned as the national telephone monopoly in the United States. Monopolies have never rested quietly with the body politic in the United States; AT&T was subject to regulation at the federal, state, and local levels, and to periodic antimonopoly lawsuits and legislation. In 1974, MCI Communications Corporation sued AT&T on antitrust grounds; the lawsuit was subsequently joined by the U.S. Department of Justice (DOJ). A jury awarded MCI $1.8 billion in damages in 1980; and the DOJ pressed its suit to break up the monopoly. Surprisingly, the directors of AT&T agreed to do just that, and in 1982, settled the government antitrust suit by signing a consent decree that separated the long-distance and local telephone operations. AT&T kept the long-distance business, the Western Electric equipment manufacturing business, and Bell Labs, a research organization. Seven independent regional phone companies (Baby Bells) emerged.

The breakup occurred in 1984, upon which AT&T entered the computer equipment manufacturing business. Thereafter, the firm sought to develop a computer systems business that would compete on world markets with the likes of IBM. Management of the new AT&T committed itself to a bet on convergence between computing technology and telecommunications, providing customers with integrated computing and communications systems. In 1991, Richard Bodman, senior vice president of AT&T described the strategy as follows:

> AT&T's mission is broad and deep: to be the world leader in information
> technology—a technology that inescapably involves the best of both

computer and communications technology. AT&T has a well-defined strategy for establishing leadership in this field:

1. Maintaining leadership in its core business like network services.
2. Establishing world leadership in networked computing, which is the technology driving the growth of electronic transactions.
3. To firmly establish AT&T as a truly global company.[9]

On the face of it, the marriage of computing and communications seemed like a plausible strategy. AT&T had the largest captive market in long-distance telecom. It had some manufacturing expertise in Western Electric. And its Bell Labs was the incubator of UNIX, the computer language that was the basis for open-source system architecture.

Unfortunately, the entry into computing was unsuccessful. AT&T accumulated $2 billion to $3 billion[10] of losses over its initial internal development effort. Its systems were neither leaders, nor likely to be competitive. For instance, AT&T's joint venture with Ing. C. Olivetti & Company, made computers for AT&T since 1983 that were viewed as overpriced and poor performers. And generally it seems that AT&T picked its fights poorly.

> Part of AT&T's problem has been that, despite its technological strength, it has not brought much new to the computer business. The company already had more than $30 billion in revenues from its long-distance business, and it wanted its computer business to generate several billion dollars in revenue, at least. As a result, it has tended to enter larger, established markets, which have entrenched competition, rather than pioneer new, smaller markets where the growth is. AT&T entered the computer business with large minicomputers just as the industry was shifting to smaller desktop models. Worse, the AT&T 3B minicomputers, having been designed primarily for use in telephone switches, were not well received.[11]

Computer segment revenues had risen from $900 million in 1986 to $1.5 billion in 1990. Further, a pretax loss of nearly $1 billion had been reduced to about $300 million in 1990. These numbers were enough for AT&T to conclude that it needed an acquisition to stay competitive in the computer business. Moreover, the adverse impact of AT&T's divestiture was beginning to emerge: AT&T reported net income of $2.5 billion, while the

Baby Bells had a combined net income of $8.5 billion. The cumulative market–adjusted returns on AT&T shares from the breakup in 1984 to 1990 (see Figure 8.1) were erratic; AT&T was holding its own relative to the market, but not creating value on a relative basis. And the firm's return on total capital sagged below its cost of capital following the breakup (see Figure 8.2). The computer business was not the path to new value. One critic wrote:

> It says it must be in the computer business to pursue its strategy in computer networking. But this is as logical as claiming that one must manufacture ovens to be in the restaurant business. These problems make me wonder whether AT&T has lost its way, whether it has any overall realistic strategy. Is the ship rudderless in the high seas of competition, while the captain searches for the New World of computers?[12]

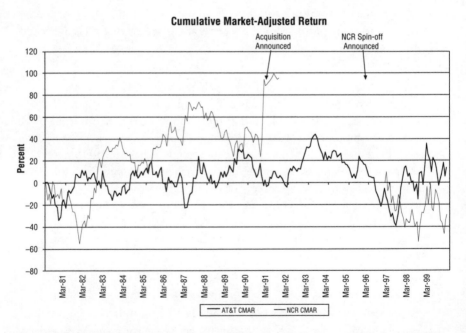

Figure 8.1 **Cumulative Market–Adjusted Return on Shares of AT&T and NCR, 1980 to 2000**

Source of data: Datastream.

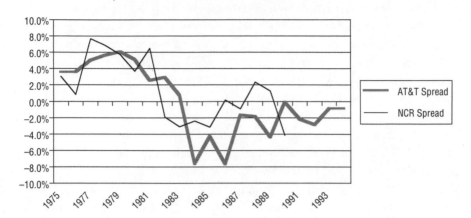

**"Spread" Between Return on Capital and
Cost of Capital for AT&T and NCR**

Figure 8.2   **Returns Spread on AT&T and NCR Common Stock**

Source of data: Company annual reports and Bloomberg Financial Services. Computations are author's estimates.

Charles Exley of NCR called it a "failed strategy."[13] And a third critic said, "It would be cheaper shutting it down. But that would be admitting failure."[14]

AT&T was at a crossroads: It needed to fix the unit or to exit the business. Exit would require a major redirection of the firm's strategy. Aside from the ambiguity about what the firm would do instead, there would be sizable writeoffs, recriminations, and loss of face. Given how rapidly computing technology was changing, Robert Allen, the CEO of AT&T, chose to raise the bet rather than to fold and leave the game. Analysts believe that AT&T ultimately decided that the potential benefits of being able to provide integrated communication and computing systems outweighed the business risks. Charles Ferguson of MIT said, "Everything AT&T has done to stay in the computer business has been kind of irrational."[15]

NCR: FROM CASH REGISTERS TO COMPUTING

"We have reinvented ourselves several times," said Charles Exley.[16] Founded in 1884, National Cash Register became a national icon selling registers and other business machines. But it hastily adapted to the advent of electronic cash registers in the 1970s, and entered the manufacture of minicomputers, mainframes, and PCs. Charles Exley became CEO in the mid-1980s when yet another change was required: One analyst said, "They were on the verge of collapse. They had mainframes that nobody wanted anymore. The minicomputer business was dying. They had no software to speak of."[17] Thus, NCR reinvented itself again, to a line of computing equipment configured by open systems architecture that was based on networks of PCs, rather than on a mainframe computer hub. Success required a broad line of equipment to meet the diverse computing requirements of clients. The first computers (Series 3000) under this new line were produced in September 1990.

At that moment, the process of reinvention meant that NCR was vulnerable. Its recent share price performance was evident in Figure 8.1: The cumulative market-adjusted returns show a declining trend from March of 1987 to the takeover announcement. And the firm's spread over cost of funds turned sharply negative in 1990, reflecting heavy capital spending to bring on the Series 3000 product line (see Figure 8.2).

NCR offered a number of attractive attributes to AT&T including profitability of operation, larger competitive scale (NCR was the fifth-largest computer company in the United States), global reach, a strong position in commercial transaction processing with its ATMs and sophisticated cash registers, and above all, complementarity. The equipment of NCR and AT&T used the UNIX operating system; NCR had special competencies in computing, AT&T in telecommunications; NCR was strongly positioned among business customers in retailing, financial services, and state and local governments; AT&T was strongly positioned among customers in telecommunications, transportation, manufacturing, and the federal government. NCR had a strong revenue base outside the United States; AT&T was focused domestically.[18] Finally, several observers thought that both firms had a "Midwestern ethos" in their corporate cultures.[19]

Unfortunately, by the winter of 1990/1991, NCR's big bet on Series

3000 was weakening. The early stages of recession did not favor corporate capital spending on new computer gear. As all producers tried to move inventory, pricing turned cutthroat. NCR was finding it difficult to keep up with the rapid pace of innovation required for survival. And it discovered that its costs were too high.[20] In September 1991, NCR revised downward its forecasts in filings with the SEC.

THE TAKEOVER

In 1988, Robert Allen met with Charles Exley to explore the possibility of a friendly combination between the two firms. Exley demurred, but indicated that if NCR were ever the subject of a hostile raid, he would consider calling upon AT&T to act as a "white knight." A year later, the two men met on the same subject, and with the same result.

On November 15, 1990, AT&T extended an offer of $85 per share to NCR, by a confidential message from Robert Allen to Charles Exley. In response to the secret bid, NCR chairman Charles Exley replied that he would not sacrifice a successful computer company to save AT&T's failing computer group and that AT&T's bid was just an attempt to salvage its failure in computing. Exley also threatened to quit if AT&T acquired his company. Analysts believed that NCR's response was aimed at getting AT&T to raise its offer. Indeed, NCR was prepared to negotiate at a price of $125 per share ($8.5 billion) but AT&T viewed that price as "outrageous and totally unjustified." At the same time, NCR took steps to boost its antitakeover measures.

Following the rejection by NCR's board, AT&T commenced a public tender offer for NCR at $90 per share, on December 2, 1990. The cash-for-stock bid was valued at about $6.1 billion. The hostile bid was seen as being highly unusual for AT&T, "which generally uses its dominant position in the telephone industry and the reputation of its research staff to find willing partners."[21] AT&T sought to portray the offer as friendly, but NCR reacted negatively to the offer. Dennis Block, an NCR lawyer, said, "A marriage of the companies makes no business sense." Exley told a reporter, "There's not only no synergy, there's a direct contradiction."[22]

On December 14, 1990 NCR's board rejected AT&T's takeover offer, describing the $90 per share bid as "grossly inadequate and unfair." Two days later, AT&T announced that it would mount a proxy fight to unseat NCR's board. A special meeting of the shareholders could be called by 25 percent of NCR's shares, but 80 percent of the shareholders would be needed to vote out the board of directors. Institutional investors owned about 60 percent of NCR's stock. For the next month, AT&T and NCR jousted with lawsuits in various courts either aimed at stopping or delaying AT&T, or limiting the ability of NCR to delay the takeover process. These lawsuits included claims about violations of federal securities laws, antitrust laws, bank holding company laws, and federal communications rules.

On January 16, 1991 AT&T reported that it had received tenders for about 70 percent of NCR's common stock. With proxies in hand, AT&T called for a special meeting of shareholders to elect directors; the meeting was scheduled for March 28. The growing feeling among analysts and investors was that Exley should negotiate an acquisition for a suitably high price, rather than let AT&T win NCR at the existing $90 per share bid. But Exley continued to defend the independence of NCR.

In late February NCR tried to create a $500 million employee stock ownership plan (ESOP) that could control eight percent of the company's stock (the purchase of 5.5 million shares for the program would not require outside financing). A court subsequently threw out the ESOP defense. NCR also approved a special $1 billion dividend payment as well as an increase in its regular quarterly dividend from 35 cents to 37 cents.

These defenses notwithstanding, it became apparent to all including Exley, that AT&T would gain four seats on the board after the special shareholders meeting on March 28, and gain control of the board one year later. On March 10, AT&T indicated that it would be willing to raise its offer to $100 a share ($6.77 billion) if NCR's board dropped its objections to the deal. Once again Exley reacted negatively to the offer saying, "If AT&T wants to proceed in a professional and responsible manner, they should deal directly with us and submit a serious proposal in writing—rather than posturing in the media."[23] Nine days later, AT&T announced that it would definitely raise its offer for NCR to $100 per share if shareholders voted to remove the board at NCR's special stockholders meeting.

Then, just four days before the special shareholders' meeting, Exley announced, "The board authorized management to initiate a process that will help AT&T understand the basis for the board's conclusion that [NCR's] value is substantially above $100 per share. Accordingly, I have advised AT&T that we are prepared to meet with them and make appropriate information available." NCR and AT&T negotiators met for two days, and then parted bitterly over the valuation of NCR. AT&T vowed to press on with its takeover efforts in the absence of talks.

At the special meeting, AT&T fell short of gaining the necessary 80 percent shareholder support to replace NCR's entire board. However, AT&T did win 4 of 12 seats on the board. On April 8, 1991 Exley announced that NCR would be willing to restart merger talks with AT&T—but not at a price below $110 per share ($7.48 billion).

Two weeks later, AT&T raised its bid to $110 share, provided it could pay for the transaction with its own stock and account for the transaction under the pooling-of-interests method. The offer was also conditional on an agreement with Exley to stay on for the transition period, as well as on reaching a new employment arrangement with seven other top executives to retain their leadership in the new company. NCR indicated that it would approve the new bid if shareholders were assured of getting $110 when the deal was completed. Therefore, AT&T offered to include a collar, which would guarantee the $110 per share price as long as AT&T stock stayed within a targeted price range.

NCR finally agreed on May 6 to AT&T's takeover bid in a deal for $7.4 billion of AT&T shares. NCR was to retain its corporate identity, as well as its headquarters in Dayton, Ohio. Exley said that his company would move swiftly to combine operations with AT&T, with six to eight managers from each company working solely toward this effort. Transition teams were chartered to explore how the two firms could best combine their manufacturing, products, finances, marketing, and personnel.

A month later AT&T announced that it would divest its 19 percent stake in Sun Microsystems, the fast growing leader in computer workstations. AT&T's 19.1 million shares in Sun were worth about $692 million. The partnership had led to the development of a unified version of UNIX, but did not have any further strategic significance. This sale was ironic: Sun remained profitable, continued to grow rapidly, and went on to create the hugely popular Java software that would enable computers to run other software applications off the Internet. Every Internet provider (including Microsoft) ultimately embraced Java.

At the time of its bid, AT&T announced its intent to hand over its computer business to NCR to be run by NCR's management at its existing headquarters in Dayton, Ohio. Layoffs and other cost reductions were to come from the AT&T side. In July, AT&T announced better-than-expected earnings for the second quarter at $828 million (up 26 percent), but said it would take a write off of as much as $4 billion ($2.5 billion after taxes) by the end of the year in charges[24] related to its takeover of NCR as well as a number of cost cutting programs. Jack Grubman, a research analyst, concluded that this amounted to a total write-off of AT&T's computer operations: "You can finally say, eight years after they started to break up the old AT&T, that the ship has turned and is headed in the right direction."[25] Earlier he had said, "You can consider this a reverse acquisition. AT&T is getting out of the computer business by a $6 billion acquisition of NCR."[26] But another analyst asked, "Can you execute a vision that isn't yours? This is AT&T's vision for what the future should hold, not NCR's."[27] Ultimately, the 7,500 employees of AT&T's computer segment were laid off, though 2,000 were re-hired by NCR.

On September 13, 1991, NCR's shareholders overwhelmingly approved the takeover by AT&T. The merger was consummated on September 19.

AFTERMATH

Following the acquisition in September 1991, AT&T was silent for several quarters regarding the performance of its new business unit. The firm announced some costs related to the acquisition, and various restructuring charges totaling $2.65 billion. But in general the presentation to the public was upbeat. In June 1992, NCR chairman Gilbert Williamson said his company was growing and was profitable across all divisions. This was reconfirmed in September 1992, and January and May 1993.

In March 1993, NCR chairman Gilbert Williamson announced his retirement effective May 1. He was to be replaced by Jerre Stead, an AT&T executive who had successfully turned around AT&T's office phone systems business. Williamson said that he was not being forced to retire; the decision was his own choice. He simply wanted to spend more time with his family.

The management transition in 1993 proved to be the equivalent of a belated postmerger integration. AT&T installed one of its own senior managers to run NCR. As John Keller reported:

[AT&T] let many top NCR executives exit, then rankled an embittered and balky work force and hostile management by imposing its own culture on the new property. . . . AT&T waited through a voluntary two-year hands-off period to take full management control of NCR. Then it appointed its own executives to run the unit—even though AT&T managers had flopped in steering the parent company into computers. The AT&T team tried to put in a financial-reporting system that made it tougher to gauge profitability as products moved from production to market. They reorganized sales, confusing customers. And they ultimately dumped the NCR name . . . in favor of the sterile [Global Information Solutions]."[28]

Roughly coincident with Stead's arrival, the financial performance of NCR deteriorated sharply. Figure 8.3 gives the operating income for NCR and its ratio of EBIT to invested capital. Plainly, the business turned sharply for the worse after Gil Williamson left. Though NCR recovered profitability in 1996, never again was it as prosperous as earlier. What changed? AT&T paid $500 million in restructuring costs associated with closing the old AT&T computer segment. But the firm also noted that "we faced fierce competitive pricing, particularly for lower-end computer products, and weak economic and market conditions in Europe and Japan."[29] Later, the firm noted:

All parts of our business face substantial and intensifying competition. Product pricing and technology are under continual competitive pressure, and business and market conditions are changing rapidly. . . . Price competition for personal computers was severe. Most personal computers from different manufacturers use the same or comparable microprocessors and software, leading customers to focus increasingly on price. We plan to make NCR a stand-alone business focused on transaction-intensive computing. The new strategy centers around more profitable products such as massively parallel computer processors, automated teller machines and retail scanning equipment. This

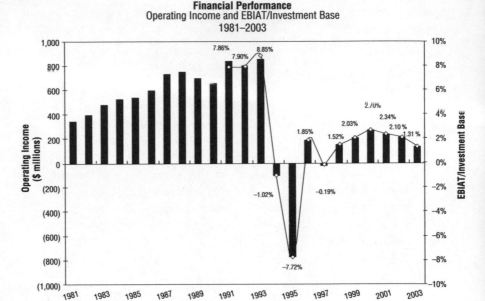

Figure 8.3 **NCR Operating Profit and EBIT/Investment**

Sources of data: Company annual report and author's computations.

direction also enhances the company's primary strategy which is to help businesses use new technology to collect and use information to enhance customer service. Although NCR is ceasing the manufacture of personal computers, it will continue to offer personal computers manufactured by others as part of its total solutions approach. NCR, as a result of continuing operating losses, has taken decisive action in 1995 to create a smaller, more focused business, concentrating on the three industries in which it has a leading position—retailing, financial and communications. This resulted in restructuring and other charges in the third quarter of 1995, of approximately $1.6 billion before taxes ($1.2 billion after taxes). The pretax charges reflect $698 million for employee separations and other related costs, $564 million for asset write-downs, $196 million for closing, selling and consolidating facilities and $191 million for other items.[30]

One analyst wrote:

> The problem, in a nutshell, is that business is horrible and the cost structure is too bloated. NCR's domestic business actually saw a double-digit revenue increase, but international was down as weak overseas orders from last year carried over into weak revenues in the first quarter. In addition, the product mix at NCR was skewed to the areas with the most pricing pressure, hence, the worsening of losses despite the top-line pickup.[31]

Another analyst said:

> NCR wasn't a bad asset; it's just that AT&T merged it into its own money-losing computer operations and tried to do too much with it too soon. In addition, NCR's customer segments fell into a global swoon, and some of its product lines were too early or inefficiently targeted (we think the in-house PC business has always been a disaster, while first-generation massively parallel systems lacked generic software).[32]

On November 24, 1993, NCR announced a plan to reduce its workforce by as much as 15 percent in order to cut costs and regain its competitiveness. The company had been suffering all year from intense price competition and tight markets, and NCR had announced a $49 million operating loss for the third quarter (versus a $50 million profit the year before). NCR hoped to eliminate 7,500 jobs through voluntary measures, rather than layoffs.

A year later, Jerre Stead announced that the business unit's losses had narrowed, and that he would resign to become chairman and CEO of Legent Corporation. In March 1995, AT&T announced that Lars Nyberg, an executive from Phillips Electronics with a reputation as a cost-cutter, would take over as chairman and CEO of AT&T Global Information Solutions. Nyberg had been brought in to cut jobs and costs. In May the business unit was losing money at the rate of $2 million per day. Results for the first nine months of 1994 included an operating loss of $501 million, compared with earnings of $63 million in the first nine months of the merger year. Analysts saw a need for the computer unit to gain market share "in whatever part of the business they are competing in or get out."[33] In short, by the summer of 1995, AT&T found itself facing the decision it had faced in 1990: Raise the bet or exit the industry.

On July 28, 1995, AT&T announced that it would shrink its computer unit and focus on its core strengths in the financial, retail, and communications industries. Then on September 21, 1995, AT&T announced a three-way breakup into units focused on telecommunications (the new AT&T), equipment manufacturing (Lucent Corporation), and computer equipment manufacturing (NCR). AT&T's stock rose 11 percent on the announcement. Analysts attributed the increase to the elimination of a diversification discount. AT&T Chairman Robert Allen said, "The market value of AT&T was being buried. Investors will clearly understand now." Employees of NCR celebrated with balloons and champagne. After the announcement of the NCR spin-off, John Myers, an NCR programmer candidly said, "I think it's great to get rid of the ball and chain around us. They've been slowing us down for five years now. We can really focus more now in the areas we know about."[34]

The spinoff of NCR occurred on January 2, 1997, yielding a market value of NCR of $3.4 billion, less than half of what AT&T had paid five years earlier. AT&T sold its remaining stake in NCR by year-end 1997. A rough estimate of AT&T's internal rate of return on investment would be −40 percent.[35] Considering that from September 1991 to January 1996 the S&P 500 index grew by an average annual rate in excess of 15 percent, the return to AT&T shareholders adjusted for the lost opportunity of investing in the market was −50 percent. Possibly foreshadowing this loss was the dramatic movement in AT&T's share prices during the takeover fight. Thomas Lys and Linda Vincent (1995) studied these movements, and concluded that the takeover fight reduced AT&T shareholder wealth by about $3 billion.

Journalists and securities analysts viewed the acquisition of NCR by AT&T as a disaster. "Part of the problem, according to analysts, was that AT&T bought NCR right at the time it was making the transition from traditional mainframe computers to so-called massively parallel computers powered by collections of smaller, cheaper processors running in tandem. The unit has also been hit by a decline in its traditional cash register business as low-margin personal computers have made up a rising proportion of such sales. And on the hardware side, it has found it difficult to compete with efficient producers such as Compaq Computer."[36] *The Economist* suggested that the failure was due to the absence of a useful marketing fit, a clash of cultures (unionized at AT&T, nonunion at NCR; conservative at NCR and "politically correct" at AT&T), and the huge cost in terms of capital and people.

A COMPLEMENTARY DEAL FROM HELL: MERCK AND MEDCO

For a comparative example to the case of AT&T and NCR, consider another unhappy case, Merck's acquisition of Medco. The latter differs from the former in one important dimension: Medco was prospering greatly under Merck's ownership at the time that Merck decided to spin it off to shareholders. As such, it offers a lesson about the forces necessary to overcome cognitive biases favoring retaining a unit. As AT&T and NCR showed, sunk cost mentality and the escalation of commitments are powerful contributors to M&A failure. But are they inevitable in M&A?

The facts of the acquisition are as follows. On July 12, 1993, Roy Vagelos, CEO of Merck, announced that he was holding talks to acquire Medco Containment Services, Inc., in a deal that would total $6 billion and that would be consummated on November 18. Ten years later, Merck spun off Medco to its shareholders in a deal that valued Medco at about $6 billion, a virtual giveaway in light of Medco's sixfold growth and strong profitability over the decade of ownership by Merck. The large question is not why Merck exited from this sound business, but rather, why it took so long.

Merck was a leading producer of prescription pharmaceuticals and had been recognized by *Fortune* magazine as the most-admired company in the United States. Medco was a pharmaceutical benefits manager (PBM), a mail-order supply house that provided prescription fulfillment services under contract to corporate clients and HMOs. Through its bulk purchasing and other management efforts, Medco reduced prescription drug costs for its clients.

Vagelos saw that the explosive growth in health care costs would intensify cost-containment pressures on patients and health care providers.

Merck's annuity drugs were drawing close scrutiny by lawmakers and regulators. Figure 8.4 shows the sagging share prices of pharmaceuticals companies as the reality of the expected price pressure hit investors. Accordingly, Vagelos focused on means of offsetting the price cuts through volume increases. Medco offered a solution: As manager of pharmacy fulfillment for 33 million people, Medco could push Merck-brand products over its competitors' and give Merck insights into prescription trends. Furthermore, Medco's selling and administrative efforts were done by telephone, which was much cheaper than Merck's 5,500 direct field sales people. Medco's revenues were growing at 35 percent annually. Vagelos said, "I've always thought there would be a better way. This is it. This is eureka."[37] Other big pharmaceutical companies followed suit with purchases of other PBMs.

The only problem was that Medco shifted from a neutral cost-cutter to a partisan product-promoter. For example, Medco used aggressive telemarketing tactics to steer physicians toward Merck products. One physi-

Figure 8.4   **Price Trends of the S&P 500 Index and S&P Drugs Index**
Source of data: Datastream.

cian wrote, "By acquiring Medco, Merck will be in a position through the large mail-order drug dispenser to sway physicians to prescribe Merck products. Consumers and health reformers both have a stake in the outcome. To the degree that individual Merck drugs are the best on the market, this will be beneficial. To the degree that other drugs are better, the public interest will not be served. And in either event, companies attempting to bring forth competing products will be at a disadvantage."[38] "It's putting the fox in charge of the henhouse," he later added.[39]

Economically, Merck's strategy of dominating the channel of distribution made sense. Ethically the implementation of this strategy did not. Prescription-switching was conducted by Medco's telephone pharmacists without disclosing to physicians that they ultimately represented Merck and had a potential conflict of interest between the welfare of the patient and the welfare of Merck. Whether this practice crossed the line of illegality was the focus of lawsuits and government investigations for the next several years.

Just two years after the deal, beginning in 1995, the legal challenges gained traction. In February, Merck settled a lawsuit by agreeing to offer other manufacturers' drugs in the Medco formulary (a list of recommended drugs for treating diseases) and to limit the exchange of certain information about drug prices quoted by other manufacturers. In October, Merck settled with 17 states in litigation that Merck had violated consumer-protection laws. Merck agreed to disclose to physicians that the Medco pharmacists were calling on behalf of Medco, owned by Merck, and to disclose the manufacturers of recommended drugs. In November, the Government Accounting Office (GAO) reported on practices adopted by PBMs after their acquisition by pharmaceutical firms—Merck/Medco, SmithKline Beecham's Diversified Pharmaceutical Services, and Lilly's PCS Health Systems. The GAO found that Medco had dropped from its formulary some drugs that competed with Merck.[40]

The U.S. Federal Trade Commission (FTC) was concurrently investigating these competitive practices, and found that those at Merck/Medco raised "the most difficult issues."[41] In 1998, Merck signed a settlement with the FTC finding that "Medco has given favorable treatment to Merck drugs. As a result, in some cases, consumers have been denied access to the drugs of competing manufacturers."[42] Merck agreed to adopt practices diminishing preferential treatment for Merck's drugs. Also in 1998, the U.S. Food and Drug Administration began a study of possibly regulating the

PBMs. Later, the FDA relented after intense resistance from PBMs and drug companies.

Medco succeeded in building Merck's share of market, despite these interventions. Table 8.1 shows substantial disparities in sales of Merck products through Medco, as compared with the open market. Merck defended the share of market gains by noting that simply focusing on share ignored rebates and discounts that Medco won for its clients.

In 2002 the U.S. Attorney's office in Philadelphia launched an investigation into Medco's practices. And separately, the State of West Virginia sued Merck, alleging that Medco had steered state employees to more expensive drugs and had kept rebates that should have been passed along to the state. Medco countersued, alleging that it had saved West Virginia *more* money than expected, and that some of the savings should be shared with Medco. Merck settled a similar five-year lawsuit with clients, who charged that Medco kept rebates due to them. Merck agreed to pay $42.5 million and change its disclosure practices. Merck also noted that plaintiffs' attorneys would garner 30 percent of the settlement.

The settlement sparked the interest of more state attorneys general. In January 2003, 25 of them joined West Virginia in opening inquiries into Medco's PBM practices. Medco denied favoring one manufacturer over another. In March, a large union and a consumer group sued the four

TABLE 8.1   SELECTED MARKET SHARES OF MERCK DRUGS WITHIN MEDCO AND IN OPEN MARKET

		At December 1999	
Product	Treatment for	% Share of Medco Prescriptions	% Share of All Prescriptions in Market
Zocor	High cholesterol	41%	22%
Prinzide	High blood pressure	27%	9%
Prinivil	High blood pressure	39%	13%
Pepcid	Heartburn	29%	21%
Vasotec	High blood pressure	24%	17%
Vioxx	Arthritis pain relief	19%	12%
Fosamax	Osteoporosis	19%	14%

Source of data: Court documents, reported in B. Martinez, "Merck's Ties with Medco Detailed," *Wall Street Journal,* January 8, 2003, D6. Copyright © 2003 by Dow Jones & Co. Inc. Reproduced with permission of Dow Jones & Co. Inc. in the Format Trade Book via Copyright Clearance Center.

largest PBMs for failing to pass savings onto health plans and consumers. "In the early 1990s, they told us PBMs were the key to controlling drug costs. . . . But now its clear that PBMs have not only failed to deliver any savings, but they have built all kinds of new profit-shaving into the system," said a spokesperson for the consumer group.[43] In June, the U.S. Attorney in Philadelphia finally moved: The Department of Justice joined a whistleblower lawsuit that claimed Medco put profits before patients. Later that year, the DOJ charged Medco with fraud. Medco contests the charge; the litigation is ongoing.

As if the litigation weren't sufficient to motivate an exit, Merck encountered fierce challenges to its leading drug lines. Studies found that Vioxx and Celebrex were no more effective as pain cures than older and cheaper drugs. In 1997, Zocor was suddenly displaced as the leading anticholesterol drug by Lipitor, produced by Warner–Lambert. And the patents on five important Merck drugs accounting for one-third of Merck's medicine sales would expire in 1999. Though Merck introduced 17 new drugs to the market between 1995 and 2002, the financial impact of the sudden reverses was sharp. Merck informed investors that earnings would be lower than forecasted. Merck's market value fell nine percent on June 22, 2001, the date of announcement. In 2001, Merck lost one-third of its market capitalization.

Meanwhile, the other large pharmaceutical companies that had acquired PBMs were bailing out of the industry. Eli Lilly sold PCS Health Systems for a $2.4 billion loss in 1997; SmithKline Beecham sold Diversified Pharmaceutical Services for a $1.9 billion loss in 1999.

In response to these difficulties, Merck decided to exit from the PBM business, announcing on January 29, 2002, a prospective carve-out of Medco. Merck aimed to sell 20 percent of Medco in an initial public offering (IPO) in mid-year. Later, Merck would distribute the balance of the shares to its shareholders. The prospectus for the deal disclosed that Medco would be obligated to continue to promote the sale of Merck drugs for five years. Then the IPO was cancelled when Merck disclosed that from 1998 to 2001, it had recognized $12.4 billion in drug co-payments (collected through Medco) as revenue. Professor Charles Mulford said, "While it doesn't alter net income, clearly they're taking an aggressive stance relative to other companies in the industry. It overstates total economic activity at the company."[44] In contrast, Robert Willens of Lehman Brothers opined that "the accounting was appropriate because Medco served as the obligor of the payments."[45] But in July, Merck and the underwriters decided to cancel the offering.

Nine months later, Merck announced that it would spin off Medco, distributing shares in Medco directly to Merck shareholders. The spin–off would be accompanied by two features. First, as with the carve–out, Medco would be required to push Merck drugs for a period of time. Second, Medco would borrow and pay a $2 billion dividend to Merck. Under the earlier carve–out plan, Merck had anticipated receipts of $2.5 billion. The spin–off occurred on August 19, 2003.

As with AT&T and NCR, one wonders why it took so long for Merck to decide to exit. In both cases, the companies were awash in bad news long before the spin–offs. But in Merck's case, the story is more complicated than just sunk cost mentality. Medco was just too profitable to let go. Figure 8.5 shows that Medco's operating profit was rising rapidly, during the time of difficulty for Merck. Given that Merck was facing a worsening position in its leading drugs, and then a worsening economic climate starting in 2000, the prospect of lost earnings must have been par-

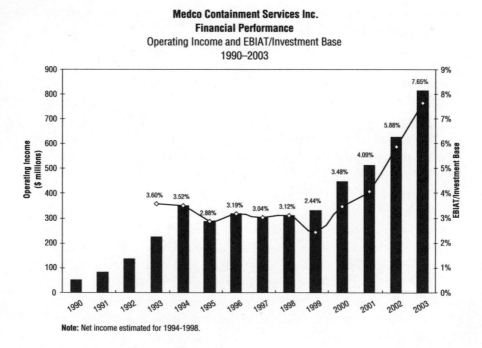

Figure 8.5   **Medco Operating Profit**

Sources of data: Company annual reports and author's computations.

ticularly unappealing. Offsetting this, of course, would be the sizable payment to Merck, to help fund its R&D efforts.

CONCLUSION

The M&A failure framework highlights the many dimensions of the disastrous deal between AT&T and NCR. *Business was not as usual* given the rapid shift toward open-architecture computing, rapid technological innovation, price competition, and the onset of a recession in 1991. AT&T was smarting from a six-year failed attempt to establish a viable foothold in the industry. Unknown to all was NCR's impending distress. Both AT&T and NCR were in the midst of reinventing themselves and would discover only in 1993 that their reinvention was too late.

On the surface, it would seem that this deal offered little *complexity*: AT&T simply erased its existing computer group and brought its existing client base to NCR. But complexity appears in NCR's own corporate transformation to open-architecture computing as of 1991. Such transformations require the migration of employees, customers, and suppliers to new products and processes in virtually every dimension of the business. And they require high coordination. This, plus the high purchase price sapped flexibility from the situation: NCR's fortunes were *tightly coupled* to its shift to open-architecture computing.

The fundamental *management choice* that predetermined its difficulties was the strategic decision to enter the computer industry in 1984. *Cognitive biases*, particularly overoptimism, sunk cost mentality, and escalation of commitments spurred Robert Allen onward through the operational losses and major investment in NCR. Finally, cultural differences dragged on *team effectiveness*, particularly after the departure of Gil Williamson and the arrival of Jerre Stead in 1993.

The cognitive biases in this case received special attention. A careful study of the AT&T/NCR case by Thomas Lys and Linda Vincent led them to reflect that the acquisition was a manifestation of the *escalation of commitments*. Decision-makers can become "bound" to an earlier decision when it is difficult to reverse, is clear and public, is freely taken, and has large personal implications for the decision-maker.[46] To become "bound" to a decision means to follow through with it even in the face of information, opinion, or outcomes to the contrary. Escalation occurs when decision-makers who feel bound to a course of action "raise the ante" in an effort to make their gambles pay. AT&T's managers had freely consented to the court decree dividing the firm, and then committed themselves to a strategy that would marry computing and telecommunications. Management wanted to prove the value of the strategy they had adopted after agreeing to the court decree. AT&T's initial efforts in computers failed, motivating AT&T to acquire NCR. Even though the assessment of the equity market was sharp and adverse, AT&T's management slogged ahead. Lys and Vincent estimated that the cumulative wealth loss to AT&T shareholders because of the acquisition was $6.5 billion. Even after acquiring NCR, AT&T's management raised the bet further by absorbing ongoing losses.

The complementary deal, Merck's acquisition of Medco, would qualify as another deal from hell in the damage it wrought to Merck's reputation. Though it was moderately successful in economic terms, the deal created enormous conflicts of interest, the evidence of which will occupy trial lawyers for years to come. Merck was the first pharmaceutical company to enter the PBM field and the last to leave. Its delay is easily explained by the economic *success* of Medco, in contrast to AT&T, which delayed the exit in disbelief that the losses were chronic.

NOTES

1. This chapter was prepared with research assistance from Sean Carr, David Eichler, Chad Rynbrandt, and Sanjay Vakharia.

2. Quotation of Robert Allen in Nikhil Deogun and Steven Lipin, "Deals & Deal Makers: Cautionary Tales," *Wall Street Journal*, December 8, 1999, C1.

3. Quotation of Robert Allen in Cindy Skrzycki, "NCR Corp. Agrees to AT&T Merger," *Washington Post*, May 7, 1991, C1.

4. Quotation of Robert Allen in "Deals and Deal Makers: Cautionary Tales: When Big Deals Turn Bad," *Wall Street Journal*, December 8, 1999, C1. Copyright © 1999 by Dow Jones & Co. Inc. Reproduced with permission of Dow Jones & Co. Inc. in the Format Trade Book via Copyright Clearance Center.

5. Raju Narisetti, "History Holds Some Hard Lessons for Compaq," *Wall Street Journal*, January 28, 1998, B1.

6. Nicholas Booth, "NCR Rejoins the Road to Success," *The Times of London*, June 25, 1997, Interface 12.

7. Quotation of Robert Allen in "Fatal Attraction," *Economist*, March 23, 1996, 74.

8. Quotation of Robert Allen in "Deals and Deal Makers: Cautionary Tales: When Big Deals Turn Bad," *Wall Street Journal*, December 8, 1999, C1.

9. Letter to the Editor from Richard Bodman, *New York Times*, April 14, 1991, Section 3, 11. Copyright © 1991 by the New York Times Co. Reprinted with permission.

10. The extent of losses by AT&T before the NCR deal is not known for certain. Three billion dollars is the figure most commonly cited. Three billion dollars is an upper-bound given in Andrew Pollack, "Big Deal That Poses Little Threat," *New York Times*, May 7, 1991, D6.

11. Andrew Pollack, "Coming to the Rescue of a Computer Venture," *New York Times*, December 4, 1990, D1. Copyright © 1990 by the New York Times Co. Reprinted with permission.

12. Figures given in Michael Noll, "The Failures of AT&T Strategies," *New York Times*, March 31, 1991, Section 3, 9. Copyright © 1991 by the New York Times Co. Reprinted with permission.

13. Quoted in Eben Shapiro, "Cash Offer by AT&T after Rebuff," *New York Times*, December 6, 1990, D1.

14. Keith Bradsher, "NCR and AT&T: Would the Combination Work?" *New York Times*, December 9, 1990, Section 3, 12.

15. Quotation of Charles Ferguson in L. J. Davis, "When AT&T Plays Hardball," *New York Times*, June 9, 1991, Section 6, Part 2, 14.

16. Quotation of Charles Exley in L. J. Davis, "When AT&T Plays Hardball," *New York Times*, June 9, 1991, Section 6, Part 2, 14.

17. Quotation of Judith Hurwitz at Patricia Seybold's Office Computing Group in L. J. Davis, "When AT&T Plays Hardball," *New York Times*, June 9, 1991, Section 6, Part 2, 14.

18. The points of complementarity are paraphrased from Rick Whiting, "NCR/AT&T: One Era Ends . . . Another Begins," *Electronic Business*, May 1993, 34.

19. Eben Shapiro, "AT&T Is Offering $6 Billion to Buy a Computer Maker," *New York Times*, December 3, 1990, A1.

20. Points of downturn are abstracted from Edmund Andres, "AT&T Acquisition, Soon to Be Spun Off, Regains NCR Name," *New York Times*, January 11, 1996, D5.

21. Eben Shapiro, "AT&T Is Offering $6 Billion to Buy a Computer Maker," *New York Times*, December 3, 1990, A1.

22. Keith Bradsher, "NCR and AT&T: Would the Combination Work?" *New York Times*, December 9, 1990, Section 3, 12.

23. Eben Shapiro, "AT&T Pressures NCR Board," *New York Times*, March 11, 1991, D1.

24. From advising in the AT&T–NCR deal, Dillon Read (NCR's advisor) received fees of $18.5 million; Morgan Stanley (AT&T's advisor) was paid $13.3 million.

25. Barnaby Feder, "AT&T Expects Big Write-Off," *New York Times*, July 19, 1991, D1.

26. Andrew Pollack, "Coming to the Rescue of a Computer Venture," *New York Times*, December 4, 1990, D1.

27. Carla Lazzareschi, "Will This Marriage Succeed?" *Los Angeles Times*, May 7, 1991, D1

28. Keller (1995).

29. Quoted from AT&T Form 10-K, 1994, filed with the Securities and Exchange Commission.

30. Quoted from AT&T Form 10-K, 1996, filed with the Securities and Exchange Commission.

31. Salomon Brothers, U.S. Equity Research, Telecommunications, "AT&T—The Clear Winner in Telecom," May 3, 1994.

32. AT&T Corporation Company Report, Prudential Securities, M. Elling, R. Walsh, C. Larsen, October 12, 1995, 11. "GIS Free to Find a New Home."

33. *New York Times*, May 5, 1995.

34. Quotation of John Myers, NCR programmer, in James Hannah, "NCR Celebrates Independence from AT&T," Associated Press Newswires, January 2, 1997.

35. This estimate is based on the following assumptions. AT&T's initial outlay was the sum of $7.48 billion for NCR's common stock, plus the equity value of its own computer business, which for simplicity I assume was nil. From 1990 to 1995, the computer business lost an accumulated $3.85 billion. It is not possible to obtain a clear pattern of these losses over time from AT&T's annual reports. But news reports suggest that the losses began after Gilbert Williamson's departure in March 1993. For simplicity, I assume that the computer business operated at breakeven from 1991 to 1992, and that the losses were spread evenly across 1993, 1994, and 1995. Also for simplicity, I assume that ongoing outlays for working capital or fixed assets are zero. The exit value for this calculation was the market value of NCR at the date of spin-off, $3.4 billion. The simplifying assumptions bias the negative return toward zero, suggesting that a more accurate estimate is probably worse by a wide margin. However, the refinements would add little to the qualitative conclusion that the investment in NCR was sharply value-destroying.

36. *New York Times*, July 29, 1995.

37. Brian O'Reilly, "Why Merck Married the Enemy," *Fortune*, September 20, 1993, 60.

38. Philip R. Alper, "Health Care: Report from the Trenches—High-Pressure Tactics Raise Doctor's Pressure," *Wall Street Journal*, November 17, 1993, A22.

39. Quotation of Philip R. Alper in Elyse Tanouye, "Changing Minds: Owning Medco, Merck Takes Drug Marketing the Next Logical Step," *Wall Street Journal*, May 31, 1994, A1.

40. The GAO finding is summarized in "Merck Settles Arm-Twisting Charges," *Business & Health*, December, 1995, at www.findarticles.com/p/articles/mi_m0903/is_n12_v13/ai_178575492.

41. Elyse Tanouye and Laurie McGinley, "GAO Report Says Merck-Medco Merger Raises Issues That Warrant Scrutiny," *Wall Street Journal*, November 13, 1995, B12.

42. Barbara Martinez, "Merck's Ties with Medco Details—Drug Maker Used Unit to Increase Market Share, Court Documents Show," *Wall Street Journal*, January 8, 2003.

43. Quoted in Barbara Martinez, "Pharmacy-Benefit Managers Are Stiffing Consumers, Suit Says," *Wall Street Journal*, March 19, 2003, D3.

44. Quotation of Charles Mulford in Barbara Martinez, "Merck Included Co-payments among Revenue," *Wall Street Journal*, June 21, 2002, C1.

45. Paraphrase of Robert Willens in Martin Sikora, "Merck to Get a Cash Payment in Spinning Off Medco," *Mergers and Acquisitions*, June 2003, 16.

46. See, for instance, Salancik (1977) and Keisler (1971).

9

December 1993: Renault's Proposed Merger with Volvo

On September 6, 1993, the CEOs of AB Volvo and Renault announced plans to merge Volvo's auto business with Renault.[1] This triggered a dramatic contest that temporarily destroyed a fifth of Volvo's market value, ousted Volvo's longstanding CEO and four directors, distracted the diplomatic relationship between Sweden and France, and when the proposal was finally withdrawn in December, set in motion changes in the firm's governance, ownership structure, and strategy and ended a major strategic alliance between Volvo and Renault. Renault/Volvo remains probably the most significant failure of a merger proposal within Europe.

A counterpoint to the story of Renault/Volvo is the contest to approve Hewlett-Packard (HP)'s acquisition of Compaq Computer in 2002. HP/Compaq is strikingly similar to Renault/Volvo in several respects: charismatic CEOs, depressed industrial conditions, declining market positions and profitability due to overcapacity in the industry, large prospective synergies, and fierce opposition by employees and influential shareholders. Yet in HP's case, the merger was approved. The comparison of these two cases highlights the vital roles of credibility of synergies, careful deal design and communication.

MOTIVES FOR MERGER: RENAULT AND VOLVO

In the early 1990s, three developments seemed to indicate a fundamental shift in competition in the worldwide automobile industry. First, growth in unit demand was slackening, reflecting in part the economic recession that had begun in North America in 1990 and in Europe in 1992. Second, the industry's capacity utilization was declining. In 1993, capacity utilization in Europe was 66 percent; worldwide it was 73 percent. Third, bases of quality, research breakthroughs, new product cycle times, and new forms of organization increasingly decided the winners and losers in fierce industry competition. For various reasons, smaller manufacturers had been slow to adopt these techniques or resisted adopting them altogether.

In 1993, Maryann Keller, a leading auto industry analyst, published an assessment of the leading automobile manufacturers concluding that "these companies and others would increasingly collide with each other. Too many countries are employing the same systems and technology to produce an excess of the same kinds of products for markets that are not growing fast enough to accommodate them all."[2]

Volvo was a small player in the global automotive industry. With an annual output of around 208,000 cars, it ranked 27th in the world. Pehr Gyllenhammar, Volvo's CEO, argued that Volvo was strategically vulnerable and needed a sizable partner with whom it could obtain advantageous purchasing arrangements, over whose volume of output it could amortize rising new product development costs, and whose deeper financial pockets could sustain Volvo through a moderately severe recession such as it had experienced in 1992. Some observers blamed Volvo's predicament on Gyllenhammar, pointing out that Volvo's share price had dramatically underperformed the Swedish stock market index (see Figure 9.1). Although he never discussed other strategic alternatives, he probably faced at least two possibilities, either exit from the auto business, or form a network of smaller, highly focused alliances. Volvo's strategic predicament suggested that some form of restructuring or change of strategy would be necessary, if not immediately, then over the medium term, but there is relatively little to suggest that a single, comprehensive partnership necessarily dominated other alternatives.

Volvo and Renault had a relatively long history of association, beginning with a components swap agreement in 1971, and deepening with

Share Price Performance:
Volvo vs. Swedish Stock Market Index

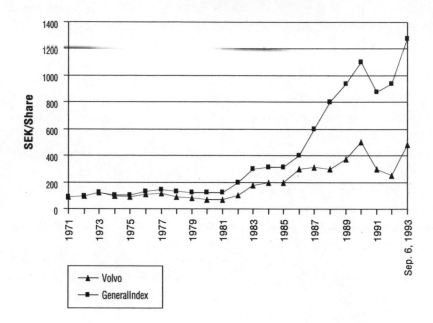

This figure gives the time-series of AB Volvo's >B' share prices and the Affarsvärlden Swedish stock market index from 1971 (the year of Pehr Gyllenhammar's appointment as CEO of Volvo) to 1993 (the year of the merger proposal and Gyllenhammar's resignation). For comparability, the market index is pegged at the beginning of the time series to Volvo's share price. The time-series of the >A' shares gives a similar indication, and for simplicity is ignored here.

Figure 9.1   **Price of Volvo's Shares, 1971 to 1993**

Renault's purchase of a minority equity interest in Volvo in 1980. Renault sold those shares at the time of its near-bankruptcy in 1985. With the installation of new management in 1986, Pehr Gyllenhammar offered to acquire Renault's truck-manufacturing business. Renault's CEO, Raymond Levy, demurred at the time, saying that, as a new executive, he wanted to settle into his new job before deciding on any such proposals. The two CEOs resumed discussions in earnest in the fall of 1989. Levy told me that initially the CEOs explored the concept of a cross-border merger along the lines of Royal Dutch and Shell. For political reasons, a merger was not an option then. The possibility of a merger, however, appears to have colored the thinking of managers in both companies as they announced in January 1990, a "joint venture." The details of this association did not emerge until September 1990, when it became apparent that this was to be a far-ranging strategic alliance.

The alliance agreement had been a complex engagement of the two firms—indeed, Levy called it a "marriage." Not only would each ally own a minority interest in the other ally, but also each would own a large minority interest in the other's auto and truck manufacturing units. The CEOs argued that the direct stakes in each other's manufacturing units would align the firms with each other's fortunes and promote industrial cooperation. Not discussed publicly was a complex poison pill provision, which would make it costly for either party to seek to unwind the alliance. In sum, this agreement constituted a significant escalation of commitment between the two firms, and dedicated them to the path of intimate industrial cooperation. Commitment escalated again in 1993 when the two firms proposed to merge.

The firms consummated the alliance with cross-acquisition of shares in January 1991, and over the next two years their endeavor showed modest success. Although slow to gain momentum, purchasing benefits could be foreseen more clearly by 1993. However, important projects for joint design of an auto and rationalization of truck manufacturing were stalling. Interviewees point to many causes, including French protectionism, Swedish–French cultural conflicts, a ponderous alliance bureaucracy of 21 committees, and distant senior leaders. Worse, Volvo's principal market, North America, slid into recession in late 1991, prompting one of the worst declines in reported financial performance in the firm's history.

In late 1992, Gyllenhammar and Louis Schweitzer (appointed CEO of Renault upon Levy's retirement in 1992) secretly began negotiating a merger of the two businesses. Unfortunately, the French Socialist Party, which was in power at the time, vetoed the proposal to privatize the country's largest state-owned enterprise. When the conservatives came to power in the elections of March 1993, negotiations between the two firms reopened. These talks culminated in the merger proposal announced on September 6, 1993, to form Renault–Volvo RVA.

The Volvo merger prospectus pointed to three main reasons for the merger: (1) to increase competitive advantages, (2) to improve financial strength and the ability to meet new capital requirements (estimated in Volvo's case to amount to between SEK 5 and 8 billion), and (3) to exploit operating efficiencies in procurement, research and development, and production. Gyllenhammar projected these merger economies to amount to SEK 16.4 billion on an undiscounted basis between 1994 and 2000, over and above those expected from the alliance alone.

The proposed transaction would affect the interests of Volvo shareholders in several important ways:

- The Renault management team would dominate the management of Renault–Volvo RVA. Pehr Gyllenhammar, Volvo's executive chairman, would be nominated chairman of RVA's supervisory board. The French government would nominate the chairman of the management board and the CEO of RVA; the likely nominee was Louis Schweitzer, CEO of Renault.

- The business relationship would change from a strategic alliance in which the partners enjoyed 50:50 control, to an acquisition. The French state would have 65 percent ownership of RVA, and Volvo 35 percent, though the actual voting of shares would take place through a holding company. The proposed control structure was complicated, and, as my interviews revealed, contributed to the difficulty in understanding the deal. Gyllenhammar argued to me that the holding company structure would have given AB Volvo a stronger voice in the control of RVA, and that a similar holding company structure had been used in other major cross-border mergers, such as the merger of Asea and Brown–Boverie.

- Initially, the shares in the company surviving from the combination (Newco) would be illiquid. The French government announced that it intended to privatize Renault–Volvo RVA in 1994, and that it would sell its shares principally to a *noyau dur* (or "hard core") of investors. Observers believed that leading candidates for this hard core included Matra-Hachette (a French industrial firm and co-producer with Renault of the Espace minivan) and French state-owned banks and insurance companies.

- The French government would retain an unusual right, an *action specifique* (literally, "specific share" and popularly called a "golden share") that reserved for the government the ability to prevent an investor from acquiring (or voting) more than a 17.85 percent (later amended to 35%) direct interest in RVA. Like a poison pill or control share antitakeover amendment, the golden share could change the voting power of certain (i.e., powerful) shareholders. The French had discretion in using the golden share, however, as the limitation was not automatic. Golden shares are now a common feature in the privatization of state-owned enterprises. Their origin is difficult to ascertain, although many observers cite the wave of British privatizations in the 1980s as the first in Europe to include golden shares. This right would last indefinitely.

In summary, the merger proposal offered Volvo's shareholders participation in the benefits of potential new synergies in exchange for a short position in a bundle of control options (i.e., the golden share, a privatization option concerning the timing and magnitude of any public offering of RVA shares, as well as a *noyau dur* option concerning the targeted purchasers of any shares offered). Collectively, these options granted the French state significant rights to determine RVA's strategy.

At the time of the merger announcement, 19.1 percent of Volvo's votes were presumed to support the merger.[3] Gyllenhammar's task was to increase the supporting coalition to more than 50 percent. The 17 largest investors in Volvo, mainly investment institutions, held 65.4 percent of the votes; the remainder was widely dispersed. Curiously, Gyllenhammar was slow to approach the institutional investors for their support; many of the meetings that ultimately did occur happened at the initiative of the institutions. He seemed inclined to let the deal speak for itself, rather than to be an advocate. Many interviewees suggest that this was consistent with Gyllenhammar's leadership style focused on grand strategy and vision.

REACTION TO THE MERGER PROPOSAL

Volvo's share prices fell dramatically following the announcement of the merger proposal on September 6, 1993. Over the following seven weeks, the abnormal returns to Volvo's shareholders accumulated to −22 percent, a decline in equity value of about SEK 8.3 billion (US$ 1.055 billion). A large portion of this wealth destruction is associated with the release of detailed information about the merger terms.

Newspapers and activist investors fanned the growing disbelief of the institutional investors. Two Swedish tabloids immediately condemned the

merger, largely on nationalistic grounds. The Association of Individual Investors, a shareholder advocacy group, requested information and met with
Volvo's management twice following the merger announcement. The Association voiced opposition to the merger on October 7 and solicited
proxies from its members. It also threatened to sue Volvo's directors. The
opposition coalition accounted explicitly for only about one-third of
Volvo's votes. But this eliminated any chance for a clear larger-than-two-
thirds majority and ensured that the directors would have to deal with a
lawsuit. Volvo's blue-collar union expressed support for the merger, believing that the deal would preserve their jobs and possibly seeing some benefit in allying with the Confederation Générale du Travail, Renault's leftist
trade union, but this support for the deal repelled, rather than attracted, the
institutional investors. Volvo's white-collar union, representing 5,000 employees, voiced opposition, as did the union of Volvo's engineers, representing 900 employees. Three former senior executives of Volvo wrote
newspaper columns opposing the deal. Until the end of October, however,
Volvo's institutional investors offered no public comments.

In mid-October, Swedish investors witnessed the spectacle of a management coup at Air France, another French state-owned enterprise. The
CEO, Bernard Attali, had sought to cut wages and jobs and to change
work rules at France's worst-performing state ward. The unions struck and
began to pressure the government to sack Attali. Swedish investors viewed
this confrontation as an acid test of the French government's resolve to run
state enterprises in a businesslike fashion, a crucial condition for them to
realize acceptable returns from RVA. When Attali was fired on October 16,
investors' doubts about the French connection gained momentum.

The institutional investors remained silent until they saw the formal
merger prospectus, published on October 26. Several institutional investors
had hoped that the prospectus would present a detailed justification for the
projected merger synergies, and that it would value Renault and Volvo's
automotive assets as a foundation for justifying the share exchange ratio in
the merger. However, the prospectus gave no information beyond what
was already in the public domain. The patience of the institutional investors snapped.

Within three days, two institutions, the 92–94 Fund (2.5 percent of
Volvo's votes) and SPP Insurance (4.5 percent), declared their opposition
to the deal, and a third, Skandia Insurance indicated that it would delay its
decision. Two of Stockholm's leading investment managers published a

newspaper article condemning the deal and calling for Gyllenhammar's resignation. They wrote, "We don't like the proposed Renault agreement, and we don't like the way Volvo has been abused over the years."[4] Reeling from the tide of institutional opposition, Gyllenhammar agreed to postpone the shareholder meeting by one month in order to give the institutions added information and time for them to assess it.

On November 4, Volvo's operating managers, at a golf outing in Marbella, Spain, told journalists that nine-month profits in Volvo's truck segment would be up sharply, indicating a strong recovery from a year earlier. This was confirmed at the formal release of nine-month figures on November 18. These revelations triggered a fresh round of accusations from the institutions that the merger had been negotiated when Volvo had been at a cyclical low in cash flows and that now, in the face of a buoyant recovery, the automotive business was being given away. More importantly, the buoyant reports turned the merger debate toward the central issue of valuation. An institutional investor was quoted as saying:

> Renault is basically making a bid for Volvo's cars and trucks and paying with its shares. As Volvo shareholders, we cannot assess what those Renault shares are worth until Renault has a market value.[5]

Lars-Erik Forsgårdh, president of the Association of Individual Investors, said, "The fundamental point is that Volvo has not succeeded in showing that this deal is good for its shareholders."[6]

In mid-November, Gyllenhammar undertook two efforts to elicit institutional support for the merger. First, he tried to reopen its merger negotiations with France, only to be rejected. The French minister of industry did issue a letter guaranteeing that the government would not exercise its golden share against Volvo as long as Volvo's equity interest in RVA did not exceed 35 percent. This letter was unsatisfactory to the institutions. Second, Volvo said that it would initiate a large (SEK 5 billion) rights offering if the merger were not approved. The institutions viewed this as an attempt to intimidate them, as it ignored the possibility of selling nonautomotive assets to finance the car and truck segments.

Two more funds expressed their opposition on November 24 and 29, and on November 30 Skandia Insurance announced that it would vote against the proposal. Volvo's largest institutional investor, the Fourth Fund, announced that it would vote for the deal. Six days later, however, the

Fourth Fund announced that it would reconsider its previous commitment to vote in favor. The Fourth Fund's board had barely approved its support for the deal, with a vote of 8 to 6, and only after very heavy lobbying by Volvo's blue-collar union representatives on the board.

As Volvo's board meeting approached on December 2, the largest bank in Scandinavia, S-E Banken (SEB) announced that it would vote "no." In explaining SEB's opposition, the CEO said:

> The information was not up to the standard we like to have in such an important case as this. . . . [Also] we are very concerned about the doubts among Volvo's personnel, especially the engineers. If you don't have your employees with you going into a merger like this it will be very damaging.[7]

In a surprise move on December 2, twenty-five senior managers informed the board of their opposition to the merger, leaving Pehr Gyllenhammar, Volvo's executive chairman, isolated in his own company. On that date, the board withdrew the proposal; Gyllenhammar and four directors resigned.

The significance of certain institutional announcements in the final days before the board meeting is worth noting. S-E Banken was the largest bank in Scandinavia, on whose board Gyllenhammar served as a director. Skandia Insurance was the largest insurance company in Scandinavia, and a firm with which Gyllenhammar had personal ties. Gyllenhammar's father had been CEO of Skandia, as had Gyllenhammar himself in his early thirties. Gyllenhammar's inability to sway these two "lead steer" institutions may have signaled to Volvo's board the strong hostility of institutional investors to the deal.

From publication of the prospectus (October 26) to the withdrawal of the proposal (December 2), the period when institutions expressed their "voice," the returns are significantly positive. The abnormal return on shares over all trading days was +28.33 percent. Investor activism rewarded Volvo's shareholders.

Following the board's rejection of the deal, a coalition of the activist Swedish institutional investors jointly nominated a new board of directors in December 1993 and called for a special shareholders' meeting, which elected them in January 1994. Volvo's management negotiated a dissolution of the strategic alliance with Renault. This reversed the cross-shareholdings in the two firms' operating units. Also, Volvo's management announced a new strategy for the firm that entailed focusing on the automotive industry. Volvo would sell investments in other businesses and use the proceeds to finance the development of new products. In addition, Volvo would remain independent, possibly exploiting small highly focused alliances but avoiding mergers and complex alliances. Volvo's share prices recovered dramatically in the weeks following the withdrawal of the merger proposal, nearly doubling by the annual meeting in April 1994. The French government partially privatized Renault in October 1994.

Ultimately, Gyllenhammar's strategic assessment of Volvo's vulnerability was sustained. Unable to achieve major efficiencies through a loose network of alliances, AB Volvo sold its automobile manufacturing operation to Ford Motor Company on March 31, 1999.

COUNTERPOINT: HEWLETT-PACKARD/COMPAQ

Founded in 1939 by Bill Hewlett and Dave Packard in a Palo Alto, California, garage, HP became an icon for the technology revolution. Hewlett and Packard remained closely identified with the firm long after their retirements (Hewlett retired as vice chairman in 1987 and Packard retired as chairman in 1993). Their corporate philosophy and values were known and appreciated throughout the organization; The HP Way,[8] which came to symbolize innovation, integrity, flexibility, teamwork, and individual contribution, did not materially change throughout the company's meteoric growth over the next half century.

By 1999, however, it was a matter of debate whether The HP Way was an effective response to the new challenges in the technology sector. Although innovation was still critical to long-term success, HP's industry was maturing. With that came the additional pressure of slimming margins, the importance of distribution efficiencies, and a need for developing long-term relationships with customers. Simply being a component manufacturer was not a viable mission for HP.

In July 1999, HP's CEO, Lewis Platt, retired. The board of directors named Carleton (Carly) S. Fiorina as president and CEO. After nearly 20 years at AT&T and Lucent Technologies, she had become the first company outsider named CEO in HP's 60-year history. Fiorina's challenge to lead "HP's reinvention as a company that makes technology work for businesses and consumers"[9] was no small task. She sought to transform HP "into the hottest new company of the Internet era without losing contact with the old-time commitment to quality and integrity that made the Hewlett-Packard name so trusted."[10] As an outsider she faced many existing HP managers who had developed under Bill Hewlett and Dave Packard's tutelage and subscribed to The HP Way.

In the midst of an increasingly competitive business environment, throughout 1999 and 2000, Hewlett-Packard's board of directors and executive management evaluated numerous alternatives for business growth to secure the company's viability. Although HP's Imaging and Printing Group (IPG) dominated its market segment, the company did not rank among the top three among competitors in personal computers, servers, storage, or services. Furthermore, HP's long-term dominance in imaging and printing was continually being challenged by Lexmark and Epson, who were selling inexpensive, lower quality printers in a bid for market share.

Recognizing the need to build strong complementary business lines while maintaining its strength in imaging and printing, the board of directors evaluated a range of strategic alternatives aimed at improving the company's position in enterprise computing and services.

Perhaps influenced by IBM's very successful 1990s turnaround, by mid-2000, HP's board and management settled on a strategy of developing the company's IT services business. IBM's Global Services group, which offered tailored "end-to-end" hardware, software, and business process solutions to customers, was the success story that emerged from the outmoded, pre-turnaround Big Blue. In gaining and retaining technology customers by viewing them as the business clients they ultimately were, IBM Global Services really had no other single solutions competitor in the highly fragmented IT services sector. As described by Louis Gerstner in his account of the IBM turnaround, in 1994 IBM had seen services as key to growth:

> . . . I believed that the industry's disaggregation into thousands of niche players would make IT services a huge growth segment of the industry overall. All of the industry growth analyses and projections, from our own staffs and from third-party firms, supported this. For IBM, this clearly suggested that we should grow our services business, which was a promising part of our portfolio. . . . Services, it was pretty clear, would be a huge revenue growth engine for IBM.

However, the more we thought about the long-term implication of this trend, an even more compelling motivation came into view. If customers were going to look to an integrator to help them envision, design, and build end-to-end solutions, then the companies playing that role would exert tremendous influence over the full range of technology decisions—from architecture and applications to hardware and software choices.

This would be a historic shift in customer buying behavior. For the first time, services companies, not technology firms, would be the tail wagging the dog. Suddenly, a decision that seemed rational and straightforward—pursue a growth opportunity—became a strategic imperative for the entire company. . . ."[11]

In 2000, HP was pursuing a strategy to expand its services business through both organic growth, fueled by increased investment in its services business, and possible acquisitions. HP subsequently entered into discussions to acquire the consulting services business of PricewaterhouseCoopers LLP (PwC). However, by fall 2000, these discussions had stalled. In early 2001, HP retained the services of McKinsey & Company to assist in its continued effort to implement the new strategy.

Also in 2000, Compaq directors had grown impatient with Compaq's poor performance and were encouraging Compaq's CEO, Michael Capellas, to explore a potential business combination with another computer company. Capellas subsequently presented to the board the relative strengths and weaknesses of potential pairings with companies such as Dell, Sun, EMC Corporation, and Hewlett-Packard among others, and according to Capellas, the strengths of a combined HP and Compaq were "intuitively obvious." "We wanted to be the next IBM," Capellas said.[12]

Discussions of a business combination between Hewlett-Packard and Compaq began in June 2001, during licensing conversations between the two companies. Carly Fiorina contacted Michael Capellas to discuss Compaq's interest in licensing HP-UX software. After a period of deliberation, Capellas contacted Fiorina to discuss the potential for a broader strategic relationship based on synergies between the two companies. By June 29, 2001, HP and Compaq had executed a confidentiality agreement, and the companies commenced mutual business due diligence investigations. However, by August 5, the merger negotiations had stalled due, in part, to disagreement over Michael Capellas's role in the combined company.

Compaq called off the talks and the deal remained on hold until late August.[13] The discussions resumed when Capellas agreed to accept the role of president and chief operating officer of Newco, reporting to Fiorina. On September 2 and 3, 2001, HP and Compaq executives, along with their respective financial and legal advisors met to negotiate the final terms of the merger agreement. Both boards unanimously approved and executed the merger agreement as of September 4, 2001. During the evening of September 3, 2001, HP and Compaq issued a joint press release announcing the merger agreement.

RATIONALE FOR THE MERGER OF HP AND COMPAQ

Described by insiders as a "merger of equals," HP and Compaq had different strengths in their lines of business, which together produced a complementary set of products and services, better able to serve customers at lower cost.

Prior to merger discussions, HP and Compaq had been focused on growing their enterprise computing and Information Technology (IT) services businesses, two areas in which each company had areas of strength—Compaq was the more significant player in enterprise systems in general—but in which neither company was dominant across the board. By merging, the newly combined company would be a major force in enterprise computing and perhaps within the top three in services. Furthermore, with customers looking to maintain strong relationships with fewer technology vendors, the merger better positioned the combined company to provide their clientele with a wider spectrum of products and services.

In February 2002, HP's three primary lines of business were: (1) Imaging and Printing, (2) Computing, consisting of desktops, notebooks, servers and storage products, and (3) IT Services. Although the market leader in imaging and printing, HP's Computing and IT Services businesses noticeably lagged the competition, and the company did not have an organic growth strategy for these businesses. Unlike Compaq, which had moved toward a direct distribution model in response to Dell's cost competitiveness and now shipped a majority of its PC's direct, HP shipped only 15 percent of its PC's direct to customers.[14] To lower costs, HP had recently announced plans to outsource its PC manufacturing operations, although it still acknowledged the need for further cost reductions.

Compaq's three primary divisions were: (1) Access, consisting of commercial and consumer PCs, (2) Enterprise Computing, which included servers and storage products and (3) Global Services. The company was the market leader in PCs and shipped more units internationally than within the United States. Although direct distribution had helped lower its costs, Access still operated at a negative margin. By merging with HP's PC business, management believed that positive operating margins could once again be achieved through economies of scale. Compaq was also the market leader in fault-tolerant computing and industry standard servers, where in the former, HP did not have a presence and in the latter, HP's position was not strong. Conversely, Compaq was not strong in the UNIX market, where HP-UX was a top supplier. On a revenue basis, Compaq was the leading supplier of storage systems in the world, and HP was strong in high-end servers.[15]

In combination, the merged company would be a dominant leader in servers and well positioned to exploit the fast growing "storage area networks" trend in the storage market. By combining these complementary server and storage lines, the merged company reduced costs, offered a comprehensive array of products for enterprise customers and could more effectively allocate R&D for growth in its enterprise computing business.

In addition to strategic benefits, the merger would deliver significant financial benefits to shareholders as well. Through both significant cost savings and improved profitability of business lines, substantial earning improvements for shareholders would be realized. By mid-2004, management projected recurring, annual, pretax cost savings of $2.5 billion. Management projected these cost savings to have a value of $5.00 to $9.00 per share, even taking into consideration annual revenue losses of $4.1 billion in 2004 (of total projected 2004 revenue of $92.8 billion) resulting directly from the merger. After realizing anticipated cost savings from synergies, management anticipated a substantial improvement in operating margins beginning in the company's 2003 fiscal year, in which they projected an overall operating margin of 8 percent to 10 percent. Segment operating margins were anticipated to improve.

REACTION BY THE MARKET AND WALTER HEWLETT

At the close of trading on September 4, 2001, the first day of trading after the merger was announced, HP's stock price dropped 18.7 percent to close at $18.87 and by September 10, 2001, HP's shares had fallen 22.9 percent (see Figure 9.2).

On November 6, 2001, Walter B. Hewlett announced his intent to vote against the proposed business combination of Hewlett-Packard and Compaq. In response, HP shares, which were still lower than their announcement day levels, closed up 17.3 percent.

Son of HP co-founder William R. Hewlett and a member of HP's board of directors, Walter B. Hewlett had attended five of HP's eight summer 2001 board meetings where the merger was discussed. He also had attended the September 3, 2001, HP board meeting where he joined other board members in voting unanimous support for the merger. However, on November 6 Hewlett said, "After careful deliberation, consultation with my financial advisor and consideration of developments since the announcement of the merger, I have decided to vote against the transaction."[16]

Citing the market's strong negative reaction to the announcement, Hewlett expressed concerns over diluting HP's high margin printing and imaging business with Compaq's low margin, fiercely competitive PC business. "With this transaction, we get what we don't want, we jeopardize

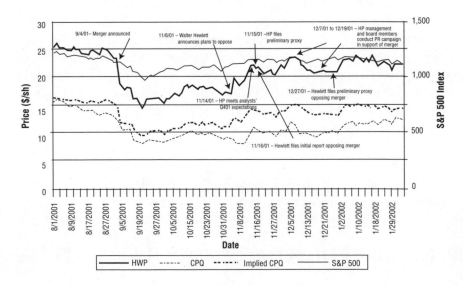

Figure 9.2 **Market Prices for HWP, CPQ, Implied CPQ, and S&P 500 (8/1/01–2/4/02)**

what we already have, and we compromise our ability to get what we need," said Hewlett.[17]

On November 16, 2001, Walter Hewlett filed with the SEC a 71-page report, which detailed his reasons for opposing the merger. In addition to the business portfolio shift away from imaging and printing in favor of PCs, Hewlett's filing identified three other areas of concern: (1) the merger would not solve HP's strategic problems, as he believed the company would still be poorly positioned to lead in either enterprise computing or services; (2) the financial impact on shareholders was unattractive, substantiated by the dramatic postannouncement decline in HP's stock price since the announcement date; and (3) integration risk was substantial, as the two companies were widely believed to have very different cultures and values.[18]

Thus began an active campaign by Walter Hewlett for a negative vote on the merger proposal. Over the following months leading to the proxy vote, Hewlett amended his initial information filing with the SEC numerous times by providing hundreds of pages of documentation supporting his claim that the merger rationale was flawed. Hewlett succeeded in creating a public relations battle that sought to sway the opinions of shareholders, analysts, and industry observers. As Hewlett managed to keep the HP–Compaq merger controversy at the forefront of coverage by business news reporters and Wall Street analysts, other high profile dissenters entered the fray.

On December 7, the Packard Foundation, controlling 10 percent of outstanding HP shares and the single largest HP shareholder, decided to oppose the merger. This prompted the following comments from Patrick McGurn of Institutional Shareholder Services, an independent advisory group that analyzes proxies and advises clients on how to vote. "If they lose both families, I can't see it going through. . . . It's a real mess now."[19]

While much of Walter Hewlett's basis for opposing the merger was related to strategic issues, he also claimed that it was just a bad deal financially. Largely discounting the value of synergies, Hewlett contended that HP was paying too much for Compaq and that shareholder value would be destroyed by the merger.

At a time when the NASDAQ had suffered a 30 percent drop during the past 12 months of highly volatile trading activity, markets were still skittish as a result of the September 11, 2001, terrorist attacks and many technology firms were projecting continuing losses for 2002, understanding the value of the HP–Compaq merger was no small undertaking for shareholders. Arguably, the world was a much different place in early 2002 than it had been on September 3, 2001, when the deal was announced, and it was certainly fair to question whether a good deal had been struck. Valuation multiples for comparable companies as well as recent comparable transactions varied widely, due to the uncertain but largely negative outlook for the tech sector, specifically, and the economy overall.

TERMS OF THE MERGER

In comparison to the complexity of the Renault/Volvo deal, the HP/Compaq deal structure was simple. It would entail a straightforward exchange of shares: Each Compaq shareholder would receive 0.6325 shares of HP common stock, resulting in an approximate 36 percent ownership of the newly merged company by former Compaq shareholders. At the announcement on September 3, 2001, the implied acquisition premium was 18.9 percent. But by February 2002, the premium had dwindled to 14.3 percent.

The company was to retain the Hewlett-Packard name, and the HWP ticker symbol would be changed to HPQ. Carly Fiorina, HP's chairman and CEO, was to maintain those positions in the merged company, and Michael Capellas, Compaq's chairman and CEO was to be named president of the new HP. The resulting board of directors would have 11 members with a maximum of two employee directors; six directors would come from HP. The merger was described as a tax-free reorganization, in which a Hewlett-Packard subsidiary, Heloise Merger Corporation, was created solely for the purposes of merging with Compaq. This was a reverse triangular merger that would result in a tax-free reorganization in which HP would control Compaq's assets through a wholly owned subsidiary, thereby limiting HP's exposure to Compaq's liabilities. The transaction would be tax-free to Compaq's shareholders. Although a shareholder vote of the target was required, if necessary, a minority freeze-out could be accomplished. This form of transaction would limit HP's ability to sell or spin off assets immediately prior to the transaction.

Carly Fiorina and Michael Capellas described the business combination as a merger of equals (MOE), a mutually beneficial marriage of two technology companies each with different strengths and areas of contribution. Whether from euphemism or earnest intent, informed observers could be justifiably dubious of the MOE characterization. In spite of its presumably positive intended consequences, Walter Hewlett took issue with the "merger of equals" and later stated his view to the Council of Institutional Investors:

> A merger of equals is the toughest kind of integration to pull off. It is much harder than an acquisition, and certainly much harder than a spin-off. A spin-off creates focus, creates winners, and doesn't require integration. In mergers of equals there is invariably a battle for power, sometimes subtle at first but often becoming quite blatant, and there is no reason to think it will be different this time. Who will win two years from now? Texas or Silicon Valley? *The Dallas Morning News* is already placing its chips on Michael Capellas, and the *Houston Chronicle's* technology columnist has said that Compaq would be better off without HP and the huge problems integration would bring."[20]

The MOE described a merger of firms that are approximately equal in size and where a low (or zero) acquisition premium is paid. By indicating that neither party is strongly dominant in the combined company, the term often conveys an attitude of teamwork and cooperation. Although both buyer and target benefit from the realization of synergies that result from the merger, given the lower acquisition premium typically paid, the target's shareholders are believed to bear more of the cost of an MOE structure. It might facilitate getting a deal done and be beneficial to the buyer's shareholders in the short term.

By acquiring Compaq with equity, HP would be issuing more than one billion new shares of stock. The merger would likely dilute earnings per share for HP shareholders if full synergies were not realized.

THE CAMPAIGN FOR VOTES

In light of the growing block of "no" votes, as well as Hewlett's intensified public relations efforts to encourage shareholders' rejection of the merger, HP began its own PR campaign. On December 19, 2001, HP filed with the SEC a package of slide presentation materials that it had prepared for shareholders rebutting Hewlett's criticisms. In summary, HP claimed that Walter Hewlett had (1) presented a static and narrow view of HP and the industry, (2) selectively ignored synergies in several keys areas of analysis, (3) displayed simplistic antimerger bias by ignoring empirical evidence of successful mergers, and (4) offered no alternatives.[21]

Embarking on the spoiler's version of a proxy road show, between December 2001, and March 2002, Walter B. Hewlett traveled the country meeting with fund managers, trusts, and other investor groups soliciting their support for a "no" vote on the merger. Hewlett continued utilizing the services of the boutique advisory firms Friedman Fleischer & Lowe and The Parthenon Group to present his analysis supporting a shareholder rejection of the merger. Full-page ads were run in prominent newspapers and business journals, a web site was launched to facilitate the public's access to information regarding rejection of the merger, and the opposition campaign gained steam. Hewlett had conducted a sophisticated investor relations campaign.

As the March 19 shareholders' meeting approached, Hewlett continued fanning the flames in the hope of keeping HP embroiled in the contentious proxy vote contest. During late February and early March, Hewlett's presentations, SEC filing, and press releases described the rich compensation packages Ms. Fiorina and Mr. Capellas would receive if the merger occurred, as well as the results of customer surveys and employee opinion polls, all of which suggested that HP shareholders would be better off without a Compaq merger. Foreseeing a failed merger vote, Hewlett began to suggest that Ms. Fiorina would need to be replaced for the company to move successfully beyond the proxy battle and to pursue a go-it-alone strategy. This elicited a forceful response from HP:

> The reported action of Walter Hewlett to recruit former HP CEO Lew Platt as a replacement CEO for Carly Fiorina is an outrage and blatant disregard of a director's responsibilities. In addition, an erroneous headline in an early posting of the article on FT.COM, which is being corrected by the publication, said that HP itself was involved in the recruiting of the former CEO, which is clearly false.
>
> This proxy contest is not about the office of the Chairman and CEO. It is about a business strategy strongly supported by management and all of the members of the Board of Directors other than Walter Hewlett.

Walter Hewlett intends to mislead and distract shareowners by raising this issue. His unilateral action, without conferring with his fellow board members, to publicly engage in an attack on the CEO position and to recruit for that position is a blemish on the character and quality of HP. All of HP's directors other than Walter Hewlett have declared their unequivocal support for Carly Fiorina and believe that his calls for her departure are presumptuous, baseless and irresponsible.[22]

Ever aware of the importance of institutional investors, during a presentation to the Council of Institutional Investors on March 11, 2002, Hewlett summarized his views on the flawed strategy:

> First, with this merger, HP would be committing itself to be the world's largest provider of commodity computing: this is a terrible business, where the profits go to Intel, Microsoft and Dell.
>
> Second, it is a business in which scale alone does not lead to profitability. If scale were the answer, HP which is smaller than Compaq, would be less profitable. In fact the case is just the opposite: HP is more profitable. If scale were the answer, Dell would not have overtaken Compaq as the number one supplier of PC's.
>
> Third, HP's goal of "end to end" solutions for everyone will lead to lack of focus. Trying to do too much has been the downfall of many conglomerates. As *Business Week* said, it is like a chef trying to simultaneously compete with McDonalds and Le Cirque. HP can't out Dell-Dell and out IBM-IBM at the same time; and make no mistake, that is what this merger would require.
>
> Fourth, HP has some key strategic gaps in services and software that this merger does not fill."[23]

In early March, 2002, Institutional Shareholder Services (ISS) was scheduled to deliver its proxy vote recommendation to HP shareholders. Leading up to the ISS announcement, shareholder sentiment had begun to swing against the deal as Hewlett's vote "no" campaign gained momentum. Led by Fiorina, HP had stepped up its efforts to discredit the antimerger movement by criticizing the Hewlett camp for not having an alternative plan, and personal attacks were exchanged between Fiorina and Hewlett.

Both sides of the HP proxy battle had made presentations to ISS in the hope of influencing the independent advisory group's decision. As many clients vote according to the ISS recommendation, the odds for merger approval improved with the ISS nod but were still by no means certain.

On March 5 and 6, 2002, ISS recommended that the respective shareholders of both HP and Compaq vote in favor of the merger. There were several key reasons for the ISS endorsement: (1) ISS agreed with management on the strategic and financial outlook for the deal, determining that cost synergies were achievable and revenue losses were realistic; (2) integration efforts made by the two companies had progressed well; and (3) ISS was unable to "confidently embrace" Walter Hewlett's plan to maintain significant strategic focus on HP's imaging and printing business.[24]

Undeterred by the ISS recommendation, Walter Hewlett continued his campaign to defeat the merger and issued a critique of the ISS report, summarized by the following conclusions:

- ISS' recommendation contradicts the stock market's clear assessment of the proposed merger.
- ISS neglected to provide any financial analysis of the proposed merger.
- ISS assumes that the substantial integration risk is mitigated by management's planning process despite management's lack of merger experience and the extensive history of failed merger integrations in the industry.
- ISS does not evaluate the risk/reward trade-off between the "focus and execute" strategy and the proposed merger.[25]

THE OUTCOME: HEWLETT-PACKARD/COMPAQ

Approaching the March 19, 2002, vote deadline, both sides had made extensive efforts to meet with institutional shareholders to present their positions on the merger. The lobbying efforts by both Walter Hewlett and HP were also focused on individual shareholders, with those owning as few as 200 shares receiving phone calls and mailings of proxy materials urging them to vote.[26]

The rift that had developed between Hewlett and the rest of HP's directors and management characterized the mood of shareholders present at the meeting, as Hewlett received a standing ovation and Fiorina was booed several times. There were even accusations made by Walter Hewlett's associates that the meeting had gotten off to a late start due to last minute lobbying by HP of Deutsche Asset Management who purportedly had switched their votes at the meeting.

After the vote deadline, HP claimed a "slim but sufficient" margin of victory, but Walter Hewlett, who said the outcome remained "too close to call," refused to concede defeat until all shareholder votes were tallied. At a news conference, Mr. Hewlett maintained his optimism that the antimerger campaign would prevail but also said that he would like to remain on the HP board, believing that he could "add value to the company."

By April 17, 2002, more than four weeks since the shareholder vote, HP announced that a preliminary vote tally had confirmed shareholder approval of the merger. On May 1, 2002, HP announced that it had won the election with 51.39 percent of votes cast. The deal was closed May 3, 2002. The newly merged Hewlett-Packard Company began trading under its new HPQ ticker symbol on May 6, 2002.

Walter Hewlett sued HP alleging that HP had obtained votes by "improper means" and that the company had seriously misled investors regarding the progress of its integration plans with Compaq. The court decided in HP's favor. Thereafter, the company announced that it would not nominate Walter Hewlett as a candidate for its board, based on his "ongoing adversarial relationship with the company."

By the end of the second quarter after the merger had closed, HP reported cost savings above plan. One year after the merger Fiorina reported that HP had successfully met its targeted cost savings of $3.5 billion. But after three years, HP showed volatile quarterly EPS and operating margins below target. Fiorina noted that the computer industry had endured its worst recession since the merger and that higher volatility was to be expected. In February 2005, Carly Fiorina resigned at the request of HP's board, who refused to call the merger with Compaq a mistake, and instead cited problems in her execution of the firm's strategy.

REFLECTION: THE VALUE OF COMMUNICATION, CREDIBILITY, AND CONTROL

The collapse of the proposed Volvo/Renault merger bears many similarities with other deals from hell. The story features a number of *cognitive bases* (hubris, bad judgment, sunk cost mentality, escalation of commit-ments, and path dependence).[27] *Business conditions* were turbulent, driven by the grinding overcapacity in the global auto industry. The merging companies and the deal were *highly complex*; the deal terms and the long-standing joint venture between the firms *tightly coupled* their fortunes. What distinguishes this case, however, are failures in *management choices* and in *team execution*. Especially prominent is the failure in communica-tion with investors regarding the value of synergies, and the control pro-visions for the new firm. Hung in the balance, the benefits of potential synergies were judged to be less than the value of diminished control by the Swedish investors over their automotive assets. To succeed in a con-tested merger campaign, Carly Fiorina showed what is required: A clear plan, credible savings, solid support from the board of directors, meeting the voters face-to-face, and a blow-for-blow response to criticism that gives back as hard as it receives.

Gyllenhammar himself explained the failure of the merger proposal in behavioral terms: irrationality, Swedish cultural chauvinism, or an en-vious vendetta against him. In April 1993 the Association of Individual Investors compelled Gyllenhammar to reveal that his compensation was SEK 9.5 million, revealing that he was the highest-paid executive in Scandinavia at a time when Volvo reported losses and was closing plants. CEO compensation is a lightning rod for criticism. Gyllenhammar states that he was opposed by a secret coalition centered on the Wallenberg in-terests, the only other Swedish industrial group of size and significance comparable to Volvo, which sought to bring an independent Volvo under their influence. Several interviewees, however, discount the significance of this fact. A journalist, Sven-Ivan Sundqvist,[28] argues that over time Gyllenhammar had amassed enough enemies in the Swedish business community that he had no base of support with which to confront the opposition. This suggests that the merger failed because of psychology or politics. Yet such an explanation is ultimately unsatisfying, for it sheds lit-tle light on the roots of opposition to *this* deal. For instance, if the merger of Renault and Volvo were to have created shareholder value, it seems doubtful that Gyllenhammar's opponents would have successfully defeated the proposal.

A counter-assessment, offered by Swedish institutional investors in interviews and by Sundqvist, explains the failure to merge as follows. Volvo's shares materially underperformed the Swedish stock market over the term of Gyllenhammar's leadership. Gyllenhammar led the firm into a number of alliances and diversifying acquisitions that failed to deliver the performance improvements investors expected. The strategic alliance with Renault that Gyllenhammar personally crafted was not going well, and institutional investors surmised that otherwise Gyllenhammar would not have advocated merger. In 1993 the merger proposal was a bad deal, presented badly: The control provisions were confusing, and the projected synergies were not justified. Eventually it was learned that the synergies were estimated not by Volvo's staff, but by outside advisers to Gyllenhammar. Rather than lending credibility, this served to heighten suspicions that Gyllenhammar was manipulating the estimates to serve his own ambitions. Eventually the investors discounted the merger synergies and concluded that the control rights represented an expropriation of Volvo equity value by the French state. From this perspective, the deal failed on its economics.

An internal study by Volvo supports this view. It claims that the golden share and uncertainty about the privatization of Renault were the key drivers of the collapse of the merger proposal. Reflecting on the predicted synergies, the author of the study, Arne Wittlov, said, "People quite simply did not believe in the benefits of co-operation."[29]

In the abstract, the synergy benefits seemed reasonable. No interviewee or published source disputes Gyllenhammar's strategic rationale for the alliance or merger. In an industry characterized by scale economies, the small producer will have a cost disadvantage and therefore an incentive to increase size through alliances and mergers. In other words, the merger did not fail for want of a sound strategic motive. At issue, however, was Gyllenhammar's credibility in estimating the size of those synergies, and in actually harvesting them.

Compounding Gyllenhammar's credibility problem was the alteration in control. In essence, the proposed deal would transform the Volvo shareholders from being complete owners of their automotive assets into being minority shareholders in a larger enterprise, where the partner was one of the most interventionist European governments. The French would enjoy 65 percent voting control, a golden share (i.e., a veto over strategic changes in the new firm), discretion over the timing and pace of privatization, and likely sale of a controlling bloc of shares to French corporations. The negative abnormal returns at the release of new information about the terms of merger is consistent with investors' growing clarity about the value transfer implicit in the French control options, and with their incredulity at the projected synergies. My analysis[30] suggests that the control options were worth at least SEK 3.12 billion under conservative assumptions, or 8.3 percent of AB Volvo's market value of equity just before the merger announcement. This case suggests that *control is valuable; CEOs underprice it at their own risk.* In his public statements, Gyllenhammar seemed to minimize the importance of the control options in the deal. Yet, if he truly believed in the synergy forecasts that Volvo published, the implied value of the control options would be material. This internal inconsistency supports the claims of Sundqvist and various interviewees that the proposed merger of Volvo and Renault failed in no small part because of doubts about the credibility of its chief advocate.

The importance of these considerations is highlighted in the comparison with the HP/Compaq merger contest. Table 9.1 summarizes the main

TABLE 9.1   KEY DIFFERENCES: RENAULT/VOLVO VERSUS HP/COMPAQ

	Renault/Volvo	*HP/Compaq*
CEO, Advocate	Pehr Gyllenhammar: distant, "imperial." Strategist: frames alternatives, analytic.	Carly Fiorina: aggressive communicator. Marketer: listens, sells, handles objections.
Campaign	Issue reports. Let proposal speak for itself. Solo act by Gyllenhammar.	Active campaign for votes. Personal outreach by CEO. Large coordinated effort including senior executives and board of directors.
Synergies	Doubted to the end.	Credible to ISS and many major institutional investors.
Liquidity	Shares of Newco will be illiquid. General commitment for a public offering.	Shares of Newco will be liquid from time of merger. Listing on NYSE.
Control and Social Issues	Deal structure gives valuable control options to French government. Volvo managers and shareholders will be minority.	Structured as a merger of equals, though some power advantage accrues to HP (in appointment of CEO and board seats).

differences in the two cases. First, we see a remarkable difference in the key advocates for the deals. Gyllenhammar was a distant leader, removed from both employees and investors, a visionary of the integrated Europe, arrogant, and in the view of some, "imperial." Fiorina was an aggressive communicator, eager to take her case for the merger to investors and employees. A saleswoman by experience, she could read the customer and handle objections. No less a visionary than Gyllenhammar, she conveyed a sense of urgency about the need for transformation. As a result of their differing leadership styles, Gyllenhammar and Fiorina led very different campaigns for votes. Gyllenhammar offered a prospectus and consultants' reports, preferring to let the deal speak for itself. Fiorina conducted an active campaign, personally contacting all major shareholders and leading a large coordinated effort of the senior executives of HP.

The differences in communication and leadership led to very different perceptions about the benefits of merger. The credibility of synergies was challenged in both mergers, but Fiorina was successful in persuading major investors that the savings could be realized. Gyllenhammar, on the other hand, hindered by a legacy of financial underperformance and previous deals that had fizzled, failed to make a credible case for the savings. As a result, the Volvo shareholders became wary of the implications of the deal for liquidity and control.

Finally, the two deals presented very different value propositions to investors. Volvo's deal meant marriage to a French state-owned enterprise, anathema to a private investor. The deal offered Volvo's investors illiquid shares in a firm about which the French government had made vague promises to privatize and in which the government held perpetual rights to intervene in major business decisions. The control options represented material transfers of value from the Volvo shareholders to France. In contrast, the HP/Compaq deal was straightforward: relatively little change in liquidity and control with which to distract shareholders from the value of synergies or the strategic motives of the deal.

NOTES

1. The analysis of Renault/Volvo derives from 20 field interviews of executives at both Volvo and Renault, as well as of knowledgeable observers, and draws from insights originally presented in Bruner (1999) and my collaborative work with

(Bruner and Spekman, 1998). The segment on HP/Compaq draws from case studies prepared by Anna Buchanan, research assistant, under my direction. I am grateful for the comments of numerous students, friends, and colleagues.

2. Keller (1993), 213.

3. The "committed" camp included Renault, which owned 10 percent of Volvo's votes, and two investment companies that had sizable cross-shareholdings with Volvo.

4. Quoted in David Bartal and Ian Hardin, "Pressure Mounts on Car Chief," *The European*, November 9, 1993, 14.

5. Quoted in Carnegy and Ridding (1993).

6. Quoted in Brown-Humes (1993).

7. Quoted in Carnegy (1993b).

8. For additional reading, see "The HP Way: How Bill Hewlett and I Built Our Company," by David Packard (David Kirby and Karen Lewis, editors), originally published in 1995, with a paperback version in June, 1996 (HarperBusiness).

9. HP Company web site, www.hp.com, "HP History and Facts—Timeline: 1990's."

10. Robert M. Fulmer, Philip A. Gibbs, and Marshall Goldsmith, "The New HP Way: Leveraging Strategy with Diversity, Leadership Development and Decentralization," *Strategy & Leadership*, October–December 1999, 22.

11. Quoted from "Who Says Elephants Can't Dance?" by Louis V. Gertsner Jr., published by HarperBusiness, 2002, 124.

12. Quoted from "Perfect Enough: Carly Fiorina and the Reinvention of Hewlett-Packard," by George Anders, published by the Penguin Group, 2003, 117.

13. As described in "Backfire: Carly Fiorina's High Stakes Battle for the Soul of Hewlett-Packard," by Peter Burrows, published by John Wiley & Sons, 2003, 184.

14. Joint proxy statement/prospectus delivered by Hewlett-Packard and Compaq, February 4, 2002, 58.

15. Joint proxy statement/prospectus delivered by Hewlett-Packard and Compaq, February 4, 2002, 58.

16. "Hewletts against Compaq," *CNN Money*, November 6, 2001.

17. "A Stunning Reversal for HP's Marriage Plans," *BusinessWeek* online, November 19, 2001.

18. This information appears in "Report to the Trustees of the William R. Hewlett Revocable Trust on the Proposed Merger of Hewlett-Packard and Compaq," prepared by Friedman Fleischer & Lowe and The Parthenon Group, filed with the SEC by Walter B. Hewlett, November 16, 2001.

19. "Family Affair: H-P Deal's Fate Rests with Skeptical Heirs of Company Founders—A No from Packard Bloc Could Doom Takeover of Struggling Compaq—New Courtship of Investors," *Wall Street Journal* (Eastern edition), November 9, 2001, A1.

20. "Council of Institutional Investors Presentation Comments," made by Walter Hewlett, March 11, 2002, and filed with the SEC March 12, 2002, 8.

21. This information appears in the "Summary Observations on Walter Hewlett Filings" section of HP's presentation slide package, "HP Position on Compaq Merger," provided to shareholders and filed with the SEC on December 19, 2001.

22. HP press release: "HP Issues Statement Regarding Hewlett Action to Recruit New CEO," March 2, 2002.

23. "Council of Institutional Investors Presentation Comments," made by Walter Hewlett, March 11, 2002, and filed with the SEC March 12, 2002, 10.

24. "H-P Garners Major Endorsement of Deal—ISS Advisory Firm Backs Acquisition of Compaq; Vote Seen as Still Close," *Wall Street Journal* (Eastern edition), by Pui-Wing Tam and Gary McWilliams, March 6, 2002, A3.

25. "A Critique on the ISS Report," by Walter B. Hewlett, filed with the SEC on March 8, 2002.

26. "Divided Electorate: For Fund Managers, Hewlett-Compaq Vote Is Agonizing Choice—Personal Lobbying by Fiorina Helped Turn a Rout into a Very Tight Race—Early Results Possible Today," *Wall Street Journal* (Eastern edition), Pui-Wing Tam, March 19, 2002, A1. Copyright © 2002 by Dow Jones & Co. Inc. Reproduced with permission of Dow Jones & Co. Inc. in the Format Trade Book via Copyright Clearance Center.

27. Volvo's commitment to an alliance with Renault in 1990 created a path dependence that contributed to the destruction of wealth in the merger attempt. This case illustrates other hypothesized sources of wealth destruction in mergers, such as hubris, Roll (1986); managerial entrenchment, Morck, Schleifer, and Vishny (1988); Jensen (1986); bad judgment, Morck, Schleifer, and Vishny (1990); and the escalation of commitment, Lys and Vincent (1995).

28. Sundqvist (1994).

29. Quoted in Carnegy (1994b).

30. Bruner (1999).

10

December 1994:
The Acquisition of Snapple
by Quaker Oats

O n November 2, 1994, Quaker Oats announced an agreement to acquire Snapple Beverage Corporation for $1.7 billion, merely two percent more than the closing price a day earlier and 48 percent *below* Snapple's high share price of the year.[1] Notwithstanding the apparently low acquisition premium, Quaker's share price fell 9.9 percent on the announcement day, a loss in market value of over $1 billion. Quaker had been rumored to be a takeover target. This acquisition would reduce the likelihood of takeover. Moreover, many observers believed that even at the low acquisition premium, Quaker had paid perhaps $1 billion too much.[2]

Twenty-nine months later, Quaker announced an agreement to sell Snapple for $300 million and take a $1.4 billion write-off on the sale. In addition to accumulated operating losses and certain tax benefits, analysts estimated that the total undiscounted loss ranged between −$1.2 and −$1.5 billion. Soon afterward, William Smithburg, a 30-year veteran of the firm and CEO since 1979, announced that he would resign. Smithburg's departure was the last of a string of senior executive resignations and dismissals related to the brand. One reporter[3] noted a steady "brain drain" from the company, and low morale in the organization. And in financing the acquisition of Snapple, Quaker sold profitable pet food and candy businesses, which, had they been kept, would have sustained a much higher level of performance for the firm.

A counterpoint to the story of Quaker/Snapple is the acquisition of the Jif and Crisco businesses by J.M. Smucker from Procter & Gamble in 2001. That case is similar to Quaker/Snapple in several respects: branded consumer foods; product line extensions that built on existing strengths; and acquisitions aimed at restoring growth to maturing firms. In Smucker's case, the merger was successfully concluded, value was created, and expectations for the new brands were met or exceeded. The comparison of these two cases highlights the negative impact of competitor reactions and the resistance within a company's own supply chain.

SNAPPLE BEVERAGE CORPORATION

Snapple was founded in 1972 to distribute healthy beverages such as fruit juices, natural sodas, and fruit drinks to health food stores. In 1987 the firm began distributing its own ready-to-drink (RTD) tea and was recognized as a segment innovator, inventing the hot package manufacturing process that would eventually be adopted by competitors. Demand for the Snapple teas spread rapidly mainly through word-of-mouth and acquired a loyal following, almost defining a new segment of "new age" beverages. The brand developed a loyal clientele and within a year grew to be the best-selling RTD teas in the United States. The company attracted the attention of financier Thomas H. Lee, who acquired the firm in a leveraged buyout in 1992, and then took it public in 1993. Exploiting growing consumer awareness of health and fitness issues, the brand was taken national and enjoyed a period of explosive growth. At the core of the firm's culture was a high value placed on collaboration that extended to its system of distributors and co-packers. Distributors earned high profit margins on the Snapple products and were permitted to carry other beverages on their trucks, thus enhancing their profitability and granting Snapple a high degree of loyalty. As of July 1994, the firm showed the highest growth rate of all beverage companies.

Facing Snapple were a range of smaller firms and two giants: Coca-Cola and Pepsico, each with its own brand. By late 1994 it was clear that the RTD tea industry was maturing. Growth in shipments for the industry was declining from 60 percent in 1993, small in historical terms but unsustainable for long. And competition was rising. New independent brands entered the market, including Arizona Iced Teas, Nantucket Nectars, and Mystic. More ominously, Coca-Cola and Pepsico, who had formed in 1992 tea-based joint ventures (for Nestea and Lipton, respectively) were making serious inroads into the market through supermarkets and vending machines. In late 1994, Snapple reported that the distribution chain had developed material overstocks of product, owing, it said, to the cool temperatures that summer and lags in adapting production.

MOTIVES FOR QUAKER'S ACQUISITION OF SNAPPLE

Quaker Oats offered a range of explanations that seem like standard fare for many acquisition announcements. But on closer scrutiny, the motives raise flags of concern.

Reinvigorate Quaker's growth. Quaker's grain-based products (breakfast cereals and pet foods) were mature businesses. Smithburg's fundamental aim was to raise the company's growth rate. Snapple represented an opportunity to restore growth to the firm. The firm's SEC filing noted that Quaker's growth in the most recent five years had lagged its rates for the 1985–1989 period as shown in Figure 10.1. But the difference is difficult to interpret in light of the substantial decline in inflation over the 1980s. Moreover, the focus on financial reporting results obscures the growth that matters: increase in market value—on this basis, the firm was a laggard. Quaker's share price had been essentially unchanged since 1991, in com-

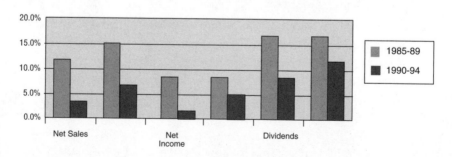

Figure 10.1   **Growth Rates in Selected Financial Performance Measures for Quaker Oats**

Sources of data: SEC filings, Quaker Oats Corporation.

parison to a buoyant stock market. Figure 10.2 and Figure 10.3 summarize financial and stock price performance for Quaker Oats up to the acquisition, and during the period in which it operated Snapple. More importantly, Quaker's performance had not escaped the notice of takeover arbitrageurs and potential buyers: In the months before the acquisition of Snapple, Quaker was the focus of several takeover rumors.

Position Quaker in strategically important new areas. Quaker's decision to acquire Snapple grew from a strategy to expand into noncarbonated consumer beverages, especially "healthful drinks." Consumers were plainly looking beyond colas and other carbonated drinks to slake their thirst. All the major consumer beverage producers had noticed this segment. Quaker's strategy seemed more like following the herd than seeking out and exploiting market inefficiencies.

Repeat Gatorade success story. In 1983, Smithburg had acquired Gatorade from Stokeley-Van Camp Corporation over the objections and derision from observers who claimed that he had paid too much. Over the ensuing eight years, Quaker turned the moribund specialty drink into a vibrant, growing brand. In late 1994, Gatorade dominated its segment with an 85 percent share of market. By then, no one doubted the wisdom of Smithburg's acquisition. Looking for growth opportunities to reinvigorate Quaker's financial performance, Smithburg sought to repeat the story. Generally, Snapple shared a number of

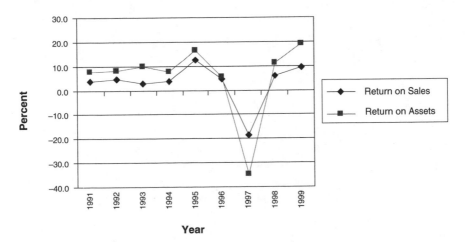

Figure 10.2 **Quaker Financial Performance**

Quaker Stock Price

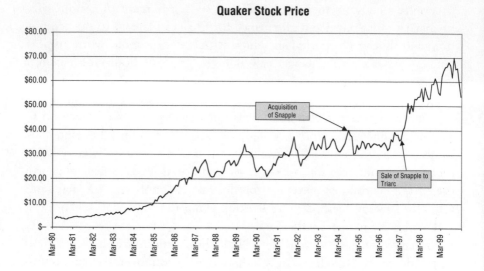

Cumulative Abnormal Return

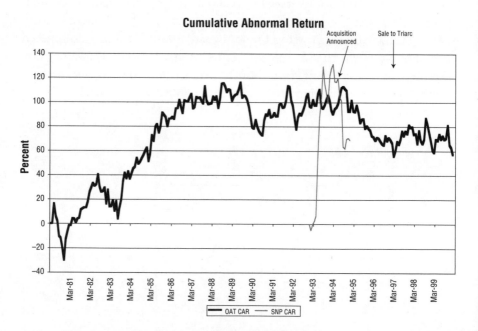

Figure 10.3 **Quaker Stock Price and Abnormal Returns**

characteristics with the Gatorade story: rapid growth, dominance in a specialty niche, and excellent opportunities for the application of Quaker's skills in brand management. Quaker thought it could leverage Snapple/Gatorade into a superior combined offering. Potential benefits notwithstanding, one is struck by the difference between Snapple and Gatorade. Table 10.1 suggests that the brands, culture, marketing, and manufacturing systems offered little similarity. A news article reporting on the acquisition said:

> Analysts said that an early indication of compatibility will come as the two companies seek to create what Quaker Chairman and Chief Executive William D. Smithburg termed "the most innovative distribution system in the beverage industry." The intent is to give both Gatorade and Snapple's line new outlets and, hopefully, new customers. But today, Snapple and Quaker are distributed very differently. Gatorade goes

TABLE 10.1   COMPARISON OF SNAPPLE WITH QUAKER/GATORADE

	Snapple	*Quaker/Gatorade*
Culture and Brand	New wave Entrepreneurial Speedy decision-making Upstart, novel advertising Flout tradition	Button-down Large corporation Professional marketing culture
Competitive Strengths of Product	East and West coasts Strong representation in restaurants, delicatessens, convenience stores, vending machines	Strong in Southern U.S. Strong in supermarkets
Distribution	Factory to independent distributors to stores	Factory to retailer warehouses to stores
Manufacturing	Independent manufacturers under "co-pack" contracts	Company-owned plants
Corporate Strengths	Start-up capabilities Segment-defining brand	Marketing management Cost management Contacts Experience Money

from factory to retailer warehouses, where grocers take what they need to restock their shelves. Snapple, however, goes directly to stores, on trucks driven by independent distributors often carrying an assortment of branded beverages. "You'll have a lot of independents out there who are going to scream if Quaker tries to change that network" predicted [a consultant.][4]

Run Snapple more efficiently. Quaker's plan was to combine the Snapple organization with its own Gatorade group and achieve synergies through more efficient operation.

- *Gain scale efficiencies by combining manufacturing and distribution into a unified supply chain.* Snapple had employed a distribution scheme that relied on independent distributors. These independents had exclusive rights to distribute products in their regions and were adept in penetrating restaurants, delicatessens, clubs convenience stores, and vending machines, but were inefficient in servicing the truly high-volume channel, supermarkets. Quaker's distribution system for Gatorade was the reverse: depending on large warehouses to service supermarkets. Quaker wanted to have their efficient warehouse system service the high-volume outlets for the sake of economies of scale. They proposed to take the high-volume outlets from the independents and give them Gatorade to distribute to convenience stores and mom-and-pop outlets in return. This was the so-called "revolution on a truck." After the acquisition, Quaker would actually use both systems, each delivering product that exploited its strengths. Looking upstream, Snapple had relied on "co-pack" bottlers, who manufactured the finished product under license for Snapple. These independents offered Snapple little flexibility: It took three weeks to fill an order by a distributor. Quaker aimed to shift production from the co-packers to company-owned plants. The motive of this shift was to gain scale efficiencies by combining manufacturing and marketing into a unified supply chain system.
- *Rationalize the product line.* Snapple offered consumers 55 different flavors, not all of which had a strong following. Quaker proposed to reduce the range to the top 40 flavors. This would generate savings in manufacturing, distribution, and brand management.

- *Penetrate new geographic markets.* Snapple had significant market presence on the East and West coasts of the United States, but not in the center or southern tier of states. Gatorade was strongest in the Midwest and South and had overseas distribution that would help Snapple gain an international franchise. Quaker believed that it could roll out the brand to these other market regions.

HOW THE ACQUISITION PLAYED OUT

Quaker consummated its acquisition of Snapple on December 6, 1994. The price of $1.7 billion was high relative to valuations currently prevailing in the industry. The cash payment for Snapple was financed from asset sales of pet food, Mexican chocolates, and other operations that had yielded positive, but low-growth, cash flows to the firm.

The downward spiral for Snapple took public form in an announcement on November 7, 1994, four days after Quaker Oats had disclosed its deal: Snapple stunned the business community by cutting its internal projection of earnings per share 38 percent, from $0.65 to $0.40. In May, Snapple had announced an expectation of $0.86 per share. Snapple acknowledged that this was a surprise even to Quaker: Snapple had given Quaker a forecast of earnings per share (EPS) at $0.55 during the negotiations. This was a continuation of a trend: Snapple had reduced its EPS forecast at several points during the year

The EPS news suggested that Snapple was a declining brand in a growing segment. Quaker would need to either take share of market back from its competitors, or hope that growth in the segment would produce the brand growth it wanted. Analysts pessimistically noted that in 1994 Quaker had doubled the advertising budget for Gatorade (to $50 million) and still had lost five percentage points of market share. Thus, it was an ominous development when on November 11, 1994, Coca-Cola announced that it would spend $150 million to expand its Fruitopia brand. In the face of these developments, Quaker nevertheless completed its acquisition of Snapple on the terms originally announced and resorted to selling other assets to finance the acquisition.

In March 1995, Quaker's CFO, Terry Westbrook, resigned. He had been the architect of the Snapple acquisition and related divestitures. Smithburg explained only that Westbrook's departure was part of an effort to streamline the organization by eliminating layers of management. Also, the firm announced that it would take an extraordinary charge against earnings of $90 million related to the sale of businesses to finance the Snapple acquisition. Charges for the sale of noncore businesses are not unusual, though securities analysts viewed the charge and departure as evidence that "things are not totally smooth at Quaker."[5]

During the summer of 1995, Quaker revised downward Snapple's anticipated performance from the crucial summer selling season, and announced that as a result, the unit would operate at or below financial breakeven for the year. Quaker offered several explanations. Snapple did not have the infrastructure in place to support Quaker's growth plan. The co-packers couldn't fill orders in timely fashion. And Quaker had been trying to renegotiate distribution agreements with Snapple's independent distributors, and found them obstinate in their refusal to let Quaker circumvent them to gain entry into supermarkets. Coca-Cola and Pepsi were mounting strong competitive marketing efforts. And finally, Smithburg charged that Snapple's previous owners had crammed the distribution pipeline full of inventory before the acquisition,[6] perhaps to justify a higher acquisition price. These problems notwithstanding, Smithburg suggested that action had been taken (new managers appointed, line of flavors reduced, and advertising budget tripled), and the unit would return to profitability in 1996.

Part of Quaker's transformation of Snapple was to revamp completely the brand's advertising. Discarded was the quirky, homespun, new age theme that featured Snapple employee, Wendy Feldman, reading letters from satisfied customers. In was a message that Snapple was competing with Coke and Pepsi and that it is okay to be number three, a big-corporation theme that alienated Snapple's ardent customers.

Yet again, in mid-autumn, Quaker reduced investors' expectations: Snapple would not break even in 1995; it would lose $35 million to $40 million. This announcement was followed on October 23 by the resignation of Philip Marineau, Quaker's president and chief operating officer. The 8-K filing by Quaker Oats stated:

> As we have restructured our business portfolio for growth over the past year, we have also reconfigured our management structure to remove layers, shorten lines of decision making and bring senior level focus to bear upon major challenges. [Smithburg said.] Our entire portfolio, including the important Snapple acquisition, will receive my full attention.

Marineau had personally assumed leadership for the Snapple unit; his departure suggested that things were going particularly badly there.

On December 22, 1995, Quaker again revised downward Snapple's performance: The unit would lose an estimated $75 million. This was driven not only by weaker-than-expected sales, but also by inventory write-offs, and $40 million in charges associated with the revision of contracts with co-packers and other suppliers. Later, Donald Uzzi, the president of Snapple Beverage, explained that Snapple's independent distributors simply wouldn't accept the proposed swap of Gatorade distribution for direct supermarket access: Snapple was much more profitable per case than Gatorade. The co-packaging contracts had also locked Snapple into unrealistic production levels with the independent suppliers. And Snapple itself had no new products in the pipeline, and no new advertising or promotions on the way. Finally, Quaker had been too slow to respond to the problems in the unit.

Despite these ominous developments, Quaker estimated that Snapple would return to profitability and growth in 1996. The grounds for this outlook were numerous actions that Quaker had taken to improve the unit. Quaker's accomplishments included reduced delivery time to distributors from three weeks to three days by processing orders faster, and running plants more efficiently; cut inventory costs by half; reduced delivery lag to the stores; reduced the number of flavors; improved the taste; introduced seasonal flavors; improved packaging; pushed the product into supermarkets; and linked the top 50 distributors by computer to the firm.[7]

On June 27, 1996, Quaker announced that Snapple was not achieving planned sales gains, and would probably incur significant operating losses. Donald Uzzi resigned a month later. And two weeks after that, Quaker estimated that the operating losses could exceed $120 million for the year. Also, the firm noted that Snapple had slipped to the second-ranked position in iced tea.

In a move perceived by some as a mark of desperation, Quaker mounted a free giveaway marketing campaign in August 1996, that would ultimately cost the firm $40 million and result in no gain in share of market. Indeed, in October 1996, the firm revealed that Snapple's unit sales had fallen 20 percent despite the giveaway. Quaker explained that it had been a cool and rainy summer in Snapple's key Northeastern U.S. market. Yet analysts observed that shipments of competing brands had fallen only four percent to five percent.

The investment community began pressuring Quaker's management in earnest. Standard and Poor's, the investment rating agency, lowered Quaker's debt rating from A– to BBB+. Takeover rumors swirled in November and December. Quaker began to hint at a possible sale of the unit and then quashed the hint.

Snapple's share of market sagged to third place (with a 15 percent market share), behind Lipton (33 percent) and Nestea (18 percent). What had been a commanding lead was now history. Worse, Coke and Pepsi shifted production to cold-fill bottling that allowed faster line speed and lower costs compared to Snapple's hot-fill system. This gave the competitors a pricing advantage that they used to great effect.

On March 28, 1997, Quaker announced that it would sell Snapple for $300 million, and take a $1.4 billion write-off. Many observers noted the very stiff competition Quaker had met from Coca-Cola and Pepsi: "The Empire [struck] back" said one; and "We crushed Snapple," crowed Pepsi's beverage chief.[8] A month later, William Smithburg announced his resignation.

The Snapple debacle was the start of a slide in performance for the company that ultimately resulted in a decision to sell Quaker Oats. After some negotiation, Quaker agreed to a $13.7 billion all-stock bid from Pepsico in early December 2000. The vaunted "revolution on a truck" became just that: Distributors resisted revisions in the supply chain that might have delivered the value Quaker Oats sought. Observers derided the "gulp fiction" that Quaker's overoptimistic earnings forecasts came to be called. In contrast, three years later in October 2000, Triarc sold the Snapple brand to Cadbury Schweppes for approximately $1 billion.

COUNTERPOINT: SMUCKER'S ACQUISITION OF JIF AND CRISCO

In October 2001 J.M. Smucker Company agreed to purchase the Jif peanut butter and Crisco cooking oil and shortening businesses from Procter & Gamble (P&G) for $810 million in stock. Smucker was the number-one U.S. producer of jams, jellies, and preserves, and also made dessert toppings, peanut butter, juices, and specialty fruit spreads under various brand names. The firm had been incorporated in 1921 and had remained substantially under the control of the Smucker family. At the time of the acquisition, Smucker did not have its own sales force. Because of its small size, it sold its products through brokers. Smucker had recently finished a three-year $35 million overhaul in its inventory and customer-service systems. The company was an active acquirer, completing 11 deals from 1996 to 2001, and sought to grow sales 4 percent annually through acquisitions.

Procter & Gamble was a large consumer goods manufacturer that marketed more than 250 brands to nearly 5 billion consumers in over 140 countries. P&G had conducted an auction for the businesses and chose Smucker to be the buyer because Smucker's offer was tax-free to P&G shareholders. Jif and Crisco accounted for two manufacturing plants, 400 employees, and $571 million in annual sales in fiscal year 2003.

Procter & Gamble sought to sell the two businesses in light of their low growth prospects—Crisco's sales fell by 11 percent, and Jif's by 3 percent in 2001—and a desire to focus on global brands (the two businesses were focused on North America). Smucker had had an interest in acquiring Jif for 25 years and had approached P&G with an offer to buy on previous occasions. In contrast to Quaker's interest in Snapple, Smucker's interest in Jif reflected long-standing strategic intent. Smucker sought to buy the businesses to exploit two important trends in consumer eating: (1) "dashboard dining," handheld food that can be eaten in transit; and (2) nutritional cuisine. Peanut butter, though high in fat and calories, has been found to combat cholesterol and to slake appetites. Pundits named the deal, "peanut butter and jelly" in reference to the marriage of Jif and Smucker's jams. Adding Jif and Crisco was expected to double Smucker's projected revenues to an estimated $1.3 billion in fiscal 2003. Due to the acquisition, Smucker's market share would rise to 41 percent in jam, 38 percent in peanut butter, and 24 percent in cooking oils, making Smucker the dominant force in these segments. Co-CEO, Richard Smucker, emphasized a "center of the store" strategy (products in the central store-aisles in supermarkets) that would give the firm larger mass, bargaining power with its food brokers, and general leadership.

The deal was a stock-for-assets exchange, giving P&G shareholders shares in Smucker. The total payment of about $1 billion reflected a valuation multiple in a reasonable range. Analysts expected the deal to be accretive to Smucker's earnings per share, increasing them by 30 percent. This deal would shift 53 percent of Smucker stock into the hands of

P&G shareholders, and would roughly double its total shares outstanding. An unusual provision allowed for "super voting" shares. All shareholders at completion of the deal would own shares with 10 votes each. If the shares were sold, the new owner would have only one vote per share until owned consecutively for four years. The Smucker family had significant shareholdings in the firm and would represent a major voting block if, as was expected, the P&G shareholders sold their Smucker shares. P&G was heavily owned by index funds who would have to sell Smucker stock because unlike P&G, Smucker was not in the Standard & Poor's 500 index. Other institutional investors, too, might sell if they believed Smucker would not be actively traded or enjoy good growth prospects. An important effect of the deal would be to triple the liquidity and trading volume in Smucker shares—but whether the improved liquidity would be enough to entice more institutional investors remained an open question.

The deal closed in April 2002. It appears to have created new economic value for Smucker's shareholders as shown in Figure 10.4. This is evident in the sustained positive difference between Smucker's share price and a benchmark, the S&P 500 index. Smucker's positive returns could be due to several reasons: reasonable acquisition price; a focusing, not diversifying, investment for Smucker; increased clout with brokers

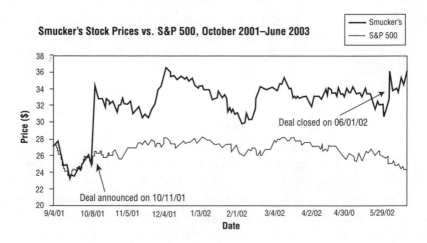

Figure 10.4   **Stock Price of J.M. Smucker**
Source of data: Datastream.

and retailers; and credible synergies through economies of scale and purchasing. One analyst estimated cost savings of around $20 million annually.[9]

Following the acquisition, Jif and Crisco performed well for Smucker. In the fiscal year 2004, both brands achieved material growth in sales of 14 percent (or 70 percent of Smucker's overall increase in sales). This resulted from increased market shares under the new management. However, the volume gains were offset somewhat by price reductions, suggesting to observers that Smucker was buying share of market.

REFLECTION: THE ROLE OF STRATEGIC REACTION

All of the six drivers of M&A failure appear in the case of Quaker and Snapple. *Business was not as usual*: Consumers were shifting from fizzy to healthy drinks and the largest competitors, Coca-Cola and Pepsi were entering Snapple's domain. The manufacturing and distribution systems of Quaker and Snapple were *complex* and *tightly coupled* by means of long-term contracts. The erosion of the senior management team suggests breakdowns in due diligence, integration, and implementation of the new strategy for Snapple. The *operating team* seemed unable to gain traction in pursuing the potential Quaker had seen in Snapple. And the strong optimism about the future of Snapple under Quaker's ownership, stemming from Quaker's previous success with Gatorade suggests a *cognitive bias* that interfered with the ability of Quaker to respond to the worsening situation. Of all the drivers, however, the Quaker/Snapple story emphasizes the dramatic effect of poor *management choices*. At the center of this failure was an error about strategic *reaction*, an important consideration in any setting where there are multiple players and competing interests.[10] The reaction of competitors has been a venerable subject of study[11] and is a concern for thoughtful practitioners. Jack Levy, head of Merrill Lynch's M&A department, said, "Companies ignore deal physics: For every reaction there's more often than not an equal competitive reaction."[12] Quaker's strategic plans for Snapple embraced two bets about the reactions of others:

- *Competitors.* The relatively high purchase price must have been premised on the belief that Coca-Cola and Pepsi would allow Snapple to continue to dominate the flavored tea market space.

- *Distributors and co-packers.* The strategic plan assumed that the distributors would swap their rights for supermarket distribution of Snapple in exchange for the right to distribute Gatorade to their atomistic clientele. Quaker did not anticipate that the distributors would view this as an unfair exchange. Also, it appears that Quaker presumed an easier exit from co-pack manufacturing contracts than was realistic.

The failure of the Quaker–Snapple acquisition displays other causes, some of which are common to deals discussed in other chapters. Table 10.2 summarizes the differences between these two cases.

Price and capital market conditions: It appears that Quaker paid top dollar for Snapple. It may be coincidental that the stock market was buoyant and Quaker's stock price relatively stagnant, making it a takeover target. We know from the research findings summarized in Chapter 2 that acquisition premiums balloon during buoyant market conditions. Smucker, on the other hand bought Jif and Crisco during an economic recession, announced shortly after the 9/11 attacks and in the midst of the unfolding Enron debacle. The price was in line with prevailing multiples in the market.

Seller: The research evidence suggests that private deals are more successful for buyers than are companies purchased on the public market. This distinction is borne out in this comparison: Smucker purchased a division in a private deal, whereas Quaker acquired a publicly-listed firm.

Product market conditions: In both cases demand for the targeted consumer foods brands was declining. But in Snapple's case, the adjustment in expectations was severe: What had been the dominant product in a high-growth segment was becoming an also-ran in a crowded field. Jif and Crisco, on the other hand, retained their segment dominance in mature fields. Smucker was able to restore the volume growth for Jif and Crisco; Quaker was unsuccessful in doing so for Snapple.

Difficulty of transformational M&A: Ultimately, Quaker imposed a very high performance test on itself by changing so many things about Snapple at the same time. Resistance to change and propensity to fail rise in proportion to the scale of change. Given the declining performance of Snapple at the date of the deal, Smithburg no doubt felt a sense of urgency about the need to act decisively. But the distributors had the power to reject this change, much like a body rejects a virus.

TABLE 10.2   COMPARISON OF QUAKER/SNAPPLE AND SMUCKER/JIF AND CRISCO

	Quaker/Snapple	*Smucker/Jif and Crisco*
Seller	Public firm.	Division of public firm.
Price	Relatively high, but much lower than peak.	Low.
Capital Markets	Buoyant capital market conditions.	Economic recession. Index "flow back."
Strategy	Related diversification.	Focusing in core markets.
Management	Two of three top managers cash out and leave. Many HQ personnel leave, along with half of Snapples field sales force.	Management carries over.
Manufacturing	Changes require $30 million to buy out contracts of co-pack bottlers.	No significant changes contemplated.
Demand	Declining due to intensifying competition and passing of fad.	Demand stable.
Advertising	Discontinued Wendy Kaufman ad campaign.	No major change.
Distribution	Distributors resist shift to more efficient system.	No change in distribution (continued through food brokers).
Product Line	Fad-like. Discontinued 20 flavors. Quaker dumped 1 million cases of discontinued product and materials.	Staples.
Competitor Reaction	Serious inroads from Coke and Pepsi.	No significant competitor reaction.
Implementation	Delays with distributors prevented implementation of marketing plans.	No material delays in implementation.
Culture	Mismatch of big corporate culture with that of quirky entrepreneurial firm.	Adjustment to family-style culture of J.M. Smucker.
Due Diligence	Adverse surprises.	No significant surprises.

NOTES

1. The research contributions of Chad Rynbrandt and Christine Shim are gratefully acknowledged as are comments and suggestions from Paul Reiner. I also thank Thomas MacAvoy, a Director of Quaker at the time of the Snapple acquisition, for his comments and suggestions on an earlier draft of this chapter. The research sources on which this chapter draws are in the public domain.

2. A journalist noted that the price was equivalent to 32 times Snapple's earnings (Burns, November 14, 1994). John D. Bowlin, President of Kraft Foods International estimated that Snapple was really worth only $700 to $800 million (see Greg Burns, September 23, 1996).

3. See Greg Burns, April 14, 1997.

4. Richard Gibson and Laurie M. Grossman, "Snapple's Lowering of Profit Projection Underscores Continuation of Problems," *Wall Street Journal*, November 11, 1994.

5. Quotation of Nomi Ghez of Goldman, Sachs & Co. in Gibson, March 9, 1995.

6. See Sellers, June 10, 1995.

7. Moukheiber (1996).

8. See McCarthy et al., March 28, 1997.

9. John M. McMillin, Jeffrey G. Kanter, and Greer O. Tobin, "The J.M. Smucker Company," Equity Research, Prudential Finance, December 11, 2001, 3.

10. Simple examples of competitive reaction can be found in board games such as checkers and chess: You move to gain some advantage, and I in turn move to deny you the advantage and perhaps take it myself. Play a few games, and you gradually learn the importance of *thinking strategically*, that is, several moves ahead, anticipating your opponent's responses to your moves, and constructing a path of moves to get you to your goal despite your opponent's responses. (The opposite of strategy is myopia, thinking only in the near term, or just one move ahead.)

11. In 1838, the French economist, Augustin Cournot, modeled the reaction of two firms in an industry (i.e., a duopoly) *who refuse to collude and fail to learn from the past actions of their rival*. Cournot's model is a study in the consequences of failure to anticipate the reaction of a rival. One competitor initially is the only supplier in the market. Then a second competitor enters at a lower price aimed at absorbing the part of demand left unfulfilled by the first firm. This triggers a competitive dance in which the two firms keep adjusting their prices in the belief that the other side will not respond. The net result is that both firms undersupply the demand, and fail to maximize their joint profit. Cournot tells us that ignoring the rival is costly. The German economist, Heinrich von Stackelberg (1952) extended Cournot's model to recognize that a sophisticated competitor might correctly anticipate the moves of the rival. His

conclusion is that the sophisticated competitor effectively harvests the profits of a monopolist. Thus attention to the likely reaction of the rival is profitable. These little thought exercises are remarkably applicable to the observed behavior of Quaker and its competitors.

12. Nikhil Deogun and Steven Lipin, "Deals & Deal Makers: Cautionary Tales: When Big Deals Turn Bad—Some Hot Mergers Can Come Undone for Many Reasons," *Wall Street Journal*, December 8, 1999, C1.

11

May 1999:
Mattel's Acquisition of
The Learning Company

MATTEL'S ANNOUNCEMENT OF THE DEAL

Jill E. Barad was a standout figure in an industry that depended on the ability to stand out. As CEO of Mattel Inc.,[1] a leading toy manufacturer, she could dictate trends. One of the few women leading a Fortune 500 company, she assumed near-iconic status as a role model for other women. She was style-setting industrially and personally, with movie-star charisma and fashionable attire. Having joined Mattel in 1981 as a product manager, she rose through the marketing ranks at Mattel and proved that she could win a customer, close a sale, and build business. And at 48 years old, she was comparatively young for a CEO.

On December 14, 1998, Barad announced that Mattel would acquire The Learning Company (TLC) for about $3.8[2] billion in stock, a deal she declared would be accretive to earnings in 1999. The acquisition was described as a turning point in the strategic direction of Mattel. She told journalists, "This isn't a bet on the Internet. It's a bet on technology and how we are going to communicate to customers."[3] She expressed the possibility that the firm might use TLC's leading figure, Reader Rabbit, as the basis for an interactive doll, or that a line of educational software might be created around Mattel's Barbie doll. Barad said, "Today, the computer—that's [the kids'] play, that's where they are spending their time."

In the same news conference, she also announced that Mattel's sales would fall $500 million below forecast, and that as a result, the firm's earnings per share would be off 35 percent (from expectations that had been reaffirmed just six weeks earlier). By the end of the day share prices of both Mattel and TLC plummeted.

Fifteen months later, Mattel's share price had fallen 70 percent since the announcement of the TLC deal. Jill Barad and other senior executives had left the firm. And Mattel's board of directors determined to sell TLC at a loss.

Origins of the Deal

As of late 1998, the toy industry was in the midst of profound change due to shifting competitive power, technological innovation, and fluctuations in consumer demand. Large retailers grew in power. Toys R Us dictated tough terms: Mattel conceded to them the right to revise orders until shortly before the end of the holiday selling season. In addition, the sales of traditional toys, such as Mattel's Barbie doll, were in steep decline. The rise of interactive toys and changes in parents' tastes accounted for the drift away from Mattel's core money-making product.

Mattel, one of the dominant toy manufacturers in the United States, produced a variety of well-known toy products including the Barbie fashion dolls and accessories, GI Joe, Disney-licensed toys, Fisher-Price toys, *Sesame Street* characters, Hot Wheels vehicles and playsets, Matchbox vehicle toys, Scrabble games, and Cabbage Patch dolls. The firm noted that its business was dependent in great part on its ability each year to redesign, restyle, and extend existing core products and product lines and to design and develop innovative new toys and product lines. New products have limited lives, ranging from one to three years, and generally must be updated and refreshed each year.

Mattel enjoyed an apparently impregnable competitive position. Nevertheless, its financial performance in 1998 faltered. As shown in Figure 11.1, revenues and operating earnings had declined since 1996, reflecting changing consumer buying patterns, especially toward Mattel's flagship product, the Barbie doll. Reversing this trend became Jill Barad's priority,

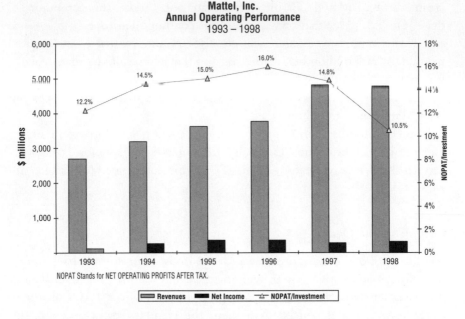

Figure 11.1 **Operating Results for Mattel Inc.**

Source of data: Value Line Investment Survey.

to find the next big hit product that would restore the company's growth and prosperity.

Since the late 1970s the industry had experienced a declining average product life as fad toys (often associated with entertainment figures), or new technology (such as game software) gained a greater share of market. Increasingly, internal product development efforts were supplemented by acquisitions as a means of ensuring that a given toy company would be able to offer retailers a high-volume product. Retailers wanted fad products and gave preferential shelf-space positions to toy makers who produced them. Toy retailing was experiencing its own revolution with the appearance of high-volume channels such as the enormously successful Toys R Us. Toys that couldn't generate sufficient volume wouldn't garner the support of the powerful retailers.

In the fall of 1998, Mattel engaged Goldman Sachs to explore possible acquisition targets for Mattel. On November 2, 1998, Jill Barad met with Michael Perik, TLC's CEO to explore the possibility of an acquisition. Eight days later, the two firms signed a confidentiality agreement and swapped internal financial information. By November 13, the two firms were in due diligence research. On December 2, the two firms began to discuss the price for the target company and other details regarding the structure of the transaction, such as a share-for-share exchange with a collar. On December 13, the boards of the two firms approved the deal.

The Learning Company was a leading publisher of consumer software for home personal computers (PCs). The company's products included software in several segments: educational (the *Reader Rabbit* software for younger children; *Carmen Sandiego* and *Oregon Trail* software for school-age children, and the Princeton Review line of test preparation software); reference (*Compton's Encyclopedia* and *National Geographic* software) and lifestyle, productivity and entertainment software (including *PrintMaster*, *Print Shop*, *Calendar Creator*, *Tomb Raider*, *Myst*, *Riven*), which it produced and sold both in North America and internationally. In addition, the company was developing a growing line of products that linked to or benefited from the Internet, such as *Cyber Patrol*, which allowed parents to filter access to inappropriate web sites.

TLC was founded in 1978, emerged from a three-way merger in 1994 among SoftKey, WordStar, and Spinnaker Software, and assumed the name SoftKey International. In 1996, the firm changed its name to The Learning Company, signaling its emphasis on educational software. From 1996 until the announced acquisition by Mattel, TLC grew substantially by acquisition. A report by Booz Allen Hamilton listed two of SoftKey's acquisitions as among the 10 worst U.S. acquisitions for 1994–1996 as measured by shareholder value two years after the deal.[4]

TLC introduced 100 new and upgraded products in 1998, and noted that 90 percent of its U.S. revenues in 1998 were derived from products that were internally developed. However, analysts were concerned about TLC's aging product lines and absence of material research and development that might replace the aging products. Also, competition in the educational software industry was fierce and characterized by price erosion. One analyst said, "It's a battle for the hearts and minds of children. The publishers are desperate to lock in those consumers."[5] In the years leading up to the acquisition announcement, The Learning Company had reported annual losses, as shown in Figure 11.2.

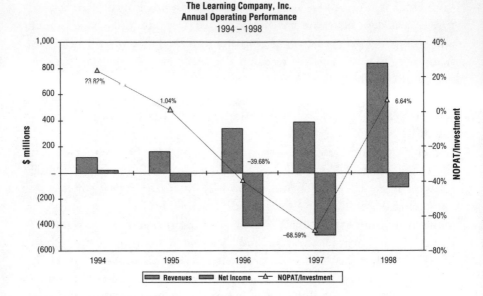

Figure 11.2   Operating Results for The Learning Company

Source of data: Value Line Investment Survey.

Objectives of the Acquisition

The joint merger proxy statement/prospectus filed by Mattel and TLC with the Securities and Exchange Commission on February 2, 1999, declared:

> Mattel, Inc. and The Learning Company, Inc. are proposing to merge because we believe the resulting combination will create a stronger, more competitive company capable of achieving greater financial strength, operational efficiencies, earning power and growth potential than either company would have on its own.
>
> The combined company will feature a portfolio of well-known brands including, among others, BARBIE, FISHER-PRICE, AMERICAN GIRL, READER RABBIT, HOT WHEELS, MATCHBOX, CARMEN SANDIEGO and OREGON TRAIL. We intend to leverage these brands across software, toy and related product categories to capitalize on Mattel's global distribution strength and to exploit opportunities in Internet e-commerce.[6]

The proxy statement mentioned "expected synergies" in the combination but nowhere stated what they were or described their sources. A review of the facts surrounding the merger suggests two main objectives for the deal.

First, Mattel's acquisition of TLC was part of an opportunistic search for the next hot thing in toys. Jill Barad's purpose for acquiring TLC was to help Mattel devise a new line of interactive toys. This would move the firm into the high-growth product arena.

The acquisition of TLC perhaps served a second, cosmetic, purpose, to mask Mattel's earnings hit from its $500 million shortfall in sales for 1998. One analyst termed the earnings impact of the sales decline to be "a catastrophe."[7] A similar pattern of acquisition announcement timed with an adverse earnings announcement had occurred six months earlier, in June 1998, when Mattel had announced an agreement to acquire Pleasant Company. At the time, journalists questioned the timing of these two announcements and were told "the timing just happened that way."[8] With the announcement of the dramatic shortfall in December, securities analysts and investors became very skeptical: "It's Wall Street's version of 'wag the dog,' . . . Was the timing [of the earnings announcement] just a coincidence?" wondered a journalist.[9] Securities regulations may have required Mattel to disclose its earnings results at the same time as its acquisitions, *given that* it had chosen to announce those deals at the end of their respective quarters. Mattel's own press releases carried the earnings announcements after the report of the acquisitions, suggesting an intentional spin on the news. And in any event, newspaper articles reported the earnings results after the announcement of the acquisition.

M&A activity can affect reported corporate financial results in at least three ways, by altering the mix of assets, the mix of debt and equity, and the mix and trend of earnings over time. This complicates the reading of financial statements and perhaps affords managers the opportunity to mask a deteriorating financial condition. In addition, the rules for accounting for acquisitions make it possible for buyers to present a growing trajectory of revenue and earnings per share where in economic terms the operations were mature or even declining. This is "growth illusion," a profile that Mattel and TLC fit. TLC acquired 14 firms in the 19 months leading up to the acquisition. Mattel acquired seven firms in the five years up to the announcement, two of which were poolings-of-interests and required major restatements of financial results. Despite these, TLC reported large losses; and Mattel showed deteriorating performance.

Reaction to the Acquisition Announcement

The reaction of investors to the pair of announcements was swift. Mattel's share price fell 27 percent at the announcement; shares in The Learning Company fell nearly 12 percent. One columnist, Herb Greenberg,[10] summarized the disbelief in the financial community as follows:

> Sounds to some skeptics like two desperate companies doing one desperate deal. Why else, they wonder, would Mattel, which trades at 2 times sales, swap its stock for a company that trades at 4.5 times projected sales?
>
> Why else, they wonder, would Mattel buy a company that has been the target of charges, for years, of stuffing the distribution channel to make its numbers look better than they really are? Along those lines, why else, they wonder, would Mattel buy a company whose receivables in recent quarters, have been rising faster than sales—if you included the amount of receivables that had been sold off to investors?
>
> Why else, they wonder, would Mattel buy a company that itself had done upwards of $1.3 billion in takeovers, with much of the combined purchase price being written off? (Makes some critics wonder what was in those writeoffs, and adds further doubt to the quality of TLC's earnings.) And why else, they wonder, would Mattel buy a company that has bought numerous other companies, including Broderbund, whose fundamentals have been failing?
>
> Why else, they wonder, would Mattel buy a company whose operating earnings are an unusually robust 26%, twice the margins of Electronic Arts, which is with little doubt one of the best operators in the game industry? (Such a big discrepancy doesn't sit well with some critics.)
>
> Why else, they wonder, would TLC's management sell the company, at this time, if the biz is so good?
>
> Maybe the answer is that before getting into the software biz, TLC Chairman and CEO Michael Perik was a currency trader in Canada. Mattel's purchase of TLC, it would appear, is the ultimate trade.

Aftermath: Decline and Fall

Seeking to shore up the sagging share price, Mattel issued a statement in February 1999 that was mildly buoyant: While at the end of the fourth quarter 1998, Mattel's share price was down 70 percent, Mattel announced that earnings per share in the next year would be up 25 percent over 1998. Barad stated that the forecast would "leave room for other unforeseen events . . . We would rather underpromise than underdeliver."[11] This was supplemented by tough talk that Mattel would require retailers to place firm orders by Thanksgiving, and that the firm would avoid building inventory. Barad said, "If the retailer is not going to be aggressive, we'll find another way to put our products in front of the consumer."[12] Finally, Mattel would mount an electronic retailing strategy.

The launch of Mattel.com was announced in April. Mattel disclosed that it would spend $50 million on the new channel. In the same announcement, however, the firm said that it would take a pretax charge of $300 to $350 million to digest TLC, and reposition it as a "diversified family products company." The restructuring would save Mattel $450 million in costs annually over four years. Mattel's share price rose 8.9 percent on the announcement.

The acquisition of TLC was consummated on May 13, 1999. In July, Mattel reaffirmed that the firm was "on track" to meet a forecasted earnings per share of $1.50 for 1999. Ominously, it noted that sales of the Barbie doll declined again. In August, the two senior executives of TLC, who had been the founders and principal owners of the firm before the acquisition, sold the bulk of their shares, but remained with the firm.

Then in October 1999 Mattel announced that its third quarter EPS estimate would be cut 40 percent to 55 percent due to problems at TLC. The losses were attributable to a revenue shortfall at TLC, higher advertising costs, returned goods, write-offs of bad debt, and the failure of a licensing agreement to materialize. Critics added that Mattel had simply paid too much for a target with aging brands and a history of accounting trouble, and that took the firm afield from its familiar business. Mattel's share price fell 20 percent in anticipation of the earnings announcement.

Criticism of Mattel and of CEO Barad was intense. "People feel they were lied to," said one investment manager; another said, "We're very upset, and we're very critical of management at this point."[13] Barad replied that she had been unaware of the full extent of problems at TLC. She initiated an investigation of the losses and uncovered no fraud or irregularities. The product returns, bad debts, and licensing agreement problems had come to light when the headquarters of TLC was moved from Cambridge, Massachusetts, to Novato, California. At the end of October, Barad declared that she remained "very satisfied" with the TLC acquisition.[14]

Nineteen ninety-nine drew ominously to a close. Pretax losses in the third quarter were –$100 million; in the fourth quarter, they slid to –$184 million. In November, the chairman and president of TLC left the company with a severance package of $5.2 million each. A journalist reported that they had not told Barad of the difficulties at TLC until a week before the October announcement. One institutional investor announced that it was offering to buy 11.3 million Mattel shares with a view toward establishing a control position.

On January 4, 2000, Mattel announced that its chief financial officer would retire. He was responsible for the due diligence research on TLC. At about the same time, Bernard Stolar joined Mattel to assume responsibility for its interactive products—essentially to fill the leadership vacuum created by the exit of TLC's leadership. It took him 10 days to determine that more write-offs and a significant restructuring would be necessary. This discovery proved to be the final straw for the directors of Mattel.

In the first week of February, Jill Barad announced her departure from the firm. Simultaneously, Mattel disclosed that it had lost four cents per share in the fourth quarter of 1999, compared to a profit of two cents per share in the prior year's fourth quarter. Mattel also announced that it would take another restructuring charge of $75 to $100 million in the first quarter of 2000, related to TLC. Later, it was disclosed that Barad had received a severance pay package estimated to be nearly $50 million (including $26.4 million in cash, forgiveness of $7.2 million in loans, payment of $3.3 million in taxes triggered by the loan forgiveness, and a pension of $709,000 per year for life.)[15] The payment outraged investors in light of the firm's performance under her leadership.

In April 2000, Mattel's board of directors announced that it would sell TLC for no cash, but a claim on 50 percent of the profits for a period of time. This triggered a write-down of $441 million on the investment in The Learning Company. The board had estimated that a turnaround of TLC would take two years, a length of time they refused to endure.

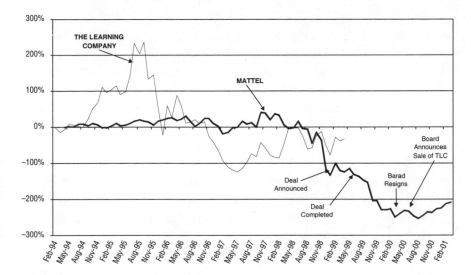

Figure 11.3 **Mattel and The Learning Company Cumulative Market-Adjusted Returns (CMARS), February 1994–March 2001**

Source of data: Datastream.

From the date of the announcement of acquisition until February 2000, Mattel's shares lost 70 percent of their market value. Figure 11.3 graphs the cumulative market-adjusted return on Mattel and Learning Company shares from 1994 to 2001. The graph suggests that The Learning Company had declined dramatically from the summer of 1995 to spring of 1997, a tell-tale of the turbulence in TLC's business and of the difficulties Mattel would experience following the acquisition. The graph also confirms that the deal was announced following a sharp decline in Mattel's cumulative market-adjusted returns, consistent with the view of some critics that the deal announcement was an attempt to obscure the decline in Mattel's core business.

COUNTERPOINT: IBM'S ACQUISITION OF LOTUS DEVELOPMENT CORPORATION

On June 5, 1995, Louis Gerstner, CEO of IBM Corporation, called James Manzi, CEO of Lotus Development Corporation, to say that IBM was commencing a hostile tender offer for Lotus, suing Lotus to rescind its poison pill defense, and mounting a consent solicitation to replace Lotus's directors with IBM's nominees. Such an attack was unheard of at that place and time. The hostile tender offer was an unusual tactic, amounting to perhaps two percent of all M&A transactions among large firms. It was virtually never used in industries where the key asset walks out the door each night, since alienating the human capital could quickly render the target company a shell of its former self, with few prospects for growth. Hostile deals were extremely rare in technology and software. IBM had a strong tradition of organic growth, rather than growth by acquisition. It preferred to develop new technology internally rather than acquire it. An icon of conservative corporate America, IBM had never gone hostile before. And when it did acquire other firms, the track record was not impressive: Most notably, IBM sold Rolm at a loss three years after acquiring it in 1985. Finally, the pricing was very rich—virtually a 100 percent acquisition premium to be paid in cash. The cash payment would enrich those employees of Lotus who held options on the firm's stock, and thus loosen the bonds holding them to Lotus—Jim Manzi owned 1.2 million shares of Lotus, putting a value of $73 million on them at IBM's bid price. IBM's $3.2 billion bid for Lotus was large in absolute terms and relative to IBM's market capitalization. The astonished reaction of many was, "What can Gerstner have been thinking?"

Motives for the Acquisition of Lotus

Louis Gerstner joined IBM as CEO in 1992 following stints as consultant with McKinsey and executive positions at American Express and RJR Nabisco. At the time, IBM was a declining company, hurt by the shift to distributed computing, the rise of Microsoft and Intel as leaders of the computing industry, an arrogant culture of "we know what's best for the customer," and a focus on selling hardware rather than solutions. In his first three years, Gerstner triggered a major transformation in the way IBM did business.

By 1994 it became clear to Gerstner that the integration of computing software with hardware into business solutions was necessary to restore the firm. He found:

> A software business that was big but fragmented and unmanaged; a software portfolio that was closed in a world destined to be open; software

built for mainframes rather than for smaller and more widely dispersed systems; and a business that, aside from operating systems tied to the hardware, was losing huge sums of money. We needed far more focus.[16]

IBM's software portfolio contained 4,000 products each with separate names, brands, and identities. Gerstner reorganized the software business under a single executive and embarked on a process of strategic repositioning that would prepare IBM to compete in the future. Strategic analysis considered three segments of the software industry. Operating systems that ran the computer comprised a relatively low-growth segment, dominated by a few players. At the other extreme, application software that the end-user could see and use, was also dominated in business applications by firms such as SAP, PeopleSoft, and J.D. Edwards. The analysis focused instead on software products sandwiched in between, the "middleware," as the attractive opportunity for development. Middleware focused on transaction management, database management, and the management of large networked systems of computers and users. The key development was the rise of networks internal to corporations and, of course, networks to arise over the Internet. Gerstner and his colleagues foresaw a wave of collaborative computing and wanted to position IBM to exploit it.

Lotus would help to meet that wave. Often thought of as the developer of the first mass-market computer spreadsheet program, Lotus 1-2-3, Lotus had broadened its product portfolio. Key to Gerstner's thinking was Lotus Notes, the seminal software for file sharing among a large number of users. Lotus claimed a 34 percent share of the networking market, with Microsoft in second place at a distant 12 percent.[17] Surely other large firms recognized the promise in Lotus Notes and might be contemplating some kind of combination. If IBM wanted Notes, it would need to move decisively.

Accordingly, IBM approached Lotus over several months in 1994 and early 1995 to solicit Lotus's interest in an acquisition by IBM. Manzi suggested that Lotus sell its troubled desktop applications business (including Lotus 1-2-3 and a word processing program). But on each occasion, Lotus sharply rebuffed the advances to buy the entire firm. So firmly opposed to the idea was Manzi, that he did not even convey the news of the offer to Lotus's board.[18] This meant that Gerstner's only alternative was to make a hostile bid.

Implementation of IBM's Offer and Its Aftermath

Gerstner later recounted that the conversation with Manzi was "noncommittal, cold but polite—and very brief."[19] Manzi immediately resisted the offer. Gerstner believed that retaining Lotus's employees was the key to a successful acquisition and that this depended on communicating directly to them through the Internet. Moments after Gerstner's call to Manzi, IBM's web site went live with a series of communications that sought to explain IBM's motives, express its intentions to grow, not dismember, Lotus, and address fears that the employees might have. Rumors circulated in the market about possible white knight acquirers, including AT&T, Oracle, and General Motors's EDS subsidiary. But in the final event, none of these came forward with a bid.

As abruptly as the offer became public, the defenses were withdrawn. On June 11, 1995, Manzi and Gerstner announced an agreement to merge Lotus into IBM. IBM had raised its bid by $200 million and agreed to maintain Lotus as a separate subsidiary of the corporation, thus preserving its identity and infrastructure. IBM would immediately fully vest the stock options of all Lotus employees. Manzi would become a vice president of IBM. Raymond Ozzie, 39, the lead developer of Notes and manager of a team of 100 software engineers, told a reporter, "Now Notes needs an infusion of resources that one of the suitors might be able to bring that Lotus, in its financial condition, might not . . . From that perspective, I can be positive. IBM is a tremendous company. They have a lot of interesting technologies and resources that could be brought to bear at a scale that's never been available to Lotus before."[20]

The acquisition was consummated on July 5. IBM announced that it would write off almost two-thirds of the acquisition price as goodwill over five years, diluting earnings per share about 15 cents per quarter. IBM's write-off of purchased R&D in this deal was the largest seen to that date. Such write-offs tend to understate the book value of assets and overstate return on equity. IBM and Lotus chartered five integration teams to plan the operational merging of the two firms. By the end of July, the two firms had contacted most of the Lotus customers, announced a new combined product line, and engaged customers in the design of new business processes. The new firm would offer a bundle of products to Lotus customers that would prominently feature Lotus's core products, Notes, and CC: Mail. This signaled the prominence and sustainability of the Lotus culture.

Though IBM successfully retained most of Lotus's pool of talented software engineers, Jim Manzi resigned from the company three months after the close of the merger. Manzi concluded that "I'm not the right person to lead this company inside IBM."[21] Louis Gerstner appointed two long-time Lotus managers to be co-presidents of Lotus, signaling a commitment to the culture and autonomy of Lotus.

Some observers believed that the advent of the corporate intranet in late 1995 would displace Notes as a groupware tool. But Notes contained sophisticated security, communication, and collaboration features that intranets could not match. And IBM responded quickly with Domino, a Web server with Notes features. Many observers of the merger thought that IBM's culture would stultify the Lotus organization. Ray Ozzie and other talented designers left beginning in 1997, but Lotus retained its autonomy and flourished. IBM's deep financial pockets enabled Lotus to accelerate its new product development. Under IBM's management, Notes surged into the marketplace, growing from 2 million "seats" in 1995 to 90 million in 2001, outdistancing the growth in Microsoft's Exchange, a competitor product. Gerstner argued that "Lotus is in the sweet spot of knowledge management" and that IBM became the "leading software company in networked computing."[22] Part of the success of Lotus stemmed from its own profitability, but another large component drew from its impact on IBM's sales generally. "IBM generates about $4 in additional hardware and consulting revenue for every $1 in Notes sales," said one analyst.[23] The Lotus acquisition proved to be just the beginning of a major makeover for IBM. From 1995 to 1999, IBM spent about $8 billion to acquire 60 software and services firms.[24]

CONCLUSION

The case of Mattel/TLC displays the drivers of merger failure. Especially prominent in this case is the adverse impact of momentum thinking.

The Drivers of Merger Failure

All six failure factors drove the demise of the Mattel/TLC deal. *Complexity* stemmed from the large scale of Mattel, the rapid technological change in software, and the challenges in monitoring changes in children's preferences. All of this would have made it difficult for Jill Barad to know what was happening inside TLC and at the interface of the merging firms. But it also appears that Mattel's due diligence research on TLC was inadequate, which, combined with the apparent haste to do a deal, increased the probability that Jill Barad really did not understand the risks in TLC. Mattel paid a full price for TLC, leaving little room for error in attaining a reasonable return on investment. The large outlay *tightly coupled* the operating decisions and financial results. The key *management choice* in this case, the decision to diversify Mattel's product line into software, took the company beyond its area of expertise, from the physical toy into digital amusement. While in 2004 this seemed to be a major trend in the play of children, Mattel was unprepared to evaluate or manage its new business. As Chapters 2 and 3 suggest, acquisition into less-related fields of business is a determinant of poor performance. Mattel bought TLC at a moment when *business was not usual*. Both companies faced dramatic changes in consumer demand for their products and in the power of retailers. The Internet, while booming, remained an uncertain quantity. Under the circumstances, it would have taken a management *team* that was very reliable to chart a sensible response. The steady departure of operating executives over the 15 months following acquisition hints at the fundamental instability of Mattel's response team. Finally, Jill Barad's statements and actions suggest overoptimism and momentum thinking, *cognitive biases* that may have impaired the action-taking in response to the worsening crisis.

Momentum Thinking as a Cognitive Bias

The contrasting experiences of Mattel and IBM in making software acquisitions reveal the fundamental importance of strategy. Table 11.1 compares the two transactions. Mattel's deal was driven heavily by opportunism, IBM's by strategic planning. Mattel, like the rest of the toy industry, looked for the next big hit; IBM looked to position itself well over the long run versus Microsoft and with customers seeking middleware. Mattel reached far beyond its expertise. IBM reached into a related field and in fact had its own software division on whose expertise it could rely for judgments about the quality of Lotus's products.

A second point of contrast is due diligence. Mattel engaged Goldman

TABLE 11.1 Comparison of Mattel/The Learning Company with IBM/Lotus

	Mattel/Learning Company	*IBM/Lotus*
Target	Software, $3.5 billion price.	Software, $3.5 billion price.
Why	Opportunism: searching for next big hit. Mask declining financial performance.	Strategic positioning for IBM. Bet that "middleware" will be of strategic importance in computing.
How	Negotiated deal.	Attempted negotiation followed by hostile bid that results in agreement to merge.
Endgame	TLC performance deteriorates. Discovery of accounting irregularities. Barad fired. Mattel sells TLC at significant loss.	Kept talent. Grew the business.
Lessons	Vice of opportunism and accounting cosmetics. Plunged outside of area of expertise. Value of due diligence.	Virtue of strategic focus and discipline. Reached into areas of related competence.

Sachs in the fall of 1998 to find an acquisition target. Negotiations with TLC commenced in November. The deal was done by mid-December. Events subsequently suggested hasty due diligence by Mattel. IBM, on the other hand, had been courting Lotus for at least 18 months. Through its own software operations, IBM had an excellent due diligence assessment of Lotus's position and operations. IBM's hostile bid was the final act in a relatively careful process of acquisition.

Third, we see a sharp difference in accounting effects. Jill Barad announced that the TLC acquisition would be immediately accretive to Mattel's earnings. The announcement seemed timed to make up for sharp underperformance by Mattel. IBM, on the other hand, announced that the Lotus acquisition would be dilutive to IBM's earnings. Plainly, accounting cosmetics were not foremost in IBM's thinking. Mattel was trying to construct the *appearance* of growth, whereas IBM shrugged off appearances in favor of strategic advantage and the substance of economic growth.

Finally, though both deals were richly priced, IBM had the capacity to absorb adverse surprises (because of its size), whereas Mattel did not (because of its smaller size and deteriorating earnings). At the announcement to acquire The Learning Company, Mattel was in its second year of decline. The timing of this decline could not have been worse for Jill Barad: It began when she assumed the title of CEO in 1997. Her strategic challenge was to return Mattel to a trajectory of growth and value creation.

The thread through all of these themes is Mattel's opportunism. While the business world applauds the nimble competitor who is able to respond to conditions as they change, opportunism is not a strategy for success. In Mattel's case it created a never-ending replacement problem. All fads eventually lose momentum. The challenge, therefore, is to create a steady growth trajectory from a portfolio of products or businesses each of which will inevitably mature, and decline. In the minds of many executives, resolving this problem is simple: Find attractive investments, and *time them* so that successive investments deliver the growth necessary to sustain the trajectory. In practice, this is a risky strategy for reasons that the Mattel–TLC case well illustrates:

- *Gamble on timing*. Delivering growth on schedule is the albatross for all executives who believe in the importance of momentum earnings. In most industries, the true economic rate of growth has a large random component. Thus, to deliver a stable trajectory of growth over time requires executives to fill in the air pockets of performance with opportunistic acquisitions, earnings management, or worse, fraud. The economic evidence is that managers are at best mediocre at anticipating key inflection points in their business. As Clayton Christensen (1997) has lucidly described, innovators eventually decline because they tend to listen to their current base of customers (who always want existing products) rather than the "customer ahead" who has a need for the new generation of product.

- *Gamble on direction*. Even if one tries to listen to a customer ahead, the feedback can be noisy and the path unclear. One almost never wants to simply replicate an existing line of business. The challenge is to break out. But where?

- *Gamble on type of growth.* Many managers seem to believe that the growth that matters is growth in revenues or earnings. But what capital markets reward is growth of market value. Sometimes, market value can be grown through a focus on revenues and earnings. But in other instances, the value–maximizing path will depend on cash flow.

- *Gamble on size.* It takes bigger and bigger acquisitions to offset the maturation of existing businesses. Acquisition strategies aimed at maximizing size of revenues or assets are ultimately doomed to fail by the paucity of very large firms to acquire. Firms simply cannot grow indefinitely at a rate greater than the global economy. Ultimately, the buyer must either abandon the strategy, or wind up owning the world economy.

- *Gamble on the health of the target.* For the strategy to succeed, the target company really must deliver new growth. This was Mattel's big stumble. TLC not only couldn't deliver growth, but actually contracted.

Many firms sustain a stable growth rate for a period of time. Thus, it is relatively easy for an executive to observe apparent successes—both within her firm and outside. The existence of these exemplars spurs imitation. But markets and errant human behavior present inexorable limits to the efficacy of this approach.

NOTES

1. The research assistance of Sean Carr and Chad Rynbrandt is gratefully acknowledged. The research in this chapter is based on public sources and especially the reporting of Lisa Bannon.

2. Mattel's share price declined following the announcement of the deal to acquire The Learning Company. After the decline, the value of the bid was $3.5 billion.

3. Kravetz and Auerbach (1998).

4. Reported in Bannon, Hechinger, and Deogun (October 8, 1999).

5. Bannon (1999).

6. Page iii, Form S-4 Registration Statement filed with the U.S. Securities and Exchange Commission by Mattel Inc. and The Learning Company, February

2, 1999, accessed via Internet on August 23, 2004, http://www.sec.gov/Archives /edgar/data/63276/0000898430-99-000319.txt.

7. Sherer (1998).

8. Sherer (1998).

9. Sherer (1998).

10. Reprinted from Greenberg, Herb, "Mattel Has Nobody to Blame but Itself for the Learning Co. Fiasco," TheStreet.com, October 4, 1999. Copyright (2005) TheStreet.com, Inc. Reprinted with the permission of TheStreet.com, Inc.

11. Kravetz (February 3, 1999).

12. Kravetz (February 17, 1999).

13. Bannon (October 5, 1999).

14. Bannon (1999).

15. Reported in Benjamin Gallander and Benjamin Stadelmann, "Mattel, the Company That Brought You Barbie, Is Hurting and Not Yet a Buy, Our Contrarians Say," *Globe and Mail*, May 27, 2000, accessed on the Internet on August 23, 2004, http://www.contratheheard.com/cth/contraguys/000527.html.

16. Louis V. Gerstner, *Who Says Elephants Can't Dance?* (HarperCollins, 2002), 140.

17. Patrick Flanigan, "IBM Positions Lotus Notes as Industry Standard," *Telecommunications*, August 1995, 15.

18. Revealed in Laurie Hays, "99 Days: Manzi Quits at IBM and His Many Critics Are Not all Surprised," *Wall Street Journal*, October 12, 1995, A1.

19. Gerstner (2002), 143.

20. Quotation of Raymond Ozzie in William Bulkeley, "Lotus's Star Developer Says He Would Work for a Friendly IBM," *Wall Street Journal*, June 8, 1995, B5.

21. Hays, "99 Days," A1.

22. Gerstner (2002), 141.

23. A quotation of Bruce Smith, an analyst with Merrill Lynch & Co. in Jeff Angus, Karen M. Carrillo, Justin Hibbard, and Bruce Caldwell, "IBM and Lotus Get Closer," *Information Week*, July 28, 1997, 73.

24. Mark Songini, "IBM's Acquisition Strategy: Shop (Quietly) Till You Drop," *Network World*, September 20, 1999, 25.

12

January 2001:
Merger of AOL
and Time Warner

INTRODUCTION

The merger of America Online (AOL) and Time Warner in 2001 offered two superlatives: the biggest deal to date and possibly the most notorious.[1] Nearly $200 billion in market value evaporated in the months following the announcement of the deal. CEOs and other senior executives of both companies resigned early or were fired. Alleged accounting chicanery triggered a government investigation. Disaffected shareholders launched class-action lawsuits. And eventually the AOL name was expunged from the corporate moniker. A sampling of some of the printable criticism about the deal includes these: "worst deal in history,"[2] "disaster of belly flop proportions,"[3] "one of the greatest train wrecks in history,"[4] "biggest and stupidest moment in the whole era,"[5] "miasma,"[6] "financial weakness . . . bamboozled . . . disaster,"[7] "like the Mongolian invasion of China,"[8] "catastrophic,"[9] and "largest annual loss in U.S. corporate history."[10]

On January 10, 2000, Steve Case and Jerry Levin, CEOs of AOL and Time Warner, respectively, issued a press release to announce an agreement to merge their two firms, to "create the world's first Internet-Age Media and Communications Company."[11] Upon announcement, the combined market capitalization implied in the deal was about $350 billion. It would be consummated with a share-for-share exchange. The exchange had no "collar" that would protect either side from adverse movements in share price. Only one-half percent of all deals (and six percent of large deals) have such protection, reflecting the desire of the deal designers not to signal apprehensions to the market. And the "break-up" fee for walking away from the deal was $5.4 billion for AOL and $3.5 billion for Time Warner. Accounted for on a purchase basis, the deal created $100 billion in goodwill, nearly 30 percent of the combined capitalization. The new entity, called AOL Time Warner Inc., had revenues of more than $140 billion.

Significantly, the deal was advertised as a "merger of equals" (MOE) a structure typically with shared governance by the two sides and no acquisition premium. The ownership of the new firm accrued 55/45 percent to AOL and Time Warner shareholders, respectively. Steve Case of AOL was to be chairman of the board, and Ted Turner vice chairman. Jerry Levin (of Time Warner) was to be CEO. Of a 16-person board of directors, one-half would be drawn from the directors of each of the merging firms. Richard Parsons of Time Warner took the position of co-chief operating officer alongside Bob Pittman from AOL. But the gush of bonhomie implied in the MOE structure evaporated quickly. The day following the announcement of the deal, the *New York Times* headline read: "America Online Agrees to Buy Time Warner for $165 Billion." And an equity analyst at Credit Suisse First Boston subsequently opined that AOL had paid a premium of $67 billion to acquire Time Warner[12]—an acquisition premium of about 70 percent.[13]

The reaction by investors to the news was mixed. On Monday, January 10, 2000, Time Warner stock closed at an all-time high of $90, up 39 percent from the previous day's closing price. In addition, the Nasdaq Composite index posted its biggest single day gain ever: a 167 point increase to above 4,000. AOL, however, fell 1.5 percent. By the closing price of Friday of that week, four days after the announcement, AOL's shares had fallen 14.4 percent, net of the change in the S&P 500 index. Time Warner's shares were up 30 percent net of market for the week. As Chapter 2 suggests, it is not unusual for the buyer's share price in a merger to fall, while the target's rises. But in this case the stock price movements suggested two sharply differing views of the deal.

Boosters of the deal predicated their outlook on convergence among print, broadcast, cable, and Internet media. The merger embodied this convergence. Convergence would lead to ubiquity of reach for advertisers that would dominate any of the individual media alone. Nearly a year after the merger announcement, Raymond Katz at Bear Stearns wrote:

> For us the "sizzle" in the AOL Time Warner story is found in the online division, which will act as the engine to create the 21st century equivalent of what the broadcast networks were at their peak: a leading mass-marketer. Even at this early development stage, we believe AOL is showing the growth potential inherent in this strategy.[14]

S.G. Cowan's analysts wrote that the merger creates "a new paradigm in consumer mass marketing of information, news, film and music entertainment content, Internet, and broadband distribution. The merger is complementary as each company has similar business models. . . ."[15]

Much of the promise of this new medium assumed a move of consumers from narrowband access (over copper wire, such as telephone dial-up service) to broadband (over coaxial cable or high-speed optical fiber such as cable TV). This permitted delivery of richer content, particularly video and telephonic services. Bear Stearns' equity research analysts foresaw the possibility that within two years AOL would have a disproportionate presence among Time Warner's cable customers, thanks to its affiliation and to the slowness of other service providers to follow suit.[16]

Early critics of the deal doubted the fundamental value of AOL's shares, likening them to "Weimar Republic money."[17] The inflation in the prices of Internet company stocks created a problem of moral hazard, the incentive to acquire companies with overvalued shares, thus transferring to the seller some of the loss that would occur when the price was corrected. Even though AOL had a fraction of Time Warner's revenue or operating cash flow, its shareholders would receive more than one-half the shares of Newco. This disparity, reflected in the huge goodwill and allocation of value to intangible assets, meant that the fairness of the deal price was founded on uncertain growth prospects rather than solid, demonstrated performance. Other critics doubted that print media content could be imported to the Internet *profitably*.[18] And finally, some critics argued that investors in each company presumably bought those shares because they wanted pure-plays in the Internet and old media, respectively. The merger would dramatically change the industrial commitment that investors were making.

ORIGIN OF THE MERGER

From first discussion to public announcement, the deal took three months to craft. In September 1999 Steve Case and Jerry Levin were thrown together in a fateful way, as co-chairs of the Global Business Dialogue on Electronic Commerce in Paris. In that capacity, they conferred intensively about the future of digital commerce. A month later in China, they met again and discussed general philosophies about the role of the corporation in society.

In mid-October, Case called Levin to propose that the two firms combine through a stock-for-stock merger of equals. Twice over the next two months, the discussion ceased, reflecting sharp differences in terms sought and offered. On both occasions, AOL's vaulting stock price and Time Warner's torpid valuation were compelling incentives to resume discussions.

On January 9, 2000, the boards of directors of America Online and Time Warner both met separately to assess the proposed deals and hear the opinions of financial advisers. The advisers told each board that the terms were "fair" to shareholders. The boards voted to approve the merger.

AOL

Founded in 1985, AOL went public in 1992 and rapidly became the leading Internet Service Provider (ISP). The corporate mission stated that AOL aimed "to build a global medium as central to people's lives as the telephone or television . . . and even more valuable." By 2000, the company was well on the way to achieving that mission. AOL led the new media revolution as the world's leader in interactive services, Web brands, Internet technologies, and electronic commerce services. As of January 2000, America Online's reach was impressive: Twenty-five million subscribers and 110 million consumers were accessing AOL's service. In another sense, AOL had arrived: In 1999, the company was included in the S&P 500 index, a signal that it had become an important firm in the American economy.

The company was driven to grow by its CEO and its culture of aggressive competitiveness. The internal mantra during the 1990s was "get big fast." In her account of the AOL–Time Warner story, *Wall Street Journal* reporter Kara Swisher recounted that

> [Steve Case's] near term goal was to be one of the biggest and most powerful media and communications companies in the world—and very, very soon. My first thought—since he did not appear to be an egomaniac, like so many executives I had interviewed—was that he might actually be insane. . . . Still, I soon learned that Case had been spinning his impossible scenario to many visitors, which was why most reporters who covered AOL considered him a bit of a crank. Besides predicting the inevitability of world domination by his tiny business, he also never seemed to let up on endless pie-in-the-sky speeches, mixing in references to "convergence" and "interactive" and all sorts of other computing hooha, and linking it with the future of all mass media.[19]

The haste and ambition of the firm were stimulated by the perception that there was a brief window of opportunity to establish a strong competitive position in the market. Like the Oklahoma land rush, if you got there first, you owned it. This was described by Robert J. Frank and Philip J. Cook as the "winner take all economy" in which the first mover in an Internet product or service would garner a commanding market position. Alec Klein, reporter for the *Washington Post*, wrote, "The hurried nature of things was in evidence everywhere in the mid-1990s. Office blackboards were scrawled with drawings, incomprehensible arrows, and lines. People were late for meetings. Executives were walking and talking in and out of rooms, cell phones attached to their ears, multitasking."[20] A focal point of this dizzying activity within AOL was the Business Affairs group (BA for short) charged with building revenue through advertising deals. BA was known for its tough culture and determination to squeeze the last penny out of counterparties. This toughness bred arrogance inside and resentment outside the firm. Kara Swisher called the firm "a disaster waiting to happen."[21]

The performance of AOL matched its aggressive intentions. Between 1995 and 2000, its revenues grew by more than 10 times; in 2000 its net income was projected to exceed $1 billion. From January 1992 to January 2000, the firm's share price grew at an astonishing 285 percent rate compounded annually. The market capitalization of the firm's equity had grown to $231 billion by October 1999. The huge run-up in share value had created an acquisition currency that would spur an additional path for growth: Rather than simply growing organically through the expansion of products and customers, the firm could *buy* growth through other companies.

One AOL executive said, "The valuation put on our company was so strong, the cost to our shareholders in making a combination was going down."[22] Of course, this is false logic: The cost of an acquisition remains the same regardless of the height of AOL's share price. The reason it may seem more attractive at higher AOL share prices is that the EPS dilution is lower, the cosmetic appearance is better, and in a share-for-share exchange, the target company shareholders bear the risk of accepting overvalued shares. Another executive said, "We all knew we were living on borrowed time and had to buy something of substance by using that huge currency. We definitely needed to trade up, and fast."[23] But based largely on this logic and the determination to get big fast, AOL embarked on an ambitious acquisition program, punctuated by the purchase in 1999 of Netscape and three other firms (Moviefone, Spinner Networks, and Nullsoft). Still, AOL's stock price kept rising: When the Netscape deal was announced in November 1998 it was valued at $4.2 billion; by closing in March 1999, it was worth $9.6 billion in AOL stock. The realization inside AOL that its lofty valuation was not sustainable created an urgency to do another big deal. "The bottom line is that there was always going to be a deal, since we felt the market was overvalued and that there was a kind of craziness. And believe me, we knew an Internet nuclear winter was coming."[24]

Along with the pressures created by a manic equity market, AOL faced an even more threatening development: the inevitable shift of consumers from narrowband to broadband. AOL was the dominant ISP in a technology that would inevitably decline as consumers demanded increasingly faster and better service. The demand for dial-up ISP service was certain to mature eventually, converting a growth business into a stable utility-like industry, or worse, a low-margin competitive slug-fest for the marginal user. Already, some ISPs were pricing their services on a flat-fee basis, or even giving it away for free. In the late 1990s, AOL was king of the hill; but was this a monarchy worth holding in the future? AOL had business and financial momentum, but could this be *sustained* by doing more of the same? "No" was the blunt answer, delivered by Steve Case himself. At a January 2000 meeting with 200 AOL executives, he said that the lofty Internet valuations would come to an end soon and that AOL needed Time Warner for capital preservation.[25]

Driven by foresight of the Internet nuclear winter and unsustainability of its current strategy, Steve Case led a strategic assessment of AOL's alternatives. Kara Swisher[26] explains that AOL management considered drilling deeper into Internet services with specialized acquisitions that would expand AOL's product offerings (eBay or Amazon were possibilities); expand the enterprise services business with a business-to-business acquisition; diversify into telecommunications; diversify into the content providers such as Disney, Bertelsmann, or Time Warner. Only after a long process of elimination did AOL arrive at targeting Time Warner.

Time Warner

Originally founded as Time, Inc., in 1922, the firm had prospered and grown in the late twentieth century through mergers and acquisitions. Its 1989 merger with Warner Communications Inc. (WCI) and its 1996 acquisition of Turner Broadcasting Systems (TBS) effectively transformed the publishing enterprise into the world's largest media and entertainment company. By merging with Warner Communications, Time got a foothold in the movie and music industry, and by acquiring Turner Broadcasting Systems, it added valuable cable channels and networks. By 2000, Time Warner had six distinct businesses: Publishing, Filmed Entertainment, Music, Cable Networks, Cable Systems, and Digital Media.

Jerry Levin, CEO of Time Warner, had begun his professional career as a lawyer. He had made his name as a rising star within the company as co-founder of the Home Box Office (HBO) business. HBO had enjoyed explosive growth, riding on the expansion of cable TV across the United States. Like the Internet challenge, the success of HBO had depended on a major bet on new technology, new products, and new creative capabilities. HBO had helped to transform Time Warner. "He saw HBO in AOL. He saw himself in Steve Case. . . . They were kindred spirits," said a Time Warner executive.[27] Even though Levin was an intellectual, a strong strategic thinker, and an effective corporate politician, his critics nonetheless saw him as distant, Ozlike and "brilliant, but fragmented. Parts of him didn't cohere, didn't fit together."[28]

While the Warner and TBS acquisitions brought a wealth of new products and content to Time, they created a culture of fiefdoms and sharply differing norms, as disparate as Ivy League print journalists versus nouveau riche film makers. While the fiefdoms delegated power closer to the business frontline, they also meant that integrated effort became more of a challenge. By several accounts the mergers left cultural divisions and animosities that later gathered around the AOL deal. Unfinished business from those earlier deals meant that AOL would face a rather hostile environment upon entry into Time Warner.

The internal fiefdoms also resisted Jerry Levin when he decided, in 1998, to enforce a "digital override" on the activities of the company. The intent was to mount a coordinated strategy to penetrate the Internet. But the divisional barons wanted to retain for themselves the key decisions about technology, products, and timing. Thus, Levin slowly turned to the idea of a transformational acquisition in the Internet space to achieve what he was unable to accomplish internally, from the inside-out.

The social problems within the firm were matched by lackluster financial performance. As Figure 12.1 shows, over the decade of the 1990s, Time Warner generally tracked the S&P 500 index, with lagging performance from 1990 to 1992 and again from 1994 to early 1997. This reflects

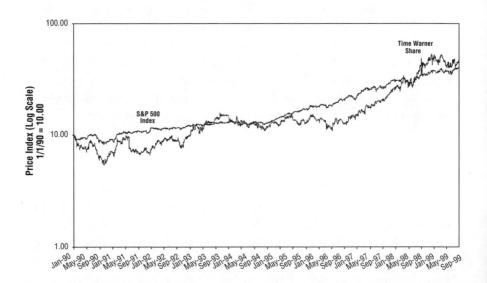

Figure 12.1 **Share Prices for Time Warner versus the S&P 500 Index, January 1990 to January 2000**

Source of data: Datastream.

the maturity of its core publishing and entertainment operations and the dilutive impact of its acquisitions. Jerry Levin, however, did not believe that the firm's stock price reflected its true value. By December 1999, Levin sent a memo to his staff. "We all feel a degree of frustration at the failure of the market to value our company in a way that approximates its superior worth."[29]

MOTIVES FOR THE MERGER

> We are proposing the merger because we believe the combined strengths of our two companies will enable us to build the world's preeminent, fully integrated media and communications company. The merger will combine Time Warner's broad array of media, entertainment and news brands and its technologically advanced broadband delivery systems with America Online's extensive Internet franchises, technology and infrastructure to create a new company capable of enhancing consumers' access to the broadest selection of high-quality content and interactive services. By combining the leading interactive services and media companies, AOL Time Warner will create the potential for stronger operating and financial results than either company could achieve on its own.
>
> —Joint Merger Proxy Statement and Prospectus[30]

Cloaked in this language was a vision for revenue opportunities and synergies in areas such as advertising by companies; increased subscriber growth through cross-promotion; better efficiency in marketing across different platforms and distribution systems; and cost efficiencies achievable by launching and operating interactive extensions of Time Warner brands. AOL and Time Warner estimated that synergies would contribute about $1 billion toward the new firm's first full year Earnings Before Interest, Depreciation, and Amortization (EBITDA), yielding a growth rate of approximately 30 percent.[31] Salomon Brothers (financial advisor for AOL) and Morgan Stanley (financial advisor for Time Warner) opined that the transaction was fair to shareholders from a financial point of view. Skeptics viewed these motives with colorful language. "A company without assets was buying a company without a clue," wrote Kara Swisher.[32] Earlier prominent deals between content providers and distribution channels—

such as Disney/CapCities–ABC or Viacom/Paramount—had not proved the wisdom of vertical integration in that industry.

AFTERMATH

The Federal Communications Commission (FCC) announced its approval of the merger on January 11, 2001, nearly a year after the deal was first announced. The merger was consummated the same day. The long delay was due to an extensive regulatory review by European and American antitrust authorities. The FCC required that the new firm open its instant messaging service to competing ISPs when AOL entered Time Warner's cable system. And the European antitrust regulators required that Time Warner drop the merger of its music subsidiary with recording and music publisher, EMI Group.

Approval by the Federal Trade Commission (FTC) occurred on December 14, 2000, and was contingent on the new company opening its cable system to competing ISPs of AOL and offering AOL's digital subscriber line (DSL) services to subscribers in Time Warner cable areas where affiliated cable broadband service is available in the same manner and at the same retail pricing as they do in those areas where affiliated cable broadband ISP service is not available. Finally, the FTC required the appointment of a Monitor Trustee to check on the new firm's observance of the order.

After the closing on January 11, the two organizations turned toward integration. Bob Pittman, co-chief operating officer, commenced a process of trying to realize the $1 billion in synergies promised at the announcement. But the divisional fiefdoms within Time Warner frustrated the process. Most importantly, the open access requirements of the regulators meant that Time Warner's cable systems division would have to carry ISP rivals and offer DSL alternatives to their broadband services, unacceptable to the division chiefs. As the drive for synergies stalled, it became clearer that AOL's revenue base had weakened considerably and that the new firm would miss its earnings targets.

Securities analysts had predicated their optimistic forecasts for the merger on the migration of AOL's large subscriber base to Time Warner's cables. This was a foundation for the cross-selling opportunities envisioned in the synergies for the merger. Bear Stearns said, "In our opinion, broad-

band is necessary to create the new online mass-market medium."[33] Kara
Swisher quoted sources that "Cable was the driver of everything. Without
it, the merger made a lot less sense."[34] But the cable system executives in
Time Warner resisted carrying AOL on their system. This reflected linger-
ing hostility about AOL's premerger maneuvers, especially its attempts to
force cable operators to open their lines to online companies like AOL,
belief that AOL would hijack consumers from the cable systems, and a desire to protect Time Warner's own ISP service, Road Runner. Kara
Swisher concluded, "The fact of the matter was this: The company's failure
to make any progress in linking AOL to Time Warner's cable assets was the
single clearest indicator that the merger was never going to work."[35] As
customers switched from narrowband connections to broadband connections, AOL would atrophy.

During the year that it took government regulators to approve the
merger, the Internet bubble collapsed in the U.S. equity markets. From
March 28 to April 30, 2000, the Datastream Internet Index lost 41 percent,
and AOL lost 18 percent. The broader market followed: From September
2000 to November 2001, the Internet index lost 81 percent of its value; in
comparison, AOL's share value lost 39 percent. After November 2001,
AOL's decline in value accelerated. Without a collar to protect Time
Warner's shareholders, AOL's share price decline dissipated the acquisition
premium up to the date of closing.

Figure 12.2 gives the share prices of AOL, Time Warner, Newco,
and two equity market benchmarks, the S&P 500 and Internet stocks, as
indexed to 1.00 as of January 1, 1998. Most apparent is the astonishing
tenfold rise in share price in the early stage of the Internet boom, 1998
and early 1999. Rather sharp volatility in AOL's share price during the
peak, 1999, is followed by the fall in 2000. Figure 12.3 shows that the
consummation of the merger with Time Warner commences more
moderate performance in the firm's share price: For the first year after
merger the shares of AOL Time Warner roughly tracked the S&P 500
index; thereafter the shares slumped sharply, to align more closely with
the Internet index.

Coincident with the decline of the Internet equities came the onset of
recession in the United States. Between January and April 2001, the Federal Reserve Bank cut interest rates four times, yet stocks kept falling. Bad
financial news was the harbinger of senior management changes. Jerry
Levin resigned on December 5, 2001, after losing an internal battle to ac-

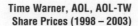

Figure 12.2   **Share Prices from 1998 to 2003**
Source of data: Datastream.

quire some cable assets from AT&T and amid recriminations about financial performance. Richard Parsons of the Time Warner side stepped in as CEO. The earnings report in January 2002 was below target. In April the firm adopted new accounting policies that required a $54 billion charge to earnings, the largest in corporate history, to reflect the impairment of goodwill. On April 9, the CEO of the AOL division was reassigned and Bob Pittman was sent in to rescue the operation: Subscriber growth was stalling and AOL still had no effective offering in broadband.

Advertising spending, always sensitive to the economic cycle, receded generally across the media industry. For AOL, the advertising recession in 2001 had threatened to turn into a rout. Needing to save the merger, AOL pressed its advertisers hard to maintain their spending so that AOL could report the targeted revenues. In this context, AOL's Business Affairs unit, always the most aggressive in the firm, pushed into deals whose impact on reported earnings was merely cosmetic. Alec Klein of the *Washington Post*

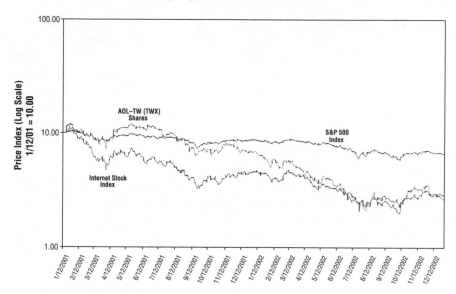

Figure 12.3 **AOL–TW Postmerger Share Prices**
Source of data: Datastream.

published two articles starting on July 18, 2002 (the same day that Bob Pittman announced his resignation), which described AOL's efforts to bolster its advertising revenues. He wrote:

> AOL converted legal disputes into ad deals. It negotiated a shift in revenue from one division to another, bolstering its online business. It sold ads on behalf of online auction giant eBay Inc., booking the sale of eBay's ads as AOL's own revenue. AOL bartered ads for computer equipment in a deal with Sun Microsystems Inc., AOL counted stock rights as ad and commerce revenue in a deal with a Las Vegas firm called PurchasePro.com Inc.[36]

Shortly after the publication of Klein's exposé, the U.S. Justice Department commenced an investigation into the financial accounting for AOL's revenues, prompting AOL Time Warner to make its own internal investigation. On August 14, 2002, the company disclosed that $49 million in revenues had been "inappropriately recognized." Though small compared to the total revenues of the firm, the revelations shattered the vulnerable confidence of investors in the new firm's management. Pittman left in July, 2002, as the news of the accounting chicanery was breaking.

This last piece of bad news precipitated the final act of the tragedy. Gordon Crawford, the highly respected portfolio manager, organized other significant shareholders to lobby for firing Steve Case. Crawford told me, "I met with Case and told him to resign. He took it defensively. I said, 'You're a roadblock to rebuilding esprit de corps in the company.'" Case declared in December that he would step down as chairman at the next annual meeting. In 2003, "AOL" was removed from the firm's name, symbolically closing the chapter on this deal. Gordon Crawford said:[37]

> This was a breathtaking deal. Everyone was surprised by it. But it turned out to be the wrong company at the wrong time and at the wrong price. The crux of the issue here is Levin's ego. If he had waited a year, he could have bought Yahoo! Then everyone would have thought he was brilliant. Yahoo! is at the core of the global Internet business. It was there at the birth of paid search, where you connect buyers and sellers. Today the company [Yahoo!] has a $30 billion market cap and is growing rapidly. AOL was just an ISP, tied to narrow-band communication—Steve Case's big mistake was in the negotiations with regulators: He traded away the ability to offer AOL broadband on Time Warner's cable systems. I was stunned later at how quickly broadband took off.
>
> Levin got caught up in his self-image as a leading thinker about transformative technology. His experiences with HBO and satellite communication were key. He had the right concept in 2000, that the Internet would be a transforming medium.
>
> There was a lot of unhappiness caused by the management structure in this deal. No one believed Steve Case would simply sit by as chairman and not meddle in the business. The people at Time Warner didn't like Steve; they thought he was arrogant, incompetent, and insensitive. But if AOL Time Warner had hit its expected performance targets, all the management stuff wouldn't have mattered. I discount the cultural side of the failure. If the two sides had gotten along, it is unlikely that the game would have played out differently.

There is not a clear path to success for AOL. Time Warner could sell it, merge it into a competitor, or keep it and milk it for the cash. It could keep its profits steady by sharply reducing costs. AOL has gone from 34 million subscribers to 24 million. The number of subscribers is in long-term secular decline.

The Internet had a huge bubble; the stock prices slumped. But the promise of the Internet has never wavered. As a channel of mass-market communication, the Internet (firms like Yahoo! and Google) will take huge market share from the other media. The entertainment companies are incompetent in integrating new media; they've blown every transition to new technology, just as they did with the advent of TV and cable.

A lot of the difficulty at AOL Time Warner was exogenous. I don't fault them for that part of it. You couldn't have anticipated the economy in the summer of 2001. The really fatal error was that the insiders knew that it would be increasingly difficult to make the numbers; yet they kept the projections strong.

THE DRIVERS OF FAILURE

The merger of AOL and Time Warner displays prominently the six drivers of M&A failure. Given their size and range of technologies, the two firms individually and together were *complex*. Much like the Pennsylvania/New York Central deal 32 years earlier, the fixed exchange ratio *tightly coupled* the operating performance of the two firms. Failure on AOL's part to report expected quarterly earnings growth might derail the deal. The recession starting in 2001 and the collapse of the Internet bubble (both reflected in receding equity markets and in the spectacular failures of various e-business models) shows that *business was not as usual*. The accounts suggest some unusual *cognitive biases* at work: hubris, momentum thinking, and recency bias. A number of *management decisions elevated risks*: Time Warner's decision to diversify into the Internet and to receive payment in shares of AOL, and Steve Case's agreement with the Federal Trade Commission (FTC) to give up exclusive carriage for AOL on the Time Warner cable system. Finally, the cultural clashes between the AOL and Time

Warner sides, and the competition among Time Warner fiefdoms impaired the ability of Pittman and others on the *integration team* to realize the values hoped for in the deal.

COUNTERPOINT: YAHOO! ACQUIRES GEOCITIES AND BROADCAST.COM

During the heady days of the Internet boom in the late 1990s, Yahoo! was the chief rival to AOL. From the customer's perspective, the two firms offered similar attributes: an entryway into the Internet. Both firms earned a profit in 1998, unusual for companies in the Internet field. But from there the comparisons differed. AOL was an Internet service provider (ISP) depending on dial-up service, earning revenues from both customer subscriptions and advertising. Yahoo! was a "portal" that attracted visitors on the Web to its services. It was the first navigational guide to the Web and offered a network of branded communications, shopping, and information services. Yahoo!'s revenues ($203 million in 1998) depended entirely on advertising. Its services were without charge to the end user. And since Yahoo! was not tied to a mode of access like AOL (i.e., through telephone dial-up), it was prepared for the advent of broadband and wireless communications.

One of the sharpest differences between the stories of AOL and Yahoo! is in their acquisition strategies. Both active acquirers during the boom, they steered different paths at the end of the boom. AOL diversified, acquiring old economy assets. Yahoo! concentrated within the Internet sphere, in effect, betting that the Internet would pay. AOL closed its acquisition program with a huge acquisition that transformed the firm. Yahoo! consummated a string of relatively small acquisitions that did not. While AOL's acquisition strategy had its critics, so did Yahoo's!. The former CEO of Lycos (a competitor of Yahoo!) wrote:

> Yahoo's failure to use its $130 billion plus market cap to create a transforming event will be looked back upon as one of the greatest missed business opportunities of all time. Yahoo! could have purchased virtually any business it chose, yet its determination to remain pure to an Internet-only model deprived the company of the chance to build scale on a

grand dimension. Only time will tell. But I believe the company left a massive opportunity on the table and will ultimately be owned by one of the old-economy companies it should have acquired.[38]

My focus of comparison of AOL and Yahoo! is Yahoo!'s acquisition in 1999 of two firms, GeoCities and Broadcast.com. Both were transformative deals for Yahoo! That same year, Yahoo! acquired three smaller firms in 1999, Encompass ($130 million), Online Anywhere ($80 million), and log-me-on ($9.9 million). These deals were dwarfed in impact by GeoCities and Broadcast.com.

The GeoCities Deal

On January 28, 1999, Yahoo! announced an agreement to acquire GeoCities for $4.66 billion in stock, representing a 52 percent acquisition premium. The deal took shape quickly, over six weeks. The timing of the deal was spurred perhaps by rumors that AOL was considering an acquisition of GeoCities, too. The land rush described earlier, motivated aggregators like AOL and Yahoo! to preempt one another. Four key deals in the months before threatened heightened competition: Disney/Infoseek, AOL/Netscape, @Home/Excite, and USA Networks /Lycos. All were competitors of GeoCities and Yahoo! before their deals, and would be stronger competitors after. From 1997 to 1998, GeoCities' revenues quadrupled and gross profits grew 11 times. In the same period, Yahoo!'s revenues and gross profits tripled and its net income turned solidly positive for the first time. Also, Yahoo! had made a small investment in the firm in late 1997, acquiring 2.1 percent of GeoCities' stock. The acquisition in 1999 cemented two firms who knew each other relatively well.

GeoCities, founded in 1994, invented the concept of the Web community, a site for personal home pages. About 3.5 million "homesteaders" created sites that attracted 19 million visitors in December 1998, making GeoCities the third most-visited site on the Internet. Web users, "homesteaders," published their own personal web sites in one of 41 themed GeoCities neighborhoods such as personal finance, politics, and so on. These neighborhoods offered navigational advantages to visitors and compelling targets for advertisers and merchants. The business concept was to exploit feelings of affinity among users with common interests who had personalized their engagement with the Web. Though the firm lost $20 million in 1998 on revenues of $18 million, its losses were shrinking over time.

Yahoo!'s aim in the acquisition was, quite simply, to broaden its reach: The combined Yahoo!/GeoCities would stretch to 58 percent of the users of the Internet, making it the second-largest network on the Internet. The acquisition would create the largest Web "community." It would give Yahoo! access to personal publishing and editing tools, in which GeoCities had a leading position. And Yahoo! services could be sold to homesteaders on the GeoCities platform. The merger proxy statement said:

> This merger will combine two of the largest and most popular services on the Internet. Following the merger, you will have a stake in one of the world's leading global branded Web networks. Overall, both Yahoo! and GeoCities believe that the merger will provide added value to all of their respective stockholders. However, both Yahoo! and GeoCities note that their goals in the merger are subject to risks . . .

Neither the proxy nor the other communications about the deal disclosed the sources of the added value.

THE ACQUISITION OF BROADCAST.COM

Barely three months later, on April 21, 1999, Yahoo! agreed to acquire Broadcast.com in a share-for-share exchange worth $4.73 billion. Broadcast streamed on-demand audio and video programs over the Internet to users 24 hours a day, 7 days a week. Covering 385 radio stations, 40 TV stations and cable networks, and 420 college and professional sports teams, the company had reached more than 800,000 unique users by December 1998. Broadcast.com boasted a number of firsts, including the first Internet distribution of live commercial radio station programming, a live sporting event, a quarterly earnings call, and a stockholders meeting. The company's sites ranked sixteenth of all sites on the Web for visitors. Founded in 1995, the company went public in July 1998.

RealNetworks, the prime competitor to Broadcast.com, was the pioneer of the technology to stream audio and video content over the Internet. Broadcast, however, had been the pioneer of licensing and distributing programming. Yahoo! understood the distribution of text and graphics but did not have the capability to distribute audio and video content. Broadcast's growth depended on the size of the population of users with broadband access to the net (narrowband access was too slow). As of 1999, only four percent of the households had broadband access, a percentage that was expected to grow rapidly over the next decade. Thus, Yahoo!'s acquisition of Broadcast.com was a bet on the technological enrichment of the Internet and growing sophistication of consumer demand.

The unfolding of the Broadcast acquisition had a similar pattern to that of the GeoCities deal. Broadcast was running deficits and was expected to continue to do so as it built out its business. Though it was a public company, it needed deeper financial pockets than its own capacity to raise capital would provide. Therefore, the executives of Broadcast hoped to attract possible buyers. National Broadcasting Company (NBC) and AOL each contemplated acquiring Broadcast.com, but Broadcast liked Yahoo! best. Yahoo! had invested a small amount ($1.2 million) in Broadcast in 1997, as a basis for building a business acquaintance.

Motives

SEC filings and analysts' reports from the time suggest that Yahoo!'s acquisitions were a manifestation of a strategic drive for market position in a volatile and rapidly changing field. Some critics viewed these businesses as shams with which executives were paying a cynical game to hype share prices through maximization of whatever metric du jour investors seemed to value. The classic metric was "eyeballs" or number of visitors to a site. An Internet business that was losing money could still be positively valued in the stock market based on expectations of acquiring an audience that might eventually turn profitable. Thus, Karen Angel wrote, "The main motivation behind both the GeoCities and Broadcast.com buys was this: to expand Yahoo's audience so it had more eyeballs to monetize."[39] Yahoo!'s formal public relations efforts surrounding these deals did nothing to discourage an eyeballs-centric view. The industry was in very rapid consolidation in 1999 as the economic realities about Internet products and services began to sink in. Yahoo!'s executives were focused on building a defensible share of market through M&A. A reporter for *Wired News* wrote:

> The acquisition is part of a mad dash by the Internet industry to buy the attention of as many people as possible. The idea is to build an all-encompassing service, so that one company reaps all the revenue, no matter where Internet surfers spend their time and money. Just last week, At Home, with the backing of AT&T, proposed to buy Excite, a Yahoo rival. 'This whole wave of mergers was triggered by AOL's buy of Netscape,' said Anthony Blenk, an analyst with Everen Securities. 'You can expect to see a lot more of this.'. . . Yahoo would get a big boost in traffic from the purchase. With GeoCities folded in, Yahoo's reach on the Web will shoot even farther past rivals like Lycos, and settle in just behind the proposed combination of America Online and Netscape Communications.[40]

GeoCities argued that the mergers would create synergies:

> . . . combining GeoCities and Yahoo! would result in potential operating synergies and cost savings, including the elimination of duplicate expenses in sales and marketing, business development, administration, and product development, and increased buying power due to the size of the combined entity.[41]

Absent more detailed information about the sources and size of the benefits, investors could not have been able to ascribe much value to the merger synergies.

AFTERMATH: YAHOO!

The timing of both acquisitions was more propitious in Yahoo!'s case than was AOL's acquisition. Yahoo! enjoyed a relatively fast resolution of the uncertainty surrounding antitrust approval for the deals. And through the end of the calendar year, the stock market continued to regard the Internet sector favorably. Rather impulsively, Yahoo! tried to assert a copyright interest on all private materials posted on GeoCities' private sites. The homesteaders responded violently, which compelled Yahoo! to retreat from its "rights grab." And Yahoo! restructured the organizations of both GeoCities and Broadcast.com. For instance, Yahoo! laid off 200 of GeoCities' 300 employees.

Yahoo!'s fortunes turned down with the bursting of the Internet bubble in the spring of 2000 and the onset of recession later that year. Figure 12.4 gives the stock price for Yahoo! versus the Nasdaq and S&P 500 index from December 1998 to December 2003. From nearly $200 per share at the end of 1999, Yahoo!'s shares had slumped to about $20 at the end of 2000, a meltdown of epic proportions. In the process, the leading Internet analyst, Mary Meeker, downgraded Yahoo! in her investment recommendations.

On February 27, 2001, Yahoo!'s directors met to assess the damage to the firm, and decided to seek new operational leadership for the company. The CEO, Tim Koogle, was to step down and assume the role of chairman of the board once a successor had been found. At the announcement of the management change, the firm also disclosed that it was lowering its expectations for revenues and earnings for the quarter. Investors reacted by bidding down Yahoo!'s share price by 11 percent.

Jerry Yang, founder, director, and titular Chief Yahoo of the firm, took a personal role in the search for a new CEO. His attention turned to Terry Semel, former co-chairman of Warner Brothers. Nontechnical where Koogle was technical, pragmatic where Koogle was visionary, and formal where Koogle was casual, Semel marked a sharp break in the leadership style of Yahoo! Karen Angel wrote that "he was Koogle's opposite in almost every respect."[42]

Joining the firm on May 1, 2001, Semel declared that a firm with 44 business units reporting directly to the CEO was unmanageable and had no focus. He initiated a restructuring program to reorganize the operations into six broad divisions, to shift the mix of revenues toward a lower reliance on advertising, and to push to generate revenue. In particular he focused on revamping advertising sales from simple order-taking to planned selling and marketing. In November 2001, he announced a major partnership with SBC Communications to combine Yahoo!'s content with SBC's broadband.

Figure 12.4 shows a modest recovery in Yahoo!'s share price in 2003. In large part this reflects a dramatic recovery in Yahoo!'s revenues and profitability. Figure 12.5 gives the time series of revenue, net income, and employees. During the same period, Yahoo!'s main pure-play competitors, Lycos, Infoseek, and Excite@Home, declined more sharply, leaving Yahoo! well positioned in the competitive field.

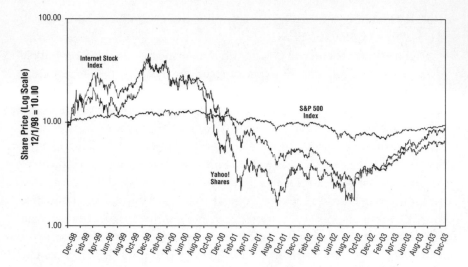

Figure 12.4   **Share Prices of Yahoo! versus the S&P 500 Composite Index and an Index of Internet Stocks, December 1998 to December 2003**

Source of data: Datastream.

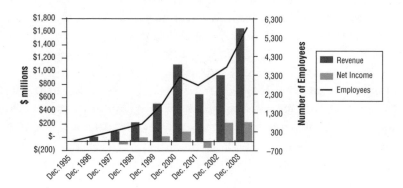

Figure 12.5   **Revenues, Net Income, and Employees of Yahoo!**

Source of data: Hoover's Online.

CONCLUSION

The AOL/Time Warner transaction dwarfs other deals from hell in almost all respects. It leads the field in the meltdown in value. The executive firings and resignations, the civil litigation, criminal investigation, and the erasure of AOL from the corporation's name reveal a remarkable wipeout of the vision of the deal's architects. Plainly, rendering judgment on the entire deal ignores the enormous asymmetry in welfare for the AOL and Time Warner shareholders. The Time Warner side bore more of the damage. What should Case and Levin have done differently? Less hubris, less gushiness and more sobriety, more honesty in financial reporting, better due diligence, better management of the postmerger integration, higher cultural sensitivity, more teamwork, and use of a collar are obvious remedies. But these are dwarfed by the strategic dilemma facing the two firms in 1999.

Response to Changes in Internet Technology

In light of the disruptive impact of Internet technology, doing nothing was not an option for either firm. Steve Case saw clearly the inevitable atrophy of AOL's narrowband service and the rise of the broadband alternative. Jerry Levin saw clearly the digitization of news and entertainment. All of this is coming to pass, though perhaps not at the speed at which the pundits of 1999 expected. In 2005, no informed observer doubts the inexorable movement of these trends. One of the CEO's most important jobs is to position the firm for survival and prosperity. In the cases of AOL and Time Warner in 1999, Case and Levin would have been derelict in their duties not to respond to the looming threats. From AOL's standpoint, the merger with Time Warner was its solution to the threat of broadband. From Time Warner's standpoint the merger with AOL would help to digitize Time Warner (where earlier attempts to do so had failed ingloriously).

But was the theory of convergence the appropriate bet for each company? It makes sense if you believe that it is possible to lock in consumers to a particular brand or portfolio of services. For instance, Time Warner saw in the merger with AOL the opportunity to acquire a significant share of the Internet market to whom its news and entertainment

products could be sold, rather like its decision a few years earlier to acquire cable TV properties that would provide a captive pipeline for the
firm's filmed entertainment. This kind of vertical integration has a time-
honored place in the annals of M&A, most of it with a mediocre track
record. The highest returns flow to the creators of new content; distributors, suffering through each new wave of innovation and competition,
earn lower returns. With benefit of hindsight, we know that consumers
are much more fluid engagers of digital media (just ask the wireless telephone service providers), which weakens considerably the effects of
lock-in and convergence.

Yahoo! offers what would have been an alternative strategy for AOL:
Continue to invest in the Internet space to extend its range of services and
enrich the experience of subscribers. The written accounts of the process
of elimination by which AOL discarded this alternative are not as detailed
as we might like, though it is clear that a Yahoo!-style strategy would have
done little to cure AOL's looming threat of broadband.

On balance the firms' responses to the turbulent changes in Internet
technology seem reasonable and plausible, though not necessarily optimal.
Turbulence generally predicts M&A activity in an industry. The deals by
both AOL and Yahoo! are consistent with this explanation. And the trend
continues. As of 2005, we note the disruptive impact of the Internet on
musical entertainment (Napster, copying, downloading), telephone companies (VOIP technology), and retailing (the intrusions of Amazon and
eBay). It is ironic that both buyers ended up with old economy CEOs,
suggesting perhaps that the future for Internet operations lies in their integration (or convergence) with the rest of the economy. Someone criticized
Terry Semel for being a technology illiterate, to which he replied that it
was a good thing, too, since all the technology literates were producing
such large losses.

Response to the Equity Market Bubble

The two cases in this chapter reveal that the timing and volume of M&A
activity among Internet companies were influenced by the extraordinary
overvaluation in their shares. This suggests a rather cynical opportunism at
work in the conduct of these deals. The land rush mentality; winner take
all; the advantage of the first mover all suggest a Ready, Fire, Aim approach
to M&A that proves so disastrous. Yahoo!'s strategic intent to remain in the

Internet space. Its focus on building a defendable market position may have increased the market reach somewhat but did not prove to be positively transforming as reflected, for instance, in heightened profitability or share price relative to the sector. However, the firm did remain better positioned than AOL to exploit the shift of customers from narrowband Internet service to broadband.

Figure 12.6 plots the relative market values of AOL, Yahoo!, an index of Internet stocks, and an index of media and entertainment stocks from the date of the AOL/Time Warner merger announcement to 2003. We see that over the first year, AOL did better than its Internet peers and worse than its media peers. But by the end of 2003, AOL wound up in line with Yahoo! and the Internet index. In short, the merger offered a soft landing in the Internet crash for Steve Case and his AOL shareholders. However, the merger was less beneficial for Jerry Levin and Time Warner. Levin remains unrepentant about the AOL Time Warner merger. He has expressed to several reporters his faith that eventually circumstances will prove the wisdom of the deal.

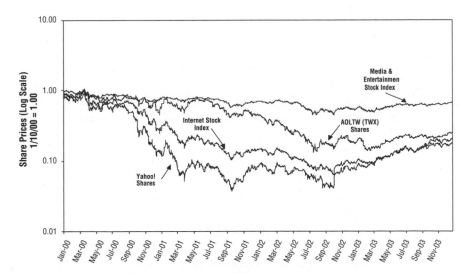

Figure 12.6 **Share Prices of AOL (and Newco) and Yahoo! versus Indexes of Internet Stocks and Media/Entertainment Stocks During and After the Internet Bust, January 10, 2000 to December 31, 2003**

Source of data: Datastream.

NOTES

1. The research assistance of Christine Shim and Sean Carr is gratefully acknowledged, as are the interviews with Gordon Crawford, Raymond Katz, and Thayer Bigelow. Key secondary sources of information on this transaction include the book-length summaries by prominent journalists who covered the events

2. Swisher (2003), 9.

3. Swisher (2003), 10.

4. A quotation of *Fortune* in Swisher (2003), 10.

5. Swisher (2003), 12.

6. Swisher (2003), 16.

7. Klein (2003), 287–288.

8. Klein (2003), 292.

9. Klein (2003), 293.

10. Klein (2003), 300.

11. Press release, January 10, 2003, filed with the U.S. Securities and Exchange Commission.

12. Research report, Credit Suisse First Boston, "AOL/TWX" January 19, 2000.

13. "Time Warner: Extracting a Premium," *Financial Times*, February 12, 2000.

14. Raymond Lee Katz, Katie Manglis, and Michael Kelman, Bear Stearns Research Report, "AOL Time Warner, Inc.," April 9, 2001, 1.

15. Edward T. Hatch, Peter J. Moirsky, and Elizabeth L. Kressel, S.G. Cowan Perspectives, "Time Warner," January 19, 2000, 1.

16. Raymond Lee Katz, Katie Manglis, and Michael Kelman, Bear Stearns Research Report, "AOL Time Warner, Inc.," April 9, 2001, 25.

17. Swisher (2003), 146.

18. J.B. Haller, "AOL: Best—or Worst—of Times?" *ZDNet News*, January 17, 2000.

19. Swisher (2003), 3.

20. Klein (2003), 61.

21. Swisher (2003), 19.

22. A quotation of George Vradenburg III, AOL's chief lobbyist, in Klein (2003), 86.

23. A quotation of Richard Hanlon, AOL's chief of investor relations, quoted in Swisher (2003), 128.

24. A quotation of an unnamed AOL executive in Swisher (2003), 128.

25. Reported in Swisher (2003), 105.

26. Swisher (2003), 129.

27. A quotation of Dave Sickert, former HBO marketing director in Klein (2003), 71.

28. Munk (2003), xiv.

29. Memo by Jerry Levin quoted in Klein (2003), 70.

30. Amendment No. 4 to Form S-4 Registration Statement, AOL Time Warner, May 19, 2000, ii.

31. AOL Time Warner revised Joint Proxy Statement-Prospectus, May 19, 2000, 48.

32. Swisher (2003), 2.

33. Raymond Lee Katz, Katie Manglis, and Michael Kelman, "The Tiffany OSP: AOL Time Warner," Bear Stearns Research Report, April 9, 2001.

34. Swisher (2003), 207.

35. Swisher (2003), 208.

36. Alec Klein, "Unconventional Transactions Boosted Sales," *Washington Post,* July 18, 2002, 1. © 2002 *The Washington Post.* Reprinted by permission.

37. Interview of Robert Bruner and Christine Shim with Gordon Crawford, April 21, 2004.

38. Bob Davis, *Speed Is Life* (New York: Currency, Doubleday, 2001), 181.

39. Karen Angel, *Inside Yahoo!* (New York: John Wiley and Sons, 2002), 163.

40. Craig Bicknell, "Yahoo Gobbles Up GeoCities," *Wired News,* January 28, 1999, accessed August 30, 2004 at http://www.wired.com/news/business /0,1367,17595,00.html.

41. GeoCities Merger Proxy Statement, April 29, 1999, 43.

42. Angel (2002), 232.

13

December 2001: Dynegy's Proposed Merger with Enron

On December 2, 2001, Enron Corporation filed for bankruptcy in what was the largest industrial filing to date.[1] The collapse capped a year that had seen the death spiral of one of the darlings of the business press. And the filing concluded a frenetic month of merger negotiations with Enron's closest competitor, Dynegy Incorporated. The failure of merger negotiations sealed the evaporation of $70 billion in market value for Enron's shareholders, the partial liquidation of the firm, layoff of 60,000 employees, and an explosion of civil and criminal litigation.

A counterpoint to the story of Dynegy/Enron is the acquisition of General Cinema Corporation by AMC Entertainment, its close competitor in 2002. AMC/General Cinema is strikingly similar to Dynegy/Enron in several respects: Both industries were in sharp contraction at the time of negotiations; both targets were in deep financial distress; both buyers were healthier but also had weathered the industry storm with difficulty. Yet in AMC's case, the merger was successfully concluded and Newco emerged from the transaction much stronger. The comparison of these two cases highlights the vital roles of leadership, market instability, credibility of managers, and underlying asset quality in determining whether a merger of companies in distress will result in a deal from hell.

THE MERGING FIRMS: ENRON AND DYNEGY

Enron was formed from the 1985 merger of two gas-pipeline firms: Houston Natural Gas and Omaha-based InterNorth, Inc., then one of the largest pipeline companies in the world. Kenneth Lay, head of Houston Natural Gas and an economist by training, took over the combined entity. As CEO, Lay transformed Enron from a gas-pipeline company into the nation's biggest energy trader.

Lay was aided in Enron's remarkable transformation by the timing of deregulatory reforms of the United States' natural gas distribution and electric utility industries. These reforms naturally led to a more open and vibrant energy market. Enron seized the opportunity to shape the wholesale power industry in transition. Enron envisioned and developed a marketplace for energy where prices could be set by open bidding, buyers and suppliers could be brought together, and power contracts could be tailored to meet the exact needs of a customer. Soon Enron was trading not just energy, but also paper, steel, bandwidth, and even dynamic random access memory (DRAM) chips; Enron had morphed into an entirely different entity. While in 1990 around 80 percent of its revenue came from the gas-pipeline business, by 2000 its trading business accounted for 95 percent of revenue.[2] Enron's forays into trading earned it the accolade Most Innovative Company from *Fortune* magazine for six years in a row. As Figure 13.1

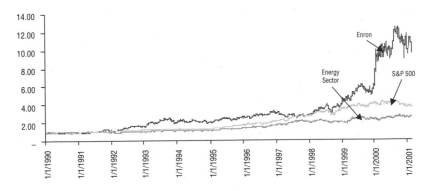

Enron Stock Performance versus Sector and Market

Figure 13.1 **Enron Share Price Performance**

shows, Enron's share price skyrocketed, while share prices of other companies in the energy sector rose only modestly.

Dynegy Inc. was in the businesses of energy trading, marketing, and generation, and electricity and natural gas transmission and distribution. In addition, like Enron, it had activities in the broadband and weather derivatives businesses. Unlike Enron, however, Dynegy had a more balanced revenue mix. In 2000, 53 percent of its business came from power generation and energy marketing and trading activities; 30 percent came from transmission and distribution, while the remaining 17 percent came from its natural gas liquids activities. Although the two companies were considered archrivals, Dynegy was far smaller than Enron. Total revenue in 2000 was $29 billion versus Enron's $101 billion; total assets were $21 billion while Enron had $65 billion.[3] Dynegy's biggest shareholder was Chevron Texaco, which held a 26 percent stake in the company.

EVENTS LEADING UP TO THE MERGER PROPOSAL

Pundits will argue endlessly about the beginning of Enron's demise. The firm's share prices suggest August 23, 2000, when the quote peaked at $90.75, the turning point after which the firm's fortunes sagged. Within a month a journalist, Jonathan Weil, published an article that questioned mark-to-market accounting and its possible abuses. A leading short-seller, Jim Chanos, read the article, and by November had taken a major short position on Enron. The accelerating decline of the firm over the next 12 months can be traced in several parallel developments:

- *Growing turbulence in Enron's product markets.* In the fall of 2000, the California electric power crisis began to appear, leading observers to query its possible adverse impact on Enron, which was a supplier to this market and could claim a positive advantage in dealing with it. The concern about California rippled through energy prices nationwide. And a populist governor sought to turn public opinion against Enron and the other energy suppliers. The growing hostility toward Enron took physical form when protesters threw a pie into CEO Jeffrey Skilling's face in June 2001.

Enron Broadband Services (EBS), a trading operation unveiled by Jeffrey Skilling in January 2000 that some analysts estimated to be worth an extra $37.00 per share, was not realizing the expected trading volume. A joint venture with Blockbuster to deliver movies on demand had fallen apart. Layoffs began at EBS on March 1, 2001. Azurix, a partially spun-off business unit that contained all of Enron's public water assets, also failed to meet projections. Enron had underestimated the resistance of municipalities to price increases in water. But the greatest threat to Enron was simply the entry of new competitors into its trading arenas. Profit margins on trading in the core gas and electricity arenas were declining, thanks to the new competition. Enron sought to create new trading arenas in pulp paper, boxcar capacity, and other commodities. But the start-up of trading operations took additional capital and was a risky proposition, as the EBS operation proved.

- *Deteriorating financial performance and aggressive use of special purpose entities.* Market turbulence translated into declining profit margins, worsening earnings per share (EPS) performance, and rising debt. But to sustain its high price/earnings multiple, Enron had carefully cultivated investors' expectations of rapid growth. To support these expectations would require raising more capital. The CFO of Enron, Andrew Fastow, raised funds off balance sheet through the use of "special purpose entities" (SPEs). Raising capital this way is legal, not uncommon in American business, and was the focus of applause by *CFO* magazine in 1999 for Fastow's innovative financing. Where SPEs can create trouble is in the structure of their teams, which, if designed aggressively, can backfire. During 2000, Fastow had rolled out three special purpose entities, called "Raptors," which offset about $1 billion in investment losses of Enron. But these hedges were a sham, since the Raptors were capitalized with Enron's own stock that would need to be "topped up" as Enron's share price fell. Thus, the Raptors did not bear meaningful risk; they mainly disguised losses. As the asset values underlying the Raptors declined, Enron was required to accommodate the investors in the SPEs with fresh capital infusions.

- *Rising objections to Enron's lack of financial transparency.* In March 2001, *Fortune* magazine asked, "Is Enron overpriced? It's in a bunch of complex businesses. Its financial statements are nearly impenetrable. So why is Enron trading at such a huge multiple?"[4] The article gave the first prominent signal of growing discontent with the lack of transparency in Enron's financial reports. Nevertheless, Wall Street analysts continued to issue strong buy recommendations even as they admitted difficulty in deciphering Enron's financial statements. "The ability to develop a somewhat predictable model of this business for the future is mostly an exercise in futility," a Bear Stearns analyst wrote.[5] Then-CEO Jeffrey Skilling told *Fortune*, "People who raise questions are people who have not gone through [our business] in detail and who want to throw rocks at us."[6] At the same time, Fastow, referring to Enron's trading operations, told *Fortune*, "We don't want to tell anyone where we're making money."

- *Management turnover.* In the year before Enron's bankruptcy, the senior management ranks of the firm changed substantially and to some extent unexpectedly. On December 13, 2000, Kenneth Lay announced that he would step down as CEO and that Jeffrey Skilling would assume that position. Lou Pai, Ken Rice, and Cliff Baxter, all senior executives and founders of the novel businesses that Enron harbored, resigned in the spring. In mid-August, Skilling unexpectedly resigned as president and CEO of Enron. He had been CEO for only six months. Largely credited with helping to transform Enron into a trading behemoth, Skilling cited family matters as the reason for his departure. He also told investors that there were "no accounting issues, trading issues, or reserve issues. . . . I can honestly say the company is in the strongest shape it's ever been in"[7]—though later he admitted that he had been distressed by the firm's falling share price.

- *Troubling financial disclosures.* On October 16, 2001, Enron reported a $618 million loss in the third quarter owing to $1.01 billion in write-downs of investments in the retail-power business, broadband telecommunications, technology, and water.[8] In addition, Enron had taken a $1.2 billion charge to shareholders' equity to repurchase 55 million shares previously issued to a limited partnership called LJM2 Co-Investment LP—a partnership that had been run by Enron CFO Andrew Fastow.

This write-off was triggered by discovery of an error by Enron's accountants, Arthur Andersen, that inappropriately boosted Enron's book value of equity by almost $1 billion, related to the Raptors. When Ken Lay returned to the CEO's post after Skilling's departure, he learned about the Raptors and the accounting error and decided to unwind the entire arrangement, at a charge to equity of $1.2 billion. Enron said that the equity reduction resulted in its debt-to-equity ratio increasing to 50 percent from 46 percent previously.[9] Enron's dealings with limited partnerships, particularly those run by Fastow, had been criticized by investors for their opacity and for the possible conflict of interest from having the Enron CFO be at the same time the general partner in the limited partnerships. In response to shareholder criticism, Enron ordered Fastow to end his involvement with the partnerships in July 2001.[10] Some analysts had been expecting Enron to report losses mainly resulting from its broadband trading and Azurix water businesses. Indeed, on October 16, Enron's stock price closed *up* 63 cents. But by the end of the week, its shares had lost a third of their value—this in response to critical reporting in the *Wall Street Journal* about Enron's asset write-downs (October 17), losses in SPEs (October 18), and Fastow's ties to the SPEs (October 19).

These financial revelations prompted Moody's to put Enron's long-term debt on review for a possible downgrade. Later Fitch followed suit while Standard & Poor's downgraded its outlook on Enron to negative from stable. On October 22, Enron disclosed that the SEC had launched an inquiry into LJM2 and other Enron partnerships. Investors, worried about the impact of more undisclosed negative news and a ratings downgrade, hammered the stock. A Goldman Sachs analyst told the *Wall Street Journal* that ". . . he heard people voice concerns about a possible 'death spiral' in which increasing credit concerns about Enron would decrease the number of people willing to do business with the company, which would in turn weaken its finances and lead to further business reductions."[11]

- *Declining share price.* As Figure 13.2 shows, Enron's share price fell 80 percent from the first of the year to October 25, 2001.

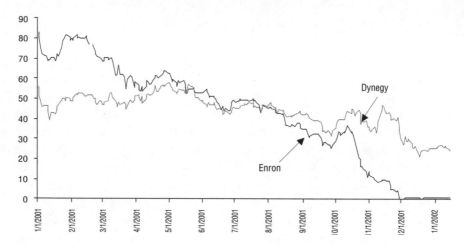

**Enron and Dynegy Share Prices:
January 2001 to January 2002**

Figure 13.2   **Enron and Dynegy Share Price Performance**

NEGOTIATIONS TO MERGE ENRON AND DYNEGY

On the evening of October 23, Enron was unable to refinance its commercial paper. Therefore, the firm drew down its $3 billion backup line of credit from the bank and discussed obtaining an additional line of credit. Enron seemed in desperate need of more cash to finance its trading operations and to unwind unprofitable positions. Transaction volume had begun to slow down and other parties grew wary of trading with Enron. Therefore Enron began discussions with buyout groups and other energy concerns to seek an additional $2 billion capital infusion.

Standing in the way of a speedy resolution of Enron's financing was Andrew Fastow, who was at the center of the firm's waning credibility. Thus on October 24, Greg Whalley (Enron's president) fired Fastow. The next day Enron approached Dynegy about the possibility of a merger. Stan Horton (Enron's pipeline executive), Greg Whalley, and Mark Frevert (Enron's vice chairman) had lunch with Steve Bergstrom, the president of Dynegy. Whalley asked Bergstrom whether Dynegy would be interested in buying Enron. The response, as Bethany McLean and Peter Elkind recorded it:

"Bergstrom was astounded. *They're in worse trouble than I thought!* When lunch was over, the Enron executives returned to headquarters and reported that the Dynegy president responded positively to their overture."[12]

The potential cost-saving synergies were large, in the neighborhood of $400 million per year. Combining the two firms' trading and distribution operations would grant huge market power and economies in head-office expenses. As the second-ranked energy trader, Dynegy aspired to conquer Enron and to stabilize an increasingly nervous industry. The steady stream of bad news about Enron was hurting business. It might be cheaper to buy Enron at the enormously discounted price currently than to weather the fallout of a larger collapse.

On Thursday evening, October 25, Ken Lay called Chuck Watson, the CEO of Dynegy, to arrange to meet to discuss merger terms. The next day, Watson hurriedly conducted due diligence and valuation research on Enron. Rebecca Smith and John Emschwiller reported that Watson didn't think Enron's broadband or international businesses were worth much. In fact, he assigned them almost no value. But he thought the trading business was basically sound. Clean up the balance sheet, sell the junk, and you would have a good company.[13]

Lay and Watson met at Lay's condo on Saturday, October 27, at 8:30 A.M. Lay asked for a merger of equals structure, a new name for Newco, and the title of Chairman. As is typical in most merger negotiations, the social issues (governance, power, and control) assumed preeminence. Lay wanted a premium paid for Enron; Watson was willing to pay only the current market price. Lay relented. In return, Watson agreed to arrange an immediate cash infusion of $1.5 billion for Enron and $1.0 billion at closing of the deal—but Watson wanted collateral for the infusion. Lay offered Enron's Northern Natural Gas Company pipeline, one of the jewels in Enron's asset portfolio. Thus, if the deal cratered for any reason, Dynegy would get the pipeline.

Starting Monday, October 29 the race was on to prepare the documents, obtain approvals from both boards of directors, and inform the SEC and capital markets of the intention to merge. Lay wanted to sign the agreement on Sunday, November 4 and to announce it to the public the next day.

On Tuesday, November 1, Enron announced a $1 billion financing from Citibank and J.P. Morgan Chase. Both large banks had been picked as advisers to the merging firms heightening the incentive to cooperate in financing the merger complete the deal. That same day, the SEC requested fuller disclosure by November 5 (later relaxed to November 8) of the extent of Fastow's participation in SPEs.

On Wednesday, November 2, Enron's board met to approve the deal, Key to the board's action were the prospective cash infusions that would restore confidence in Enron's trading operations. The scenario of recovery was crucial to the thinking of senior management and the board. An internal assessment foresaw that Enron would consume $3 billion in cash before year-end, plainly more than Dynegy's $2.5 billion infusion. Implicitly, the deal assumed the availability of other sources of financing and/or that announcement of the deal would trigger a rebound in trading volume and profitability at Enron. The board minutes show that Jeff McMahon, the new chief financial officer of Enron, "expressed concerns on the inadequate level of financial liquidity, noting that the Company had begun to defer certain trade payments currently due, noting that if the Moody's published debt rating was not maintained at investment-grade, significant obligations would become due immediately and the Company would be illiquid."[14] The merger was expected to forestall these threats.

Also at the board meeting, Enron's accountants, Arthur Andersen, revealed that the accounting for two of the SPEs would need to be revised. As a result, the write-down of $1.2 billion that had previously been announced on October 16 would need to be restated. On Monday, November 5, Enron's general counsel called the Dynegy merger team to disclose the change in accounting that would be reported to the SEC in an 8-K filing, and the firings of two senior executives related to the SPEs—one of them Ben Glisan, treasurer, who had been working on the Enron merger deal team. That same day, Fitch's cut Enron's debt rating to BBB— the borderline just above junk debt status.

A dramatic threat was narrowly averted on November 7. Moody's declared that it intended to cut Enron's debt rating to junk bond status. This would trigger billions of dollars in default provisions in the SPEs and would effectively terminate the merger. Jeff McMahon and the Enron merger team frantically renegotiated terms of the deal with Dynegy that would give Moody's sufficient comfort not to cut the debt rating. Specifically, the exchange ratio was revised downward to reflect Enron's deteriorating condition and the "material adverse change" clause of the merger agreement was strengthened to limit Dynegy's ability to exit from the transaction. In addition, the two banks, Citibank and J.P. Morgan, committed $500 million in new equity capital. Moody's relented and cut the bond rating only to BBB–. S&P followed suit.

The merger announcement and restatement to the SEC coincided on Thursday, November 8. First, Enron disclosed the restatement consolidating the SPEs and erasing $586 million in net income over the previous four years and revealed that Andrew Fastow had made more than $30 million from the SPEs. Second on November 8, Dynegy and Enron announced the merger agreement. Dynegy would exchange .2685 of its shares for each Enron share, for a total of close to $9 billion in stock. In addition, Dynegy would assume Enron's debt. Based on Dynegy's share price that day, the deal valued each Enron share at $10.41, 21 percent above Enron's previous closing price of $8.63. In addition, Dynegy would immediately inject $1.5 billion into Enron in exchange for preferred stock in a subsidiary that owned Enron's most valuable pipeline asset, the Northern Natural Gas pipeline, which consisted of 16,500 miles of pipeline running from the Great Lakes to Texas. If the merger fell apart, Dynegy would have the right to buy the pipeline subsidiary for an additional $23 million.[14] At completion, Chevron Texaco, which owned a 26 percent stake in Dynegy, would inject another $1 billion into the combined company.[16] Dynegy retained the right to walk away from the merger in the case of a "material adverse change" and if Enron's litigation liabilities topped $3.5 billion.[17] Dynegy's directors would hold 11 of the 14 board seats in Newco. Watson envisioned $400 million in annual cost savings from the merger. He planned to close all operations not currently making money, leaving the pipelines and trading operations. He argued that the deal would be 35 percent accretive to Dynegy's earnings per share.

In reaction to the announcement, Enron's share price rose 16 percent; Dynegy's rose 19 percent.

THE DYNEGY/ENRON MERGER FALLS APART

Despite the promises of new cash (and their subsequent delivery on November 13) Enron's condition continued to deteriorate. Within six days, Enron burned through $1 billion in cash as trading partners demanded more collateral or simply defected to other partners. Volume on Enron Online, the Internet-based energy trading site, dropped 50 percent.

In an effort to rebuild confidence, Greg Whalley and Jeff McMahon gave a lengthy presentation to bankers on Monday, November 19, arguing that a new leadership team at Enron had identified all the problems and was correcting them. This was a remarkably candid repudiation of the systems under which Enron had grown so large. The main objective of the presentation was to argue that Enron could survive until the closing of the Dynegy merger.

But that same day, Enron filed its third-quarter report with the SEC. In it, Enron disclosed three bad developments. First, the loss for the third quarter was −$664 million, worse than the −$618 million loss reported on October 16. Second, Enron revealed that the ratings downgrade had triggered obligations under a minority interest transaction, $690 million. And the report showed that cash was in short supply. In effect, Enron had burned through $1 billion in six days and $2 billion in the past month.[18, 19, 20]

On hearing the news on November 19, Chuck Watson was livid and embarrassed. Despite the fact that only a week earlier he had told analysts that Dynegy had done its due diligence, was aware of Enron's problems, and had obtained a good discount on the price. He wrote to Lay bitterly complaining that he had not been briefed about the surprising disclosures. Enron, he said, would need to communicate better with Dynegy for the merger to reach a successful conclusion. The surprise fueled doubts on the Dynegy side about the wisdom of the merger. The perquisites, high salaries and ample severance packages at Enron, surprised the Dynegy side.

Enron shares dropped 45 percent in value over the next two days to $5.01 per share, less than one-half Dynegy's implied purchase price. The fall in Enron's share price ignited fears that the deal with Dynegy would fall apart, even though Dynegy had already injected $1.5 billion into Enron. Trading on Enron's platform, Enron Online, slowed to a trickle as trading partners grew increasingly wary of Enron's future.

Because of the sharp price break in Enron's shares, the exchange ratio in the merger would have to be renegotiated. It remained to be seen whether the deal could be salvaged *again*.

Teams from Enron, Dynegy, and the banks negotiated intensely the weekend after Thanksgiving, 2001—*re*-renegotiating the exchange ratio by which Dynegy would acquire Enron and, more importantly, the infusion of new capital into Enron's operations. Banks had determined that Enron needed $2.25 to $3.0 billion in fresh capital to restore its balance sheet and provide liquidity for active trading. The atmosphere was tense following revelations about Enron's accounting and a nosedive in the firm's share price since November 8. On Saturday, November 24, Dynegy and the banks said they would ante up $3.0 billion. Then early on Sunday, the Dynegy team became anxious and left the negotiations, needing a few hours to regroup. Simply trying to figure out the value of assets it was acquiring and the size of liabilities it would assume was especially challenging. New information about Enron's trading book was arriving continuously and the news was not favorable. In the meantime, the Enron team and its banks discussed the possibility of a debt-for-equity swap and rescheduling of debt repayment. On Sunday afternoon the Dynegy team returned and announced its willingness to participate in a deal bringing $2.25 billion in fresh capital. By that evening, the targeted amount of financing had fallen to $750 million. The negotiations seemed to stabilize at that level. The team agreed to a new exchange ratio of .12 Dynegy shares for each Enron share, less than one-half the payment of the previous deal, $4 billion. Even so, Enron would need new capital just to hang on until closing to be supplied one-third each by Citi, J.P. Morgan, and Dynegy. Debt would need to be rescheduled for payment at a later date than 2002. And Citi and Morgan would need to convert their debt to equity. As the weekend ebbed away, so did Dynegy's resolve.

On Monday, November 26, the legal documents among Enron, Dynegy, and the banks were completed. By 4:00 P.M. the documents had been signed by the Enron side. CEO Ken Lay and the rest of his team departed for the airport, thinking that Dynegy was fully committed and ready to sign. The corporate jet, a Gulfstream V, revved its engines and began to taxi toward the runway. Then a call came in on the radiophone relaying the news that Chuck Watson, CEO of Dynegy, still had deep misgivings about the deal and warned that he could not go forward at all with the merger.

Meanwhile, officials from Enron and Dynegy, and their bankers, met with the credit rating agencies to persuade them of the viability of the renegotiated merger terms. The agencies expressed sharp doubts about the viability of Enron at the levels of cash infusion that were being discussed and were inclined to downgrade Enron to junk status. The merger teams tried to persuade the credit rating agencies to hold off from downgrading Enron while the new deal was being ironed out. At

2 A.M. on Wednesday, November 28, the talks between Enron and Dynegy broke down for the last time. Dynegy called off the planned merger, invoking a "material adverse change" clause in the merger agreement.[21] Watson said, "We worked our butts off to make this thing work." But "I wasn't about to put our balance sheet in jeopardy."[22] Later that morning, at 10:57 A.M. on November 28, Standard and Poor's announced that it had lowered Enron's rating two full grades from BBB– to B–, placing Enron in junk status. Moody's and Fitch also downgraded Enron to junk status a few hours later. The downgrades triggered immediate repayment of $3.9 billion in liabilities.[23] Trading at Enron's online system ground to a halt soon after the announcements. Enron shares fell 85 percent from the previous day's close to $0.61, while its bonds traded at 20 cents on the dollar.

On December 2, Enron filed for bankruptcy. That same day Enron filed a $10 billion lawsuit against Dynegy for backing out of the merger. Enron claimed that Dynegy had no right to invoke the "material adverse change" clause because ". . . With its eyes open, Dynegy committed itself to acquire Enron and its highly profitable energy-trading business. . . . Dynegy knew that Enron was in a precarious financial condition, was on the verge of dropping to a noninvestment grade credit rating, and was in no small measure dependent on the successful completion of the merger for its very survival."[24] Dynegy filed a countersuit against Enron the next day, insisting on its right to claim Enron's Northern Natural Gas pipeline system immediately given the two parties' initial agreement.

On January 7, 2002, Enron agreed to cede the pipeline subsidiary to Dynegy to "avoid sizeable litigation costs and the distractions of the state court suit."[25] For its part Dynegy agreed to extend the deadline for Enron to repurchase the pipeline unit from May 9 to June 30. Enron would need to repay $1.5 billion plus interest to Dynegy in order to reacquire the pipeline unit.[26] Dynegy assumed $950 million of the subsidiary's existing debt, bringing its total purchase price to around $2.5 billion.[27]

In giving up its pipeline subsidiary, Enron lost its most valuable and profitable hard asset to Dynegy. In addition, Enron's once-mighty trading operation was acquired by Swiss bank UBS AG in an auction held on January 11, 2002 as part of the bankruptcy proceedings. Although Enron fought for a 49 percent stake in the trading operations, UBS agreed only to pay Enron royalties amounting to one-third of the trading operation's pretax profit for a 10-year period. UBS did not pay any cash upfront for the trading unit.[28]

On January 23, Kenneth Lay was terminated as chairman and CEO of Enron at the request of creditors, who recommended a restructuring expert, Stephen Cooper, to take Lay's place. Cooper said he planned to reorganize the company around the steadier businesses of natural gas transportation and electricity generation. Enron's last balance sheet reported total liabilities of $13 billion, but bankers estimated that including off-balance sheet transactions, minority interest financing, prepayments, project debt, and so on, total debt was closer to $40 billion.

COUNTERPOINT: ACQUISITION OF GENERAL CINEMA BY AMC

Acquiring a target company that is in extremis is not necessarily a formula for failure. On December 17, 2001, two weeks after Enron had declared bankruptcy, David Brown, CEO of AMC Entertainment, announced an agreement to acquire General Cinema Corporation. The announcement made barely a ripple in the media, owing to the preoccupation with Enron, terrorism, and the deepening economic gloom. But what made this announcement remarkable was that the target was bankrupt; the buyer was in poor financial health itself; and the deal would create the second-largest cinema theater operator in an industry that was a mess: Most of the major cinema theater operators had declared bankruptcy in 2001. Most investors wanted to *exit* from the industry; instead, AMC was doubling-down on its investment there. The stock market had swooned; in sympathy, M&A deal activity had ground to a crawl. This hardly seemed like the time to be cutting deals, or the industry and company on which to cut them. But David Brown had a contrary view.

Movie Theater Industry

AMC had the upstart's reputation in the industry. In 1995 it triggered a wave of new construction by building the first-ever "megaplex" in Dallas,

Texas. The megaplex contained 25 to 30 individual theaters with extra-wide stadium seating, digital sound, typically located at high-traffic venues in upscale suburbs. The megaplex required an investment of between $20 and $100 million per site, dramatically raising the entry barrier to the industry. The megaplex did to the industry what the multiplex (2 to 12 screens) had done to the single-screen exhibitors a generation earlier. AMC's competitors followed suit and the industry rapidly expanded the number of screens by 6,400 over the three years from 1995 to 1998, an increase of 24 percent. This expansion was fueled in no small part by the flood of new capital into the industry from private equity investment firms looking to participate in the industry. Notably Kohlberg, Kravis, and Roberts and Hicks, Muse, Tate and Furst had teamed up to acquire the largest operator, Regal Cinemas, in 1998.

While the industry was expanding capacity, attendance remained unchanged, at about 5.5 visits per year per person. This was fueled in part by the absence of blockbuster productions that would draw more viewers to the theater and the string of movies that failed at the box office, like *1942*, *Heaven's Gate*, and *Ishtar*.

The resulting crash in industry performance starting in 1998 tarnished virtually all the major exhibitors. By December 2001, 11 major operators had declared bankruptcy, including Carmike, Edwards, United Artists, and General Cinema (GC). The largest operator, Regal Cinemas, with 4,493 screens at 418 sites, had approached its lenders with a request for relief from onerous financial requirements. Another major chain, Loews Cineplex Odeon, was in similar discussions. Industry analysts believed that 20 to 25 percent of the screens would need to be closed to restore the industry to profitability.

Filing for bankruptcy was a mechanism for the theater chains to cancel costly long-term leases and shut down unprofitable screens. The exhibitor would emerge from bankruptcy with a lightened debt load and therefore a stronger ability to compete on price. This created an unusual dynamic: It would be difficult for any competitor to *avoid* bankruptcy. Thus ensued a competitive panic to restructure. The investment opportunity attracted the interest of "vulture" investors, who purchased distressed properties in the expectation of earning a sizable return. For instance, in April 2000, Philip Anschutz, a Denver billionaire, purchased 21 percent of the debt of United Artists in an effort to gain control of the firm. Then, later, he reached agreements to acquire Regal and Edwards as well, making him the largest consolidator in the industry.

The Deal to Acquire General Cinema

AMC was the fourth-largest operator of movie theaters in the United States, with 2,774 screens in 21 states. Responding to the overcapacity in the industry, AMC had announced in January 2001 that it would close about 300 underperforming screens or about 11 percent, spread over the next four years. On April 24, 2001, AMC announced the sale of $240 million in preferred stock to Apollo Management, a vulture investment firm controlled by Leon Black. Black would control about 60 percent of the shares and 37 percent of the votes in AMC.

General Cinema Corporation was created in a spin-off in 1993 from publisher Harcourt General, Inc. Sticking to its strategy of operating multiplexes and single screen theaters, it virtually ignored the megaplex boom. An operator of 1,070 screens, it declared bankruptcy on October 12, 2000. Eight months later, in June 2001, two distressed debt specialist firms, Onex Corporation and Oaktree Capital, announced an agreement to acquire General Cinema for $36.6 million in cash and the assumption of $114 million in debt. Onex had also recently announced an agreement to acquire the Loews chain, making it likely to become the largest industry player.

U.S. bankruptcy procedure requires an auction of companies or assets sold out of bankruptcy. The first bidder, in effect, becomes a stalking horse that other buyers must top. This is an orderly process, subject to approvals by creditors and the bankruptcy court. Haste is not necessarily a consideration unless it can be shown to the court that the value of assets will be impaired by delay.

In July 2001, a month after the Onex/Oaktree bid, AMC offered $62.5 million in cash plus assumption of debt. At least two other exhibitors submitted bids. In December 2001, AMC and General Cinema announced an agreement for AMC to pay between $175 and $195 million, in cash, stock, and subordinated notes, subject to approval by the bankruptcy court and antitrust regulators. The higher amount revealed in December included the resolution of debt claims against General

Cinema. AMC forecasted annual cost savings of $8.8 million, and $3.0 million of other operating synergies. AMC's shares, traded on the American Stock Exchange, gained five percent net of the market in the week after the announcement.

In March 2002, AMC issued common stock in the amount of $95 million and planned to use the proceeds to finance the GC acquisition and for other corporate purposes. On April 1, 2002, AMC announced the completion of its acquisition of GC for a total of $167 million. This brought AMC's total number of screens to 3,520 in 247 complexes and vaulted AMC to second-largest in the industry.

WHY DYNEGY/ENRON FAILED AND AMC/GENERAL CINEMA SURVIVED

The demise of the merger of Enron and Dynegy shows the hallmarks of the six drivers of merger failure. Enron's finances and trading book were terrifically *complex*. As the news unfolded during the fall of 2001, complexity only increased: The true state of Enron's economic strength became more, rather than less, difficult to ascertain. In no small part was this due to the earnings management that came to light. As in the cases of Pennsylvania and New York Central, and AOL and Time Warner, the fixed exchange ratio *tightly linked* the viability of the deal to financial performance of the two firms in some kind of parity over the pendency of the deal. This linkage left little margin for error. The accumulated disastrous *management choices* in financing and financial reporting gutted the credibility of Enron in the marketplace, and to some extent impaired the standing of its peers. Throughout the deal development process, management displayed a level of optimism so detached from the facts of the situation as to suggest a strong *cognitive bias*. The stress of time urgency and crisis conditions, and the dramatic turnover in executives during 2001 can only have weakened the ability of the *operating team* of decision-makers at the scene. But most prominent was the fact that Ken Lay and Chuck Watson were trying to get business done when *business was not as usual*. Watson backed out of the merger with Enron because of surprises that Enron's liabilities were larger and accelerating and its profits were smaller and dwindling than previously estimated. The drumbeat of bad news and the apparent ignorance or unwillingness of Enron's senior management to deal proactively with it prompted a market "panic" or "run on the bank" that denied Enron the liquidity or market activity it needed to stay afloat. The collapse of the Dynegy–Enron deal highlights the importance of investor confidence in M&A deal-making. Too often such confidence is taken for granted. Had confidence been retained or restored, it is possible that Enron could have bought time to renegotiate the deal, or reach another satisfactory financial outcome. This case illustrates the consequences of straining the confidence of shareholders and creditors.

Table 13.1 gives a scoreboard on the two deals. The two cases differ in several important ways:

- *Pace of market movements.* The meltdown in the movie theater industry took place over years; the worst had already happened;

TABLE 13.1   KEY DIFFERENCES: DYNEGY/ENRON VERSUS AMC/
GENERAL CINEMA

	Dynegy/Enron	*AMC/General Cinema*
Market volatility	Market meltdown took place in weeks. Drumbeat of negative news between announcement of deal and withdrawal.	Market meltdown took place over years. No adverse market surprises during period of deal negotiation.
Plausibility of outlook	Deteriorating future for energy trading. Questioned assumption that core trading operations were profitable.	Volume of ticket sales was stable. Clarity about what needed to be done to restore operations to profitability.
Time available	Crisis schedule. No time for careful due diligence by Dynegy.	Plenty of time for diligence, negotiation. Deal subject to approval by bankruptcy court.
Financial reserves	Limited ability to finance deepening losses at Enron.	Backing of Apollo and ability to raise fresh capital through equity markets.
Credibility, personal and corporate	Surprising revelations destroyed confidence in Enron's management.	Confidence in AMC's management was retained.

there was broad consensus about the stability of underlying demand (albeit inadequate); and there were no adverse product market surprises during the period of deal negotiation. The deal negotiation over General Cinema was a comparatively stately process. In contrast, Enron (and Dynegy) experienced a "run on the bank," a massive contraction in business as customers abandoned the market for fear of assuming counterparty risk. It was not clear how or when equilibrium would be restored to the industry. This meant that the parties had to keep renegotiating the terms of merger under stress and uncertainty.

- *Plausibility of outlook.* In General Cinema's case, the number of total ticket sales in the industry remained fairly steady. The competitors needed to close unprofitable theaters as a basis for restoring profitability. In contrast, Enron's economic outlook was highly uncertain throughout the deal negotiation process. With the rapid changes in trading volume, the estimating Enron's cash requirements even through the end of 2001 proved extraordinarily difficult.

- *Time pressure.* The bankruptcy process under which General Cinema operated imposed an orderly process for the disposition of the firm's assets. Enron, on the other hand, could not file for bankruptcy without triggering the debt rating downgrade that it so deeply feared. This meant that a restructuring of Enron's finances had to occur *before* or *as part of* any merger. And given the burn rate on Enron's cash, the time available to conclude a deal kept shrinking. Research on negotiations shows that haste makes waste: More time results in a higher probability of settlement and in a deal structure more acceptable to all parties.[29]

- *Financial resources.* In canceling the deal because he did not want to put Dynegy's balance sheet at risk, Chuck Watson admitted that Dynegy had exhausted its financial reserves against further adverse surprises at Enron. Dynegy's pockets weren't deep enough to hedge further deterioration. In hindsight, it is hard to imagine forms of hedging other than carrying a fat wallet into the deal. Most product market risks are very difficult to hedge, such as the unwillingness of customers to do business with you.

The single best protection against this downside risk is a conservative capital structure.

- *Credibility: personal and corporate.* Of course, even the most conservative capital structure means nothing if providers of fresh capital will not believe you. The events of January to November 2001 had effectively destroyed Enron's credibility and damaged Dynegy's. In stark contrast, AMC retained and perhaps expanded its credibility with the investment by Leon Black and the Apollo Group. Despite the fact that AMC and the other players in the industry were losing money and had terrible balance sheets, AMC retained its credibility as a source of positive future cash flows.

NOTES

1. The segments on Dynegy/Enron draw upon numerous field interviews conducted with my colleague, Samuel Bodily. The product of that research is a digital case study, "Enron: 1986–2001" (UVA-G-0563-M) available from Darden Business Publishing. These interviews included Kenneth Lay, Jeffrey Skilling, Andrew Fastow, and others. Anna Buchanan and Jessica Chan gave able research support on this chapter. Additional resources were the book-length accounts by investigative journalists Bethany McLean, John Emschwiller, and Rebecca Smith.

2. Bethany McLean, "Is Enron Overpriced?" *Fortune*, March 5, 2001, 122.

3. Company SEC 10-K filings.

4. Ibid.

5. Quoted from "Is Enron Overpriced?" by Bethany McLean, *Fortune*, March 5, 2001, 122.

6. Ibid.

7. John R. Emschwiller, "Enron's Skilling Cites Stock-Price Plunge as Main Reason for Leaving CEO Post," *Wall Street Journal*, August 16, 2001, A2.

8. John R. Emschwiller, "Enron Jolt: Investments, Assets Generate Big Loss—Part of Charge Tied to 2 Partnerships Interests," *Wall Street Journal*, October 17, 2001, C1.

9. Rebecca Smith and John R. Emschwiller, "Partnership Spurs Enron Equity Cut—Vehicle Is Connected to Financial Officer," *Wall Street Journal*, October 18, 2001, C1.

10. John R. Emschwiller, "Enron Jolt: Investments, Assets Generate Big Loss—Part of Charge Tied to 2 Partnerships Interests," *Wall Street Journal*, October 17, 2001, C1.

11. Rebecca Smith and John R. Emschwiller, "Enron Replaces Fastow as Finance Chief—McMahon Takes Over Post; Move Follows Concerns Over Partnership Deals," *Wall Street Journal*, October 25, 2001, A3.

12. McLean and Elkind (2003), 391.

13. Rebecca Smith and John Emschwiller, *24 Days* (New York: HarperBusiness, 2003), 196.

14. Quoted in McLean and Elkind, (2003), 395.

15. John Emschwiller, "Enron Agrees to Sell Pipeline to Dynegy Inc.," *Wall Street Journal*, January 7, 2002, A16.

16. John Emschwiller and Rebecca Smith, "Dynegy's Enron Deal Faces Uncertainties—Potential Antitrust Worries or New Enron Liabilities Could Upset Agreement," *Wall Street Journal*, November 12, 2001, A3.

17. Ibid.

18. John Emschwiller, "Enron Stock, Bonds Receive More Hits Following Warning," *Wall Street Journal*, November 21, 2001, A4.

19. Rebecca Smith, "Enron Warns of Eroding Profit," *Wall Street Journal*, November 20, 2001, B16.

20. Rebecca Smith and John Emschwiller, "Dynegy Deal to Buy Enron Hits Crossroads," *Wall Street Journal*, November 23, 2001, A3.

21. Gregory Zuckerman and Jathon Sapsford, "Why Credit Agencies Didn't Switch Off Enron—S&P Cries 'Junk,' But the Warning Comes Too Late," *Wall Street Journal*, November 29, 2001, C1.

22. Ibid.

23. Rebecca Smith and John Emschwiller, "Running on Empty: Enron Faces Collapse as Credit, Stock Dive and Dynegy Bolts—Energy Trading Giant's Fate Could Reshape Industry, Bring Tighter Regulation—Price Quotes Suddenly Gone," *Wall Street Journal*, November 29, 2001, A1.

24. Quoted from "Enron Files for Chapter 11 Bankruptcy, Sues Dynegy—At Least $10 Billion Sought; Wrongful Termination of Merger Is Charged" by Robin Sidel, Thaddeus Herrick, and Richard Schmitt, *Wall Street Journal*, December 3, 2001, A3.

25. Quoted from "Enron Agrees to Sell Pipeline to Dynegy Inc." by John Emschwiller, *Wall Street Journal*, January 7, 2002, A16.

26. Ibid.

27. Robin Sidel, Thaddeus Herrick, and Richard Schmitt, "Enron Files for Chapter 11 Bankruptcy, Sues Dynegy—At Least $10 Billion Sought; Wrongful Termination of Merger Is Charged," *Wall Street Journal*, December 3, 2001, A3.

28. Mitchell Pacelle and Rebecca Smith, "Congressional Panel Investigates Andersen's Enron Audit—UBS Emerges as Top Bidder for Enron

Trading Unit; Big Obstacles Remain," *Wall Street Journal*, January 14, 2002, A3.

29. See Robert F. Bruner, "Understanding Merger Negotiation, Part 1: Teaching with a Merger Negotiation Exercise," *Journal of Financial Practice and Education*, Spring/Summer 1992, and "Understanding Merger Negotiation, Part 2: Testing Rational Choice and Behaviorism in a Simulated Setting," *Journal of Financial Practice and Education*, Spring/Summer 1992.

14

January 2002:
Acquisition Program
of Tyco International

TYCO'S SURPRISING NEWS

For years, Tyco International had delivered steadily growing earnings per share (EPS) and a buoyant share price.[1] A steady diet of acquisitions substantially shaped this record. Figure 14.1 shows the pattern of Tyco's M&A activity by number and volume of deals. On January 22, 2002, Dennis Kozlowski, CEO of Tyco International, Ltd., announced a radical restructuring plan for the firm that would break Tyco into four segments. The transaction would entail three spin-offs. Kozlowski argued that the firm would be worth 50 percent more after the restructuring: "Acquisitions have become far less important. The model for the future is far more for organic growth."[2] Securities analysts were mystified by the announcement. Tyco had been the target of SEC accounting investigations—so far, these had turned up nothing. But a new spate of rumors had dogged the firm since late fall 2001. An analyst was quoted as saying:

> To me, it smells a little bit fishy. If you are a public company and people are pointing the finger at you, I wouldn't think your first reaction would be to split up and make things confusing for investors. Here is a clear effort to break up one company and make it a more complicated com-

314

pany. . . . *Their goal is to show revenue and earnings momentum.* . . . The first quarter had a questionable earnings outlook going forward. They use it [stock] as a currency to make acquisitions, so the timing [of the split] is certainly questionable.[3] [Italics added.]

Other observers speculated that Tyco's profitability was declining and would create problems in trying to service its huge debt load, built up during its acquisition program. The sale of stakes in operating units would generate about $8 billion in cash to service and pay down some of the debt.

Just a week earlier, Tyco had announced that its earnings for the

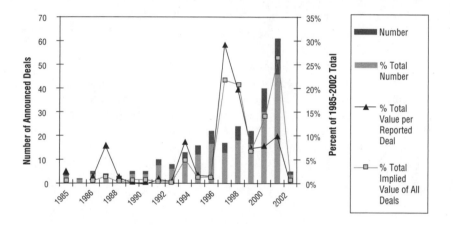

N.B.: The displayed variables are defined as follows:

Number is the number of announced M&A transactions reported in the Thomson Financial SDC Platinum database for Tyco International each year. It has been reported that Tyco did not report numerous transactions. If it can be assumed that Tyco's unreported volume of deals followed a similar distribution over time, then this series is useful mainly as an indicator of the total activity.

%Total Number is the number of announced deals each year as a percentage of the total number of Tyco deals over 1985–2002, 226 deals.

%Total Value per Reported Deal is the dollar value of reported deals each year, divided by the total value of reported deals, 1985–2002.

%Total Implied Value of All Deals is the product of the number of deals each year times the average value of reported deals each year divided by the total for all years. The value of all deals each year is implied rather than actual and is meaningful if the actual value per reported deal each year is a reasonable proxy for the actual value per unreported deal each year.

Figure 14.1 **Tyco International, Ltd. M&A Activity 1985–2002**

Source of data: Thomson Financial SDC Platinum M&A database.

current quarter would not meet forecasts. This triggered an 8.5 percent decline in the firm's shares. A journalist wrote:

> Short sellers said yesterday's report offered new evidence that Tyco's strategy of growth through acquisition was no longer working. Short sellers have aimed at Tyco for years, arguing that it is little more than a hodgepodge of slow-growing businesses. To deliver high growth in earnings, the company has pushed the limits of accounting rules, they said. Tyco's sales have soared from $19 billion in 1998 to $36 billion last year, but most of that growth has come from acquisitions. In its most recent fiscal year which ended Sept. 30, the company's sales grew 3 percent, excluding acquisitions . . . By minimizing, or marking down, the value of the tangible assets and maximizing or marking up, good will, Tyco can inflate its earnings, said James Chanos, president of Kynikos Associates, a hedge fund that has shorted Tyco's stock. The earnings lift, he said, comes because Tyco can treat the good will differently from the real assets, which under accounting rules lose value over time. In addition, if Tyco sells the products it has devalued or marked down, at the time of an acquisition, it can make an even larger profit, Mr. Chanos said. The issue may seem arcane, but it has big consequences for Tyco's profits, because Tyco generally allocates almost the entire price of an acquisition to good will, Mr. Chanos said. Over the last three years, Tyco has spent about $30 billion on acquisitions and created the same amount of good will.[4]

Tyco's Acquisition Strategy

Tyco was founded in 1960 as a scientific research boutique and was transformed later in the 1960s into a miniconglomerate by acquiring 24 companies, following the then-current fashionable model of ITT Industries Inc. After the wave of conglomerate diversification ended in the early 1970s, Tyco reverted to a more focused strategy. Yet growth by active acquiring retained its appeal, especially to Dennis Kozlowski, a lifelong employee of Tyco who had risen through the ranks from auditor to division head, president, and CEO (in 1992). In 1994 Kozlowski launched a stream of large acquisitions, with the purchase of Kendall International, a maker of disposable medical supplies. This caused Tyco's earnings to nearly double in 1995. In 1997, Kozlowski acquired ADT Security Services for $11.3 billion in a reverse takeover that moved the firm's headquarters to

Bermuda. In 2001, Kozlowski acquired CIT Group for $9.2 billion, emulating General Electric (GE), which had bought rival Heller International shortly before.

Kozlowski had articulated a strategy for growth in his letters to shareholders that would deliver a sustained rate of growth in excess of 20 percent annually. Tyco would achieve this through organic growth in the low double digits and the balance from acquisitions. Excerpts from Kozlowski's letters, given in Table 14.1 and from other aspects of the annual reports, suggest an acquisition strategy based on these elements:

- Focus on a steady percentage rate of growth in EPS. To sustain a constant percentage rate of growth requires larger and larger absolute increases in EPS. This suggests gains that beget more gains, called "momentum" by professional investors.

- Increasing number and dollar value of acquisitions per year over time.

- Avoidance of EPS dilution; focus on accretive acquisitions.

- Heavy reliance on accounting conventions that produce favorable financial results, such as pooling accounting and if purchase, heavy allocations to goodwill that (in those days) would not be depreciated for financial reporting purposes. Of particular concern was the overhang of goodwill on the firm's balance sheet. As of March 31, 2003, Tyco's book value of equity was $25.39 billion; and its goodwill was $26.03 billion "meaning the company's shareholder equity would be negative without the goodwill. Any substantial write-down in goodwill would send shareholder equity plunging, potentially putting Tyco in default" of a credit agreement, prompting Professor Abraham Briloff to conclude that Tyco's goodwill was "severely excessively overstated."[5]

- Underreporting and nondisclosure. Generally accepted accounting principles require firms to report material events. Tyco deemed numerous acquisitions it made to be immaterial and unnecessary to report though in the aggregate they amounted to $8 billion.

- Aggressive tax accounting. Tyco reduced its effective tax rate from 36 percent in 1996 to 18.5 percent in 2002 by moving its corporate headquarters to Bermuda and making heavy use of dormant subsidiaries in tax-haven countries (countries with favorable tax

TABLE 14.1   TYCO INTERNATIONAL'S ACQUISITION STRATEGY

November 30, 1998

While we are very pleased with our past performance, we are especially excited about our prospects . . . After reinvesting in plant and equipment and new product development, we will use this [free cash flow] for acquisitions that strengthen our market position and have an immediate positive impact on our earnings. . . . We continue to show that the word *synergy*, though much abused, can still have meaning in the corporate world. We bundled sales of certain products and services, folded new products into existing distribution systems and relied on some acquisitions to create a beachhead for us in previously untapped markets. . . . So far so good, but the best news of all is this: We are extraordinarily well positioned to *maintain our momentum*. We have a lot of room to run in all of our businesses. And run we will . . . We believe we can double our revenues in the next five years, with a corresponding increase in earnings, by keeping our focus precisely where it is.

Although internal growth is the core of the Company, we will continue to make strategic acquisitions. We feel no compulsion to do so; we just keep finding companies that would fit well within Tyco. At any time, we have a long list of candidates in various stages of evaluation. We're not exactly trigger-happy, though. We walk away from a high percentage of potential transactions because our criteria for acquisitions are so stringent. All acquisitions must be friendly, immediately accretive to earnings (that means in the next quarter, not "someday if everything breaks just right"), and strengthen an existing Tyco Business.

December 14, 1999

We aim for sustained earnings growth in excess of 20 percent, powered by increased revenues and margin expansion. . . . We spend hundreds of hours assessing the benefits and risks of each transaction we consider. We always ask: What's the worst-case scenario? We perform thorough due diligence every time, and we walk away from nine out of every ten transactions we evaluate. Even when we decide that the rewards significantly outweigh the risks, we spend a great deal of time planning the integration process to minimize the difficulties inherent in each acquisition. . . . the future looks bright. We think we can double our earnings over the next three years.

Note: Italics added.

Sources: Tyco International Inc. Letters to the shareholders, *Annual Reports 1999, 2000*, L. Dennis Kozlowski, Chairman of the Board and CEO, as filed with the U.S. Securities and Exchange Commission.

policies toward corporations). Foreign subsidiaries can be used to shield royalties, interest, dividends, and other passive income from U.S. taxation.

- Aggressive management of investors' expectations. One journalist reported that in 1999 Dennis Kozlowski successfully pressured the CEO of Merrill Lynch, David Komansky, to replace the securities analyst following Tyco. The new analyst lifted the research recommendation from "buy" to "accumulate." Merrill was among Tyco's leading underwriters and an important adviser for M&A transactions.[6]

- Executive compensation based on size of the firm. The compound average growth rate in Tyco's revenues was 48.7 percent annually from 1997 to 2001. Kozlowski's total compensation vaulted upward as well, with the growing portfolio of the firm's businesses: from $8.8 million in 1997, to $67 million in 1998, and $170 million in 1999.

At the core of Tyco's acquisition–growth story is a buoyant stock market that created a high-priced acquisition currency and a *feedback effect* that together create perceived *momentum* in the financial performance of the firm. The feedback of momentum acquisition growth is illustrated in Figure 14.2. The observed rate of growth of EPS influences investors to value the firm more highly. This increases the price/earnings multiple. The firm issues new (higher-priced) shares in an acquisition. If the acquisition is accretive (if it adds to earnings per share), the EPS grows faster. The faster growth promotes a higher P/E multiple and the cycle continues. What is remarkable about the momentum story is that for a time it may mask an economic rate of growth (growth in intrinsic value) that is rather mundane. Tyco's organic rate of growth was probably in line with the manufacturing sector of the United States—2 percent to 4 percent in real terms per year. But with momentum, low organic growth is offset by rapid growth from acquisitions and earnings management. Unfortunately, momentum acquisition strategies create a toxic exposure to unexpected trouble: A small negative variance from market expectations typically produces a rapid fall in stock price and often a change in management. Momentum acquiring rarely ends with a gradual adjustment of investor expectations: The outcome is generally sudden and painful to investors.

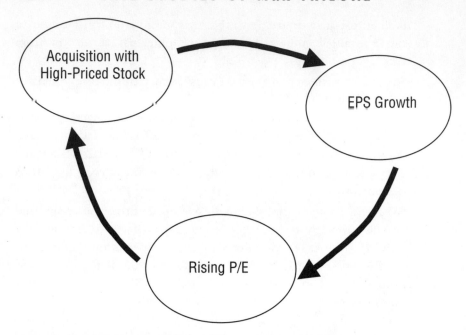

Figure 14.2   **The Feedback Effect in Momentum Acquiring**

Creating unexpected growth is the foundation for the momentum cycle. Momentum strategies can focus on a variety of targets for momentum growth. Two targets stand out with the most frequency.

- *EPS momentum.* Earnings per share (EPS) growth is the focus of momentum acquirers, who believe that stock prices are driven by changes in EPS and that therefore steady and aggressive growth in EPS will result in high stock prices (and high P/E multiples). In the context of an acquisition program, EPS can be managed through the design of acquisitions in ways that avoid EPS dilution. The avoidance of dilution motivates a focus on buying target firms that have lower P/E ratios than the buyer firm. Dilution could also be avoided or reduced through earnings management and aggressive accounting choices. Above all, negative earnings surprises are to be avoided in order not to impair the buyer's P/E ratio. The core implication of this approach for senior management is the need to establish, and continually justify, the acquirer's high P/E multiple.

Rather than give fundamental information to investors to justify the firm's share value, the momentum acquirer sends signals about the firm's value through the path of EPS growth.

• *Revenue momentum*. In some industries, the momentum focus is on revenues instead of earnings per share. Firms in some industries such as biotechnology, computing, software, and so on, may be difficult to value using more traditional approaches, since their net earnings are depressed by large R&D expenses, new product introductions, and other temporary costs associated with young firms, or firms with a large portfolio of new products. A significant portion of the market value of these firms derives from their *growth options*, which are ordinarily quite difficult to value using standard techniques, such as discounted cash flow. In these instances, some analysts advocate using revenue multiples as a basis for valuing the firm. Perceiving this, managers of these firms may focus on acquisition strategies that lift the firm's revenues, and create momentum. They view building revenue momentum with the assistance of an acquisition program as a logical supplement to internal growth efforts.

Aftermath

Accounts about development of the restructuring program for Tyco suggest confusion among the senior leadership of the firm, stimulated in no small part by the mounting investigations by the SEC and the District Attorney's Office into accounting and financial irregularities at the firm. *BusinessWeek* reported:

> On Jan. 16, Kozlowski called his directors to Boca Raton to discuss a desperate plan to boost Tyco's sinking share price by breaking the company into four parts. The directors had their doubts but gave their approval four days later at a board meeting in Bermuda. The plan will "release value," Kozlowski predicted with a touch of defiance in an announcement on Jan. 22. "We believe there is over a 50% upside compared to [Tyco's] current market value." But the hastily concocted plan both puzzled and alarmed investors who feared that Tyco was running short of cash. Within a few weeks, CIT effectively had been frozen out of the commercial paper market, forcing it and Tyco to draw down more

than $13 billion in bank lines. By early March, Kozlowski "was a changed person," says one Tyco insider. "Normally, he is very decisive, but now he was like a deer caught in the headlights."

In April, investors were flummoxed again when Kozlowski performed yet another about-face. Tyco was going ahead with the CIT sale, but not the bust-up, he said, prompting more catcalls from the Street. "We now know that it was a mistake," he admitted in an abject letter to shareholders. "I take full responsibility." A majority of directors now were convinced that Kozlowski had to go, but there was disagreement about when to act. By early may Kozlowski could feel the noose tightening.[7]

The spin-off announcement triggered a 58 percent decline in the firm's share price. But this was only the beginning of a dramatic unraveling of a strategy of growth by acquisition. The highlights of the slide included these:

- *February 2002*: Tyco revealed that it had not disclosed to investors 700 acquisitions over the past three years, worth about $8 billion. The company argued that individually, these deals were immaterial and unworthy of disclosure.[8] That same month, Tyco divested CIT Group, booking a loss of $7 billion on the acquisition.

- *July 2002*: Kozlowski and former CFO Mark Swartz were fired after news that they would be indicted following a criminal investigation. Edward Breen was hired as the new CEO.

- *September 2002*: Dennis Kozlowski and Mark Swartz were indicted on grounds that they allegedly looted $170 million from Tyco in unauthorized compensation and $430 million in fraudulent stock sales. The indictment accused them of running a "criminal enterprise." The two executives claimed innocence.

- *December 2002*: Tyco released a report of the results of an internal investigation, which revealed that the company had systematically managed its accounting to inflate earnings. Specifically cited were tapping reserves to cover unrelated expenses, and booking current charges as long-term expenses. The aggressive creation of reserves by Tyco's targets before acquisition was also cited as a means of inflating Tyco's postacquisition performance. The investigation, led by David Boies, found no "systemic or significant fraud" and that the practice had been to bend, rather than break the accounting rules. The investigators acknowledged that they did not study all transactions and might have missed something.

- *Spring 2003*: CEO Breen continued to investigate. Tyco announced that it would take charges against earnings to cover more accounting problems. The write-offs for accounting-related problems accumulated to $2.3 billion. The investment community seethed at the apparent inability of Tyco to put its problems behind itself.

- *April 2004*: The trial of Kozlowski and Swartz resulted in a mistrial when jurors could not agree on a verdict. The District Attorney sought another trial. In July, Mark Belnick, former chief counsel of Tyco, was acquitted on criminal charges.

In its 2003 annual report, Tyco enumerated the costs of its fall. The write-offs of impaired goodwill and operating losses reduced shareholders' equity by $9 billion. Senior management and the board of directors turned over. The new leadership team began to sell off businesses, such as Tyco Capital, that had not made much sense. And management committed itself to a strategy of organic growth based on operational improvements. Rejected was the aggressive role of acquisition that had appeared during Kozlowski's tenure.

COUNTERPOINT: THE ACQUISITION PROGRAM AT BERKSHIRE HATHAWAY

As Figure 14.3 shows, from 1990 to 1998, Tyco and Berkshire Hathaway showed remarkable growth in share prices, fueled significantly by acquisitions. After 1998, Berkshire was able to sustain this value, but Tyco's share price crashed. This comparison of two conglomerates yields insights into the definition of "good" and "bad" growth.

From 1982 to 2003, Berkshire Hathaway acquired companies worth $45 billion; over the same period, Tyco acquired $60 billion (this is a low estimate, owing to numerous acquisitions not publicly disclosed by Tyco). Figure 14.4 gives the publicly disclosed annual acquisition expenditures over time for each firm: Berkshire's is a fairly steady trend of smaller deals dominated by the $23 billion deal for GEICO in 1998, whereas Tyco's

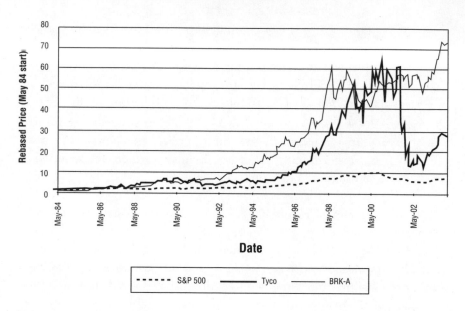

S&P 500, Tyco International and Berkshire Hathaway
(Since May 1984)

Figure 14.3 **Comparison of Stock Prices: Tyco International versus Berkshire Hathaway Inc. 1984 to 2003**
Note: **For the sake of comparison, this graph rebases Tyco, Berkshire Hathaway, and S&P 500 index values at $1.00, at May 1984.**

shows a generally rising trend over time, with multibillion dollar deals in the late 1990s. The example of Berkshire Hathaway's conglomerate acquisition strategy presents a stark alternative to momentum.

The company was incorporated in 1889 as Berkshire Cotton Manufacturing and eventually grew to become one of New England's biggest textile producers, accounting for 25 percent of the country's cotton textile production. In 1955, Berkshire merged with Hathaway Manufacturing and began a secular decline due to inflation, technological change, and intensifying competition from foreign competitors. In 1965 Warren Buffett and some partners acquired control of Berkshire Hathaway, believing that the decline could be reversed. Over the next 20 years it became apparent that large capital investments would be required to remain competitive and that even then the financial returns would be mediocre. In 1985, Berkshire Hathaway exited the textile business. For-

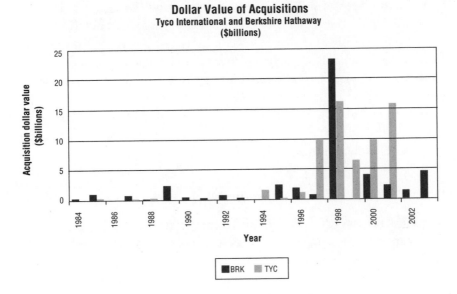

Dollar Value of Acquisitions
Tyco International and Berkshire Hathaway
($billions)

Figure 14.4   **Comparison of Annual Investments in Acquisitions by Tyco International and Berkshire Hathaway Inc.**

tunately, the textile group generated enough cash in the initial years to permit the firm to purchase two insurance companies headquartered in Omaha: National Indemnity Company and National Fire & Marine Insurance Company. Acquisitions of other businesses followed in the 1970s and 1980s.

The investment performance of a share in Berkshire Hathaway had astonished most observers. In 1977 the firm's year-end closing share price was $138.00. On September 30, 2004, the firm's closing share price was $86,650.00 for a 27 percent compound average annual growth rate. In comparison, the compound average annual return on the S&P 500 index over the same period was 9.6 percent.

Berkshire Hathaway described itself as "a holding company owning subsidiaries engaged in a number of diverse business activities."[9] Its portfolio of businesses included operations as diverse as the insurance group (focused on property and casualty insurance), the *Buffalo News* (a daily and Sunday newspaper in upstate New York), Fechheimer (a manufacturer and distributor of uniforms), Kirby (a manufacturer and marketer of home cleaning systems and accessories), Nebraska Furniture (a retailer of home furnishings), See's Candies (a manufacturer and distributor of boxed chocolates and other confectionery products), Childcraft and *World Book* (a publisher and distributor of encyclopedias and related educational and instructional material), Campbell Hausfeld (a manufacturer and distributor of air compressors, air tools, and painting systems), and three manufacturers, importers, and distributors of footwear (H.H. Brown Shoe Company; Lowell Shoe, Inc., and Dexter Shoe Company). In addition to these businesses, Berkshire owned an assortment of smaller businesses generating about $400 million in revenues.

Berkshire Hathaway's Acquisition Policy

Berkshire Hathaway's portfolio of businesses stretches the definition of "conglomerate" in comparison to Tyco, or even the paragon of conglomerate diversification, General Electric. Tyco and GE made some effort to represent their various businesses as internally linked by some theme or focus. Buffett's approach to acquisitions was much more eclectic in industrial focus and diametrically opposed to momentum acquiring; one could call Berkshire's strategy "anti-momentum." Table 14.2 gives the formal statement of acquisition criteria contained in Berkshire Hathaway's 1994 Annual Report. In general, the policy expressed a tightly disciplined strategy that refused to reward others for actions that Berkshire Hathaway might just as easily take on its own.

One prominent example to which Buffett referred was Berkshire Hathaway's investment in Scott & Fetzer in 1986. The managers of Scott & Fetzer had attempted a leveraged buyout of the company in the face of a rumored hostile takeover attempt. When the U.S. Labor Department objected to the company's use of an Employee Stock Ownership Plan to assist in the financing, the deal fell apart. Soon the company attracted unsolicited proposals to purchase the company, including one from Ivan F. Boesky, the arbitrageur. Buffett offered to buy the company for $315 million (which compared to its book value of $172.6 million). Following the acquisition, Scott & Fetzer paid Berkshire Hathaway dividends of $125 million, even though it earned only $40.3 million that year. From 1986 to 1994 the internal rate of return on investment in Scott & Fetzer was 36 percent, which compared to 12.6 percent for returns on large firms on average over the same period.[10]

TABLE 14.2   BERKSHIRE HATHAWAY ACQUISITION CRITERIA

"We are eager to hear about businesses that meet all of the following criteria:

1. Large purchases (at least $10 million of after-tax earnings),
2. Demonstrated consistent earning power (future projections are of no interest to us, nor are "turnaround" situations),
3. Businesses earning good returns on equity while employing little or no debt,
4. Management in place (we can't supply it),
5. Simple businesses (if there's lots of technology, we won't understand it),
6. An offering price (we don't want to waste our time or that of the seller by talking, even preliminarily, about a transaction when the price is unknown).

The larger the company, the greater will be our interest: we would like to make an acquisition in the $2–3 billion range.

We will not engage in unfriendly takeovers. We can promise complete confidentiality and a very fast answer—customarily within five minutes—as to whether we're interested. We prefer to buy for cash, but will consider issuing stock when we receive as much in intrinsic business value as we give.

Our favorite form of purchase is one fitting the pattern through which we acquired Nebraska Furniture Mart, Fechheimer's, Borsheim's, and Central States Indemnity. In cases like these, the company's owner-managers wish to generate significant amounts of cash, sometimes for themselves, but often for their families or inactive shareholders. At the same time, these managers wish to remain significant owners who continue to run their companies just as they have in the past. We think we offer a particularly good fit for owners with such objectives and we invite potential sellers to check us out by contacting people with whom we have done business in the past.

Charlie and I frequently get approached about acquisitions that don't come close to meeting our tests: We've found that if you advertise an interest in buying collies, a lot of people will call hoping to sell you their cocker spaniels. A line from a country song expresses our feeling about new ventures, turnarounds, or auction-like sales: "When the phone don't ring, you'll know it's me."

Besides being interested in the purchase of businesses as described above, we are also interested in the negotiated purchase of large, but not controlling, blocks of stock comparable to those we hold in Capital Cities, Salomon, Gillette, USAir, and Champion. *We are not interested, however, in receiving suggestions about purchases we might make in the general stock market.*"

Source: Berkshire Hathaway *Annual Report*, 1994, 21.

To Think like an Investor

Warren Buffett was first exposed to formal training in investing at Columbia University where he studied under Professor Benjamin Graham. The coauthor of a classic text, *Security Analysis*, Graham developed a method of identifying undervalued stocks (that is, stocks whose price was less than "intrinsic value"). This became the cornerstone of the modern approach of "value investing." Graham's approach was to focus on the value of assets such as cash, net working capital, and physical assets. Eventually, Buffett modified that approach to focus also on valuable franchises that were not recognized by the market.

Over the years, Buffett has expounded his philosophy of investing, in his CEO's letter to shareholders in Berkshire Hathaway's Annual Report. These lengthy letters accumulated a broad following because of their wisdom and their humorous, self-deprecating tone. They outline the core of what it means to think like an investor:[11]

- *Focus on economic reality, not accounting reality.* Financial statements prepared by accountants conformed to rules that might not adequately represent the *economic* reality of a business. Buffett wrote:

  > . . . because of the limitations of conventional accounting, consolidated reported earnings may reveal relatively little about our true economic performance. Charlie and I, both as owners and managers, virtually ignore such consolidated numbers. . . . Accounting consequences do not influence our operating or capital-allocation process.[12]

  Accounting reality is conservative, backward-looking, and governed by generally accepted accounting principles (GAAP). Investment decisions, on the other hand, should be based on the economic reality of a business. In economic reality, intangible assets such as patents, trademarks, special managerial know-how, and reputation might be very valuable, yet under GAAP, they would be carried at little or no value. GAAP measured results in terms of net profit; in economic reality, the results of a business were its *flows of cash*.

  A key feature of Buffett's approach defined economic reality at the level of the business itself, not the market, the economy, or the security. He was a *fundamental analyst* of a business. His analysis sought to judge the simplicity of the business, the consistency of its operating history, the attractiveness of its long-term prospects, the quality of management, and the firm's capacity to create value.

- *Reflect the cost of the lost opportunity.* Buffett compared an investment opportunity against the next best alternative, the so-called "lost opportunity." In his business decisions, he demonstrated a tendency to frame his choices as either/or decisions rather than yes/no decisions. Thus, an important standard of comparison in testing the attractiveness of an acquisition was the potential rate of return from investing in common stocks of other companies. Buffett held that there was no fundamental difference between buying a business outright, and buying a few shares of that business in the equity market. Thus, for him, the comparison of an investment against other returns available in the market was an important benchmark of performance.

- *Know that time is money: focus on present value to measure "intrinsic value."* The value that matters for Buffett's decision-making is "intrinsic value" which he defined as the

  > . . . discounted value of the cash that can be taken out of a business during its remaining life. Anyone calculating intrinsic value necessarily comes up with a highly subjective figure that will change both as estimates of future cash flows are revised and as interest rates move. Despite its fuzziness, however, intrinsic value is all-important and is the only logical way to evaluate the relative attractiveness of investments and businesses.[13] . . . In all cases, what is clear is that book value is meaningless as an indicator of intrinsic value.[14]

  To look to future flows of cash means that the analyst must convert them to present-day terms, through the mechanism of discounting cash flows. Buffett wrote:

  > [All other methods fall short in determining whether] an investor is indeed buying something for what it is worth and is therefore truly operating on the principle of obtaining value for his investments. . . . Irrespective of whether a business grows or doesn't, displays volatility or smoothness in earnings, or carries a

high price or low in relation to its current earnings and book value, the investment shown by the discounted-flows-of-cash calculation to be the cheapest is the one that the investor should purchase.[15]

The difference in value creation and destruction is driven entirely by the relationship between the expected returns and the discount rate: In the first case, the spread is positive; in the second case, it is negative. Only in the instance where expected returns equal the discount rate will "book value" equal intrinsic value. In short, book value or the investment outlay may not reflect economic reality: One needs to focus on the prospective rates of return and how they compare to the required rate of return.

- *Measure performance by gain in intrinsic value, not accounting profit.* Buffett wrote:

  Our long-term economic goal . . . is to maximize the average annual rate of gain in intrinsic business value on a per-share basis. We do not measure the economic significance or performance of Berkshire by its size; we measure by per-share progress.[16]

  The gain in intrinsic value could be modeled as the value added by a business above and beyond a charge for the use of capital in that business.

- *Risk and return.* The more risk one takes, the more one should get paid. Buffett argued that he avoided risk, and therefore should use a "risk-free" discount rate. His firm used almost no debt financing. He focused on companies with predictable and stable earnings. He or his vice chairman, Charlie Munger, sat on the boards of directors where they obtained a candid, inside view of the company and could intervene in decisions of management if necessary.

- *Diversification.* Buffett disagreed with conventional wisdom that investors should hold a broad portfolio of stocks in order to shed company-specific risk. In his view, investors typically purchased far too many stocks rather than waiting for the one exceptional company. Buffett said:

  Figure businesses out that you understand, and concentrate. Diversification is protection against ignorance, but if you don't feel ignorant, the need for it goes down drastically.[17]

- *Investing behavior should be driven by information, analysis, and self-discipline, not by emotion or "hunch."* Buffett repeatedly emphasized "awareness" and information as the foundation for investing. He said, "Anyone not aware of the fool in the market probably is the fool in the market."[18] Buffett was fond of repeating a parable told him by Benjamin Graham:

  > There was a small private business and one of the owners was a man named Market. Every day Mr. Market had a new opinion of what the business was worth, and at that price stood ready to buy your interest or sell you his. As excitable as he was opinionated, Mr. Market presented a constant distraction to his fellow owners. "What does he know?" they would wonder, as he bid them an extraordinarily high price or a depressingly low one. Actually, the gentleman knew little or nothing. You may be happy to sell out to him when he quotes you a ridiculously high price, and equally happy to buy from him when his price is low. But the rest of the time you will be wiser to form your own ideas of the value of your holdings, based on full reports from the company about its operation and financial position.[19]

Buffett used this allegory to suggest the variability of stock prices as compared to intrinsic value. Graham believed that an investor's worst enemy was not the stock market, but oneself. Superior training could not compensate for the absence of the requisite temperament for investing. Over the long term, stock prices should have a strong relationship with the economic progress of the business. But daily market quotations were heavily influenced by momentary greed or fear, and were an unreliable measure of intrinsic value. Buffett said:

> As far as I am concerned, the stock market doesn't exist. It is there only as a reference to see if anybody is offering to do anything foolish. When we invest in stocks, we invest in businesses. You simply have to behave according to what is rational rather than according to what is fashionable.[20]

Accordingly, Buffett did not try to "time the market" (i.e., trade stocks based on expectations of changes in the market cycle). His was a strategy of patient, long-term investing. As if in contrast to Mr. Market, Buffett expressed more contrarian goals: "We simply attempt to be fearful when others are greedy and to be greedy only when others are fearful."[21] Buffett also said, "Lethargy bordering on sloth remains the cornerstone of our investment style,"[22] and, "The market, like the Lord, helps those who help themselves. But unlike the Lord, the market does not forgive those who know not what they do."[23]

- *Alignment of agents and owners.* Explaining his significant ownership interest in Berkshire Hathaway, Buffett said, "I am a better business-man because I am an investor. And I am a better investor because I am a businessman."[24] As if to illustrate this sentiment, he said:

> A managerial "wish list" will not be filled at shareholder expense. We will not diversify by purchasing entire businesses at control prices that ignore long-term economic consequences to our shareholders. We will only do with your money what we would do with our own, weighing fully the values you can obtain by di-versifying your own portfolios through direct purchases in the stock market.[25]

For four of Berkshire's six directors, more than 50 percent of their family net worth was represented by shares in Berkshire Hath-away. The senior managers of Berkshire Hathaway subsidiaries held shares in the company, or were compensated under incentive plans that imitated the potential returns from an equity interest in their business unit, or both.

CONCLUSION: SOME LESSONS ABOUT MOMENTUM ACQUIRING

A definitive documentation of the fall of Tyco awaits the conclusion of litigation swirling around Kozlowski, Swartz, and the firm. But what we know about it suggests the influence of the six drivers of M&A failure. Kozlowski built a conglomerate with 2,431 subsidiaries as of September 2001, a *complex* enterprise by any standard. The huge overhang of good-will on the balance sheet and the intense focus on growing earnings *tightly linked* the reported financial performance of the firm to its share price and to its acquisitions. *Management chose* a number of policies con-sistent with the goal of rapid earnings growth; particularly unfortunate was the decision to book as goodwill much of the purchase price on its acquisitions This policy exposed the firm to significant risk of unexpected and large charges to earnings should goodwill become impaired. *Business went sour* in 2001, threatening the dreaded impairment charge. Kozlowski hastily cobbled together the plan to restructure the firm before the charge would have its devastating impact. Creditors and investors, however, saw through the attempt and stopped it. And the SEC's investigation threatened the credibility of Tyco's growth in EPS. The *inept management team response* is apparent in the double about-face. But of all the causes, *cognitive bias* in the form of momentum thinking is at the heart of this deal from hell.

The story of Tyco, in contrast with Berkshire Hathaway, offers a clear lesson that momentum acquiring is bad and that value acquiring is good. Let's consider why.

The chief claim in favor of momentum acquiring is that stock market investors appear to value it. Firms with momentum seem to enjoy higher valuation multiples than firms without. But what is the chain of causation? Does momentum create high multiples, or do high multiples stimulate momentum acquiring? The story of Tyco and other momentum acquirers associates momentum with a buoyant, or overvalued, stock market.

One argument in favor of causation is the existence of momentum-style investors. The 1990s saw the emergence of professional money managers who invested on the basis of earnings or share price momentum. These investors were the financial analogue to sports fans who believe that athletes can have a "hot hand" or a winning streak that is sustainable over some period. But the existence of momentum-style investment managers is not persuasive evidence that investors especially value momentum. Thousands of investment management companies, hedge funds, and specialty boutiques exist to invest on the basis of unusual themes or strategies—the vast bulk of them fail to beat benchmark returns with any consistency. A profitable momentum strategy is inconsistent with the existence of rational investors and an efficient market. Any success from momentum investing is just as plausibly due to luck, or the possibility that the momentum style is a proxy for investment drivers that *do* matter, or the ability to find a temporary anomaly in the stock market, but none of these proves that investors will pay a premium for momentum. The burden of proof is on momentum investors to show that momentum pays.

Research finds that momentum-style investing pays no better than other investing strategies, and may pay worse. The test is whether the strategy of buying stocks with winning momentum and selling stocks with losing momentum earns positive "alpha" returns (that is, returns in excess of a suitable benchmark). Like other investing strategies, momentum-style investing *may* generate a small positive alpha but that is swamped by taxes and transaction costs.[26] Positive alpha return from momentum investing is almost entirely explained by *industry momentum* rather than firm momentum.[27] This finding is consistent with other research suggesting that it isn't momentum that investors value, but rather the occurrence of positive developments that affect an entire industry. If true, then CEOs should be less concerned with creating earnings momentum through acquisition and more concerned about creating real economic value by responding appropriately to industry shocks.

It is difficult to find an episode of momentum acquisition that did not end in some or all of the following: sharp loss in stock price, dashed expectations among investors and securities analysts, bankruptcy or financial distress, and sacked managers. All of this is virtually inevitable. Producing a steady rate of growth through a program of acquisitions is ultimately unsustainable, for at least three reasons.

1. *The annual volume must get bigger.* A fixed percentage growth target each year dictates that the acquisition volume must grow from year to year. A growing acquisition program becomes more challenging to implement and probably stimulates the search for bigger targets, both of which expose the firm to more risk.

2. *The world is finite.* Any acquisition growth target in excess of the rate of inflation, if extended long enough will result in the momentum acquirer owning the entire world economy. The political and economic barriers to such an outcome are enormous.

3 *Stuff happens.* Unblinking expectations of steady growth fail to account for possible adversities, such as the SEC investigations and restructuring proposal at Tyco.

Against factors like these, it seems inevitable that the momentum acquirer will be thrown from the game, like a player in musical chairs. In theory a soft landing is possible, though eventually, investors settle up with momentum managers.

Specifically regarding M&A, studies by Rosen (2002) and Ang and Cheng (2003) give evidence consistent with the unsustainability of momentum benefits. Rosen found some evidence of merger momentum, that is, buyers' share prices showed larger increases at deal announcements when the market for mergers was "hot" or if the general equity market was buoyant. But these increases were not permanent: Over the long run, buyer returns were *worse* for deals announced in hot markets. Ang and Cheng found that acquirers tend to be more overvalued than their targets. As overvaluation increases, it is more likely that a firm will acquire another firm, and that stock-paying buyers are more overvalued than buyers in cash deals. But the benefits of this overvaluation are brief. The long-run returns following the overvalued stock deals are negative: As a target shareholder in these deals, it is best to bail out quickly from the buyer's stock. The unsustainability of momentum benefits is consistent with evidence that firms tend to acquire when they have an inflated currency with which to do so. Momentum helps to create the inflated currency.

Central to the momentum acquisition approach is the maintenance of a steady path of growth in EPS, revenues, or assets. Because of the difficulties of maintaining the growth trajectory, the incentives increase to use accounting cosmetics. Generally accepted accounting principles permit wide latitude in reporting financial performance. This latitude can degenerate into earnings management, misrepresentation of the performance of the firm. The fixation on accounting dilution to EPS, rather than economic reality can distort managers' M&A decision-making.

The most serious criticism of momentum acquiring is that it offers a flawed benchmark for evaluating the desirability of acquisition opportunities. For instance, the momentum acquirer would say that the decision criterion is simple: Accept all deals that build momentum, and reject deals that diminish momentum. This rule can hurt the firm and its shareholders wherever the avoidance of dilution dictates a different course of action than does the creation of value.

The antidote to the vagaries of momentum acquiring is to base an acquisition strategy on value creation, rather than momentum. Value creation, and its associated measure, discounted cash flow (DCF) respond to the defects of momentum discussed previously, and carry a number of strengths. The chief drawback to the value-based approach is its complexity of analysis. DCF valuation is difficult to explain to novices and busy executives. New analysts are easily paralyzed by endless refinements and sensitivity analyses. The resulting values are themselves uncertain, and almost surely measured with error.

Though not perfect, value based acquisition strategies have the ultimate virtue of weeding out bad deals more effectively than other approaches. In addition, the value approach highlights good deals more prominently. Regardless of the temporary robustness of momentum acquisition approaches, value creation better promotes the survival and prosperity of the firm.

The key lesson of this discussion must be that momentum acquiring is a dangerous path, both for corporate managers and their investors. It is a strategy premised on the mistaken belief that the *appearance* of growth matters more than economic reality. Some of the telltales of this strategy are a focus on EPS (or revenues), earnings management, the manipulation of goodwill and dilution, a relatively large number of acquisitions increasing in size over time, and an aggressive trajectory of performance. This chapter has argued that value creation is a superior foundation for acquisition planning. A summary comparison of the momentum and value approaches is given in Table 14.3.

TABLE 14.3   COMPARISON OF MOMENTUM ACQUISITION STRATEGY AND VALUE-ORIENTED STRATEGY

	Momentum Acquiring Strategy	*Value-Oriented Acquiring Strategy*
Focus	Contribution to earnings or revenue momentum; size, reported financial results.	Price to acquire target versus its intrinsic value. Net present value of the acquisition.
Implicit Assumptions	Reported results matter. Investors are driven by accounting reality: EPS is king.	Value matters to investors. Investors are driven by economic reality: cash is king.
Approach	Estimate the target's contribution to earnings or revenue momentum. Avoid dilution and goodwill charges.	Estimate the intrinsic value of the target. Negotiate a price. Price ≠ value. Tell investors about value.
End Game	Bubble bursts.	Value created.

NOTES

1. The research assistance of Sean Carr and Jessica Chan is gratefully acknowledged. Research for this chapter drew upon many public sources.

2. Quoted in Sorkin (2002).

3. A quotation of Ron Taylor, Schaeffer Investments in Cincinnati, in Fakler (2002).

4. Berenson (2002). Copyright © 2002 by the New York Times Co. Reprinted with permission.

5. Maremont and Weil (2003). *Wall Street Journal* Eastern Edition [staff produced copy only] by M. Maremont and J. Weil. Copyright © 2003 by Dow Jones & Co. Inc. Reproduced with permission of Dow Jones & Co. Inc. In the Format Trade Book via Copyright Clearance Center.

6. For more detail on alleged pressure on securities analysts, see Charles Gasparino, "Merrill Replaced Its Tyco Analyst After Meeting," *Wall Street Journal*, September 17, 2002, C.1.

7. Anthony Bianco, William Symonds, and Nanette Byrnes, with David Polek in New York, "The rise and fall of Dennis Kozlowski. How did he become so unhinged by greed? A revealing look at the man behind the Tyco scandal," *Business-Week*, December 23, 2002, 64. Reprinted by special permission © 2002 McGraw-Hill Companies, Inc.

8. Reported in Moore (2002).

9. Berkshire Hathaway, Inc. *Annual Report*, 1994, 6.

10. Reported in *Stocks, Bonds, Bills, and Inflation*, Ibbotson Associates.

11. This section draws structure and some content from the case study, "Warren Buffett, 1995," by Robert Bruner, and the chapter "Finance," prepared by Robert F. Bruner and appearing in Robert Bruner, R. Edward Freeman, Robert Spekman, Elizabeth Teisberg, and S. Venkataraman, *The Portable MBA*, 3rd ed. (Hoboken: John Wiley & Sons, 2002).

12. Berkshire Hathaway, Inc. *Annual Report*, 1994, 2.

13. Berkshire Hathaway Inc. *Annual Report*, 1992, 14.

14. Berkshire Hathaway, Inc. *Annual Report*, 1994, 7.

15. Berkshire Hathaway, Inc. *Annual Report*, 1992, 14.

16. Ibid., 2.

17. Quoted in *Forbes*, October 19, 1993, and republished in Andrew Kilpatrick, *Of Permanent Value, The Story of Warren Buffett*, 574.

18. Quoted in Michael Lewis, *Liar's Poker* (New York: Norton, 1989), 35.

19. Originally published in Berkshire Hathaway *Annual Report*, 1987. This quotation was paraphrased from James Grant, *Minding Mr. Market* (New York: Times Books, 1993), xxi.

20. Peter Lynch, *One Up on Wall Street* (New York: Penguin Books, 1990), 78.

21. Berkshire Hathaway *Annual Report*, 1986, 16.

22. Berkshire Hathaway *Annual Report*, 1990, 15.

23. Berkshire Hathaway *Letters to Shareholders, 1977–1983*, 53.

24. Quoted in *Forbes*, October 19, 1993, and republished in Andrew Kilpatrick, *Of Permanent Value*, 574.

25. "Owner-Related Business Principles" in Berkshire Hathaway *Annual Report 1994*, 3.

26. See, for instance, Lesmond, Schill, and Zhou (2002).

27. See Moskowitz and Grinblatt (1999).

III

AVOIDING THE
DEAL FROM HELL

15

Conclusions and Implications

THE "WHAT" OF M&A FAILURE: PREVALENCE OF FAILURE AND SUCCESS

Contrary to conventional wisdom M&A is not a loser's game. A large mass of economic research suggests that investments through acquisition pay about as well as other kinds of corporate investment: On average, they cover the buyer's cost of capital. This should not be surprising: Competition in markets tends to drive returns toward this cost.

Neither is M&A necessarily a winner's game. The returns to buyers show a wide dispersion around the average. This dispersion suggests a nontrivial chance that one can lose meaningfully from M&A. But the failure rate in M&A seems no larger than in other business pursuits that are generally applauded, such as new business start-ups, new product introductions, expansions to new markets, and investments in R&D and new technology. I suspect that if the public could see all corporate investing with the kind of clarity with which we evaluate large mergers, we could conclude that M&A tends to be in the range of tolerable risk. Business is risky. One should aim to manage risk better, not eliminate it.

Viewing the dispersion of returns to buyers, my advice to the business practitioner is to be coldly realistic about the benefits of acquisition. Structure your deals very carefully. Particularly avoid overpaying. Have the discipline to walk away from uneconomic deals. Work very hard to achieve the economic gains you hypothesized. Take nothing for granted. M&A is no money machine, and may well not offer the major career-building event you wanted. The only solace is that you could say the same about virtually any other form of corporate investment: On average and over time, your shareholders will tend to earn the cost of capital on M&A activity. Given the uncertainties in M&A as elsewhere, one must remember the ancient advice, caveat emptor (buyer beware).

THE "WHERE" OF M&A FAILURE: NEIGHBORHOODS OF FAILURE AND SUCCESS

A wide dispersion around the average experience for buyers in M&A means that you cannot be terribly confident of hitting the average return simply by acquiring naively. Something must be going on in M&A markets that can help us understand the propensity to gain or lose.

All M&A is local. Research suggests that the market for acquisitions is highly segmented. The large implication is that blanket assertions about M&A profitability are not terribly useful. It is better to have a view of M&A profitability informed by these different segments than to think in average terms.

Chapter 2 summarizes findings along 18 dimensions that explain material differences in returns to buyers. Synthesizing across these areas suggests that buyers are *more likely* to fail in M&A when:

- *The buyer enters a fundamentally unprofitable industry, or refuses to exit from one.* All sensible acquiring begins by thinking like an investor. This means making sound industry bets based on expected returns and risks.
- *The buyer acquires far away from its core business.* "Far away" can be measured in geographical terms: Research suggests that foreign buyers pay a premium for local knowledge. But distance can also be expressed in strategic terms: Acquiring into the same or related industries is associated with higher returns. The discovery and exploitation of merger synergies is more likely when you are dealing with familiar territory. However, a firm's core competency could be in managing a portfolio of unrelated businesses. Thus, the key strate-

gic driver of profitability has less to do with focus and relatedness and more to do with distance expressed in terms of knowledge, mastery, and competencies. What does your firm know? What is it good at doing?

- *The economic benefits of the deal are improbable or not marginal to the deal.* The capital market judges merger synergies skeptically. Such skepticism is fueled by long experience with hyped expectations created at deal announcements. Thus, sophisticated investors adopt a "show me" attitude toward synergies. Executives should internalize this skepticism and exercise it in the earliest stages of deal discussions.

- *The buyer fails to seek some economic advantage.* Bargaining power pays; bargaining weakness is costly. What advantage does your firm have, or can it create, in trying to do a deal with the target? What are the sources of that advantage? Can those sources be duplicated by competitors? The famous "winner's curse" is associated with auction-type settings. The research suggests that there may be a "winner's blessing" in negotiated acquisitions for private companies. The point is that you must think carefully about what special resources you have and in which settings those resources can be deployed most profitably.

- *The buyer does not adapt the deal design to the situation.* Years of capital market research show that tailoring in the design of deals and financial instruments pays. One size does not fit all. You can probably improve the returns from M&A to the buyer through artful deal design. The use of cash, debt financing, tax shields, staged payments, merger-of-equals terms, and earnout incentive structures are all associated with higher buyer returns.

- *The buyer has poor systems of governance and incentives.* The avoidance of deals from hell begins with effective checks, balances, and incentives among the board of directors and senior managers.

The survey of scientific research tells us that executives have choices in M&A that, when made thoughtfully, can tilt the odds of success in their favor. Though I doubt that success or failure in M&A is predestined, *where* you choose to do deals (in the sense of the previous elements) has a significant influence on outcomes.

THE "WHO" OF M&A FAILURE: PROFILES OF FAILURE AND SUCCESS

The best and worst transactions are significantly different from each other and from the middle of the distribution. Chapter 3 gives some new findings about the profile of buyers in the most and least successful deals. These findings are consistent with the broader mass of research in Chapter 2, especially the virtues of staying close to what you know and of tailoring the deal terms. The profiles of the standout successes and failures added two more conditions that the buyer is likely to fail where:

1. *The buyer acquires out of weakness.* How the buyer and target complement each other has a big effect on outcomes. Successful buyers bring to the acquisition capabilities that can help the target prosper. Unsuccessful buyers tend to bring weaknesses to the acquisition that they hope the target will fix. Failure may be more likely because of flaws of the buyer, rather than flaws of the target.

2. *The buyer goes "hot."* Deals done in "cool" markets and industries tend to be more successful than deals done in "hot" markets and industries. Under hot market conditions, prices are high and buyers are numerous. It is easy to get caught up in deal frenzy and overoptimism, and to overpay. In cool markets, one can be more judicious and disciplined as a buyer.

One can always find exceptions to generalizations such as these, but such exceptions merely prove the larger rule that all M&A is local. The wise M&A practitioner thinks in terms of the different neighborhoods rather than the entire metropolis.

THE "HOW" OF M&A FAILURE: THE "PARABLE"

Chapters 2 through 4 offer a glimpse into the kinds of drivers associated with financial and real disaster. From that research, I distilled six dimensions of failure: complexity, tight coupling, adverse management choices, business not as usual, execution failures associated with the malfunctioning of a team, and cognitive biases. Viewed through the lens of these dimensions, the 10 case studies of M&A failure display many points in common. Appendix 15.1 offers a summary comparison of the failure cases. The similarities are striking and might be summed as the following parable of merger failure:

One day, a buyer decided to acquire a target. Because of size, technology, and/or breadth of products or markets, each firm was complex. This made it hard for the operating managers and senior executives to know what was really going on or to take quick and decisive action in response to problems. In addition, units within each firm were interlinked so that changes in one part would be felt in the others. Thus, each firm was a "system." The proposed acquisition would increase the complexity. In addition, the nature of the companies and of the deal terms themselves offered little tolerance for error. However, the environment for the deal was uncertain; external forces made it a turbulent world. In this context, management of the buyer made some choices that seemed reasonable and perhaps innocuous but that actually amplified the stress and exposure to risk. Perhaps sounder judgment would have counseled slowing down, changing, or canceling the acquisition, but management and the organization had a different mind-set, a focus on sunk costs, overoptimism, arrogance, or a sense of momentum and deal frenzy. The team of employees who were chartered to manage the integration of the target into the buyer failed to function effectively: Inattention, miscommunication, bickering, and poor planning diverted them from resolving problems that mattered.

So . . . the acquisition occurred. Business did not go as usual, which produced errors from plan. Because of complexity and tight coupling, the errors radiated through the company and out into the marketplace. Customers complained and departed; so did key employees. The integration team reacted poorly to these errors: They disbelieved the significance of the errors, took their time, and over- or undercorrected. Thus, the errors festered and compounded. Eventually deterioration became obvious to all: Business meltdown was in progress. Under great stress, the team broke down. A new team came in, but by then the wreckage was so complete that their mission became disgorging the target with the least remaining damage to the buyer.

In addition to points of similarity among the cases, one also sees rich variation. These variations lend texture to our understanding of what can go wrong. Consider the variations we see among the deals:

- *Business complexity makes it difficult for managers to understand what is going on in the merger or to take action.* Given that these are large firms and transactions, complexity is a fact of life in the deals from hell and the comparison deals. By itself, complexity is not a predictor of failure though it is probably a necessary precondition. The pre-eminent example of the confounding role of complexity is the Pennsylvania/New York Central merger. Other cases displayed high complexity based on large size and conglomerate organization (Tyco), logistics (Revco), project diversity (Sony), organization (Renault/Volvo), and technology (AT&T).

- *Limited or no flexibility.* With tight coupling, the absence of "buffers" or flexibility to absorb shocks, the crisis radiates through the firm, leading to a compounding of problems. Trouble can travel. Overpayment or aggressive financing of the deal eliminate degrees of freedom for managers to respond to problems. Though leveraging the firm, for instance, can create incentives for management to run a tight ship, it can also asphyxiate the firm: The case of Revco Drug Stores is the classic example here.

- *Business not as usual, trouble in one or more parts of the firm.* Complexity and tight coupling mean that little errors can become big problems. Turbulence in the business environment produces errors. Every one of the 10 deals from hell featured major turbulence, including from technology (AT&T/NCR), capital markets (AOL/Time Warner, Dynegy/Enron, Revco), industry overcapacity (Renault/Volvo), rising costs (Sony/Columbia), competitor entry (Quaker/Snapple), or government action (Tyco, Penn Central).

- *Cognitive biases cause management and employees to ignore or deny risks and the crisis.* Deals from hell are typically launched with confident assertions of benefits and a happy future. Appendix 15.2 summarizes choice statements by CEOs in the 10 cases presented here. To be fair, CEOs face the task of rallying the employees and other stakeholders to meet a major challenge and will say things like these to win support. But the evidence from archives and interviews tends to suggest that the CEOs believed sentiments like these. Overoptimism (also called "hubris") is pervasive at the start of most of these failed deals. Quaker Oats suffered from recency bias: William Smithburg had succeeded with Gatorade, so doing it again with Snapple seemed like a cinch. AT&T suffered from escalation of commitments and sunk cost mentality. Having declared in 1984 that they would carve a new identity at the convergence of telecommunications and computing, Robert Allen insisted on doubling the bet in acquiring NCR. Jill Barad (Mattel) and Dennis Kozlowski (Tyco) adopted policies consistent with momentum thinking. In contrast, the evidence from case studies of successful corporate change suggests that effective leaders have a sober assessment of the situation, are candid with employees about the opportunities *and* the potential threats, are disciplined emotionally and intellectually in their evaluation of the change, and lead as servants of the enterprise and its stakeholders.

- *Adverse management choices increase the risk of the deal or the firm.* Each of these deals from hell entailed senior management choices that bore unintended consequences. The existence of unintended consequences is nothing new; most decisions have them. But in the case of the deals from hell, these decisions seem especially ill-considered. Penn Central's decision to accelerate the pace of integration triggered higher capital spending and operational chaos. Revco's decision to change merchandising strategy sacrificed profitability at a time when the firm depended on stable cash flow. Sony decided to bet the ranch on a couple of relatively inexperienced Hollywood producers. Rather than enhancing the likelihood of success, these decisions worsened it.

- *Flaws in the operational team hamper response to the crisis.* A common theme in the deals from hell is cultural difference between the buyer and target organization. Such difference can stem from nationality (Sony/Columbia, Renault/Volvo), operating rivalry (Penn Central), or different industries (AOL/Time Warner, AT&T/NCR). Lack of candor, political infighting, aberrant leadership, and failure to exploit a response window also reflect flaws in the operating team.

THE "WHY" OF M&A FAILURE: THE PERFECT STORM

Mergers and acquisitions fail because of a convergence of forces, a "perfect storm" of poor choices, poor execution, cognitive biases, and bad external conditions. It may not be necessary for all of these forces to be present, or to be individually powerful to trigger a failure. A deal between two very weak firms (such as the Pennsylvania and New York Central railroads) may be more susceptible to disaster than a deal between two robustly healthy firms. This is a fertile subject for future research; with more experience and analysis it may be possible to illuminate the "locality" or contingencies of M&A success and failure. But the perfect storm analogy can help executives understand the storm warnings of where failure is more likely. And it lends a number of important insights.

First, the foundation for failure-avoidance is systems thinking, seeing the complexity of the drivers of failure with sufficient clarity to anticipate failure. There is no *single* fatal flaw that explains merger failure. Avoid the tyranny of sound-bite explanations. All of the research, both the case studies and the large-sample work, suggest strongly the *jointness* of causes. As Victor Hugo said, "Great blunders are made like large ropes of a multiple of fibers."

Second, many of the drivers of M&A failures are not merely common; they are prevalent in business. For instance, business is almost never "as usual." Most companies and mergers immerse the decision-makers in complexity. Behavioral economists tell us that cognitive bias is the rule, not the exception. Thus, how can it be that failure is the exception rather than the norm? The answer lies in the jointness of the perfect storm. The likelihood of a whopping failure depends on the joint probability of each of these forces occurring at the same time. Just for the sake of illustration, suppose that there is a 75 percent chance that the buyer and target will be complex firms, 75 percent chance of tight coupling, 75 percent chance of business not as usual, and so on. Then the joint probability will be $(0.75)^6$ or 18 percent. One could argue that life is more complicated than this little illustration, but even with refinements, the general idea would hold: The various seeds of failure might be prevalent in the business environment, but it is when the slot machine shows all six together that you are really at risk.

Third, the drivers of failure may be mutually-reinforcing. For instance, cognitive biases such as overoptimism or momentum thinking may promote bad managerial choices or hamper the responsiveness of the operational team. Crisis conditions outside the firm (business not as usual) may distract senior executives and operating managers from the task of merger management. Complexity may promote a false sense of security that sustains cognitive biases and bad managerial choices. And so on. Where there is some correlation among the major drivers of failure, then the probability of failure outlined in the preceding paragraph will rise.

The important implication of these insights is that you can enhance the success of an acquisition by attacking the *system* of failure, the mutually reinforcing nature of the six drivers, and the likelihood that they will converge at a point in time. As the example of the probability calculation suggests, one can attack the individual probabilities of the six forces and the correlations among the forces. This is the approach of the "high reliability organization" (HRO) such as a hospital emergency room, an intensive care unit, and an aircraft carrier flight deck. Chapter 4 outlines some of the attributes of the HRO:

- *A preoccupation with failure.* HROs are obsessive about the potential for things to go wrong.
- *A reluctance to simplify.* This attribute fights "mindlessness," a reliance on rote application of decision rules, checklists, and past experience.
- *A continuous sensitivity to operations*, vigilance to changes from plan or from a benchmark.
- *A commitment to resilience.* HROs assume that surprise is around the corner and prepare for it.
- *A deference to expertise.* HROs presume that the best decisions will be made by those who are best-informed, usually people at the front lines. Thus, decision-making is decentralized.

Though I know of no organization that explicitly has adapted to M&A the terms and concepts of the HRO, my field interviews with successful serial acquirers have revealed the HRO's spirit and concepts at work.

FURTHERMORE: A FAILURE-FREE WORLD OF M&A?

Every CEO should want his or her firm to avoid the deal from hell. But do we really want a world completely devoid of M&A failure? Such a world is unimaginably costly to construct and police. All insurance is costly. You would need to insure against a range of factors within and beyond managers' control. And the policing function inside corporations ("no mistakes, never, ever") would probably suppress success as well. Economics teaches that where there is no risk, the best you can expect is, well, the risk-free rate of return. The human spirit seeks to exercise ingenuity and risk-taking in the pursuit of a better life. Is the risk-free rate all that we will settle for?

Get a grip. The huge advances in civilization came from people who, at some considerable commitment of personal wealth and comfort, took a risk. We *want* the business economy to take risks—new drugs, environmentally-efficient housing and transportation, comfortable clothing, better connectivity with others, and food that is more nutritious and better-tasting—all these are the dividends of entrepreneurial risk-taking. But to get this, we need to put up with a certain amount of trial-and-error. Failure is the price we pay for the experimentation that brings breakthroughs.

How much failure must we tolerate? As Chapter 2 outlines, material and significant economic failure in M&A is relatively rare. Some neighborhoods of the M&A field are more profitable than others. But on average, M&A does pay.

The kinds of corporate boners sketched in this book test our tolerance for corporate risk-taking. As consumers, investors, and taxpayers, we suffer when M&A fails on this scale. But rather than banning large mergers, we should mitigate the risk of failure through better systems of management. Everything begins with setting the highest expectations of corporations. These expectations should be focused on *processes* rather than on outcomes in the belief that *how* you do business has a big influence on the results. For instance, we should expect:

- Ethical behavior of corporations and their advisors. Where there is no trust, corporations forfeit their support from the public.
- Systems of governance that are loyal to the interests of stakeholders and careful in the sense of keen attention to the details of M&A proposals.
- Deal design with enough slack in their transactions to allow for adequate variance from business as usual.
- Systems of merger integration that employ best practices in planning, information, and implementation.

- Teams of executives to work together in ways that permit dissent and foster high reliability.
- Suspension of hubris and other cognitive biases at the door of each M&A transaction.

These six process-oriented expectations will not forestall all failures. But the research offered in this book suggests that adoption of practices such as these will lower the odds of failure. Managing the odds, rather than eliminating them, is what we should aim to do.

In short, the attitudes that we bring to our corporations really matter. Let us focus our intolerance for failure on promoting good processes rather than on suppressing risk-taking and the benefits that come with it.

APPENDIX 15.1   A COMPARISON ACROSS THE CASES OF MERGER FAILURE

Case	Complexity: Makes it difficult to understand what's going on.	Tight Coupling: Absence of flexibility causes the crisis to radiate through the organization.	Business Not as Usual: Trouble in one or more parts of the firm.	Cognitive Biases: Mental "filtering" causes decision-makers to discount risks and the crisis.	Management Choices: Decisions that increase the risk of the firm or deal.	Implementation by the Team: Flaws in team processes or make-up hamper response to the crisis.
Pennsylvania and New York Central Railroads	Very complex companies. Logistical systems spanning 16 states, 20,000 miles of track, and 93,000 employees. Extremely difficult integration challenge.	Fixed exchange ratio required the two firms to perform in unison over the pendency of the merger. Small and shrinking financial reserves eliminated financial flexibility. Merger protective agreement eliminated workforce flexibility.	Decline of railroad industry. Regulatory delay and uncertainty. Inflation. Rising interest rates. Recession. Severe weather.	Overoptimism. "Obsession" to complete the deal. Deception, reflected in earnings management, and optimistic public statements.	Decision to accelerate merger integration without detailed plan.	Large cultural differences: "green team" versus "red team." Clashes among senior executives. Confusion and morale problems among supervisors and customer-contact employees. Lack of training.
CSX, NS, BNSF, UP, and Conrail Split-up	Very complex companies. Large logistical systems. Extremely difficult integration challenge.	Tendency toward high prices in these deals limited the ability to achieve high rates of return.	Declining or low interest rates. Buoyant economy.	Some tendency toward hubris and overoptimism.	Decision to consolidate.	Rivalries among management teams in most of these mergers as they combined former competitors. Generally strong leadership at the top with careful integration planning. Still, some integration problems.

Revco Drug Stores (LBO)	System of 1,400 stores requiring logistical support, and coordination on pricing and costs. Highly complicated financial structure.	Very low financial flexibility producing low tolerance for error and low estimated probability of survival.	Stock market crash, October 1987. Poor holiday selling season. Revco's changed retail focus. Entry of new competitors in the discount drug retailing field.	Overoptimism, reflected in cash flow forecasts. Conflicted interest.	Decision to change merchandising strategies. Approval of capital structure.	Inexperienced LBO sponsor. Power struggles; divided staff loyalties; infighting among management. Change in CEO within three months of transaction.
Jack Eckerd (LBO)	System of more than 1,500 stores requiring logistical support and on pricing and costs. Moderately complicated financial structure.	Constrained financial flexibility, but not extremely. Moderately good probability of survival.	Stock market crash, October 1987. Poor holiday selling season. Entry of new competitors in the discount drug retailing field.	Moderate optimism.	No change in merchandising strategy.	Experienced LBO sponsor. Stable management team.
Sony and Columbia	Film production: complicated project-based business. Long lead-times. Large capital outlays. Significant risk in development and at box office.	High price reduced the tolerance for error in achieving acceptable rate of return. Large capital requirements to re-start. Columbia would draw resources from the rest of Sony.	Columbia's film pipeline was "dry." Firm was sick and needed mending. Industry shifting toward "blockbuster" strategy. Expensive technological change.	Overoptimism. Momentum thinking reflected in haste to conclude the deal. Belief in "one-of-a-kind opportunity." Sony's trust in the "experts."	High purchase price. Decision to hire Guber and Peters. Decision to diversify filmed into entertainment.	Inappropriate incentive structure. "Bet-the-ranch" behavior of CEOs. Parent was distant both culturally and geographically: engineers vs. Hollywood; U.S. vs. Japan.

(Continued)

353

APPENDIX 15.1 (Continued)

Case	Complexity: Makes it difficult to understand what's going on.	Tight Coupling: Absence of flexibility causes the crisis to radiate through the organization.	Business Not as Usual: Trouble in one or more parts of the firm.	Cognitive Biases: Mental "filtering" causes decision-makers to discount risks and the crisis.	Management Choices: Decisions that increase the risk of the firm or deal.	Implementation by the Team: Flaws in team processes or make-up hamper response to the crisis.
Unilever and Bestfoods	Moderately complicated product marketing and distribution.	Opportunities for product bundling at retail level.	Healthy firms. Improving economic climate. Industry consolidation and rise of foods conglomerates.	Aggressive approach based on intimate knowledge of industry.	Decision to expand line of similar products.	Cross-border deal, but between similar cultures.
AT&T and NCR	Computer manufacturing is highly complex.	High purchase price reduced tolerance for error in achieving acceptable rate of return.	Deregulation. Shift toward open-architecture computing. Rapid technological change. Sharp price competition. AT&T's computing business in distress. NCR's success hinged on introduction of new product line.	Overoptimism. Sunk cost mentality. Escalation of commitments.	Strategic decision to enter computer industry in 1984.	Sharp cultural differences.
Merck and Medco	Complicated technology with long lead-times for product development.	High price, limited room for variation in the achievement of financial returns.	Sizable prospective changes in government regulation. Rapid rate of R&D with consequent displacement of established products.	Hubris. Overoptimism.	Decision to lock in channel of distribution despite apparent conflict of interest.	Cohesive management team. Medco operated autonomously from Merck.

Renault and Volvo	Automobile manufacturing is highly complex. Steady changes in models and in consumer demand.	Complex joint venture structure linked both firms tightly before the merger proposal. Disparities in performance imposed stresses on the partnership.	Industry overcapacity. Consolidation among competitors. Sharply rising costs of new product development.	Hubris. Overoptimism. Sunk cost mentality. Escalation of commitments. Path dependency.	Complex transaction design. Poor communication strategy.	Sharp cultural differences. Integration team was already in distress from the JV attempt.
Hewlett-Packard and Compaq	Complex range of products and market segments. Rapidly-changing technology.	Simple deal. Fixed exchange ratio linked the financial performance of the two firms.	Economic recession. Aggressive entry by Dell. Rapid changes in technology.	Possible overoptimism.	Decision to pursue new strategy as "solutions provider" to corporations.	Strong internal coordination and effective communication by HP management team.
Quaker and Snapple	Logistical issues and distribution rendered the merger integration a complex problem.	Distributors and contract manufacturers were linked tightly to Quaker through the value chain.	Change in consumer demand toward "healthy" drinks and snacks. Entry by Coke and Pepsi into the health segment.	Recency bias: Quaker succeeded with Gatorade and can do it again with Snapple. Overoptimism.	Decision to switch independent distributors from supermarkets to convenience stores. Decision to move from contract bottling to in-house plants.	Sharp cultural differences between Snapple and Quaker. Breakdowns in due diligence and integration.
Smucker and Jif/Crisco	Moderately complex distribution and marketing.	Coordinated branding, marketing, and distribution.	Change toward healthy foods and eating on-the-go.	Rational strategic thinking over extended time period.	Decision to focus the product line.	Strong management team at Smucker.
Mattel and Learning Company	Education and entertainment software is a complex business.	High price reduced flexibility in achieving reasonable rate of return.	Declining demand for traditional products, such as Barbie. Rising computer use by children. Rapid technological change in software and in consumer demand.	Momentum logic: Use the acquisition to mask earnings decline in the core business. Opportunism.	Decision to opportunistically acquire outside of field of expertise.	Failure of due diligence. Lack of candor between target company management and Mattel. Slow action-taking on Barad's part.

(Continued)

355

APPENDIX 15.1 (Continued)

Case	Complexity: Makes it difficult to understand what's going on.	Tight Coupling: Absence of flexibility causes the crisis to radiate through the organization.	Business Not as Usual: Trouble in one or more parts of the firm.	Cognitive Biases: Mental "filtering" causes decision-makers to discount risks and the crisis.	Management Choices: Decisions that increase the risk of the firm or deal.	Implementation by the Team: Flaws in team processes or make-up hamper response to the crisis.
IBM and Lotus	Business application software is complex, rapidly changing.	High price reduced flexibility in achieving reasonable rate of return.	Rising demand for groupware. Rapid consolidation and technological change.	Strategic thinking. Rational.	Decision to position IBM as a solutions provider.	Retention of key developers.
AOL and Time Warner	Both were large firms, multidivisional and with a complicated range of technologies.	Fixed exchange ratio without a collar imposed tight linkage between operating results of the two firms.	Rapid rise, and then fall of Internet-based commerce. "Hot" equity market conditions. Regulatory uncertainty and delay. Onset of recession.	Overconfidence. Momentum thinking. Recency bias.	AOL's decision to acquire outside of the Internet space; Time Warner's decision to enter it. Choice of partner.	Sharp cultural differences between AOL and Time Warner side. "Fiefdoms" within TW limited the coordinated integration of AOL and TW.
Yahoo! and Geocities.com, Broadcast.com	Complexity of the emerging Internet economy made it difficult to assess values and market positions.	High prices reduced flexibility in achieving reasonable rate of return.	Rapid rise, and then fall of Internet-based commerce. "Hot" equity market conditions. Regulatory uncertainty and delay.	Overconfidence.	Decision to acquire within the Internet space.	Cultural similarities between buyer and targets. CEO changed, but new CEO brought business discipline to the enterprise.

Dynegy and Enron	Extremely complicated trading, instruments, and financial reporting made it difficult to understand the risks and potential returns from an investment in Enron.	Fixed exchange ratio and capital needed to stabilize Enron limited the financial flexibility for both firms.	"Run on the bank" in equity and credit markets. Crisis of confidence in Enron specifically and in the energy trading industry generally. Investigations.	Hubris (Enron). Loss aversion (Dynegy).	Lack of candor and delay in dealing with investors.	Changing management team within Enron during period of negotiation. High stress.
AMC and General Cinema	Complicated portfolios of theaters and financing.	At best moderate financial flexibility afforded by affiliation with Apollo.	Overcapacity in industry; wave of consolidation. General Cinema in bankruptcy.	Rational strategy of consolidation, closure of underperforming sites.	Choice of roll-up strategy.	Close coordination between operating team and financial backers.
Tyco	Very complicated conglomerate structure made it difficult to understand the foundations for value and sources of cash flow.	Enormous goodwill account overshadowed the rest of Tyco's balance sheet, giving the firm little room for negative reported financial results.	Long economic boom and aggressive program of acquisition, followed by recession, equity market decline, and SEC investigation into accounting eroded investor confidence.	Hubris. Momentum logic. Opportunism.	Decision to pursue a momentum growth strategy.	Change in the management team six months later owing to alleged looting and conflicts of interest.
Berkshire Hathaway	Complicated conglomerate structure, with moderately transparent financial reporting to assist valuation analysis.	Little accumulated goodwill.	Moderate program of acquisition.	Humility. Value orientation.	Decision to pursue a value investing strategy.	Stable management team at top. Stable management teams in acquired firms.

APPENDIX 15.2 CEO's Words of Hubris and Atonement

	At the Announcement	Financial Loss	At the End
Pennsylvania and New York Central Railroads	"...it is my judgment, based on my forty-five years of experience in railroading, that the merged company will be far more susceptible to efficient management than either company alone was only a few years ago." (Alfred Perlman)[1] "...no two railroads in the country [are] in a better position than the Pennsylvania and the Central, by reason of their location, duplicate facilities and services, and similarity of traffic patterns, to consolidate their operations and at the same time substantially increase efficiency and provide an improvement in service at lower cost." (James Symes)[2] "A remarkable spirit of cooperation and enthusiasm is manifest throughout our new organization. We are confident that we have a talented, experienced and well-qualified management team for the years ahead, and we consider this a very important asset" (Stuart Saunders, 1968)[3]	–$1.8 billion to shareholders and –$7.0 billion in subsequent losses to the U.S. government.	"This is the largest merger ever undertaken in this country. And to think that you can do it overnight—we said it'd take eight years. And we would have accomplished in within five if we hadn't had the recession and inflation and tight money. We'd have done it. But nobody seems to appreciate the complexity of this thing. What a tremendous undertaking it was. And the personalities you had to deal with, the problems, the complexities. I don't care if you'd had Moses or whoever it might have been running the company, it couldn't have been done." (Stuart Saunders, 1970)[4]
Revco Drug Stores	"Management believes that, on an annual basis working capital from operations will be sufficient to fund both interest expense and the surviving corporation's expected level of capital expenditures on an ongoing basis. . . . Management believes that the Merger and the limitations of the Credit Agreement will not affect adversely its ability to continue its expansion and remodeling program." (December 18, 1986)[5]	Bankruptcy filing with claims in excess of $1.4 billion.	"Revco was in trouble from the day it went private. Sales and earning projections were strictly from dreamland." (Securities Analyst)[6]
Sony and Columbia	"You don't understand how to make movies. We do. You need to give us a whole lot of money and leave us alone. Trust us." (paraphrase of sentiments attributed to Peter Guber and Jon Peters, 1989)[7]	–$2.7 billion write-off in 1994.	"It is difficult to say that our management of the studio operations has been a total success over these past five years . . . As you are well aware, studio

	"The most important thing is to raise the image of Columbia. For a start, it would be nice to get a few big hits." (Norio Ohga, 1989)[8] "I think we are making headway . . . All of the negatives we've overcome, more or less" on the integration of hardware and software. (Michael Schulhof, 1993)[9]		management is not easy. Production costs continue to increase, and it is our responsibility to manage them effectively." (Nobuyuki Idei, 1995)[10] "I had 20 great years with Mr. Morita and Mr. Ohga. Any time there is a new management, it's important to give them the latitude and flexibility they need to pursue their own course and their own destiny." (Michael Schulhof, 1995)[11]
AT&T and NCR	"I am absolutely confident that together AT&T and NCR will achieve a level of growth and success that we could not achieve separately. Ours will be a future of promises fulfilled." (Robert Allen)[12]	−$3.0 billion.	"The complexity of trying to manage these different businesses began to overwhelm the advantages of integration. The world has changed. Markets have changed." (Robert Allen)[13]
Renault and Volvo	The risk that Volvo—and Sweden—run is that our country will not be competitive. Then there is no protection in a stand-alone alternative, whereas the new company with its strength and staying power may cushion any short-term harmful effects. Also, the French party is making the biggest ever foreign investment in Sweden—this in times of crisis. It demonstrates high confidence in Volvo and in our country. There is hardly any risk that one would erode the capital so invested by destroying the base. Mergers on this scale are delicate processes. We must maintain momentum and pace in the company while building a new and common organization. . . . If we mean anything by participating from our small national base, in building Europe, we have to realize that such work requires both giving and taking." (Pehr Gyllenhammar 1993)[14]	−$1.06 billion in market value of equity before cancellation of deal.	"The conclusion I think was that you can't have a successful merger if you don't have the people with you." (Soren Gyll, Volvo, 1993)[15] [They have] turned their backs on Europe and the world. . . . The alliance will not remain. It will be dismantled by a Renault management who, understandably, has lost its confidence in Volvo . . . Volvo is right now a wounded company." (Pehr Gyllenhammar, 1993)[16]

(Continued)

	At the Announcement	Financial Loss	At the End
Quaker and Snapple	"Snapple has tremendous growth potential through increased penetration, broader distribution and international expansion."[17]	–$1.5 billion	"After reviewing all possible options, we decided it was in the shareholders' interest to remove the financial burdens and risks Snapple brought to the portfolio and better focus on our value-driving businesses."[18]
Mattel and The Learning Company	"This isn't a bet on the Internet. It's a bet on technology and how we are going to communicate to customers." (Jill Barad, 1998)[19] "We are very satisfied with this acquisition and we will prove to you we can unleash the value of these brands." (Jill Barad, 1999)[20]	–$3.0 billion	"This was a very difficult decision to make from an emotional standpoint. It was a business decision to make. She knew it, we knew it." (Directors commenting on Jill Barad's resignation, 2000)[21]
AOL and Time Warner	"News is a form of storytelling, and I thought we should get even broader to become a truly creative company. And the growth level in the entertainment industry was also important for a publishing company that did not have that. . . . I had thought for a long time that we needed what I always referred to as a 'transforming transaction,' because I didn't think we could build ourselves into this new world." (Jerry Levin)[22] "By combining the leading interactive services and media companies, AOL Time Warner will create the potential for stronger operating and financial results than either company could achieve on its own." (Merger Proxy Statement, 2000)[23]	–$200 billion in market value of equity in the year following the announcement. –$54 billion charged to earnings in 2002 to reflect impairment of goodwill.	"When the economy comes back and everyone figures out how to work together, they will reconsider me. I believed in the Internet and I believe in it now. Of course, I did trust the integrity of Case, Pittman, and Kelly. I don't believe they engaged in deception." (Jerry Levin, 2003)[24]
Dynegy and Enron	"We are confident this is good strategically and financially for Dynegy and Enron." (Chuck Watson, 2001)[25] "The merger also validates Enron's core franchise and underscores Dynegy's ongoing strategy to pursue transactions that accelerate our growth, while enabling our shareholders, partners, and customers to realize immediate and long-term benefits." (Chuck Watson, 2001)[26]	–$70 billion in Enron's market value of equity associated with its general collapse.	"We lost confidence that the deal would be consummated in a way that would keep the rating intact. Enron's credibility and viability continued to diminish." (Ron Barone of Standard & Poor's, 2001)[27] "Dynegy's CEO says he was surprised by Enron's disclosures in its earnings report, which he received just hours before it was released."[28]

| Tyco International | "In the past five years, Tyco shares have appreciated four times faster than the S&P500 . . . we will keep executing the same strategy that has brought us this far . . . I promise that we will stay focused on the business goals that matter most: seizing opportunities, generating new revenue sources, growing earnings and cash flow, and increasing shareholder value. The future looks bright." (Dennis Kozlowski, 1999)[29]

"Hopefully we can become the next GE." (Dennis Kozlowski, 2001)[30] | –$9 billion in operating losses and writeoffs of impaired goodwill, 2003. | "TYCO former executives L. Dennis Kozlowski, Mark H. Swartz and Mark A. Belnick sued for fraud. All three charged with failure to disclose millions of dollars of low interest and interest-free loans they received from the company during their employment at Tyco. Kozlowski and Swartz alleged to have forgiven without proper authorization, tens of millions of dollars of their own loans and entered into other secret transactions with the company." (U.S. Securities and Exchange Commission, 2002)[31]

"These charges are exactly that—they are accusations, and they are unproven. When they are aired in their entirety, they will prove to be unfounded." (Kozlowski's attorney, 2002)[32] |

Notes

1. Testimony of Alfred Perlman, CEO of the Central, before the Interstate Commerce Commission, as quoted in Daughen and Binzen (1971), 63.
2. Testimony of James Symes, CEO of the Pennsylvania, before the Interstate Commerce Commission, as quoted in Daughen and Binzen (1971), 52.
3. Letter to shareholders in 1967 Annual Report, dated March 15, 1968, quoted in Daughen and Binzen (1971), 223.
4. Testimony of Stuart Saunders, Chairman and CEO of Penn Central, July 29, 1970, before Senate Commerce Committee, as quoted in Daughen and Binzen (1971), 318.
5. Prospectus, Anac Merger Corporation, Salomon Brothers Inc., December 18, 1986, 30 and 31.
6. Quotation of a securities analyst in S. Phillips, "Revco's LBO Ends with A Whimper," *Business Week*, August 15, 1988, 46.
7. Paraphrase attributed to Guber and Peters, "Hollywood's Hell-Raising Duo," *Fortune*, July 22, 1996.
8. Quotation of Norio Ohga in David E. Sanger, "Sony has high hopes for Columbia Pictures," *New York Times*, September 28, 1989, D1.
9. Quotation of Michael Schulhof in Johnnie L. Roberts, "Global Entertainment (A special report): Hollywood—Missing Links: Synergy Benefits have so far Eluded the Entertainment Giants," *Wall Street Journal*, March 26, 1993, R9.
10. Quotation of Nobuyuki Idei in Steve McClellan, "Sony Wants to be in Pictures, says New President," *Broadcasting & Cable* November 27, 1995, 58.

(Continued)

APPENDIX 15.2 (Continued)

Notes

11. Quotation of Michael Schulhof in Laura Landro and Jeffrey Trachtenberg, "Ouster of Schulhof Leaves Focus Fuzzy at Sony Entertainment," *Wall Street Journal*, December 6, 1995, A1.

12. Nikhil Deogun and Steven Lipin, "Deals & Deal Makers: Cautionary Tales: When Big Deals Turn Bad—Some Hot Mergers Can Come Undone for Many Reasons," *Wall Street Journal*, December 8, 1999, C1.

13. Ibid.

14. AB Volvo, "Information Prior to Extraordinary General Meeting of Shareholders in AB Volvo, November 9, 1993," 36–37.

15. Hugh Carnegy, "Volvo Collapse of the Merger with Renault: Soren Gyll Denies That He Betrayed Pehr Gyllenhammar," *Financial Times*, December 6, 1993, 17.

16. Hugh Carnegy and Christopher Brown–Humes, "Volvo Abandons Renault Merger," *Financial Times*, December 3, 1993, 1.

17. Nikhil Deogun and Steven Lipin, "Deals & Deal Makers: Cautionary Tales: When Big Deals Turn Bad—Some Hot Mergers Can Come Undone for Many Reasons," *Wall Street Journal*, December 8, 1999, C1.

18. Ibid.

19. Quotation of Jill Barad at announcement of Learning Company acquisition in Stacy Kravetz and Jon Auerbach, "Toys: Mattel reveals profit shortfall, software deal," *Wall Street Journal*, December 15, 1998, B1.

20. Quotation of Jill Barad in Lisa Bannon, "Learning Co. is on track, says Mattel," *Wall Street Journal*, October 22, 1999, A3.

21. Lisa Bannon and Joann S. Lublin, "Jill Barad Abruptly Quits the top job at Mattel," *Wall Street Journal*, February 4, 2000, B1.

22. Quotations of Jerry Levin originally attributed to 1987 memo, and Connie Bruck, *Master of the Game*, and quoted in Kara Swisher, *There Must Be A Pony In Here Somewhere*, 2003, 71.

23. Amendment No. 4 to Form S–4 Registration Statement, AOL Time Warner, May 19, 2000, ii.

24. Quotation of Jerry Levin in 2003 in Kara Swisher, *There Must Be A Pony In Here Somewhere*, 2003, 202.

25. Quotation of Chuck Watson in John Emschwiller, "Dynegy and Enron Shares Get a Boost as Acquisition Plan is Met with Optimism," *Wall Street Journal*, November 13, 2001, A4.

26. Quotation of Chuck Watson in "Dynegy to buy Enron for $9.5B," *CNNMoney*, November 9, 2001.

27. Quotation of Ron Barone in Gregory Zuckerman and Jathon Sapsford, "Why Credit agencies didn't switch off Enron—S&P cries 'junk' but the warning comes too late," *Wall Street Journal*, November 29, 2001, C1.

28. Alexei Barrionuevo and Elliott Spagat, "Fall of a power giant: energy firms tally costs of Enron's woes," *Wall Street Journal*, November 30 2001, A8.

29. L. Dennis Kozlowski, Letter to Shareholders, 1999 Annual Report of Tyco International, December 13, 1999, 23.

30. Quotation of Kozlowski in William Symonds, "The Most Aggressive CEO," *BusinessWeek*, May 28, 2001, 74.

31. Litigation Release No. 17722, September 12, 2002, U.S. Securities and Exchange Commission, 1.

32. Quotation of Kozlowski's attorney in Mark Maremont and Jerry Markon, "Reading the News—Former Tyco Executives are Charged," *Wall Street Journal*, September 13, 2002, A3.

16

Memo to the CEO:
A Coda on Growth

D ear CEO:
  The research and cases give some direction about what you and your organization should do to avoid failure in M&A. To these I would add one last message. It concerns one of the underpinnings of M&A activity of which you are the chief architect, your choice of the annual growth goals of the firm.

Growth targets drive M&A activity. Two sources fulfill a growth target for the earnings of the firm: organic growth (such as inflation, real expansion of the economy, market share gains, and productivity gains) and inorganic growth (M&A, joint ventures, etc.). At most mature firms, organic growth is a relatively modest number and not something you can increase very easily. This means that M&A has to fill the gap between the target you have set and the modest organic growth rate your core business can realize. The result is that your business development staff is given a shopping mandate each year to produce so many more cents in earnings per share.

This is a dubious approach to M&A. It focuses the attention of your organization on earnings cosmetics rather than on creating value. Reported earnings per share is a backward-looking, one-period measure when so much of what your firm does in the current year has impact years into the future. It ignores the deployment of capital necessary to produce an EPS increase. It ignores a host of assets that matter to investors (such as brand names, patents, and creative capital) and invites gaming behavior such as the aggressive management of earnings through accounting choices. But worst of all, it implies that it is okay to do deals that generate gains in EPS even if those deals destroy economic value (as indicated by a negative net present value of cash flows).

Vastly better is to make acquisitions that are focused on the creation of intrinsic economic value rather than as means to filling some arbitrary EPS growth goal. Done this way, each deal would be evaluated as an independent investment against rigorous benchmarks of value creation. It is conceivable that your business development staff would come to you with a deal that creates true economic value for your shareholders, but dilutes EPS this year. You should openly solicit such recommendations.

CULTURE OF GROWTH MOMENTUM

The reason many CEOs resist this is because they buy into the culture of growth momentum that pervades the global business community. Momentum thinking drives strategies that seek to maintain hot streaks, such as investments that focus on buying past winners and selling past losers. It can be exciting, to be sure: One follows the pro with the hot hand.

Securities analysts pump up the excitement by amplifying the significance of small deviations of quarterly earnings from expectation. Boards of directors peg executive compensation to momentum in earnings and share price. CEOs stretch organizations to produce growth, often with serial acquisitions or bet-the-ranch investments. Accountants and chief financial officers may risk their careers to "manage" the earnings toward acceptable gains. All this feels so natural.

Unfortunately, foreseeing changes in a hot streak is impossible. It produces reactive behavior and ignores the fact that he who lives on rising momentum dies on its descent. Given the grinding nature of capitalism—Joseph Schumpeter's process of creative destruction—high growth rates prove extremely hard to maintain over time.

AOL's stock price, for example, grew at 285 percent compounded annually from January 1998 to January 2000, when Steve Case announced the deal with Time Warner. The world economy during the same period grew at perhaps 7 percent annually. Each growing at those different rates, AOL would have owned the world economy in about five years, an astonishing result were it attainable: But business history teaches that enterprises mature as they grow large, that growth slows, and that strong economic and political forces militate against such domination.

Yet, momentum can be a powerful narcotic to decision makers: The habit is hard to kick and, because of the exponential shape of its early growth curve, produces an increased craving that ultimately leads to the downfall of the firm.

Interviews of senior managers at Enron, conducted by Samuel Bodily and me in 2000 and 2001, reveal a firm that created true economic growth in the early 1990s. But as the company's growth slowed because of rising competition, losses on big investments, and the difficulty of opening new markets for its trading model, Enron—struggling to maintain its high rate of growth—embraced the excesses for which it is now damned.

Tyco hit the wall when the stock market slumped and it no longer had high price-to-earnings ratios with which to continue its strategy of rapid growth by acquisition. WorldCom shifted expenses into capital expenditures in an effort to maintain its earnings growth rate. Business history offers numerous other examples of momentum thinking: Insull Utilities in the 1920s, Ling-Temco-Vought and Automatic Sprinkler in the 1960s, and Boston Chicken and US Office Products in the 1990s.

What the tragedies of Enron, Tyco, WorldCom, and the others share is that, like Peter Pan, these companies refused to grow up. They refused to admit frankly to shareholders and to themselves that their rates of EPS growth were unsustainable.

THE KIND OF GROWTH THAT MATTERS

All of these business failures teach a fundamental economic truth: The growth that matters most is growth in economic value, not in earnings, assets, or revenue. The momentum manager seeks growth for its own sake. The value manager knows that not all growth is good (i.e., some growth may be too risky or unprofitable). The momentum manager seeks to sustain growth. The value manager seeks to sustain economic profitability.

The momentum manager seeks to present a smooth, seamless record of advance. The value manager embraces the quirkiness of business: Opportunities and threats are surprising, large economic profits are usually only temporary and localized in market space. The momentum manager trusts illusion; the value manager trusts reality.

MANAGING IN A HIGGLEDY-PIGGLEDY WORLD

Abandoning the narcotic lure of momentum thinking may call for a deeper transformation of companies and their leaders than is comfortable to most. Managing for economic value requires a shift in thinking among CEOs, corporate directors, CFOs, accountants, media pundits, securities analysts, and investors. What would a business world without growth momentum look like?

Firms could let go the employees and consultants whose job was to smooth earnings—along with the expensive cosmetic hedges they concocted. Business development would shift from filling an earnings gap to searching for value-creating deals. Corporate earnings growth would be higgledy-piggledy, rather than smooth. But such volatility would at last begin to mirror the kind of volatility in *cash flow* that the sharpest analysts have observed for years. Companies would have to rise to new heights of candor with their owners. Such candor might include ditching the quarterly pantomime of EPS "guidance" in favor of more penetrating discussion of cash flow fundamentals.

Benchmarks to alert investors to outsized performance (good or bad) would be rooted in fundamental questions about operations and customers. Analysts would have to focus on such metrics as economic profit, discounted cash flow, or expected internal rate of return compared with cost of capital. The content of their work would shift intensively toward analysis and away from financial journalism.

It is possible that the plaintiff's bar and media pundits would have a field day in a world of higgledy-piggledy growth—at least until judges, juries, and the public accepted it as normal. But CEOs already dance through the slings and arrows of these folks and should be well-trained for the new growth world. More importantly, the opposition will get past it.

Investors, too, would need to change. Central to this would be to accept greater volatility in reported results. There is good evidence that investors have already done so. The fall of Bretton Woods, the advent of inflation-fighting at central banks and floating currencies, trade liberalization, rapid technological change, the advent of managed health care, and the wave of deregulation have inserted volatility into the lives of Everyman and Everywoman. And they have shown a remarkable resilience to deal with it. Indeed, they are probably making more intelligent choices in a world of volatility than in a world where some higher authority aims to shield them from it. And it rightly shifts the focus of public policy debates toward insuring against the ravages of extreme volatility: catastrophic illness, pension-fund wipeouts, industry-wide bankruptcy (as seen among airlines), and the like. In this context, the managed momentum of corporate growth is a vestige of the old Bretton Woods era.

There is no obvious reason why smart, ethical, well-trained, well-informed, and highly motivated CEOs and directors should cling to a mentality of momentum growth with its baggage of adverse effects. We can envision the business world under the alternative growth perspective: It doesn't look so bad.

WAKE UP AND SMELL THE SULFUR

Ideas have consequences. At the core of merger failures are mistaken ideas about the growth that markets truly value. More laws and regulations about accountants, transparency, governance, and compensation may help at the margin, but until CEOs, analysts, and investors reject momentum thinking, one can predict with confidence the periodic recurrence of the merger failures we belatedly condemn.

Wake up and smell the sulfur. The way you analyze and communicate growth goals could be incubating the next deal from hell. Critically challenge the growth mentality that underpins your firm's M&A program. The growth that matters is growth in economic value. The rest is smoke.

References

AB Volvo. 1990. Information on the alliance between Volvo and Renault.

AB Volvo. 1993a. Merger of Volvo's automotive operations with Renault: Information prior to extraordinary general meeting of shareholders in AB Volvo, November 9.

AB Volvo. 1993b. Merger of Volvo's automotive operations with Renault: Supplementary information to the shareholders.

Abarbanell, J., B. Bushee, and J. Raedy. 1998. The effects of institutional investor preferences on ownership changes and stock prices around corporate spin-offs. Unpublished working paper.

Abernathy, W.J., and K. Wayne. 1974. The limits of the learning curve. *Harvard Business Review* 52 (No. 5, September–October): 109–119.

Abrahams, J. 1999. *The Mission Statement Book: 301 Corporate Mission Statements from America's Top Companies*, 2d ed., Berkeley, CA: 10-Speed Press.

Adolph, G., I. Buchanan, J. Hornery, B. Jackson, J. Jones, T. Kihlstedt, G. Neilson, and H. Quarls. 2001. Merger integration: Delivering on the promise. Company report. New York: Booz-Allen & Hamilton.

Aggarwal, R., and A. Samwick. 2003. Why do managers diversify their firms? Agency reconsidered. *Journal of Finance* 58, 71–118.

Agrawal, A., J. Jaffe, and G. Mandelker. 1992. The post-merger performance of acquiring firms: A re-examination of an anomaly. *Journal of Finance* 47 (No. 4, September): 1605–1621.

Agrawal, Anup, and Gershon N. Mandelker. 1987. Managerial incentives and corporate investment and financing decisions. *Journal of Finance* 42 (No. 4, September): 823–837.

Ahn, S., and D. Denis. 2001. Internal capital markets and investment policy: Evidence from corporate spin-offs. Working paper, downloadable from http://papers.ssrn.com/abstract=291-527.

Alchian, A. 1969. Corporate management and property rights. In Henry Manne, ed., *Economic Policy and the Regulation of Corporate Securities*, Washington, DC: American Enterprise Institute.

Alexander, G.J., P.G. Benson, and J.K. Kampmeyer. 1984. Investigating the valuation effects of announcements of voluntary corporate selloffs. *Journal of Finance* 39, 503–517.

Alexandrou, G., and S. Sudarsanam. 2001. Shareholder wealth experience of buyers in corporate divestitures: Impact of business strategy, growth opportunities and bargaining power. Cranfield University working paper. Available by e-mail from p.s.sudarsanam@cranfield.ac.uk.

Allan, Philip, and M. Wright. 1984. Auditing the efficiency of the nationalized industries: Exit the comptroller and auditor general. *Public Administration* 62(1), 95–101.

Allen, J. 1998. Capital markets and corporate structure: The equity carve-outs of Thermo Electron. *Journal of Financial Economics* 48, 99–124.

Allen, J., S. Lummer, J. McConnell, and D. Reed. 1995. Can takeover losses explain spin-off gains? *Journal of Financial and Quantitative Analysis* 30(4), 465–477.

Allen, J., and J. McConnell. 1998. Equity carve-outs and managerial discretion. *Journal of Finance* 53(1), 163–186.

Allen, J., and G. Phillips. 2000. Corporate equity ownership, strategic alliances, and product market relationships. *Journal of Finance* 55(6), 2791–2816.

Amihud, Y., J. Kamin, and J. Ronen. 1979. Revenue vs. profit maximization: Differences in behavior by the type-of-control and by market power. *Southern Economic Journal* 45, 838–846.

Amihud, Y., and B. Lev. 1981. Risk reduction as a managerial motive for conglomerate mergers. *Rand Journal of Economics* 12, 605–618.

Anac Merger Corporation. 1986. *Prospectus* (December 18).

Anderson, A. 2002. Selecting the key to unlock hidden value. University of Arizona working paper. Copy may be obtained by e-mail from anea@mailbpa.arizona.edu.

Andrade, G., and S. Kaplan. 1998. How costly is financial (non-economic) distress? Evidence from highly leveraged transactions that became distressed. *Journal of Finance* 53 (No. 5, October): 1443–1493.

Andrews, W. and M. Dowling. 1998. Explaining performance changes in newly privatized firms. *Journal of Management Studies* 35(5), 601–618.

Ang, J., and Y. Cheng. 2003. Direct evidence on the market-driven acquisitions theory. Florida State University working paper (March). Available by e-mail from jang@garnet.acns.fsu.edu or by download from http://papers.ssrn.com/sol3/papers.cfm?abstract_id=391569.

Angel, Karen. 2002. *Inside Yahoo!. Reinvention and the Road Ahead.* New York: John Wiley & Sons.

Anslinger, P.L., and T.E. Copeland. 1996. Growth through acquisitions: A fresh look. *Harvard Business Review* (January–February): 126–135, reprint 96101.

Asquith, P. 1983. Merger bids, uncertainty, and stockholder returns. *Journal of Financial Economics* 11 (No. 1, April): 51–83.

Asquith, P., R. Bruner, and D. Mullins, Jr. 1983. The gains to bidding firms from merger. *Journal of Financial Economics* 11 (No. 1, April): 121–139.

Asquith, P., R. Bruner, and D. Mullins, Jr. 1987. Merger returns and the form of financing. *Proceedings of the Seminar on the Analysis of Security Prices* 34 (No. 1, May): 115–146.

Bagwell, S., and J. Zechner. 1993. Influence costs and capital structure. *Journal of Finance* 48, 975–1008.

Bahree, B. 1999. Oil mergers often don't live up to the hype. *Wall Street Journal,* July 23, A10.

Baker, G.P., and G.D. Smith. 1998. *The New Financial Capitalists.* Cambridge: Cambridge University Press.

Baker, G.P., and K.H. Wruck. 1989. Organizational changes and value creation in leveraged buyouts: The case of the O.M. Scott & Sons Company. *Journal of Financial Economics* 25 (December): 163–190.

Bannon, Lisa. 1999. Learning Co. is on track, says Mattel. *Wall Street Journal,* October 22, A3.

Bannon, Lisa. 1999. Mattel's new profit shortfall punishes stock and raises questions about CEO. *Wall Street Journal,* October 5, A3.

Bannon, Lisa, John Heckinger, and Nikhil Deogun. 1999. Mattel still doesn't grasp snafu at Learning Company. *Wall Street Journal,* October 8, A3.

Barabba, V., and G. Zaltman. 1991. *Hearing the Voice of the Market.* New York: McGraw-Hill.

Barclays de Zoete Wedd Securities. 1993. Volvo company report, September 3. Electronically retrieved through Investext, Thomson Financial Networks.

Barney, J. 1995. Looking inside for competitive advantage. *The Academy of Management Executive* 9(4), 49–61.

Barron, Kelly. 1999. What was she thinking? In the battle for market share, software players like Mattel's Learning Co. have forgotten about profit. *Forbes*, November 1, 54.

Bathel, J., J. Porter, and T. Opler. 1998. Block share purchases and corporate performance. *Journal of Finance* 53(2), 605–634.

Beatty, A. 1994. An empirical analysis of the corporate control, tax and incentive motivations for adopting leveraged employee stock ownership plans. *Managerial and Decision Economics* 15, 299–315.

Beatty, A. 1995. The cash flow and informational effects of employee stock plans. *Journal of Financial Economics* 38, 211–240.

Bebchuk, L., and A. Guzman. 1999. An economic analysis of transnational bankruptcies. *Journal of Law and Economics* 17, 775–808.

Becketti, S. 1986. Corporate mergers and the business cycle. *Federal Reserve Bank of St. Louis Economic Review*, 13–26.

Beitel, P., D. Schiereck, and M. Wahrenburg. 2002. Explaining the M&A-success in European bank mergers and acquisitions. Working paper, University of Witten/Herdecke, Germany (January).

Berenson, A. 2002. Tyco shares fall as investors show concern on accounting. *New York Times*, January 16. Download from: http://query.ny times.com/search.restricted/article?res=F50D14FC385C0C758DDD A80894DA404.

Berger, P.G., and E. Ofek. 1995. Diversification's effect on firm value. *Journal of Financial Economics* 37 (No. 1, January): 39–65.

Berger, P.G., and E. Ofek. 1999. Causes and effects of corporate refocusing programs. *Review of Financial Studies*, Summer 12(2), 311–345.

Berkovitch, E., and M.P. Narayanan. 1993. Motives for takeovers: An empirical investigation. *Journal of Financial and Quantitative Analysis* 28 (No. 3, September): 347–362.

Berman, P. 1999. Tom Lee is on a roll. *Forbes*, November 17, 127–131.

Best, R.W., R.J. Best, and A.M. Agapos. 1998. Earnings forecasts and the information contained in spin-off announcements. *The Financial Review* 33, 53–67.

Bhattacharyya, S., and R. Singh. 1999. The resolution of bankruptcy by auction: Allocating the residual right of design. *Journal of Financial Economics* 54(3), 269–294.

Billett, M., T. King, and D. Mauer. 2003. Bondholder wealth effects in mergers and acquisitions: New evidence from the 1980s and 1990s. Working paper. Forthcoming. *Journal of Finance*.

Billett, M., and D. Mauer. 1998. Diversification and the value of internal capital markets: The case of tracking stock. Unpublished working paper.

Billett, M., and D. Mauer. 2000. Diversification and the value of internal capital markets: The case of tracking stock. *Journal of Banking and Finance* 24, 1457–1490.

Billett, M., and A. Vijh. 2002. The wealth effects of tracking stock restructurings. University of Iowa working paper downloadable from http://www.biz.uiowa.edu/faculty/mbillett/billett.html.

Billings, et alia. 1980. *A Study of Near Midair Collisions in U.S. Terminal Airspace*, NASA–TM81225, August.

Blackwell, D.W., M.W. Marr, and M.F. Spivey. 1990. Plant-closing decisions and the market value of the firm. *Journal of Financial Economics* 26, 277–288.

Bleeke, Joel, and David Ernst. 1995. Is your strategic alliance really a sale? *Harvard Business Review* 73, 97–106.

Bohmer, Richard M.J., Amy C. Edmondson, Michael A. Roberto, Laura R. Feldman, and Erika M. Ferlins. 2004. *Columbia*'s final mission. Harvard Business School case study 9-304–090.

Boone, A.L., and J.H. Mulherin. 2001. Valuing the process of corporate restructuring. Penn State University working paper (January). Available by e-mail from aboone@psu.edu.

Boone, A.L., and J.H. Mulherin. 2002. Corporate restructuring and corporate auctions. Working paper, College of William and Mary (November). Available from the first author at audra.boone@business.wm.edu.

Bradley, M. 1980. Interfirm tender offers and the market for corporate control. *Journal of Business* 53 (No. 4, October): 345–376.

Bradley, M., A. Desai, and E.H. Kim. 1982. Specialized resources and competition in the market for corporate control. Working paper, Ann Arbor, MI: University of Michigan.

Bradley, M., A. Desai, and E.H. Kim. 1983. The rationale behind interfirm tender offers: Information or synergy? *Journal of Financial Economics* 11 (Nos. 1–4, April): 183–206.

Bradley, M., A. Desai, and E.H. Kim. 1988. Synergistic gains from corporate acquisitions and their division between the stockholders of target and acquiring firms. *Journal of Financial Economics* 21 (No. 1, May): 3–40.

Brealey, R., and S. Myers. 1996. *Principles of Corporate Finance*, 5th ed. New York: McGraw-Hill.

Bruner, R. 1988. The use of excess cash and debt capacity as a motive for merger. *Journal of Financial and Quantitative Analysis* 23 (No. 2, June): 199–217.

Bruner, R. 1995. *Warren Buffett.* 1995. Charlottesville, VA: Darden Business Publishing (UVA-F-1160).

Bruner, R. F. 1999. An analysis of value destruction and recovery in the alliance and proposed merger of Volvo and Renault. *Journal of Financial Economics* 51, 125–166.

Bruner, R.F. 2004. *Applied Mergers and Acquisitions.* Hoboken, NJ: John Wiley & Sons.

Bruner, R., and E. Brownlee. 1990. Leveraged ESOPs, wealth transfers, and "shareholder neutrality": The case of Polaroid. *Financial Management* 19(1), 59–74.

Bruner, R., M. Davoli, G. Geneletti, M. Ghiotto, and D. Rezende. 1992. Glaxo Italia S.p.A.: The Zinnat marketing decision. Charlottesville, VA: Darden Case Collection, catalogue number UVA-F-1014, available by e-mail from dardencases@virginia.edu.

Bruner, R., and K.M. Eades. 1992. The crash of the Revco LBO: The hypothesis of inadequate capital. *Financial Management* 21 (No. 1, Spring): 35–49.

Bruner, R., R. Glauber, and D. Mullins. 1979. UV Industries Inc. Boston: Harvard Business School.

Bruner, Robert F., and Miguel Palacios. 2004. Valuing control and marketability, Batten Institute working paper (May 28). Available from http://ssrn.com/abstract=553562.

Bruner, Robert F., and Robert E. Spekman. 1998. The dark side of strategic alliances: Lessons from Volvo–Renault." *European Management Journal,* April.

Buchel, B. 2000. Framework of joint venture development: Theory-building through qualitative research. *Journal of Management Studies* 37(5), 637–661.

Bulkeley, William. 1995. Lotus's star developer says he would work for a friendly IBM. *Wall Street Journal,* June 8, B5.

Bull, I. 1989. Management performance in leveraged buyouts: An empirical analysis. In Y. Amihud, ed., *Leveraged Management Buyouts* (Chapter 3), Homewood, IL: Dow Jones-Irwin.

Burgelman, R., and A. Grove. 1996. Strategic dissonance. *California Management Review* 38(2), 8–28.

Burns, Greg. 1994. Tea and Synergy? Gulping Snapple could really aid Quaker, but not right away. *Business Week*, November 14, 44.

Burns, Greg. 1996. Crunch time at Quaker Oats: Is there time for Smithburg to solve the Snapple mess? *Business Week*, September 23, 70.

Burns, Greg. 1997 What price the Snapple debacle? *Business Week*, April 14, 42.

Burrough, Bryan, and John Helyar. 1990. *Barbarians at the Gate: The Fall of RJR Nabisco*. New York: HarperCollins.

Burzawa, S. 2000. ESOPs in transition: Two companies discuss issues their ESOPs faced over time. *Employee Benefit Plan Review* 55(1), 46–49.

Butz, D. 1994. How do large minority shareholders wield control? *Managerial and Decision Economics* 15(4), 291–299.

Byrd, J., and K. Hickman. 1992. Do outside directors monitor nanagers? Evidence from tender offer bids. *Journal of Financial Economics* 32 (No. 2, October): 195–214.

Callahan, J., and S. MacKenzie. 1999. Metrics for strategic alliance control. *R&D Management* 29(4), 365–377.

Campa, J., and S. Kedia. 2002. Explaining the diversification discount. *Journal of Finance* 57, 1731–1762.

Capen, E.C., R.V. Clapp, and W.M. Campbell. 1971. Competitive bidding in high-risk situations. *Journal of Petroleum Technology*, June, 641–653.

Carhart, M. 1997. On persistence in mutual fund performance. *Journal of Finance* 52, 57–82.

Carline, N., S. Linn, and P. Yadav. 2002. The impact of firm-specific and deal-specific factors on the real gains in corporate mergers and acquisitions: An empirical analysis. University of Oklahoma working paper (February).

Carnegie International. 1993. Volvo—company report, September 9. Electronically retrieved through Investext, Thomson Financial Networks.

Carnegy, Hugh. 1993. Hostile chorus to Volvo deal reaches crescendo. *Financial Times*, 19.

Carnegy, Hugh. 1993. Sinking in a sea of opposition. *Financial Times*, 30.

Carnegy, Hugh. 1994. Volvo finds key to merger failure. *Financial Times*, 21.

Carnegy, Hugh. 1994. Volvo pays the cost of a failed merger. *Financial Times*, 19.

Carnegy, Hugh, and John Ridding. 1993. Time-out called as strains start to show. *Financial Times*, 24.

Carow, K. 2001. Citicorp-Travelers Group merger: Challenging barriers between banking and insurance. *Journal of Banking and Finance* 25, 1553–1571.

Carr, C. 1999. Globalization, strategic alliances, acquisitions, and technology transfer: Lessons from ICL/Fujitsu and Rover/Honda and BMW. *R&D Management* 29(4), 405–421.

Caves, R. 1989. Mergers, takeovers, and economic efficiency. *International Journal of Industrial Organization* 7 (No. 1, March): 151–174.

Chan, S.H., J.W. Kensinger, A.J. Keown, and J.D. Martin. 1997. Do strategic alliances create value? *Journal of Financial Economics* 46, 199–221.

Chandler, Al D. 1977. *The Visible Hand.* Cambridge, MA: Belknap Press.

Chang, S. 1990. Employee stock ownership plans and shareholder wealth: An empirical investigation. *Financial Management* 19, 29–38.

Chaplinsky, S., and G. Niehaus. 1990. The tax and distributional effects of leveraged ESOPs. *Financial Management* 19, 29–38.

Chatterjee, R., and G. Meeks. The financial effects of takeover: Accounting rates of return and accounting regulation. *Journal of Business Finance & Accounting* 23 (No. 5/6, July 1996): 851–868.

Chatterjee, S., and M. Lubatkin. 1990. Corporate mergers, stockholder diversification, and changes in systematic risk. *Strategic Management Journal* (May/June): 255.

Chaudhuri, S., and B. Tabrizi. 1999. Capturing the real value in high-tech acquisitions. *Harvard Business Review* 5 (No. 5, September/October): 15–21.

Chemmanur, T., and I. Paeglis. 2001. Why issue tracking stock? Unpublished working paper available by e-mail from chemmanu@bc.edu.

Chen, H., M.Y. Hu, and J.C. Shieh. 1991. The wealth effect of international joint ventures: The case of U.S. investment in China. *Financial Management* 20, 31–41.

Chen, S., K. Ho, C. Lee, and G. Yeo. 2000. Investment opportunities, free cash flow and market reaction to international joint ventures. *Journal of Banking and Finance* 24(11), 1747–1765.

Chen, Z., and T. Ross. 2000. Strategic alliances, shared facilities, and entry deterrence. *RAND Journal of Economics* 31(2), 326–344.

Chew, D., ed. 1999. *The New Corporate Finance: Where Theory Meets Practice.* Burr Ridge, IL: Irwin McGraw-Hill.

Chiles, James R. 2001. *Inviting Disaster: Lessons from the Edge of Technology.* New York: HarperBusiness.

Chowdhury, I., and P. Chowdhury. 2001. A theory of joint venture life-cycles. *International Journal of Industrial Organization* 19, 319–343.

Christensen, Clayton M. 1997. *The Innovator's Dilemma*. Boston: Harvard Business School Press.

Churchill, N.C., and J W Mullins. 2001. How fast can your company afford to grow? *Harvard Business Review* (May), 135–143.

Coase, R. 1937. The nature of the firm. *Economica* 4, 386–405.

Comment, R., and G. Jarrell. 1995. Corporate focus and stock returns. *Journal of Financial Economics* 37 (No. 1, June): 67–87.

Conrad, Jennifer, and Gautam Kaul. 1998. An Anatomy of Trading Strategies. *Review of Financial Studies* 11, 489–519.

Cournot, Augustin. 1927. *Researches into the Mathematical Principles of the Theory of Wealth*. translation by N.T. Bacon. New York: Macmillan.

Coutu, Diane L. 2003. Sense and reliability: A conversation with celebrated psychologist Karl E. Weick. *Harvard Business Review*, April (reprint 3418): 1–8.

Crutchley, C.E., E. Guo, and R.S. Hansen. 1991. Stockholder benefits from Japanese–US joint ventures. *Financial Management* 20, 22–30.

Cusatis, P., J. Miles, and J. Woolridge. 1993. Restructuring through spin-offs: The stock market evidence. *Journal of Financial Economics* 33, 293–311.

Daley, L., V. Mehrotra, and R. Sivakuma. 1997. Corporate focus and value creation: Evidence from spin-offs. *Journal of Financial Economics* 45(2), 257–281.

Das, T., and B. Teng. 1999. Managing risks in strategic alliances. *The Academy of Management Executive* 13(4), 50–62.

Dasgupta, S., V. Goyal, and G. Tan. 2000. Active asset markets, divestitures, and divisional cross-subsidization. Hong Kong University of Science and Technology working paper available by e-mail from dasgupta@ust.hk.

Datta, D.K., G.E. Pinches, and V.K. Narayanan. 1992. Factors influencing wealth creation from mergers and acquisitions: A meta-analysis. *Strategic Management Journal* 13 (No. 1, January): 67–86.

Datta, D.K., and G. Puia. 1995. Cross-border acquisitions: An examination of the influence of relatedness and cultural fit on shareholder value creation in U.S. acquiring firms. *Management International Review* 35, 337.

Daughen, Joseph R., and Peter Binzen. 1971. *The Wreck of the Penn Central*. Boston: Little, Brown & Company.

Davidson, K. 1989. Evolution of a new industry. *Journal of Business Strategy* 10 (January/February): 54–56.

Davis, A., and M. Leblond. 2002. A spin-off analysis: Evidence from new and old economies. Queen's University working paper available by e-mail from adavis@business.queensu.ca.

DeAngelo, H., L. DeAngelo, and E. Rice. 1984. Going private: Minority freezeouts and stockholder wealth. *Journal of Law and Economics* (October): 367–402.

DeLong, G. 2001. Stockholder gains from focusing versus diversifying bank mergers. *Journal of Financial Economics* 59 (No. 2, February): 221–252.

DeLong, G. 2003. Does long-term performance of mergers match market expectations? Evidence from the U.S. banking industry. *Financial Management* (Summer): 5–25.

Deming, W. Edwards. 1982. *Out of the Crisis.* Cambridge: Massachusetts Institute of Technology, Center for Advanced Engineering Study.

Dempsey, S., G. Labor, and M. Rozeff. 1993. Dividend policies in practice: Is there an industry effect? *Quarterly Journal of Business and Economics* 32, 3–13.

Denis, D., D. Denis, and A. Sarin. 1997. Agency problems, equity ownership, and corporate diversification. *Journal of Finance* 52, 135–160.

Denis, D., D. Denis, and K. Yost. 2002. Global diversification, industrial diversification, and firm value. *Journal of Finance* 57, 1951–1979.

Dennis, D., and J. McConnell. 1986. Corporate mergers and security returns. *Journal of Financial Economics* 16 (No. 2, June): 143–187.

Deogun, N. 1999. Merger wave spurs more stock wipeouts. *Wall Street Journal* (November 29), C1.

Desai, H., and P. Jain. 1999. Firm performance and focus: Long-run stock market performance following spin-offs. *Journal of Financial Economics* 54(1), 75–101.

Desai, M., C.F. Foley, and J.R. Hines. 2002. International joint ventures and the boundaries of the firm. Harvard University NOM Research Paper no. 02–29 (July), downloaded from http://ssrn.com/abstract_id=324123.

Dhillon, U., and G. Ramirez. 1994. Employee stock ownership and corporate control: An empirical study. *Quarterly Journal of Business and Economics* 18, 9–26.

Dickerson, A., H. Gibson, and E. Tsakalotos. 1997. The impact of acquisitions on company performance: Evidence from a large panel of U.K. firms. *Oxford Economic Papers* 49 (No. 3, July): 344–361.

Dittmar, A., and A. Shivdasani. (undated). Divestitures and divisional investment policies. Working paper, Indiana University and University of North Carolina.

Dodd, P. 1980. Merger proposals, management discretion and stockholder wealth. *Journal of Financial Economics* 8 (No. 2, June): 105–138.

Dodd, P., and R. Ruback. 1977. Tender offers and stockholder returns: An empirical analysis. *Journal of Financial Economics* 5 (No. 3, December): 351–374.

Donaldson, G. 1978. New framework for corporate debt policy. *Harvard Business Review* (September–October): 149–164.

Donaldson, G. 1990. Voluntary restructuring. *Journal of Financial Economics* 27, 117–141.

Donaldson, Gordon. 1961. *Corporate Debt Capacity*. Harvard Business School Division of Research.

Dong, M., D. Hirschleifer, S. Richardson, and S. Teoh. 2003. Does investor misvaluation drive the takeover market? Working paper.

Dorner, Dietrich. 1996. *The Logic of Failure: Recognizing and Avoiding Error in Complex Situations*. Cambridge, MA: Perseus Books.

Doukas, J., M. Holmen, and N. Travlos. 2001. Corporate diversification and firm performance: Evidence from Swedish acquisitions. Working paper available by e-mail from jdoukas@odu.edu.

Doz, Y., and G. Hamel. 1998. *Alliance Advantage: The Art of Creating Value through Partnering*. Boston: Harvard Business School Press.

D'Souza, J., and J. Jacob. 2000. Why do firms issue targeted stock? *Journal of Financial Economics* 56, 459–483.

Eberhart, A., E. Altman, and R. Aggarwal. 1999. The equity performance of firms emerging from bankruptcy. *Journal of Finance* 54(5), 1855–1868.

Eckbo, B.E. 1983. Horizontal mergers, collusion, and stockholder wealth. *Journal of Financial Economics* 11 (No. 1–4, April): 241–274.

Eckbo, B.E. 1992. Mergers and the value of antitrust deterrence. *Journal of Finance* 47 (No. 3, July): 1005–1030.

Eckbo, E., and K. Thorburn. 2000. Gains to bidder firms revisited: Domestic and foreign acquisitions in Canada. *Journal of Financial and Quantitative Analysis* 35 (No. 1, March): 1–25.

Economist. 1997. The coming car crash. (May 10): 21–23.

Edmondson, Amy C., Michael A. Roberto, Richard M.J. Bohmer, Erika M. Ferlins, and Laura R. Feldman. 2004. The recovery window: Organizational learning following ambiguous threats in high-risk organizations. Harvard Business School working paper.

Elder, J., and P. Westra. 2000. The reaction of security prices to tracking stock announcements. *Journal of Economics and Finance* 24(1), 36–55.

Erickson, M., and S. Wang. 2000. The effect of transaction structure on price: Evidence from subsidiary sales. *Journal of Accounting and Economics* 30(1), 59–97.

Evans, J., and C. Green. 2000. Marketing strategy, constituent influence, and resource allocation: An application of the Mile and Snow typology to closely held firms in Chapter 11 bankruptcy. *Journal of Business Research* 50(2), 225–231.

Evans, Philip, and Thomas S. Wurster. 1999. *Blown to Bits: How the New Economics of Information Transforms Strategy*. Boston: Harvard Business School Press.

Fakler, J. 2002. Splitsville for Tyco, worry for analysts. *South Florida Business Journal*, January 28. Downloaded from http://southflorida.biz journals.com/southflorida/stories/2002/01/28/story1.html?t=printable.

Fan, J., and V. Goyal. 2002. On the patterns and wealth effects of vertical mergers. Hong Kong University of Science and Technology working paper, January.

Fauver, L., J.F. Houston, and A. Naranjo. 2002. Capital market development, integration, legal systems, and the value of corporate diversification: A cross-country analysis. Working paper, downloaded from http://papers.ssrn.com/sol3/papers.cfm?abstract_id-320220.

Fellers, Gary. 1994. *Why Things Go Wrong*. Gretna, LA: Pelican.

Ferris, S., and K. Park. 2001. How different is the long-run performance of mergers in the telecommunications industry? University of Missouri working paper (March).

Ferris, S.P., N. Sen, C.Y. Lim, and G.H.H. Yeo. 2002. Corporate focus versus diversification: The role of growth opportunities and cash flow. *Journal of International Financial Markets, Institutions and Money* 12: 231–252.

Finnerty, J.E., J.E. Owers, and R.C. Rogers. 1986. The valuation impact of joint ventures. *Management International Review* 26, 14–26.

Firth, M. 1980. Takeovers, shareholder returns, and the theory of the firm. *Quarterly Journal of Economics* 94 (No. 2, March): 235–260.

Fisher, A.B. 1994. How to make a merger work. *Fortune* (No. 2, January 24): 66–69.

Flanagan, D. 1966. Announcements of purely related and purely unrelated mergers and shareholder returns: Reconciling the relatedness paradox. *Journal of Management* 22, 823.

Floreani, A., and S. Rigamonti. 2001. Mergers and shareholders' wealth in the insurance industry. Working paper, Universita Cattolica del S. Cuore (March).

Fluck, S., and A. Lynch. 1999. Why do firms merge and then divest? A theory of financial synergies. *Journal of Business* 72, 319–346.

Frank, Robert H., and Philip J. Cook. 1996. *The Winner-Take-All Society: Why the Few at the Top Get So Much More than the Rest of Us.* New York: Penguin Books.

Franks, J., R. Harris, and S. Titman. 1991. The postmerger share-price performance of acquiring firms. *Journal of Financial Economics* 29 (No. 1, March): 81–96.

Freiman, H. 1990. Understanding the economics of leveraged ESOPs. *Financial Analysts Journal* 46, 51–55.

Friedman, J. 2000. *Dictionary of Business Terms*, 3d ed. Hauppauge, NY: Barron's Educational Series.

Fuller, K., J. Netter, and M. Stegemoller. 2002. What do returns to acquiring firms tell us? Evidence from firms that make many acquisitions. *Journal of Finance* 57 (No. 4, August): 1763–1793.

Gartner, W.B. 1988. Who is an entrepreneur is the wrong question. *American Journal of Small Business* (Spring): 11–32.

Gerstner, Louis V. 2002. *Who Says Elephants Can't Dance?* New York: HarperCollins.

Gertner, R., E. Powers, and D. Scharfstein. 2002. Learning about internal capital markets from corporate spin-offs. *Journal of Finance* 57(6), 2479–2506.

Ghosh, A. 2001. Does operating performance really improve following corporate acquisitions? *Journal of Corporate Finance* 7 (No. 2, June): 151–178.

Ghosh, A. 2002. Increasing market share as a rationale for corporate acquisitions. Baruch College working paper (May).

Gibson, Richard. 1995. Quaker Oats president quits posts. *Wall Street Journal*, October 24, A3.

Gibson, Richard. 1995. Quaker Oats says finance chief quits, plans hefty charge on pet food sales. *Wall Street Journal*, March 9, B12.

Gil, M., and P. Gonzalez de la Fe. 1999. Strategic alliances, organizational learning, and new product development: The cases of Rover and Seat. *R&D Management* 29(4), 391–404.

Gish, Al, Z. Gu, and P. Jain. 2003. Price-earnings multiples and sustained earnings and revenue growth. Working paper downloaded from http://papers.ssrn.com/sol3/papers.cfm?abstract_id=404840.

Gleick, J. 1998. *Chaos: Making a New Science.* New York: Penguin Books.

Goergen, M., and L. Renneboog. 2003. Shareholder wealth effects of European domestic and cross-border takeover bids. European Corporate Governance Institute, Finance working paper no. 08/2003 (January).

Golbe, D., and L. White. 1988. Mergers and acquisitions in the U.S. economy: An aggregate and historical overview. In A. Auerbach, ed., *Mergers and Acquisitions*, 25–47, Chicago: University of Chicago Press.

Golbe, D., and L. White. 1993. Catch a wave: The time series behavior of mergers. *Review of Economics and Statistics* 75 (August): 493–499.

Gort, M. 1969. An economic disturbance theory of mergers. *Quarterly Journal of Economics* 83 (November): 624–642.

Grabowski, Martha, and Karlene Roberts. 1997. Risk mitigation in large-scale systems. *California Management Review* 39 (No. 4, Summer): 152–162.

Graham, J., M. Lemmon, and J. Wolf. 2002. Does corporate diversification destroy value? *Journal of Finance* 57, 695–720.

Greenberg, Herb. 1999. Mattel has nobody to blame but itself for the learning Co. fiasco. *TheStreet.Com*, October 4, 1999, accessed October 8.

Gregory, A. 1997. An examination of the long run performance of U.K. acquiring firms. *Journal of Business Finance and Accounting* 24 (No. 7/8, September): 971–1002.

Griffin J., and A. Karolyi. 1998. Another look at the role of the industrial structure of markets for international diversification strategies. *Journal of Financial Economics* 50, 351–373.

Grinblatt, M., S. Titman, and R. Wermers. 1995. Momentum investment strategies, portfolio performance, and herding: A study of mutual fund behavior. *American Economic Review* 85, 1088–1105.

Grubb, Thomas M., and Robert B. Lamb. 2000. *Capitalize on Merger Chaos.* New York: Free Press.

Gupta, A., and L. Misra. (undated). Regulatory change, profitability, and managerial motives in financial mergers. Bentley College working paper.

Hadlock, C., M. Ryngaert, and S. Thomas. 2001. Corporate structure and equity offerings: Are there benefits to diversification? *Journal of Business* 74(4), 613–635.

Haig, Matt. 2003. *Brand Failures*, London: Kogan Paige.

Hambrick, D., and L. Crozier. 1985. Stumblers and stars in the management of rapid growth. *Journal of Business Venturing* 1(1), 31–45.

Hammonds, Keith. 2002. Five habits of highly reliable organizations. *Fast Company* (May): 124–128.

Harford, J. 1999. Corporate cash reserves and acquisitions. *Journal of Finance* 54 (No. 6, December): 1969–1997.

Harrigan, K. 1984. Formulating vertical integration strategies. *Academy of Management Review* 9(9), 638–652.

Harrigan, K. 1985. *Managing for Joint Venture Success*. New York: Praeger.

Harrigan, Kathryn. 1988. Strategic alliances and partner asymmetries, *Management International Review* 28, 53–72.

Harris, M., and A. Raviv. 1996. The capital budgeting process: Incentives and information. *Journal of Finance* 51, 1139–1174.

Harrison, J.S., and C.H. St. John. 1994. *Strategic Management of Organizations and Stakeholders: Theory and Cases*. St. Paul, MN: West Publishing.

Hass, J. 1996. Directional fiduciary duties in a tracking stock equity structure: The need for a duty of fairness. *Michigan Law Review* 94, 2089–2177.

Haushalter, D., and W. Mikkelson. 2001. An investigation of the gains from specialized equity: tracking stock and minority carve-outs. University of Oregon working paper.

Hax, A., and N. Majluf. 1984. *Strategic Management: An Integrative Perspective*. Englewood Cliffs, NJ: Prentice-Hall.

Healy, P., K. Palepu, and R. Ruback. 1992. Does corporate performance improve after mergers? *Journal of Financial Economics* 31 (No. 2, April): 135–175.

Healy, P., K. Palepu, and R. Ruback. 1997. Which takeovers are profitable: Strategic or financial? *Sloan Management Review* 38 (No. 4, Summer): 45–57.

Hearth, D., and J.K. Zaima. 1986. Divestiture uncertainty and shareholder wealth: evidence from the U.S.A. (1975–1982). *Journal of Business Finance and Accounting*, 71–85.

Hellerman, M., and B. Jones. 2000. The would'ves, could'ves, and should'ves of spin-offs. *Journal of Business Strategy* 21(4), 10–14.

Hennessy, D. 2000. Corporate spin-offs, bankruptcy, investment, and the value of debt. *Insurance: Mathematics and Economics* 27, 229–235.

Herman, E. and L. Lowenstein. 1988. The efficiency effect of hostile takeovers. In J.C. Coffee Jr., L. Lowenstein, and S. Rose-Ackerman, eds. *Knights, Raiders, and Targets*, 211–240. New York: Oxford University Press.

Heron, R., and E. Lie. 2002. Operating performance and the method of payment in takeovers. *Journal of Financial and Quantitative Analysis* 37, 137–155.

Hietala, P., S. Kaplan, and D. Robinson. 2002. What is the price of hubris? using takeover battles to infer overpayments and synergies. NBER working paper no. W9264 (October).

Hite, G., and J. Owers. 1983. Security price reactions around corporate spin-off announcements. *Journal of Financial Economics* 12, 409–436.

Hite, G., J. Owers, and R. Rogers. 1987. The market for inter-firm asset sales: Partial sell-offs and total liquidations. *Journal of Financial Economics* 18, 229–252.

Hitt, M.A., M.T. Dacin, E. Levitas, J-L. Arregle, and A. Borza. 2000. Partner selection in emerging and developed market contexts: Resource-based and organizational learning perspectives. *Academy of Management Journal* 43 (3), 449–467.

Hitt, M.A., R.D. Ireland, and R.E. Hoskisson. 1995. *Strategic Management: Competitiveness and Globalization*. St. Paul, MN: West Publishing.

Hitt, M.A., R. D. Nixon, R. E. Hoskisson, and R. Kochhar. 1999. Corporate entrepreneurship and cross-functional fertilization: Activation, process and disintegration of a new product design team. *Entrepreneurship: Theory and Practice* 230: 145–167.

Hogan K., and G. Olson. (undated) A comparison of equity carve-outs and original initial public offers: The differential impact of information asymmetry related variables and underpricing. St. Joseph's University working paper available by e-mail from hogan@sju.edu.

Holmstrom, B., and S. Kaplan. 2001. Corporate governance and merger activity in the U.S.: Making sense of the 1980s and 1990s. NBER working paper W8220.

Holmstrom, B., and J. Tirole. 1993. Market liquidity and performance monitoring. *Journal of Political Economy* 101, 678–709.

Hoskisson, R., R. Johnson, and D. Moesel. 1994. Divestment intensity of restructuring firms: Effects of governance, strategy and performance. *Academy of Management Journal* 37, 1207–1251.

Houston, J., C. James, and M. Ryngaert. 2001. Where do merger gains come from? Bank mergers from the perspective of insiders and outsiders. *Journal of Financial Economics* 60 (No. 2/3, May/June): 285–331.

Huang, Y., and R. Walkling. 1987. Target abnormal returns associated with acquisition announcements: Payment, acquisition form, and managerial resistance. *Journal of Financial Economics*. 19 (No. 2, December): 329–350.

Hubbard, G., and D. Palia. 1999. A re-examination of the conglomerate merger wave in the 1960s: An internal capital markets view. *Journal of Finance* 54, 1131–1152.

Hulburt, H., J. Miles, and R. Woolridge. 2000. Value creation from equity carve-outs. *Financial Management* (Spring): 83–100.

Hyland, D., and J. Diltz. 2002. Why firms diversify: An empirical examination. *Financial Management* (Spring): 51–81.

Ingham, H., I. Kran, and A. Lovestam. 1992. Mergers and profitability: A managerial success story? *Journal of Management Studies* 29 (No. 2, March): 195–209.

Inkpen, A. 2000. Learning through joint ventures: A framework of knowledge acquisition. *Journal of Management Studies* 37 (No. 7, July): 1019–1043.

Jackson, P. 1983. *The Political Economy of Bureaucracy*. Totowa, New Jersey: Barnes & Noble Books.

Jain, P. 1985. The effect of voluntary sell-off announcements on shareholder wealth. *Journal of Finance* 40, 209–224.

Jarrell, G., and M. Bradley. 1980. The economic effects of federal and state regulations of cash tender offers. *Journal of Law and Economics* 23 (No. 2, October): 371–407.

Jarrell, G., J. Brickley, and J. Netter. 1988. The market for corporate control: The empirical evidence since 1980. *Journal of Economic Perspectives* 2 (No. 2, Winter): 49–68.

Jarrell, G., and A. Poulsen. 1989. The returns to acquiring firms in tender offers: Evidence from three decades. *Financial Management* 18 (No. 3, Autumn): 12–19.

Jayaratne, J., and C. Shapiro. 2000. Simulating partial asset divestitures to "fix" mergers. *International Journal of Economics of Business* 7(2), 179–200.

Jegadeesh, N., and S. Titman. 1993. Returns to buying winners and selling losers: Implications for stock market efficiency. *Journal of Finance* 48, 65–91.

Jensen, M. 1989. Active investors, LBOs, and the privatization of bankruptcy. *Journal of Applied Corporate Finance* 2 (Spring): 39.

Jensen, M. 1986. Agency costs of free cash flow, corporate finance, and takeovers. *American Economic Review* 76 (No. 2, May): 323–329.

Jensen, M. 1988. Takeovers: Their causes and consequences. *Journal of Economic Perspectives* 2 (Winter): 21–48.

Jensen, M. 1993. The modern industrial revolution, exit, and the failure of internal control systems. *Journal of Finance* 48 (July): 831–880.

Jensen, M., and R. Ruback. 1983. The market for corporate control: The scientific evidence. *Journal of Financial Economics* 11 (No. 1–4, April): 5–50.

Jensen, M.C. 1986. Agency costs of free cash flow, corporate finance, and takeovers. *American Economic Review, Papers and Proceedings* 76 (May): 326–329.

Jensen, M.C. 1989. The eclipse of the public corporation. *Harvard Business Review* (September–October): 61–74.

Jensen, M.C. 1993. The modern industrial revolution, exit, and the failure of internal control systems. *Journal of Finance* (July), reprinted in D. Chew, *The New Corporate Finance*. Burr Ridge, IL: Irwin McGraw-Hill, 1999.

John, K., and E. Ofek. 1995. Asset sales and increase in focus. *Journal of Financial Economics* 37, 105–126.

Johnson, S., D. Klein, and V. Thibodeaux. 1996. The effects of spin-offs on corporate investment and performance. *Journal of Financial Research* 19: 293–307.

Johnson, S.A., and M.B. Houston. 2000. A reexamination of the motives and gains in joint ventures. *Journal of Financial and Quantitative Analysis* 35(No. 1, March): 67–86.

Jovanovic, B., and P. Rousseau. 2002. Mergers as reallocation. NBER working paper 9279 (October).

Kahneman D., and A. Tversky. 1979. Prospect theory: An analysis of decision under risk. *Econometrica* (March): 263–291.

Kahneman D., and A. Tversky. 1984. Choices, values and frames. *American Psychologist* (April): 341–350.

Kaiser, K., and A. Stouraitis. 2001. Reversing corporate diversification and the use of the proceeds from asset sales: The case of Thorn EMI. *Financial Management* 1, 63 102.

Kale, P., H. Singh, and H. Perlmutter. 2000. Learning and protection of proprietary assets in strategic alliances: Building relational capital. *Strategic Management Journal* 21, 217–237.

Kaplan, S. 1989. Campeau's acquisition of Federated: Value destroyed or value added? *Journal of Financial Economics* 25 (No. 2, December): 191–212.

Kaplan, S. 1989. The effects of management buyouts on operating performance and value. *Journal of Financial Economics* 24 (No. 2, October): 217–254.

Kaplan, S., M. Mitchell, and K. Wruck. 1997. A clinical exploration of value creation and destruction in acquisitions: Organizational design, incentives, and internal capital markets. Working paper, Chicago, IL: Center for Research in Security Prices (March).

Kaplan, S., and M. Weisbach. 1992. The success of acquisitions: Evidence from divestitures. *Journal of Finance* 47 (No. 1, March): 107–138.

Kaplan, S.N. 1989. Sources of value in management buyouts. In Y. Amihud, ed., *Leveraged Management Buyouts*, Chapter 4, Homewood, IL: Dow Jones-Irwin.

Kaplan, S.N., and J.C. Stein. 1991. The evolution of buyout pricing and financial structure in the 1980s. Working paper, University of Chicago.

Keisler, Charles A. 1971. *The Psychology of Commitment*. New York: Academic Press.

Keller, John J. 1995. Disconnected line: Why AT&T takeover of NCR hasn't been a real bell ringer. *Wall Street Journal*, September 19, A1.

Keller, Maryann. 1993. *Collision: GM, Toyota, Volkswagen and the Race to Own the 21st Century*. New York: Doubleday.

Kelly, J., C. Cook, and D. Spitzer. 1999. *Unlocking Shareholder Value: The Keys to Success*. New York: KMPG LLP.

Kelly, K. 1994. *Out of Control: The New Biology of Machines, Social Systems, and the Economic World*. Reading, MA: Addison-Wesley.

Kenc, T. 2000. Discussion of optimal entrepreneurial financial contracting. *Journal of Business Finance and Accounting* 27, 1375–1378.

Kennedy, R. 2000. The effect of bankruptcy filings on rivals' operating performance: Evidence from 51 large bankruptcies. *International Journal of the Economics of Business* 7(1): 5–25.

Khanna, T., and K. Palepu. 1997. Why focused strategies may be wrong for emerging markets. *Harvard Business Review* (July–August): 41–51.

Khanna, T., and K. Palepu. 2000. Is group affiliation profitable in emerging markets? An analysis of diversified Indian business groups. *Journal of Finance* 55, 867–891.

Kim, C., and R. Mauborgne. 2002. Charting your company's future. *Harvard Business Review* (June): 77–83.

Kim, E.H., and J.D. Schatzberg. 1987. Voluntary corporate liquidations. *Journal of Financial Economics* 19: 311–328.

Kim, Y., and R. McElreath. 2001. Managing operating exposure: A case study of the automobile industry. *Multinational Business Review* 9(1), 21–26.

Klein, A. 1986. The timing and substance of divestiture announcements: Individual, simultaneous and cumulative effects. *Journal of Finance* 41, 685–696.

Klein, A., J. Rosenfeld, and W. Beranek. 1991. The two stages of an equity carve out and the price response of parent and subsidiary stock. *Managerial and Decision Economics* 12 (December): 449–460.

Klein, Alec. 2003. *Stealing Time: Steve Case, Jerry Levin, and the Collapse of AOL Time Warner.* New York: Simon & Schuster.

Klein, P. 2001. Were the acquisitive conglomerates inefficient? *RAND Journal of Economics* 32(4), 745–761.

Koh, J., and N. Venkataraman. 1991. Joint venture formation and stock market reaction: An assessment in the information technology sector. *Academy of Management Journal* 34, 869–892.

Kohers, N., and T. Kohers. 2000. The value creation potential of high-tech mergers. *Financial Analysts Journal* 53 (No. 3 May/June): 40–48.

Kohers, N., and T. Kohers. 2001. Takeovers of technology firms: Expectations vs. reality. *Financial Management* (Autumn): 35–54.

Kohn, L.T., J.M. Corrigan, and M.S. Donaldson, eds. 1999. *To Err is Human: Building a Safer Health System.* Washington, DC: National Academy Press.

Krakauer, Jon. 1997. *Into Thin Air.* New York: Doubleday.

Kravetz, Stacey. 1999. Mattel forecasts sluggish sales, posts 70% drop in 4th-quarter net. *Wall Street Journal*, February 3, B14.

Kravetz, Stacey. 1999. Mattel revamps retail plan to reduce dependence on traditional outlets. *Wall Street Journal*, February 17, B8.

Kravetz, Stacey, and Jon Auerbach. 1998. Toys: Mattel reveals profit shortfall, software deal. *Wall Street Journal*, December 15, B1

Krishnaswami, S., and V. Subramaniam. 1999. Information asymmetry, valuation, and the corporate spin-off decision. *Journal of Financial Economics* 53, 73–112.

Kruse, T. 2002. Asset liquidity and the determinants of asset sales by poorly performing firms. *Financial Management* 4, 107–129.

Kruse, T., H. Park, K. Park, and K. Suzuki. 2002. The value of corporate diversification: Evidence from post-merger performance in Japan. Working paper, University of Arkansas, available by e-mail from tkruse@walton.uark.edu.

Kuipers, D., D. Miller, and A. Patel. 2003. The legal environment and corporate valuation: Evidence from cross-border mergers. Texas Tech University working paper (January).

Kully, T. R. 1984. Revco D.S. research report. William Blair & Co. (June 19).

Kummer, D., and R. Hoffmeister. 1978. Valuation consequences of cash tender offers. *Journal of Finance* 33 (No. 2, May): 505–516.

Lajoux, A.R., and J.F. Weston. 1998. Do deals deliver on postmerger performance? *Mergers and Acquisitions* (No. 2, September–October): 34–38.

Lambrecht, B. 2002. The timing of takeovers under uncertainty: A real options approach. University of Cambridge working paper (April).

Lamont, O. 1997. Cash flow and investment: Evidence from internal capital markets. *Journal of Finance* 52, 83–110.

Lamont, O., and C. Polk. 2001. The diversification discount: Cash flows versus returns. *Journal of Finance* 56, 1693–1721.

Lamoreaux, N.R. 1985. *The Great Merger Movement in American Business, 1895–1904*. Cambridge: Cambridge University Press.

Lang, L., A. Poulsen, and R. Stulz. 1995. Asset sales, firm performance, and the agency costs of managerial discretion. *Journal of Financial Economics* 37, 3–37.

Lang, L., R. Stulz, and R. Walkling. 1989. Managerial performance, Tobin's Q, and the gains from successful tender offers. *Journal of Financial Economics* 24 (No. 1, September): 137–154.

Lang, L., R. Stulz, and R. Walkling. 1991. A test of the free cash flow hypothesis: The case of bidder returns. *Journal of Financial Economics* 29 (No. 2, October): 315–335.

Langer, Ellen J. 1989. *Mindfulness.* Reading, MA: Perseus Books.

Langer, Ellen J. 1997. *The Power of Mindful Learning.* Reading, MA: Addison-Wesley.

Langetieg, T. 1978. An application of a three-factor performance index to measure stockholders gains from merger. *Journal of Financial Economics* 6 (No. 4, December): 365–384.

Lee, I., and S.B. Wyatt. 1990. The effects of international joint ventures on shareholder wealth. *Financial Review* 25, 641–649.

Leeth, J., and J.R. Borg. 2000. The impact of takeovers on shareholder wealth during the 1920s merger wave. *Journal of Financial and Quantitative Analysis* 35 (No. 2, June): 217–238.

Lerner, J., H. Shane, and A. Tsai. 2003. Do equity financing cycles matter? Evidence from biotechnology alliances. *Journal of Financial Economics* 67, 411–446.

Lesmond, D., M. Schill, and C. Zhou. 2002. The illusory nature of momentum profits. Darden School, University of Virginia working paper 03–06. Downloaded from http://papers.ssrn.com/sol3/papers.cfm?abstract_id=256926.

Levine, J.B., and J.A. Byrne. 1986. Corporate odd couples. *Business Week*, July 21, 100–106.

Levinsohn, A. 2000. Tracking stock. *Strategic Finance* 82(3), 62–67.

Levy, H., and H. Sarnat. 1970. Diversification, portfolio analysis, and the uneasy case for conglomerate mergers. *Journal of Finance* 25, 795–802.

Levy, Matthys, and Mario Salvadori. 1992. *Why Buildings Fall Down.* New York: W.W. Norton.

Levy, R. 1967. Relative strength as a criterion for investment selection. *Journal of Finance* 22, 595–610.

Lewellen, W. 1971. A pure financial rationale for the conglomerate merger. *Journal of Finance* 26, 521–537.

Lichtenberg, F., and D. Siegel. 1990. The effects of leveraged buyouts on productivity and related aspects of firm behavior. *Journal of Financial Economics* 27, 165–94.

Linn, S., and J. Switzer. 2001. Are cash acquisitions associated with better postcombination operating performance than stock acquisitions? *Journal of Banking and Finance* 25, 1113.

Lins, K., and H. Servaes. 1999. International evidence on the value of corporate diversification. *Journal of Finance* 54, 2215–2239.

Lins, K., and H. Servaes. 2002. Is corporate diversification beneficial in emerging markets? *Financial Management* (Summer): 5–31.

Loderer, C., and K. Martin. 1990. Corporate acquisitions by listed firms: The experience of a comprehensive sample. *Financial Management* 19 (No. 4, Winter): 17–33.

Loderer, C., and K. Martin. 1992. Postacquisition performance of acquiring firms. *Financial Management* 21 (No. 3, Autumn): 69–79.

Logue, D., J. Seward, and J. Walsh. 1996. Rearranging residual claims: A case for targeted stock. *Financial Management* 25, 43–61.

Long, W., and D. Ravenscraft. 1993. LBOs, debt and R&D intensity. *Strategic Management Journal* 14, 119–135.

Longhofer, S. 1997. Absolute priority rule violations, credit rationing and efficiency. *Journal of Financial Intermediation* 6, 249–267.

Loree, D., C. Chen, and S. Guisinger. 2000. International acquisitions: Do financial analysts take note? *Journal of World Business* 35, 300.

Loughran, T., and A. Vijh. 1997. Do long-term shareholders benefit from corporate acquisitions? *Journal of Finance* 52 (No. 5, December): 1765–1790.

Louis, H. (undated). The causes of post-merger underperformance: Evidence from successful and unsuccessful bidders. Pennsylvania State University working paper.

Lubatkin, M., and H. O'Neill. 1987. Merger strategies and capital market risk. *Academy of Management Journal* 30 (December): 665.

Lubatkin, M., N. Srinivasan, and H. Merchant. 1997. Merger strategies and shareholder value during times of relaxed antitrust enforcement: The case of large mergers during the 1980s. *Journal of Management* 23, 59.

Lutz, S. 1994. Epic ESOP participants hit a home run with sale. *Modern Healthcare* (January 17): 3.

Lynch, H. 1971. *Financial Performance of Conglomerates*. Boston, MA: Division of Research, Graduate School of Business Administration, Harvard University.

Lyroudi, K., J. Lazaridis, and D. Subeniotis. 1999. Impact of international mergers and acquisitions on shareholder's wealth: A European perspective. *Journal of Financial Management and Analysis* 12 (No. 1, January–June): 1–14.

Lys, Thomas, and Linda Vincent. 1995. An analysis of value destruction in AT&T's acquisition of NCR. *Journal of Financial Economics* 39 (No. 2/3 October/November): 353–378.

Macksey, Kenneth. 2003. *Military Errors of World War Two*. New York: Barnes & Noble Books.

Makino, S., and K. Neupert. 2000. National culture, transaction costs, and the choice between joint venture and wholly owned subsidiary. *Journal of International Business Studies* 31(4), 705–713.

Maksimovic, V., and G. Phillips. 2001. The market for corporate assets: Who engages in mergers and asset sales and are there efficiency gains? *Journal of Finance* 56(6) (December): 2019–2065.

Maksimovic, V., and G. Phillips. 2002. Do conglomerate firms allocate resources inefficiently across industries? Theory and evidence. *Journal of Finance* 57 (April): 721–767.

Malatesta, P. 1983. The wealth effect of merger activity and the objective functions of merging firms. *Journal of Financial Economics* 11 (No. 1–4, April): 155–181.

Mandelker, G. 1974. Risk and return: The case of merging firms. *Journal of Financial Economics* 1 (No. 4, December): 303–335.

Manoocheri, G., and B. Jizba. 1990. How to use ESOPs as an effective tool in corporate strategy. *Journal of Compensation and Benefits* 4, 272–277.

Mansi, S., and D. Reeb. 2002. Corporate diversification: What gets discounted? *Journal of Finance* 57(5), 2167–2183.

Maquieria, C., W. Megginson, and L. Nail. 1998. Wealth creation versus wealth redistributions in pure stock-for-stock mergers. *Journal of Financial Economics* 48 (No. 1, April): 3–33.

Maremont, M., and J. Weil. 2003. Tyco's problems on accounting may not be over, *Wall Street Journal*, May 5, C1.

Markham, J. 1955. Survey of the evidence and findings on mergers. In NBER, ed., *Business Concentration and Price Policy*, Princeton, NJ: Princeton University Press.

Markides, C. 1998. Strategic innovation in established companies. *Sloan Management Review* 39(3), 31–42.

Mata, J., and P. Portugal. 2000. Closure and divestiture by foreign entrants: The impact of entry and post-entry strategies. *Strategic Management Journal* 21, 549–562.

McCarthy, Michael J., Richard Gibson, and Nikhil Deogun. 1997. Quaker to sell Snapple for $300 million—Unit's sale to Triarc Cos. to mean pretax charge of about $1.4 billion. *Wall Street Journal*, March 28, A3.

McCoid, J., II. 1996. Discharge: The most important development in bankruptcy history. *American Bankruptcy Law Journal* 70, 163–193.

McConnell J., and T. Nantell. 1985. Corporate combinations and common stock returns: the case of joint ventures. *Journal of Finance* 40, 519–536.

McHugh, C. 1996. *The 1996 Bankruptcy Yearbook and Almanac.* Boston: George Putnam.

McLean, Bethany, and Peter Elkind. 2003. *The Smartest Guys in the Room.* New York: Penguin.

McNeil, C., and W. Moore. 2001. Spin-off wealth effects and the dismantling of internal capital markets. University of South Carolina working paper.

Meeks, G. 1977. *Disappointing Marriage: A Study of the Gains from Merger.* Cambridge: Cambridge University Press.

Megginson, W., A. Morgan, and L. Nail. 2002. The determinants of positive long-term performance in strategic mergers: Corporate focus and cash. Working paper, University of Alabama (August). Available from the authors by e-mail at lnail@uab.edu.

Megginson, W.L., A. Morgan, and L.A. Nail. (undated). Changes in corporate focus, ownership structure, and long-run merger returns. Working paper available from Social Science Research Network Electronic Paper Collection: http://papers.ssrn.com /paper.taf?abstract_id=250993.

Melicher, R., J. Ledolter, and L. D'Antonio. 1983. A time series analysis of aggregate merger activity. *Review of Economics and Statistics* 65 (August): 423–430.

Mergers and Acquisitions. 1999. The Internet bounce for equity carve-outs. 33(5), 27–34.

Michel, A., and I. Shaked. 1990. The LBO nightmare: Fraudulent conveyance risk. *Financial Analysts Journal* (March–April): 41–50.

Miles, J., and J. Rosenfeld. 1983. An empirical analysis of the effects of spin-off announcements on shareholder wealth. *Journal of Finance* 38, 1597–1606.

Miller, M., and F. Modigliani. 1961. Dividend policy, growth and the valuation of shares. *Journal of Business* 34 (October): 411–433.

Mitchell, M., and J. Mulherin. 1996. The impact of industry shocks on takeover and restructuring activity. *Journal of Financial Economics* 41 (June): 193–209.

Mitchell, M.L., and E. Stafford. 2000. Managerial decisions and long-term stock price performance. *Journal of Business* 73 (No. 3, July): 287–329.

Moeller, S., F. Schlingemann, and R. Stulz. 2003. Do shareholders of acquiring firms gain from acquisitions? Ohio State University working paper (February).

Moeller, S.B., F.P. Schlingemann, and Rene Stulz. 2003. Do shareholders of acquiring firms gain from acquisitions? NBER working paper W9523 (March).

Moeller, S., F. Schlingemann, and R. Stulz. 2003. Wealth destruction on a massive scale? A study of acquiring-firm returns in the recent merger wave. Ohio State University working paper (August).

Moeller, S., F. Schlingemann, and R. Stulz. 2004. Firm size and the gains from acquisition. *Journal of Financial Economics* 73, 201–228.

Moore, R. 2002. Fool on the hill: The breaking point. *The Motley Fool*, February 21. Downloaded from http://222.fool.com/Server.FoolPrint.asp?file=/news/foth/2002/foth020221.htm.

Morck, R., A. Shleifer, and R. Vishny. 1990. Do managerial objectives drive bad acquisitions? *Journal of Finance* 45 (No. 1, March): 31–48.

Morck, R., and B. Yeung. 1997. Why investors sometimes value size and diversification: The internalization theory of synergy. University of Alberta, Institute for Financial Research, working paper No. 5–97.

Morck, Randall, Andrei Shleifer, and Robert Vishny. 1988. Management ownership and market valuation: An empirical analysis. *Journal of Financial Economics* 20, 293–315.

Moskowitz, T., and M. Grinblatt. 1999. Do industries explain momentum? *Journal of Finance* 54, 1249–1290.

Moukheiber, Zina. 1996. He who laughs last: Was Quaker Oates taken when it paid $1.7 billion for Snapple? *Forbes*, January 1, 42.

Mueller, D. 1979. Testimony before U.S. Senate, Committee on the Judiciary; Subcommittee on Antitrust, Monopoly, and Business Rights; 96th Congress, 1st Session; Serial No. 96–26, 302–312.

Mueller, D. 1980. *The Determinants and Effects of Mergers: An International Comparison*. Cambridge: Oelgeschlager, Gunn & Hain.

Mueller, D. 1985. Mergers and market share. *Review of Economics and Statistics* 67 (No. 2, May): 259–267.

Mulherin, H. 2000. Incomplete acquisitions and organizational efficiency. Working paper, State College, PA: Penn State University.

Mulherin, J., and A. Boone. 2000. Comparing acquisitions and divestitures. *Journal of Corporate Finance* 6, 117–139, and Penn State University working paper, available by e-mail from jhm14@psu.edu.

Munk, Nina. 2003. *Fools Rush In: Steve Case, Jerry Levin, and the Unmaking of AOL Time Warner.* New York: HarperBusiness.

Muscarella, C., and M. Vetsuypens. 1990. Efficiency and organizational structure: A study of reverse LBOs. *Journal of Finance* 45 (No. 5, December): 1389–1413.

Myers, S., and N. Majluf. 1984. Corporate financing and investment decisions when firms have information that investors do not have. *Journal of Financial Economics* 13, 187–221.

Nail, L., W. Megginson, and C. Maquiera. 1998. How stock-swap mergers affect shareholder (and) bondholder wealth: More evidence of the value of corporate "focus." *Journal of Applied Corporate Finance* 11(3), 153–172.

Nanda, V. 1991. On the good news in equity carve-outs. *Journal of Finance* 46, 1717–1737.

Nanda, V., and M. Narayanan. 1999. Disentangling value: Financing needs, firm scope, and divestitures. *Journal of Financial Intermediation* 8(3), 174–204.

Nasar, S. 1989. The foolish rush to ESOPs. *Fortune*, September 25, 120, 141–150.

Nathan, J. 1999. *Sony.* Boston: Houghton Mifflin.

Nelson, R. 1959. *Merger Movements in American Industry 1895–1956.* Princeton, NJ: Princeton University Press.

Nelson, R. 1966. Business cycle factors in the choice between internal and external growth. In W. Alberts and J. Segall, eds., *The Corporate Mergers*, Chicago: University of Chicago Press.

Newton, C. 2001. Strategic alliances: Collaborate or evaporate. *Journal of Financial Planning* 14(3), 72–80.

Nyman, S., and A. Silberston. 1978. The ownership and control of industry, *Oxford Economic Papers* 30, 74–101.

Opler, T. 1992. Operating performance in leveraged buyouts: Evidence from 1985–1989. *Financial Management* 21 (No. 1, Spring): 27–34.

Oster, Clinton V., John S. Strong, and C. Kurt Zorn. 1992. *Why Airplanes Crash: Aviation Safety in a Changing World.* New York: Oxford University Press.

Parrino, J.D., and R.S. Harris. 1999. Takeovers, management replacement, and post-acquisition operating performance: Some evidence from the 1980s. *Journal of Applied Corporate Finance* 11(No. 4, Winter): 88–97.

Parrino, J.D., and R.S. Harris. 2001. Business linkages and post-merger operating performance. Working paper, Charlottesville, VA: Darden Graduate School of Business, University of Virginia.

Parrino, R. 1997. Spin-offs and wealth transfers: The Marriott case. *Journal of Financial Economics* 43, 241–274.

Perotti, E., and S. Guney. 1993. The structure of privatization plans. *Financial Management* 22(1), 84–98.

Perrow, Charles. 1999. *Normal Accidents: Living with High-Risk Technologies.* Princeton, NJ: Princeton University Press.

Petersen, M., and R. Rajan. 1997. Trade credit: Theories and evidence. *Review of Financial Studies* 10(3), 661–691.

Petroski, Henry. 1982. *To Engineer Is Human: The Role of Failure in Successful Design.* New York: Vintage Books.

Pettit, B. 2000. The long-horizon performance of acquiring firms: The French evidence. Working paper, American Graduate School of International Management (November).

Phillips, G. 1995. Increased debt and industry product markets: An empirical analysis. *Journal of Financial Economics* 37, 189–238.

Phillips, S. 1988. Revco's LBO ends with a whimper. *Business Week*, August 15, 46.

Pool, Robert. 1997. When failure is not an option. *Technology Review* (July), 38–45.

Porter, M. 1979. How competitive forces shape strategy. *Harvard Business Review* (March–April): 137–145, Reprint number 79208.

Porter, M. 1980. *Competitive Strategy: Techniques for Analyzing Industries and Competitors.* New York: Free Press.

Porter, M. 1985. *Competitive Advantage: Creating and Sustaining Superior Performance.* New York: Free Press.

Porter, M. 1987. From competitive advantage to corporate strategy. *Harvard Business Review* 65 (May–June): 43–59.

Prezas, A., M. Tarimcilar, and G. Vasudevan. 2000. The pricing of equity carve-outs. *The Financial Review* 35, 123–138.

Rajan, R., H. Servaes, and L. Zingales. 2000. The cost of diversity: The diversification discount and inefficient investment. *Journal of Finance* 55, 2537–2564.

Rau, R.P., and T. Vermaelen. 1998. Glamour, value and the post-acquisition performance of acquiring firms. *Journal of Financial Economics* 49 (No. 2, August): 223–253.

Ravenscraft, D. 1987. The 1980s merger wave: An industrial organization perspective. In L. Brown and E. Rosengren, eds., *The Merger Boom*, Boston: Federal Reserve Bank of Boston.

Ravenscraft, D., and F.M. Scherer. 1987. Life after takeovers. *Journal of Industrial Economics* 36 (No. 2, December): 147–156.

Ravenscraft, D., and F.M. Scherer. 1987. *Mergers, Sell-Offs, and Economic Efficiency*. Washington, DC: Brookings Institution.

Reason, James. 1990. *Human Error*. Cambridge: Cambridge University Press.

Reier, S. 1990. Bankruptcy boondoggle. *Financial World* (October 16): 36–40.

Resende, M. 1999. Wave behaviour of mergers and acquisitions in the U.K.: A sectoral study. *Oxford Bulletin of Economics and Statistics* 61 (February): 85–94.

Reuer, J., and M. Leiblein. 2000. Downside risk implication of multinationality and international joint ventures. *Academy of Management Journal* 43(2), 203–214.

Revco D.S., Inc. 1986. *Prospectus*. December 18.

Revco D.S., Inc. 1986. *Proxy Statement*. November 14.

Rhodes-Kropf, M., and S. Viswanathan. 2000. Corporate reorganizations and non-cash auctions. *Journal of Finance* 55(4), 1807–1854.

Rhodes-Kropf, M., and S. Viswanathan. 2003. "Market valuation and merger waves. Downloaded from http://papers.ssrn.com/sol3/papers .cfm?abstract_id=334944 (April).

Rice, B., and B. Spring. 1989. ESOP at the barricade: Polaroid uses a novel anti-takeover defense. *Barron's* 69 (February): 38–39.

Ritter, J. 1991. The long-run performance of initial public offerings. *Journal of Finance* 46, 1717–1737.

Roberto, Michael A. 2002. Lessons from Everest: The interaction of cognitive bias, psychological safety, and system complexity. *California Management Review* (Fall): 136–158.

Roberto, Michael A., and Gina M. Carioggia. 2002. Mount Everest— 1996. Harvard Business School case study 9–303–061.

Roberts, Karlene. 1990. Managing hi reliability organizations. *California Management Review* (Summer): 101–113.

Roberts, Karlene, and Robert Bea. 2001. Must accidents happen? Lessons from high-reliability organizations. *Academy of Management Executive* 15(3), 70–79.

Robinson, D.T. 2001. Strategic alliances and the boundaries of the firm. Columbia University working paper (November 15). Available by e-mail from dtr2001@columbia.edu.

Robinson, D.T., and T. Stuart. 2002. Financial contracting in biotech strategic alliances. Columbia University working paper. Downloadable from http://papers.ssrn.com/sol3/papers.cfm?abstract_id=328881.

Roll, R. 1986. The hubris hypothesis of corporate takeovers. *Journal of Business* 59 (April): 197–216.

Rondinelli, D., and S. Black. 2000. Multinational strategic alliances and acquisitions in Central and Eastern Europe: Partnerships in privatization. *The Academy of Management Executive* 14(4), 85–98.

Rosen, C. 1989. Employee stock ownership plans: Myths, magic and measures. *Employee Relations Today* 16, 189–195.

Rosen. C., and M. Quarrey. 1987. How well is employee ownership working? *Harvard Business Review* 106, 15–19.

Rosen, R. 2002. Merger momentum and investor sentiment: The stock market reaction to merger announcements. Indiana University working paper, downloaded from http://papers.ssrn.com/sol3/papers.cfm?abstract_id=343600.

Rosenfeld, J. 1984. Additional evidence on the relation between divestiture announcements and shareholder wealth. *Journal of Finance* 39(5), 1437–1448.

Rouwenhorst, K.G. 1998. International momentum strategies. *Journal of Finance* 53, 267–284.

Ruback, R. 1982. The Conoco takeover and stockholder returns. *Sloan Management Review* 23, 13–33.

Rumelt, R. 1974. *Strategy, Structure, and Economic Performance*. Boston: Harvard Business School Press.

Rumelt, R. 1982. Diversification strategy and profitability. *Strategic Management Journal* 3 (No. 4, October–December): 359–369.

Rytherband, D. 1991. The decision to implement an ESOP: Strategies and economic considerations. *Employee Benefits Journal* 16, 19–25.

Salancik, Gerald R. 1997. Commitment and the control of organization behavior and belief. In Barry M. Staw and Gerald R. Salancik, eds., *New Directions in Organizational Behavior*, Chicago: St. Clair Press.

Salisbury, Stephen. 1982. *No Way to Run a Railroad: The Untold Story of the Penn Central Crisis*. New York: McGraw-Hill.

Salmon, F. 1999. Mega-mergers bring a new spate of carve-outs. *Corporate Finance* (May), 10–11.

Salter, M., and W. Weinhold. 1979. *Diversification through Acquisition: Strategies for Creating Economic Value*. New York: Free Press.

Sarasvathy, S., and A. Menon. 2002. Failing firms and successful entrepreneurs: Serial entrepreneurs as a serial machine. Working paper, University of Washington.

Saunders, Richard, Jr. 2003. *Main Lines: Rebirth of the North American Railroads, 1970–2002*. DeKalb, IL: Northern Illinois University Press.

Scanlon, K., J. Trifts, and R. Pettway. 1989. "Impacts of relative size and industrial relatedness on returns to shareholders of acquiring firms. *Journal of Financial Research* 12 (Summer 1989): 103.

Scharfstein, D., and J. Stein. 2000. The dark side of internal capital markets: Divisional rent-seeking and inefficient investment. *Journal of Finance* 55, 2537–2564.

Schein, Edgar. 1985. *Organizational Culture and Leadership*. San Francisco: Jossey-Bass.

Scherer, F.M. 1988. Corporate takeovers: The efficiency arguments. *Journal of Economic Perspectives* 2 (Winter): 69–82.

Schill, M., and C. Zhou. 2001. Pricing an emerging industry: Evidence from internet subsidiary carve-outs. *Financial Management* (Autumn): 5–33.

Schipper, K., and A. Smith. 1983. Effects of recontracting on shareholder wealth: The case of voluntary spin-offs. *Journal of Financial Economics* 15, 153–186.

Schipper, K., and A. Smith. 1986. A comparison of equity carve-outs and seasoned equity offerings. *Journal of Financial Economics* 15, 153–186.

Schipper, K., and A. Smith. 1989. Equity carve-outs. In J. Stern, G. Stewart, and D. Chew, (eds.), *Corporate Restructuring and Executive Compensation*, Cambridge, MA: Ballinger.

Schipper, K., and R. Thompson. 1983. Evidence on the capitalized value of merger activity for acquiring firms. *Journal of Financial Economics* 11 (April): 437–467.

Schleifer, A., and R. Vishny. 2001. Stock market driven acquisitions. University of Chicago working paper, downloadable from http://papers.ssrn.com/sol3/papers.cfm?abstract_id=278563.

Schlingemann, F.P., R.M. Stulz, and R.A. Walkling. 2000. Asset liquidity and segment divestitures. Ohio State University working paper.

Schlingemann, F.P., R.M. Stulz, and R.A. Walkling. 2002. Divestitures and the liquidity of the market for corporate assets. *Journal of Financial Economics* 64, 117–144.

Schoar, A. 2002. Effects of corporate diversification on productivity. *Journal of Finance* 52, 2379–2403.

Schoeffler, S., R.D. Buzzell, and D.F. Heany. 1974. Impact of strategic planning on profit performance. *Harvard Business Review* 52 (April): 137–145.

Schoenberg, R., and R. Reeves. 1999. What determines acquisition activity within an industry? *European Management Journal* 17 (February): 93–98.

Scholes, M., and M. Wolfson. 1990. Employee stock ownership plans and corporate restructuring: Myths and realities. *Financial Management* 19, 12–28.

Schumpeter, J. 1942; 2d ed., 1947. *The Theory of Economic Development*, New York: Harper & Bros.

Schumpeter, J.A. 1950. *Capitalism, Socialism and Democracy*, 3d ed. New York: Harper & Bros.

Schut, G., and R. van Frederikslust. (undated). Shareholder wealth effects of joint venture strategies: Theory and evidence from The Netherlands. Working paper, Erasmus Universiteit Rotterdam. Available by e-mail, rfrederikslust@fac.fbk.eur.nl.

Schwert, G.W. 1996. Markup pricing in mergers and acquisitions. *Journal of Financial Economics* 41 (No. 2, June): 153–162.

Securities and Exchange Commission, Staff Report to the Special Subcommittee on Investigations. 1972. *The Financial Collapse of the Penn Central Company.* August 1972, Washington, D.C.: Special Subcommittee on Investigations, U.S. Government Printing Office.

Sellers, Patricia. 1995. Can Coke and Pepsi make Quaker sweat? *Fortune* (June 10): 20.

Servaes, H. 1991. Tobin's Q and the gains from takeovers. *Journal of Finance* 46 (No. 1, March): 409–419.

Serwer, A. 1999. The deal of the next century. *Fortune*, September 6, 154–162.

Seth, A. 1990. Sources of value creation in acquisitions: An empirical investigation. *Strategic Management Journal* 11(6), 431–446.

Shapiro, A. 1999. Corporate strategy and the capital budgeting decision. In D. Chew, ed., *The New Corporate Finance*, 2d ed., Burr Ridge, IL: Irwin McGraw-Hill.

Sharma, D., and J. Ho. 2002. The impact of acquisitions on operating performance: Some Australian evidence. *Journal of Business Finance and Accounting* 29 (No. 1, January, March): 155–200.

Shekerjian, Denise. 1990. *Uncommon Genius: How Great Ideas Are Born*. New York: Penguin Books.

Sherer, Paul. 1998. Heard on the Street: Timing question dogs Mattel, Coke, too. *Wall Street Journal*, December 18, C1.

Shiller, R. 1988. Fashions, fads, and bubbles in financial markets. In J.C. Coffee Jr., L. Lowenstein, and S. Rose-Ackerman, eds., *Knights, Raiders, and Targets*, 56–68. New York: Oxford University Press.

Shiller, Robert J. 1989. *Market Volatility*. Cambridge: MIT Press.

Shiller, Robert J. 1995. Conversation, information, and herd behavior. *AEA Papers and Proceedings*, (May): 181–185.

Shleifer, A., and R. Vishny. 1988. Value maximization and the acquisition process. *Journal of Economic Perspectives* 2 (Winter): 7–20.

Shleifer, A., and R. Vishny. 2001. Stock market driven acquisitions. Working paper (June). Downloaded from http://papers.ssrn.com /sol3/papers.cfm?abstract_id=278563.

Shleifer, A., and R. W. Vishny. 1988. Management buyouts as a response to market pressure. In A. Auerbach, ed., *Mergers and Acquisitions*, Chicago: University of Chicago Press.

Shleifer, Andrei, and Robert Vishny. 1986. Large shareholders and corporate control. *Journal of Political Economy* 94, 461–488.

Shleifer, Andrei, and Robert Vishny. 1989. Management entrenchment: The case of manager-specific investments. *Journal of Financial Economics* 25, 123–139.

Shughart, W., II, and R. Tollison. 1984. The random character of merger activity. *Rand Journal of Economics* 15 (Winter): 500–509.

Sicherman, N., and R. Pettway. 1987. Acquisition of divested assets and shareholders' wealth. *Journal of Finance* 42 (No. 5, December): 1261–1273.

Singh, H., and C.A. Montgomery. 1987. Corporate acquisition strategies and economic performance. *Strategic Management Journal* 8 (No. 4, July/August): 377–386.

Sirower, M. 1997. *The Synergy Trap: How Companies Lose the Acquisition Game.* New York: The Free Press.

Skrzycki, Cindy. 1991. Exchanging marriage vows without a mate. *Washington Post*, March 27, C1.

Slovin, M., M. Sushka, and S. Ferraro. 1995. A comparison of the information conveyed by equity carve-outs, spin-offs, and asset sell-offs. *Journal of Financial Economics* 37, 89–104.

Smith, A. 1990. Corporate ownership structure and performance. *Journal of Financial Economics* 27 (No. 1, September): 143–164.

Smith, C. 1986. Investment banking and the capital acquisition process. *Journal of Financial Economics* 15, 3–31.

Smith, R., and J. Kim. 1994. The combined effects of free cash flow and financial slack on bidder and target stock returns. *Journal of Business* 67 (No. 2, April): 281–310.

Smith, Rebecca, and John Emschwiller. 2003. *24 Days.* New York: Harper-Business.

Sorkin, A. 2002. Market place: Investors react negatively to Tyco's new, and abrupt, breakup strategy. *New York Times*, January 24. Downloaded from http://query.nytimes.com/search/restricted/article?res=F70810FE35 5F0C778EDDA80894DA4044.

Stackelberg, Heinrich von. 1952. *The Theory of the Market Economy*, trans. A.T. Peacock. London: William Hodge.

Steensma, H., and M. Lyles. 2000. Explaining IJV survival in a transitional economy through social exchange and knowledge-based perspectives. *Strategic Management Journal* 21, 831–851.

Stein, J. 1997. Internal capital markets and the competition for corporate resources. *Journal of Finance* 52, 111–133.

Steiner, P. 1975. *Mergers: Motives, Effects, and Policies.* Ann Arbor: University of Michigan Press.

Stewart, G.B., and D.M. Glassman. 1999. The motives and methods of corporate restructuring: Part I. In D. Chew, ed., *The New Corporate Finance: Where Theory Meets Practice*, Burr Ridge, IL: Irwin McGraw-Hill.

Stigler, G. 1950. Monopoly and oligopoly power by merger. *American Economic Review* 40 (May): 23–34.

Stillman, R. 1983. Examining antitrust policy toward horizontal mergers. *Journal of Financial Economics* 11 (Nos. 1–4, April): 225–240.

Sumway, T. 2001. Forecasting bankruptcy more accurately: A simple hazard model. *Journal of Business* 74(1), 101–124.

Sundaram, A., and B. Yeung. 2001. Divestitures as good news or bad news: The role of creditors and management. Unpublished working paper.

Sundqvist, Sven-Ivan. 1994. *Exit PG.* Stockholm: Bokförlaget T. Fischer & Co.

Surowiecki, James. 2004. *The Wisdom of Crowds.* New York: Doubleday.

Swanson, Z., and C. Mielke. 2000. To what extent are majority shareholders affected by the presence of minority stockholders? Unpublished working paper, 1–21.

Swisher, Kara. 2003. *There Must Be a Pony in Here Somewhere: The AOL Time Warner Debacle and the Quest for a Digital Future.* New York: Crown Business Books.

Switzer, J. 1996. Evidence on real gains in corporate acquisitions. *Journal of Economics and Business* 48, 443.

Tenner, Edward. 1996. *Why Things Bite Back: Technology and the Revenge of Unintended Consequences.* New York: Vintage Books.

Thaler, Richard H. 1992. *The Winner's Curse: Paradoxes and Anomalies of Economic Life.* Princeton: Princeton University Press.

Thompson, A.A., and A.J. Strickland. 1992. *Strategic Management: Concepts and Cases.* Homewood, IL: Richard D. Irwin.

Thorburn, K. 2000. Bankruptcy auctions: Costs, debt recovery, and firm survival. *Journal of Financial Economics* 58(3), 337–368.

Town, R.J. 1992. Merger waves and the structure of merger and acquisition time-series. *Journal of Applied Econometrics* 7 (December):83–100.

Toxvaerd, F. 2002. Strategic merger waves: A theory of musical chairs. Working paper (December).

Trimbath, S. 2002. *Mergers and Efficiency: Changes across Time.* Santa Monica, CA: Milken Institute.

Turner, B.M. 1978. *Man-made Disasters.* London: Wykeham Press.

Turner, B.M. 1976. The organizational and intraorganizational development of disasters. *Administrative Science Quarterly* 21, 378–397.

United States Senate, Committee on Commerce. 1972. *The Penn Central and Other Railroads.* Washington, D.C.: U.S. Government Printing Office, December.

Varaiya, N. 1985. A test of Roll's hubris hypothesis of corporate takeovers. Working paper, Dallas, TX: Southern Methodist University School of Business.

Varaiya, N., and K. Ferris. 1987. Overpaying in corporate takeover: The winner's curse. *Financial Analysts Journal* 43 (No. 3, May/June): 64–70.

Veld, C., and Y. Veld-Merkoulova. 2002. Do spin-offs really create value? The European case. Working paper, Tilburg University. Http://ssrn .com/abstract=296092.

Vijh, A. 1994. The spin-off and merger ex-date effects. *Journal of Finance* 49(2), 581–609.

Vijh, A. 1999. Long-term returns from equity carve outs. *Journal of Financial Economics* 54, 273–308.

Vijh, A. 2002. The positive announcement-period returns of equity carve outs: Asymmetric information or divestiture gains? *Journal of Business* 75(1), 153–190.

Villalonga, B. 1999. Does diversification cause the "diversification discount"? Working paper, University of California, Los Angeles.

Villalonga, B. 2003a. Diversification discount or premium? New evidence from BITS establishment-level data. *Journal of Finance* (forthcoming), Harvard Business School working paper, downloadable from http://papers.ssrn.com/sol3/papers.cfm?abstract_id=253793.

Villalonga, B. 2003b. Research roundtable discussion: The diversification discount. Social Science Research Network, paper downloadable from http://papers.ssrn.com/sol3/papers.cfm?abstract_id=402220.

Walker, M. 2000. Corporate takeovers, strategic objectives, and acquiring-firm shareholder wealth. *Financial Management* 29 (No. 1, Spring): 53–66.

Wansley, J., W. Lane, and H. Yang. 1983. Abnormal returns to acquired firms by type of acquisition and method of payment. *Financial Management* 12 (No. 3, Autumn): 16–22.

Wasserstein, B. 1998. *Big Deal*. New York: Warner Books.

Weech-Maldonado, R. 2002. Strategic relatedness in mergers and financial performance: The case of the health maintenance organization industry in the United States. *Health Services Management Research* 15, 264.

Weick, Karl E., and Kathleen M. Sutcliffe. 2001. *Managing the Unexpected: Assuring High Performance in an Age of Complexity*. San Francisco: Jossey-Bass.

Weick, Karl E., Kathleen M. Sutcliffe, and David Obstfeld. 1999. Organizing for high reliability: Processes of collective mindfulness. *Research in Organizational Behavior* 21, 81–123, JAI Press Inc.

Weidenbaum, M., and S. Vogt. 1987. Takeovers and stockholders: Winners and losers. *California Management Review* 29 (No. 4, Summer): 157–167.

Weisinger, J., and P. Salipante. 2000. Cultural knowing as practicing: Extending our conception of culture. *Journal of Management Inquiry* 9(4), 376–390.

Weston, J. 1953. *The Role of Mergers in the Growth of Large Firms*. Berkeley: University of California Press.

Weston, J.F. 1970. The nature and significance of conglomerate firms. *St. John's Law Review* 44, 66–80.

Weston, J.F. 1989. Divestitures: Mistakes or learning. *Journal of Applied Corporate Finance* (Summer): 68–76.

Weston, J.F., and S.K. Mansinghka. 1972. Tests of the efficiency performance of conglomerate firms. *Journal of Finance* 26 (No. 3, September): 919–936.

Weston, J.F., K.V. Smith, and R.E. Shrieves. 1972. Conglomerate performance using the capital asset pricing model. *Review of Economics and Statistics* 21 (No. 4, November): 357–363.

Wheatley, C., R. Brown, and G. Johnson. 1997. Accounting disclosure and valuation revisions around voluntary corporate spin-offs. Unpublished working paper.

Whipple, J. 2000. Strategic alliance success factors. *Journal of Supply Chain Management* (Summer): 21–28.

Whited, T. 2001. Is it inefficient investment that causes the diversification discount? *Journal of Finance* 56, 1667–1691.

Wier, P. 1983 The costs of antimerger lawsuits: Evidence from the stock market. *Journal of Financial Economics* 11 (Nos. 1–4, April): 207–225.

Williamson, O. 1970. *Corporate Control and Business Behavior*. Englewood Cliffs, NJ: Prentice-Hall.

Williamson, O. 1975. *Markets and Hierarchies: Analysis and Antitrust Implications*. New York: Free Press.

Winter, R.E. 1986. Revco profit rose 20% for 3rd quarter; analysts' reaction mixed on buyout bid. *Wall Street Journal*, March 13, A7.

Wruck, K.H. 1991. What really went wrong at Revco? *Journal of Applied Corporate Finance* (Summer), 79–92.

Wulf, J. 2004. Do CEOs in mergers trade power for premium? *Journal of Law Economics and Organization* 20 (April): 60.

Yeheskel, O. 2001. Arkia Israel Airlines' CEO Israel Borovich on strategic alliances and growth. *The Academy of Management Executive* 15(1), 12–15.

Yook, K.C. 2000. Larger return to cash acquisitions: Signaling effect or leverage effect? Working paper, Baltimore, MD: Johns Hopkins.

You, V., R. Caves, M. Smith, and J. Henry. 1986. Mergers and bidders' wealth: Managerial and strategic factors. In Lacy Glenn Thomas III, ed., *The Economics of Strategic Planning: Essays in Honor of Joel Dean*, Lexington: Lexington Books, 201–221.

Zahra, S. 1995. Corporate entrepreneurship and financial performance: The case of management leveraged buyouts. *Journal of Business Venturing* 10(3), 225–247.

Zaretsky, B.L. 1990. *Final Report of Examiner*, In re: Revco D.S., Inc., et al., debtors, Honorable Harold F. White, Bankruptcy Judge, United States Bankruptcy Court, Northern District of Ohio, December 17.

Zuckerman, A. 2000. Revisiting divestiture. *Health Forum Journal* 43(6), 53–54.

Zuta, S. 1999. Diversification discount and targeted stock: Theory and empirical evidence. Unpublished working paper.

About the Author

Robert F. Bruner is Distinguished Professor of Business Administration at the Darden Graduate School of Business Administration, University of Virginia. His areas of teaching, research, and writing are corporate finance, mergers and acquisitions, investing in emerging markets, innovation, and technology transfer. His book *Applied Mergers and Acquisitions* was published in 2004 by John Wiley & Sons. He teaches the course, "Mergers and Acquisitions" in Darden's MBA program and is the faculty director of Darden's executive education program, "Mergers and Acquisitions." He has been recognized in the United States and Europe for his teaching and casewriting. *Business Week* magazine cited him as one of the "masters of the MBA classroom." He is the author or co-author of more than 400 case studies and notes, and of *Case Studies in Finance: Managing for Corporate Value Creation* soon to be published in its fifth edition. Industrial corporations, financial institutions, and government agencies have retained him for counsel and training. He has been on the faculty of the Darden School since 1982 and has been a visiting professor at various schools including Columbia, INSEAD, and IESE. Formerly he was a loan officer and investment analyst for First Chicago Corporation. He holds the BA degree from Yale University and the MBA and DBA degrees from Harvard University. He has served the Darden School, professional groups, and community organizations in various positions of leadership. Copies of his papers and essays may be obtained via his web site, http://faculty.darden.edu/brunerb/. He may be reached via e-mail at brunerr@virginia.edu.

Index

The letter n *following a page number denotes a note.*